THE CONTEST OF
LANGUAGE

THE CONTEST OF
LANGUAGE

Before and Beyond Nationalism

Edited by

W. MARTIN BLOOMER

University of Notre Dame Press
Notre Dame, Indiana

Manufactured in the United States of America

Library of Congress Cataloging in-Publication Data
The contest of language : before and beyond nationalism /
edited by W. Martin Bloomer.
    p.   cm.
Includes bibliographical references and index.
ISBN 0-268-02190-2 (cloth : alk. paper)
ISBN 0-268-02191-0 (pbk. : alk. paper)
1. Language and languages—Political aspects.   2. Linguistic minorities.
I. Bloomer, M. (Martin)
P119.3.C66   2005
306.44—dc22
                                                          2005025273

∞*This book is printed on acid-free paper*

Contents

Introduction   *1*
W. Martin Bloomer

APPROACHING THE POLITICAL HISTORY OF LANGUAGE

1   Latin versus Italian: The Linguistic Crisis of   *15*
the Early Italian Renaissance
Theodore J. Cachey Jr.

2   The Persistence of Syriac   *40*
Joseph P. Amar

3   *Dúthaigh* and *Dúchas* in Sixteenth-Century Ireland   *60*
Peter McQuillan

STUDIES IN SPEECH POLITICS

4   Language and Imperial Ideology in Late Antiquity   *99*
and Early Islam
Dimitri Gutas

5   "Till Some Person Attain to the Universal Monarchy":   *111*
Seventeenth-Century Language Technologies
and What They Say
Haun Saussy

6   Nationalism without Linguism: Tolerating   *134*
     Chinese Variants
     Susan D. Blum

7   Whose Language Is It Anyway?   *165*
     The Irish and the English Language
     Tony Crowley

LITERATURE AND THE PRESERVATION
OF NATIVE TONGUES

8   Speaking in *Glossai:* Dialect Choice   *187*
     and Cultural Politics in Hellenistic Poetry
     Richard Hunter

9   Marble Latin: Encounters with the Timeless Language   *207*
     W. Martin Bloomer

10   Dumbness and Eloquence: A Note on English   *227*
     as We Write It in Ireland
     Seamus Deane

AFTERWORD

     Philosophy and Its Languages: A Philosopher's Reflections   *245*
     on the Rise of English as the Universal Academic Language
     Vittorio Hösle

     Contributors   *263*

     Index   *265*

Introduction

W. MARTIN BLOOMER

The contest of language examined in these studies is both a synchronic phenomenon wherein an individual can feel at home in one language and yet be estranged from another and a diachronic process in which one language may replace another for a set of speakers or writers, for an institution or a place or community. These investigations, which range greatly in time and place and approach, share a sensitivity to the processes (and consequences) by which language becomes freighted with deeply felt metaphorical associations in contentious polyglot contexts. The investigators are cultural and intellectual and literary historians, philologists, and linguists who have put slightly to one side their strictly disciplinary interests to consider the unique logic in language users' metaphorization of languages.

At its most melodramatic, cultural understanding of language relations (and it should be clear that we are not conducting field studies of language contact but rather analyses of the ways a culture, especially but not exclusively through literature, represents its own languages) speaks of the rise and fall of a language. This organic metaphor, borrowed from political empire, may not be the most fundamental field. The deep metaphor may simply be "better" versus "worse"; that is, cultures may employ a simple hierarchy to set one language against another — holy versus profane, classical versus vernacular, orderly or well governed versus disorderly or dissentious. No inherent attribute or inevitable reason compels that a shift in language or a version of a language should occasion lament and nostalgia in some, pride in others. Yet we know too well that the use of a language may attract to itself symbolic resonances, quickening cultural, ethnic, intellectual, religious, social, or national animosities. The recovery or reuse of a language (against some preferred language) can be a force for emancipation or spark deep-seated oppositions. The homologies that languages invite or attract include parallel stories of identity, politics, culture, and religion that attach themselves to a particular variant. One speaker will condemn Irish as the language of peasants and revolutionaries; others recognize it as their birthright. Latin may be represented as a torpid language of privilege and exclusion or the living language of the word of God. We have attempted in this volume to canvass the variety of languages and issues, the vehicles and tenors in cultural metaphor making with language, but we are keenly aware of the emotional and political importance of such processes. Perhaps we should have sought to produce a typology of the ways language users reflect on the value of their language(s) against a prior language, another variant, or a succesor language. Then, most neutrally (yet it is hard to describe the process by which one language takes the place of another in neutral terms; language change or shift might serve, but we are dealing here with moments and practices in which a group or groups recognize a change in language as significant, at times personally, more often collectively), we would have to forgo such terms as loss, death, decay, also imposition, revival, restoration. We also would have missed an essential component, what Vittorio Hösle calls in the afterword the sense of feeling at home in a language. This is more than, different from, what linguists call competence. We track what a language or variant has meant to its speakers, which a neutral vocabulary or, more realistically, a strictly historical or linguistic descriptive analysis might miss.

The studies in this volume illustrate a frequent response to the process of language change, wherein language users color this process with grandiose and polemical characterizations: one language is the commanding voice of empire, another the ungovernable tongue of dissent. The use of a language does not simply follow sociolinguistic cues (where one variant is appropriate for one speaker, auditor, situation, or social or institutional setting) but helps to create and reinforce the idea of such distinctions. It also brings, as one consequence, ideas of the qualities of that language. The context and patterns of use tend to become understood as features of the language. In its varied history Latin would come to be a sacred language and a school language, whereupon claims were developed about its sacral or intellectual disposition. Language users tend to view these attributes not as social or cultural effects but as essential characteristics of their language as against another language. A consequence of language characterization is the habit of identifying patterns of life, allegiances, and identities with the language itself. In its most developed ideological form this habit has been called linguism, the identification of the linguistic group as the political group. Here, at least according to the schemes of nationalists, polyglossia or diglossia moves (declines?) to a monoglot standard with an accompanying shift in attitude from linguistic tolerance to intolerant monoglossia. When each nation has its own language, the contest of language seems to have been settled, except that ties of identity and political ambitions do not always square with the neat categorization single people, single language, and single nation. The contest of language has then the paradigmatic shape of the establishment of the European vernacular languages (as languages of state, church, schooling) against the universal (ecclesiastical or pan-European) Latin, perhaps with the added anxiety that language variety will dwindle to the perceived univocalism of the United States.

In this volume, however, we wish to explore the developing claims of one language against another in places and times and institutions that did not mirror the rise of nationalism or privilege modern statehood as the explanatory category. In part, studies such as Tony Crowley's and Seamus Deane's on the relations of Irish and English and Theodore J. Cachey Jr.'s on the paradigm for the paradigmatic model, Dante's writing on the use of the vernacular and the course of the use of the vernacular in the two centuries after his treatise, revise the equation that identifies the use of the vernacular with the birth of the nation. The various studies do begin in reaction to the persistent idea in the West that there has been or should be a single language (sometimes imagined as the universal language, sometimes as merely a single language for a single community). If humans regularly spoke or wrote in several languages (or simply were aware of different languages), yet remembered or prophesied a time of a single language (efficacious, authoritative, and integrating), the contrast would hold interest in the ways that other accounts, mythological and ideological, reduce the uncertainty and diversity of experience to idealized accounts of order and process. The very existence of a plurality of languages has been taken as an index of man's fall from grace or as a different sort of impediment, a roadblock on the march to nationhood. The desire to reunite man with the Edenic world where man controlled the names of things and spoke directly and unambiguously to God may overlap with, but is not the same thing as, political efforts to monopolize a language. Still, the idea that language makes human beings, differentiating them from the beasts, rescuing Caliban from infancy and promising him that he may be the master Alfonso, is inherently political (and emotional). Though the idea that there should be one (markedly virile) language for one people is not an invention of the modern European state; the state has pursued it with singular commitment and resources.

We, scholars of different languages, came together, at first in two conferences, not to seek a harmonious language but to query those assumptions, theories, and stories that understand the relation of languages as combat, in which inevitably one will win out. We hope we were motivated not so much by the lesser shadow play of national linguistic contest—the strife of modern academia where the various language departments compete for students (witness MLA statistics tracking the downturn in the fortunes of German and Russian and French, the current chicness of Italian, or the plodding small sameness of Latin enrollments)—but by the more scholarly possibility that we might learn from each other in discussing the forces and processes that enshrine or displace a language as a people's own, as the vehicle of a liturgy, as a subject of study, or as the medium for study. While on occasion in committee meetings, before our students, with colleagues inside and outside the humanities, we find ourselves proponents of this or that language, we were from the outset wary of the assumption that the relations of languages need be a contest or that this contest could be mapped in exclusively political, ideological, or social terms. Indeed, several of the studies in this volume argue that the model of one language supplanting the other is not simply polemical but fantastic. On a different conception, the choice of one language as the language of state, of liturgy, or of schooling might contribute no stigma to the language or variant not chosen. In a more charitable modeling of language and society, we can imagine either a harmonious society capable of polyglossia whereby one language could be used in one sphere and another in another, without creating or adding to a hierarchy of those spheres, their functions, or users; or we could perhaps more easily imagine a human society that did not employ language to mark distinctions of status, gender, class, religion, and so on. Better still and less utopian, we might think of language choice not as an act in a zero-sum game but as an inflationary investment, as Hösle exhorts (although without the mercantile metaphor) in his essay on the alleged globalism and hegemony of English. In the search for the implications of the choice and use of a language, it should be noted that the organic metaphor of rise and fall may suit a language no better than it does an empire. What the metaphor does get right is the recurrent tendency to view languages as empires. The political quality of the "choice" of a language should be clear—especially for those who have had and have now little say in the language or speakers who govern, church, or school them.

In this volume we consider various efforts to make a language dominant, which we interpret as the processes and attitudes that seek to make one language textual, institutional, academic, or literary. The enterprises we examine are political in the broad sense that the choice of a writing system or the use of a dialect for a specific context are implicated in other social and political endeavors.

Thus we examine both the pressures (whether from the state or from literary precedent or cultural rivalry) to elevate one language at the expense of another and the cultural and intellectual work this election aids. Linguistic politics are here given a wider range than, for instance, customary understanding of the adoption or revival of a language as an act of fealty to a state (or as a gesture of opposition to an official code). The default model, whether or not this was quite what Herder intended, has been not simply to interpret linguistic difference in an essentialist mode as difference in race or ethnicity but especially to consider the contest of one language against another as a contest of national or ethnic groups. Indeed, nationalism on this reading is said to arrive with the triumph of the vernacular against the old ecumenical or at least pan-European Latin. In turn, a nation spread to empire to the degree that it was successful in if not altogether blotting out the national or native languages of its conquered lands, then assuring that schooling, bureaucracy, and law were administered in the conqueror's tongue. (The precedent of Rome is often invoked and contrasted to the more thoroughgoing linguistic imperialism of the modern age; in fact, the Romans did not impose their language on conquered populations or even require its use in law.)[1] We do not deny the material realities of the imposition or loss of a language or the political dimensions that language use conveys, but we wish to constitute a countercurrent to the default model that has stressed the importance of nineteenth-century nationalism. At the same time, Haun Saussy, Vittorio Hösle, Theodore J. Cachey Jr., and Tony Crowley offer a far more nuanced analysis of early modern linguistic attitudes and policies (stressing, for instance, that the call to the vernacular was also a call for diglossia among the elite and tracing the fortunes of languages other than that of the state).

We go beyond and before nationalism. Indeed, four essays begin from the ancient Mediterranean. If we have a particular point of departure, it might be the death of Alexander. Richard Hunter's discussion of the significance of the creation of literary Doric and its use in Hellenistic Egypt considers several important issues that return throughout the book: the political pressures and meanings of dialect use, the censure of such use embedded in the literature that performs it, the creation or restoration of a variant against the language of empire. Dimitri Gutas and Joseph P. Amar, in their respective accounts of the histories of Arabic and Syriac, treat successor languages to the Greek *koinē*. Indeed, one unifying strain of all the studies (with Susan D. Blum's discussion of Chinese linguistic attitudes an important check) is the reflection on the influence and history of the classical languages Greek, Latin, and Arabic. The locus classicus of the politics of language and specifically of the elevation of one variant as the language of literature or of a people against the classical is, of course, Dante's *De vulgari eloquentia.* Cachey reexamines the *questione della lingua* in an essay that complicates the received model of the establishment of literary Italian. The neglect of Dante's recommendations in the two centuries after the *De vulgari eloquentia* and the humanists' championing of a rather specific kind of Latin reflect a vibrant if polemical linguistic landscape but one whose allegiances are not easily mapped onto the political; far less will they document the rise of nationalism. Blum's essay on linguistic tolerance in modern China offers a refreshing insight that does not so much indict Western normative ideas as offer a new metric for understanding cultures' attitudes toward linguistic diversity and di- or even polyglossia. Other studies in this volume consider the perdurance of "one" language, be it Syriac, Arabic, or Latin. These accounts of the fortunes of a language hope also to cut through misunderstandings not simply about the stability over time of a language, subjects more proper for the historical linguist, but the ways a language is remembered as the same and the cultural nostalgia that this collective memory abets. It is a fiction that, for instance, we too know Latin or that our Latin is the same as Alcuin's or Cicero's. The desire to possess an ancestral language can blind us to its original (and intermediate) use and users (see my essay, "Marble Latin"). The idea that a language embodies the ineffable and the essential of a culture is perhaps most thoroughly examined in this book by the three treatments of Irish. Crowley, who has devoted a great deal of his scholarship to the historical and theoretical issues of linguistic politics, here describes the history of the combative relations of Irish and English, from the first effort to prescribe Gaelic in 1366. Deane sees the modern experimentation of Irish literature as the reflex of a language and a culture dispossessed. The perceived inability of English to represent Irish experience thus leads both to the revival of Irish and the flowering of Irish literature in "English." English in turn emerges as the language of modernity. Peter McQuillan's methodology differs markedly from his colleagues. Like Deane, he traces the linguistic terms that seek to express a cultural crisis, except that he investigates a single key term, at an earlier period, *duchas,* which defines the ineffable, the inalienable. Here he offers insights into how language and literature themselves enshrine the contestable.

As Saussy notes in his account of language technology in the seventeenth century, a number of the contributors, scholars of classical languages, have approached the issue of the contest of language by asking how linguistic classicism is established or conveyed. This we treat not as a discrete phenomenon of stylistics or literary history but as one attempt, allied in many respects to others more recognizably governmental or institutional, to create, elevate, and preserve a single variant. Here, necessarily, we consider the claims literature makes to represent the native, the authentic, and even the timeless. The native and the eternal are often modulations in arguments for the legitimacy of political empires, yet both the classical and the vernacular can present themselves as the birthright that ties a group to an authenticating past. Classicism may be portrayed as a petrifying force, but it may also be a rallying cry. The characterization of a language as traditional or newcomer, literary medium or commercial script, classical or barbarian might constitute a binary system, except of course that people speak more than one language, linguistic groups do not necessarily share political programs or affiliations, and "one" language is itself a notoriously problematic construct.

The idea of a single language arising from a struggle between two or more languages reflects a habit of linguistic intolerance whereby only one can win out as the language of law, state, church, and school. To put aside the nexus of contemporary factors — social, political, and cultural — that influences language use, the contest of language is an inheritance from at least three sources: ancient aesthetics, scholars' perhaps excessive estimation of the story of Babel (a favorite for those seeking a sort of symbolic geography for European languages), and the development of the European vernacular languages as literary and then state forms. Ancient stylistics exhorted the writer to seek the style appropriate to his subject. In the influential account of the *Rhetorica ad Herennium* the writer-in-training was advised that one of three styles was to be chosen. As Erich Auerbach argued, Augustine had radically reworked the classical triad of the high, the middle, and the low to form and theorize a new Christian, universal, and humble style.[2] Auerbach was no doubt prone to fasten upon great stylists and theoreticians without too much regard for changes in the language, the system of education, even demographic shifts. Auerbach himself was a classicizer not in that he lamented the role of the vernacular (on the contrary, he wondered what would have happened if the Carolingians had not remodeled their writing and so broken with the living font of the spoken language) but because he clove to the classicist's sense that there is or should be one Latin or a single literary language suited to its time and audience. The Romans had taken from the Hellenistic scholars the idea that written and spoken language should reflect a purity of speech, Hellenism or Latinity. Hellenism was modeled on Attic literary Greek during a time when the spoken language had already devolved significantly in morphology, syntax, and lexicon (and of course had spread from the foundation of the successor kingdoms of the generals of Alexander the Great). The prescriptions for purity in Latin were problematic since the literary language was fashioned after the Hellenistic prescriptions (which were developed from an existing body of literature) and Latin literary language was in part modeled on Greek. There was no comparable authoritative corpus of Roman prose or verse literature — which makes the achievement of the generation of Cicero and Sallust and Caesar and then the Augustans even more remarkable. The story of the development of Latin is out of place here except to note that the poetic-literary tradition had embraced the idea of a single literary language (the first practitioners of literary Latin, the poets Livius Andronicus and Ennius, were remembered as vying for preeminence in writing Latin; Ennius's epitaph boasts he was so good that on his death men had forgotten how to speak Latin). The idea of one language written with a strongly exclusionary aesthetics (stigmatizing the vulgar, the everyday, the barbarian, the dialect, even the feminine and the servile) has shaped western ideas of the economy and consistency of literary language, and also no doubt instilled a prejudice toward one authoritative, high style.

This tendency, relentlessly schooled in the West, whether or not the influence of the Greek critics is acknowledged, compounds with another scholastic tendency — the search for a perfect or a single language and also for a significant story, an etiology of language — to enature the conviction that there is a proper language and that other languages are variant, descendants — both the legitimate and the bastards, the vernaculars (the *verna* was the home-born slave, child of free father and servile mother; Byron, who understood the etymology, calls Italian "soft bastard Latin").[3] And this story of origins is discovered (perhaps with some exaggeration of its influence) in a rather unimportant episode in the Old Testament, the story of the Tower of Babel. Both George Steiner in *After Babel* and Umberto Eco in *The Search for a Perfect Language* have founded their own investigations of hermeneutics and linguistic utopianism on the story.[4] Eco traced the theme of a perfect language in a historical study that is fecund, stimulating, and surprising. He began his wide-ranging investigation of invented languages, magical and religious languages, and select historical movements that invested certain languages with mystical powers from Genesis 2, that first and perfect speech act when God spoke and it was light. The act of naming and the confusion of Babel set the limits for the first chapter, "Da Adamo alla 'confusio linguarum.'" I suspect the movement from the transparency to the obscurancy of language continues to inform attitudes toward language and indeed spur the literary imagination, not because of the authority of the source, but because the stories address a central issue of linguistics that ancient language science could not or certainly did not reconcile. How does one reconcile two strong features of language, the arbitrariness of sound and the systematicity of sense? The rule-governed aspect of language, so apparent to the ancient theorist, stands at odds with the relation of *nomen,* name, and *res,* thing. The Stoics rationalized by positing an original nomothete, a namer whose system has been obscured by men's use through the passage of time. (Why syntax had changed does not seem to have been a significant issue; rather, the Greek and Roman critics stuck more to a verbal approach, seeking by etymology to restore the rationality of an original relationship of each individual word or group of words.) Thus disparate authoritative ancient traditions interpreted the lack of transparency in languages' relationships as an ur-language in need of repair. The Stoics would employ reason and analogy to repair the defect of men's use. The return to an Edenic language, the history of fabricated, revived, and "purified" languages, while a rich and fascinating topic, is not our primary focus here, although in charting the role of one language in another and the attitudes toward a plurality of languages, we cannot lose sight of these stories of origin. Still, I do not wish to overemphasize the importance of biblical stories for the production of attitudes that led to the suppression of languages. For in the West the idea that we should learn a single, ancestral, authoritative language and the conviction that this language will be more efficacious for the pursuit of truth and even of profit owe far more to traditional schooling in Latin, which had narrowed the ancient ideal of man as a public orator to specific virtues of style that could be learned by diligent application of the individual student to his reading and writing.[5]

The reduction of languages and the concomitant politics of language choice run as a motif throughout the essays. For all the valorization of the ideal singleness of languages, I must stress that institutionalized monoglossia is both a barbaric phrase and a literary (and bureaucratic) fantasy. I do not wish to belittle the human suffering attendant on programs of language suppression and language imposition but rather to sketch the appeal of the sort of stories that idealize the control and harmony inherent in univocalism. Without a doubt, Irish and Basque endure and have become more deeply politicized at the same time that their range of use and cultural depth have diminished. Literary fiction has its own interest in exploiting stories of the imposition of language or of the obsessive, politically inspired control of language. George Orwell imagined a condition in which language's ambiguity and range of expression had been lost, suppressed to a farcical monoglot that would serve the state. There are perhaps two leading modernist fantasies about language, the Orwellian, in which doublespeak reflects the arbitrariness of the language imposer and the anarchic fantasy, a more literary utopia, where words may drift liberated by their arbitrary relation from the signified. Both visions exploit a systematic inversion of the ordinary, but the presence of the state seems to form a line of division between the overgoverned prosaic world that allows no interpretation and the free-flowing poetic landscape of misunderstandings and partial glimpses, multiple meanings and heteroglossia. Satire and its poetic twin, absurdism, may stand against that odd combination of scope and conformity, the political empire. The satirist ancient and modern takes up irony, his sole antidote to the state's command of language and language of command. Perhaps language will not dance so conveniently to sovereign direction. Orwell was positing a language foreign to the ones being described by linguists in the tradition of Saussure, that is, a language divorced from its community of users. He remains essentially modernist, however, and in the tradition of Herderian ideas of language in believing that language can form its community.

The essays in this volume address anxieties about the use and abuse of language, not then as belated products of European nationalism or exclusively as imperfect intimations of an Edenic language, but as deeper manifestations of Western and even postcolonial experience. The languages and periods are various. We met not to publish a series of studies on Irish or Latin or Arabic but to confront ideas about the stories of the virtues of the various languages, the tolerances of one language for another, and the moments (or long drawn out processes) when one language displaces another. This is, therefore, part of an ongoing meditation about the investigations of scholars of literature and language. Perhaps it represents encounters of philologists with sociologists of language and with linguistic anthropologists. Much work remains to be done, not simply the technical studies of the relations of super- and substrate languages, the history of loanwords, the qualities of what is so cavalierly described as diglossia, but also the process of vulgarization, the role of textbooks, grammars, or university chairs in the spread of a certain variant or in the inculcation of ideas of linguistic tolerance or intolerance. We have made a start by reconsidering the rationales of appropriateness, function, and use, and we have broached these issues in languages still understudied in the West—Syriac, Arabic, Chinese—as well as in those languages in which the hot points of polemic and animosity are well known, though perhaps enshrined in caricature.

One common strain in our investigations is a critical appraisal of the culturally varying tolerances of linguistic diversity. The clarity of the analysis of the relation of minority to dominant language in China by Blum offered the conferees both a well-conceived anthropological template and a brisk corrective to default notions of linguistic intolerance. "Linguistic tolerance," which seems a more balanced and comprehensive term than "linguistic hegemony," is the focus of several of the essays. Gutas describes the lack of linguistic imperialism in the so-called spread of Arabic; Amar offers a rich, diachronic look at the uses and fortunes of Syriac. These two studies enrich greatly our picture of the relation of linguistic policy or better practice to Hellenization, and also the consequences for multilingualism of the dominance and withdrawal of Rome, and finally the Arab conquest from Beirut to Baghdad. Hunter's discussion of the literary use of the Doric dialect anticipates these studies both for reasons of the places and languages considered and, more important, because the linguistic legacy of Alexander is not transparent. The relation of one poem's Greek to the literary Greeks of the past, to Greek "dialects," and to the contemporary *koinē* and possible political colorations of all these is a useful reminder of the complexities of that blanket term "Hellenization." The claims made by poetry for the standing of language are taken up also in my essay on the perdurance of Latin and of course in Cachey's discussion of Dante. All of these are concerned with the relation of a contemporary poetry and literary language to the past. We have examined cultures in which one might expect an overwhelming sense of the burden of language—especially of the past impinging on the present. In Babylon after the tower's fall Thomas Merton has the chorus sing, "Things are beginning to lose their names." There need be no triumphalist suggestion that all will soon be restored (at the end of the play the chorus begins to sing in snippets of Latin, especially *In principio erat verbum* . . .). Gathering scholars together to consider how ideas of linguistic loss and imposition shape and are shaped by literary and cultural forms is not meant to restore one language or mode as the medium of scholarship or to reduce the contests of language users to a single story.

NOTES

1. See Jorma Kaimio, *The Romans and the Greek Language* (Helsinki, 1979) and Joseph Farrell, *Latin Language and Latin Culture* (Cambridge, 2001). Both Farrell and Kaimio follow Gibbon in seeing a deliberate policy of linguistic imperialism (see especially Farrell, pp. 2–6). I would stress that the degree to which Roman officials expected native peoples to use Latin differed by time and place.

2. See Erich Auerbach, *Literary Language and Its Public* (New York, 1965), esp. chap. 1, "Sermo Humilis," 25–66.

3. "Beppo" st. 44, cited by Farrell, *Latin Language and Culture,* 100.

4. Umberto Eco, *The Search for the Perfect Language,* trans. James Fentress (Oxford, 1995); and George Steiner, *After Babel: Aspects of Language and Translation* (Oxford, 1992). Others have not needed to go so far back. Greek seems the stuff of dreams, better and true and less attainable than Latin, a direct conduit to the New Testament or (by contrast) to durable and honest paganism; for the latter, see, e.g., Virginia Woolf, "On Not Knowing Greek," in *The Common Reader* (New York, 1953), 24–59.

5. The equality of the *tres sacrae linguae* was a short-lived ideal. Hebrew, Greek, and Latin were all authoritative languages to be pursued by the perfect humanist; in practice, of course, Latin was the medium of theology, law, diplomacy, science, and so on. The very discipline of classics would in the nineteenth century split this unity with the elevation of Greco-Roman culture at the expense both of theology and of Semitic culture. A very few institutions today offer a pan-Mediterranean approach to ancient studies.

APPROACHING THE POLITICAL HISTORY OF LANGUAGE

1 Latin versus Italian

The Linguistic Crisis of the Early Italian Rennaissance

THEODORE J. CACHEY JR.

E lo primo che cominciò a dire sì come poeta volgare, si mosse
però che volle far intendere le sue parole a donna, a la quale era
malagevole d'intendere li versi latini. E questo è contra coloro che
rimano sopra altra matera che amorosa, con ciò sia cosa che cotale
modo di parlare fosse dal principio trovato per dire d'amore.

———

[The first to begin writing as a poet in the vernacular was moved to do
so by a desire to make his words understandable to ladies who found
Latin verses difficult to comprehend. And this is an argument against
those who compose in the vernacular on a subject other than love,
since such a manner of writing was from the beginning invented for
the treating of love.]

Dante, *Vita nuova*, XXV

One might as well begin at the beginning, that is, the beginning of
literature in the modern vernacular languages according to Dante (1265–1321),
in a brief passage from his little book of poetry and prose about his love for
Beatrice called the *Vita nuova*.[1] In the midst of all the excitement about the *Divine Comedy* it is easy to overlook the fact that Dante was the most innovative
and penetrating literary theorist of his time and that he is still considered the

most influential critic of the early Italian literary tradition. His perspective and prejudices have shaped the reception of that tradition down to our own day. Among Dante's so-called minor works is the first example of a literary theory and rhetoric of vernacular letters, the *De vulgari eloquentia* (On vernacular eloquence), which he undertook shortly after his exile from Florence, between 1304 and 1305. Thanks to his highly original and impassioned defense of the vernacular in another postexilic work, the *Convivio* (The Banquet), Dante is traditionally known as the "father of the Italian language."[2] In the stirring conclusion to the first book of that treatise, which was the first example of philosophical prose in any modern vernacular, Dante speaks of his mother tongue as "the new sun that will rise there where the old sun will set, and that will give light to those who are in shadows and obscurity because the old sun does not shine for them."[3] One really ought to begin with Dante, since both in theory and in practice we encounter in Dante for the first time in all its complexity and importance the Italian "Questione della lingua," that is, the Language Question that has characterized Italian culture for more than seven centuries.[4]

This "Questione" is traditionally taken in two parts. In the first place, what shall be the language of cultured communication and literary expression, Latin or Italian? In the second place, if it is to be Italian, which of the vernacular languages of Italy shall serve as the model (Neapolitan or Venetian or Milanese or Florentine or Bergamasco?). In other words, if it is to be Italian, whose Italian? Dante, together with his fellow Florentines, Francis Petrarch and Giovanni Boccaccio, went a long way toward establishing the Florentine vernacular as the foundation for what eventually (by the end of this chapter) will come to be known as "Italian," by writing their vernacular literary masterpieces, the *Divine Comedy,* the *Songs and Sonnets* (*Canzoniere* or *Rerum vulgarium fragmenta*), and the *Decameron,* in their mother tongue.[5] For their preeminence as linguistic models, these authors eventually came to be known as the Tre Corone (Three Crowns). But first there was the matter of whether the language of Italian literature and culture was to be Latin or the vernacular language, and this prior question was very much at issue, and quite literally undecided, during the Quattrocento (fifteenth century). My aim in this essay, therefore, is to trace the main terms of this part of the debate as it developed between the first half of the century, when humanistic Latin was the dominant force, and the second half, which witnessed the forceful emergence of the vernacular, leading to the rapid resolution of both aspects of the "Questione," in terms that can only be foreshadowed in this context, during the first decades of the sixteenth century.

One would have thought that Dante had resolved the Latin versus vernacular question once and for all by writing the *Divine Comedy* in the vernacular. The *Commedia* was the first classic work of literature written in a modern vernacular, the first to receive the kind of extensive scholarly treatment by learned commentators in its own day that had until that time been reserved for the Bible and literary classics such as Virgil and Ovid; and more than six hundred surviving manuscripts of the *Comedy* testify to Dante's enormous success throughout Italy during the Trecento. Yet one need only consider the canon of the works of Petrarch and of Boccaccio to be disabused of the idea that Dante had decided the question and that the vernacular had won the day. With the exception of his lyric poetry (*Songs and Sonnets* and the Dantean *Triumphs*), everything else Petrarch wrote was composed in Latin. Even the annotations Petrarch addressed to himself in the margins of autograph manuscripts of his vernacular lyrics were written in Latin, which suggests that Petrarch's domestic everyday language, the language he used when talking to himself and presumably when dreaming, was not the vernacular but Latin. Boccaccio, on the other hand, started out writing in the Florentine vernacular tradition and very much under the influence of Dante. But after completing his hundred-novella vernacular masterpiece, the *Decameron*, between 1349 and 1351, he came more directly under the influence of Petrarch whom he met in Florence in 1350. A chronological list of Boccaccio's works reveals that he goes over almost completely to Latin after that date. The second part of Boccaccio's career is characterized by a series of works in Latin that would make his reputation as a humanist authority throughout Europe, including the encyclopedic *Genealogie deorum gentilium* (Genealogy of the gentile gods), his repertory of classical geographic sites, the *De montibus*, the *De casibus virorum illustrium* (On famous men), and the *De mulieribus claris* (On famous women), as well as the bucolic poetry.[6] Clearly, the tide had turned in the struggle between Latin and Italian in favor of Latin in the generation between Dante and Petrarch and Boccaccio. In political terms, the transition from the vernacular to Latin corresponded to the shift from the Italia of the free communes or city-states to the Italia of the *signorie*.

Petrarch first and foremost but Boccaccio right alongside him are considered the founders of humanism. They opened a path that would lead to the fifteenth century's rediscovery of the classical Latin and Greek literatures and the achievement of a renewed Latin style through the study of classical literature. Petrarch is considered the most influential of the early humanists by virtue of his study of classical and patristic authors and his rediscovery of several of the classical texts that were to become literary models and exemplars for humanism. The revolution he led entailed a radical devaluation of the vernacular between the end of the fourteenth and the beginning of the fifteenth century, as all energies came to be focused on the Latin and on the newly reintroduced Greek.[7] Petrarch himself referred disparagingly to his own love lyrics in the vernacular as so many insignificant "nugellae," or trifles. This poetry would later become the model for modern lyric poetry during the Renaissance, but its importance was obscured during the period of humanism's ascendancy in the fifteenth century. The state of the vernacular literature (which had been primarily poetic to that point) was so depressed during this period that the great Italian philosopher and critic of the last century Benedetto Croce famously described the hundred years between the death of Boccaccio in 1375 and the reemergence of vernacular literary culture at the "court" of Lorenzo de'Medici around 1475 as the "secolo senza poesia" (the century without poetry).[8]

Which brings us back to Father Dante's apparently ingenuous but in reality highly illuminating account of the origins of modern literature in the vernacular. Roughly translated, Dante informs us that "the first poet in the vernacular wrote in the vernacular because he wanted to make himself understood by the woman to whom he wanted to make love and who would have had a hard time understanding him if he had expressed himself in Latin. And this is why love is a particularly appropriate theme for those who write in the vernacular, since this type of writing was invented for talking about love." Historically, Dante refers in this passage to the itinerant court poets of twelfth-century Provence, the Troubadours, who began writing sophisticated lyric in a modern vernacular for the first time on the topic of love; they inaugurated the high lyric vernacular poetic tradition of which Dante (who places a representative troubadour in each of the three cantiche of the *Commedia*), Petrarch, and Shakespeare were inheritors, and which is still alive and well.

But literary genealogies aside, for the "Questione della lingua," what is particularly worth noting is the privileged relation that Dante establishes between poetry in the vernacular and the theme of love between the sexes. This theme from the beginning distinguished the vernacular literary system from the classical literary system and, by extension, from that of early Renaissance humanism, which did not reserve a privileged place for the theme of love but rather favored as its preeminent subject matter the heroic and virtuous actions of men, in matters of war, history, politics, or ethics as the case might be, but in any case, of men. Remember: Dante's love for Beatrice is the engine that powered the con-

struction of his antiepic epic, the *Divine Comedy*. When the early Florentine humanist Leonardo Bruni (1377–1444) wrote his "Life of Dante" he forgot to mention Beatrice but did not fail to mention Dante's stint in the Florentine cavalry.[9]
Even later in the Quattrocento when Florentine Neoplatonism had begun to shift
the balance, the ideological tension, not to say anatagonism, between humanism
and vernacular "love" persists and might be handily represented by the humanist Platina's (Bartolomeo Sacchi [Cremona, 1421–Rome, 1481]) dialogue *Contra
amores,* composed in 1471.[10]

Dante's "gendering" of the ideal audience for vernacular literature was pre-
scient from a historical perspective. For literature in the vernacular, in particular
vernacular lyric poetry, will reemerge as a prestigious literary form in courts of
Renaissance Italy around 1475, at the end of the "secolo senza poesia." It was at
this time that, as in the age of the troubadours and of Dante, poets, desiring to
make themselves understood to ladies and, more generally, to courtly audiences
for whom literature written in the Latin language would have been difficult to understand, turned to the vernacular. This development leads directly to the masterpieces of Italian High Renaissance literature that became models for early modern Europe such as the Neapolitan Sannazaro's *Arcadia,* the Ferrarese Ariosto's
Orlando Furioso, the Lombard Castiglione's *Book of the Courtier,* and the poetry of
mature Renaissance Petrarchism.

But to understand how this could occur, it is necessary to have a closer
look at the "secolo senza poesia" and the way in which developments during
the fifteenth century, in particular, the contributions of Florentine humanism,
prepared the way for the reemergence of the vernacular at the beginning of the
sixteenth century when a national model for modern "Italian" vernacular language and literature was finally established. In fact, the Florentine humanists during the time of Cosimo de' Medici (1389–1464) and his son Piero di Cosimo
(1416–1469) "il Gottoso," or "the Goutish," while taking a leading role in the
study of the Latin and Greek languages and literatures, also had reason to maintain some interest in vernacular literature since all the major achievements in
vernacular up until that time had been made by Florentines writing in the Florentine language. Humanists from other parts of Italy naturally had less stake
in the Florentine vernacular and no interest in cultivating their own regional or
municipal vernaculars, which were generally perceived to be less appropriate as
literary languages as a result of the success of Florentine literature throughout
Italy during the Trecento. For example, "Italian" humanists such as the Bolognese Antonio Beccadelli (1394–1471) known as Panormita, Guarino Veronese

(Verona, 1374–Ferrara, 1460), Lorenzo Valla (Rome, 1407–57), Biondo Flavio (Forlì, 1392–Rome, 1463), never wrote anything in the vernacular. Valla, the most important figure of the second generation of humanists, following that of the pioneers Bruni and Veronese, gives no sign of recognition that a vernacular literary tradition even existed.

On the other hand, nearly all of the major Florentine humanists made some use of the vernacular, including Leonardo Bruni, Cristoforo Landino, Poliziano, and of course Leon Battista Alberti, to whose efforts on behalf of the Florentine language I will return momentarily. While the great humanist and Florentine Coluccio Salutati (1331–1406; chancellor, 1375–1406) never wrote in the vernacular, he did uphold its prestige, citing Dante in his treatise on fortune, *De fato, fortuna et casu* (c. 1336). Significantly, he praised Dante's language (and not his poem) and spoke of "that most elegant Florentine idiom which alone among all the languages of the world, is adapted to poetic expression by virtue of its elegance and sweetness."[11]

Bruni was one of the most provocative and, some might say, pugnacious of the early humanists. Quite precociously attentive to the question of the vernacular, Bruni took it upon himself to write biographies of the classic Florentine authors Dante and Petrarch in the vernacular. But in his "Life of Dante" Bruni reveals the distance in terms of linguistic and literary culture that separated Dante and his humanist biographer when he writes that Dante composed the *Commedia* in the vernacular because his Latin was not nearly as good as his Florentine: And "the reason is," Bruni writes, "that his century was given over to rhyming while noble expression in prose or in Latin verses was unknown to men of the time who were rude and crude and without any skill in literature, educated as they were according to the scholastic and clerical methods." Bruni's "Life of Dante" praised the patriot-citizen Dante as much or more than it did the poet.[12]

The same ambivalent attitude toward the vernacular and its literary legacy found expression in another humanistic reflection on the vernacular by Bruni composed in 1401, the *Dialogi ad Petrum Histrum* (i.e., a dialogue addressed to Pier Paolo Vergerio of Capodistria).[13] This work, in two books, presents a discussion concerning the relation between the ancients and the moderns and the literary value of the works of Dante, Petrarch, and Boccaccio that was purported to have taken place in the literary salon of the Florentine chancellor Coluccio Salutati. Book 1 begins with ringing praises for the vernacular by no less than Salutati, who at one point enthuses, "I don't know why they [Dante, Petrarch, and Boccaccio] should not be numbered for the fullness of their human culture alongside the celebrated ancients. And if Dante had written in Latin, I would not be content to place him alongside those fathers of ours but I would put him ahead of them." Following Salutati's accolades, however, come the violent criticisms of Niccolò Niccoli, another Florentine humanist who is today, as he was then, particularly noted for collecting and annotating patristic and classical codexes. Niccoli is the spokesman for a fastidious and exclusive classicism that holds in disdain any form of vernacular literary expression:

> Who is this Dante, who is this Petrarch, what Boccaccio are you speaking to me about? Do you think that I judge according to the opinions of the vulgar and that I approve or disapprove that which the mob approves or disapproves of?

He goes on to accuse Dante of misunderstanding verses of Virgil cited by Dante in the *Divine Comedy*, verses that anyone who knew Latin would have easily understood:

> Shouldn't we be ashamed to call poet and to place even ahead of Virgil someone who didn't even know how to speak Latin?

And he concludes:

> I will deny that poet of yours [Dante] a place in the list of literate men and leave him with the tailors and the breadmakers and other men of that ilk. He spoke in fact in such a way as to be familiar only to such people.

The very founders of humanism, Petrarch and Boccaccio do not come off much better than Dante in Niccoli's assessment. Even Petrarch is ridiculed for the fanfare and exalted expectations associated with his epic poem in Latin, the *Africa*, which is described as a "ridiculous mouse." Wouldn't it have been better for Petrarch had he burned it? And Boccaccio's small merit is so evident in all his works that Niccoli doesn't spend any time discussing them.

It comes as quite a surprise then, given the emphatic nature of his attack on the Tre Corone in Book 1, when at the beginning of Book 2 Niccoli completely reverses position, claiming that he had assumed the earlier stance simply as a means of rhetorically stimulating Salutati to even stronger praise of the vernacular: "I didn't criticize those men because I thought them deserving of criticism,"

he says, "but to encourage Coluccio to praise them, driven by indignation."
Invited by the other interlocutors to make explicit his true viewpoint, Niccoli
launches into a generic exaltation of the Tre Corone that "comes across as less
convincing than the previous critique."[14] Bruno Migliorini was perhaps the first
to observe that while Niccoli retracts the opinions expressed in Book 1 and
praises the Tre Corone in Book 2, "some doubt about what his real opinions
were remains."[15] Indeed, according to a recent contribution by Paolo Trovato,
Book 1 was written before the death of Coluccio Salutati, and was probably initially conceived as a completed work. Book 2 was composed by Bruni only after
Salutati's death and, according to Trovato, was meant to serve as a rhetorical support for Bruni's candidacy to the chancellory of Florence.[16] But whatever the
explanation of Niccoli's abrupt change of opinion, it is clear that humanist debate about vernacular literature like the one depicted in Bruni's *Dialogi ad Petrum
Histrum* would have been impossible anywhere but in Florence during the first
half of the Quattrocento. Trovato's account of the genesis of the work underscores
the contemporary political significance of the "Questione della lingua" and the
continuing importance of the vernacular classics for Florentine cultural and political identity both at home and abroad. This political dimension of Florence's
vernacular literary legacy returns to the fore during the latter part of the century,
in its "foreign policy" implications, when the relationship between the Florentine literary tradition and Florentine political power and prestige in the peninsula becomes an important preoccupation of Lorenzo de' Medici and his circle.

But before proceeding, let us consider for a moment the impact of the
humanists' newfound knowledge of classical languages and literatures on linguistic theory of the time. Knowledge of new texts and an increasing historical
awareness of the Latin and Greek languages were decisive not only for the de-
liberation of Christian doctrinal issues like those faced by the great ecumenical
Council of Florence (1438–39). Just a few years earlier, in 1435 in Florence, in
the antechamber of Pope Eugene IV, many of the same humanist scholars who
would play a role in the Council of Florence took part in a discussion about an
important question of historical linguistics, a debate that would eventually involve virtually all of the major Italian humanists over the next fifty years.

In essence, the question was whether the spoken language of the ancient
Romans was the same as the Latin language found in Latin literature or if the
ancient Romans spoke a kind of agrammatical vernacular that was distinct from

the Latin language used in writing and surviving in the literature. The latter position was held by Leonardo Bruni, who argued in effect for a linguistic situation of substantial diglossia, that is, of two contemporaneous yet separate languages as a constant characteristic of the linguistic situation of the Latin West. The Latin literary language, according to this view (which was also that of Dante as expressed in the *De vulgari eloquentia*),[17] had always existed as an artificially created and maintained language of the elite alongside an agrammatical vernacular unsuited to culture. Bruni imagined the linguistic situation of ancient Rome to have been more or less the same as that of Quattrocento Italy, where the written language of culture was the Latin language used by the elite and the agrammatical vernacular served as the spoken language of the masses.[18]

The opposing position taken by Biondo Flavio, among others, argued for a substantial monolinguism in the ancient period that was subsequently disrupted by the trauma of the barbaric invasions and by the Fall of the Empire. What was significant about this second position for the contemporary "Questione della lingua" is the way it conceived of both the Latin and the vernacular as historical, natural languages. The vernacular is conceived of by Biondo Flavio quite accurately as the natural product of the transformation of Latin. Biondo went so far in his "De verbis romanae locutionis" (1435) as to arrive at a breakthrough formulation of the inherent grammaticality of the Italian vernaculars:

> In all speakers, even of the most corrupt vernacular, in every part of Italy, we find, inherent to the very nature of the idiom, that no one is so rustic, so crude or so obtuse of intellect that he doesn't know how to vary the cases, tenses, modes and number as required by the temporality and the logic of what he is trying to express.[19]

This debate in historical linguistics had important implications, since Bruni's position, which posited a written Latin language of the elite opposed to an agrammatical vernacular, effectively undermined any claims the vernacular might have as a language of culture. The conceptual position of Biondo Flavio, on the other hand, in spite of his own humanistic disdain for the vernacular, opened the way to a recognition of the grammaticality of the vernacular and therefore of a potential parity between the two languages. In fact, Leon Battista Alberti, the major humanist promoter of the vernacular during the first half of the Quattrocento, will take this theoretical issue of the Bruni–Biondo debate as his point of departure and undertake to demonstrate the inherent grammaticality of the vernacular.

Alberti, born in Genoa in 1404, the illegitimate son of a wealthy Florentine merchant family that had been exiled from Florence for their participation in the Ciompi revolt and the government of the guilds that had followed, was a perfectly formed humanist in both Greek and Latin. He studied canon law in Bologna and eventually assumed a post as a functionary at the papal court from around 1431. He was in Florence with Eugene IV at the time of the linguistic discussions.[20] Alberti is best known to students of the Renaissance for his treatises on painting (*Della pittura*), sculpture, and architecture (*De re aedificatoria*). Mirko Tavoni has acutely defined Alberti as an "extraordinary outsider,"[21] an outsider who applied, in the words of another recent commentator, Formentin, "to the diversity of the real the inexhausible curiosity of his intellect, pursuing a continuous experimentation which was devoid of any sort of prejudice."[22] No less than Alberti's unique combination of genius, Florentine family background and the perspective of exile were required to relaunch the vernacular as a language of culture and literature.

Alberti understood clearly that Bruni's view that the vernacular was intrinsically agrammatical led necessarily to the conclusion that it could never serve as a language of literature and culture on a plane with Latin. He therefore undertook to demonstrate the grammaticality of the vernacular by composing the first grammar of any modern vernacular language, the *Grammatica della lingua toscana,* fifty years before what is often considered the first—Nebrija's grammar of the Castilian language of 1492.[23] The brief introductory paragraph to Alberti's treatise can speak for itself as to Alberti's polemical target and his programmatic intents and purposes:

> Those who affirm that the Latin language was not common to all Romans but only to certain erudite scholastics, as today we see it possessed only by the few, I believe will put aside this erroneous opinion of theirs when they see this little book of ours, in which I have collected the usage of our language in the form of very brief annotations.[24]

Alberti went on to offer a concise description (it is a descriptive not a prescriptive grammar) of the contemporary Florentine vernacular (not the language of the Tre Corone) using the paradigms of Latin grammar as an effective means of demonstrating its inherent grammaticality. Alberti later returned again to the terms of the Bruni–Biondo debate in the prefatory letter, addressed to Francesco D'Altobianco Alberti, to the third book of what is generally considered his vernacular literary masterpiece, *Della Famiglia* (On the family). The apology or defense of his decision to write this work in the vernacular merits fuller citation and greater consideration than it can be give in this context:

> I do not think we can agree with those who, amazed by so great a loss, assert that the common language we speak today always existed in Italy, both before and after the invasions. They state that they cannot believe women in those times could know all the forms of the Latin language which today are quite difficult and obscure even for learned men. For this reason they conclude that the language in which learned men wrote was a literary art and invention understood rather than used by the majority. If I had intentions of disputing this opinion, I could ask them to tell me who among the ancients wrote in any language but Latin. . . . And I should also ask if anyone ever spoke in public or in private in any other language than the one which, being common to all, was used by all when they wrote and when they spoke to the people or to their friends. . . . Would it have been reasonable for ancient authors to strive to be useful to all their fellow citizens and yet write in a language known only to a few. . . . I do not think that any learned man will deny what I believe to be true, that is, that all ancient authors wrote so that they might be understood by all their fellow citizens. . . . Who will be so foolhardy as to condemn me for not writing in a way he cannot understand? On the contrary, wise men will perhaps praise me for choosing to be of use to many, by writing so that everyone may understand me, rather than to please just a few, for you know how few erudite people there are today. I should be very happy, however, if those who know how to criticize also knew how to earn praise through their writings. I admit that the ancient Latin language is very elegant and its vocabulary abundant. I do not see, however, why today we must scorn our Tuscan language so much that we should dislike anything written in it, no matter how excellent. . . . Let us grant that because of the many learned authors who used it this ancient language has as much authority among all peoples as they say. Ours will gain it too if learned men choose to make it elegant and polished through their efforts and studies.[25]

In this groundbreaking passage Alberti interpreted coherently and took to their logical conclusion the high ideals of Florentine civic humanism elaborated during the first half of the century and applied it to the vernacular language question. Alberti's position, in drawing attention to the fact that there were so many who knew little or no Latin, suggested that in order to be true to their own cultural ideals, it was high time for the humanists themselves to begin dedicating some of their energies to the cultivation of the vernacular. Like any civic humanist worthy of the name, Alberti sought to unite theory and practice in his own writings. In addition, he made another major contribution to the cause of the vernacular, when he organized and promoted in 1441 a special poetic competition in Florence under the patronage of Piero di Cosimo de' Medici, the Certame coronario. Organized by Alberti as a means of sanctioning the renewed dignity of vernacular poetic eloquence, a jury of the most distinguished humanists of the time, including Poggio Bracciolini and Biondo Flavio, was enlisted for the purpose. The contestants were invited to propose a composition on the classical Ciceronian topic of friendship. Indeed, the title of the contest ("Certame coronario," a crude latinism) and the choice of theme reveal the humanistic nature of Alberti's vernacular program that sought to build a modern vernacular literary and linguistic culture by taking classical Latin literature as its foundation and framework. The contestants accordingly did not write in imitation of the Duecento love poets or even Dante and Petrarch but rather actually sought to adopt the metrical structure of classical poetry (including hexameters and sapphic strophes) to the vernacular, as if to compete directly with classical models.[26]

The humanistic jurors, however, would have none of it. They refused to award the prize, a demurral that led Alberti to anonymously address a "protesta" to the members of the jury in which he reaffirmed his determined desire to break down the linguistic separation that existed between lettered and unlettered persons.[27] It is clear from the response, however, that Alberti received from the jury of the Certame coronario, that what was fatally lacking to his bold and energetic promotion of the vernacular language was the general support of humanistic culture, which was as yet unwilling to go along with his attempts to put the modern language on the same plane as that of the ancient. No less significantly (and it can only strike us today as a remarkable sign of the depths to which the literary prestige of the Tre Corone had plunged during humanism), Alberti never displayed the least bit of interest in Dante, Petrarch, and Boccaccio. He approached the problem of vernacular reform and renewal from a contemporary, not to say modernistic, Quattrocento perspective. In effect, Alberti's program called for the invention from ground zero of a modern vernacular literature based completely on the foundation of Latin humanistic culture and classical literary models. Alberti's program was tantamount to a jettisoning of Dante's *Commedia*, Petrarch's lyric poetry, and Boccaccio's *Decameron* and beginning anew. Thus, the "extraordinary outsider" found himself not only up against the rigid classicizing of the humanists of all Italy, but his program also went against the grain of the vernacular tradition itself and the considerable literary legacy that stood behind it. It was a vernacular literary tradition that had no match among any of the other modern vernacular literary traditions to that date, and eventually would serve admirably as the foundation for the modern Italian language and literature that emerged during the High Renaissance.

But how was this vernacular tradition to be resurrected? A combination of technological, cultural, and political factors needs to be considered, beginning with a technical advance (the most important since writing and until the invention of electronic media) introduced into Italy from Germany during the 1460s that became increasingly important as the Quattrocento drew to a close: movable type. The first book to be printed in Italy was a rhetorical work of Cicero's and the second was Lactantius's *Divine Institutes,* printed by Sweynheim and Pannartz in 1465 in Rome, an ornate treatise on systematic theology (in a style modeled on that of Cicero). In these first two printed books one sees the humanist harmonization of classical and Christian cultures materially expressed by the history of printing. Not long after, vernacular literary classics began to appear in print throughout Italy. Windelin of Speyer published in Venice in 1470 the lyric poetry of Petrarch, and in Naples, between 1470 and 1471, the first edition or *princeps* of Boccaccio's *Decameron* appeared; another edition of Boccaccio's masterpiece appeared in Venice above the mark of Valdarfer, and another Roman edition of the vernacular poetry of Petrarch by Lauer appeared in Rome in 1471. There were three more or less contemporaneous and independent editions of Dante's *Commedia* in 1472 (in Mantua, Venezia [o Iesi] and Foligno); another imprint of Petrarch's poetry (in Padua) and of Boccaccio's *Decameron* as well came out the same year, as did two editions of Boccaccio's *Filocolo* and one of his sentimental prose romances, written from the point of view of a woman in love, the *Fiammetta*.[28]

The priority given to the great Florentine authors of the Trecento and the quantity of editions produced throughout Italy (significantly, at least initially, Florence did not feel the need to print its own classics) reflect a strong and renewed interest in the vernacular literary tradition outside of Tuscany, especially in the Italian courts. Indeed, the emergence of a flourishing courtly culture throughout the peninsula in the second half of the Quattrocento was to put increasing

pressure on the humanists who wanted to adhere strictly to the earlier exclusionary and dismissive attitude toward the vernacular. Alberti had been right
about the relatively small number of people who were well enough educated in
Latin to participate in the humanist culture, and the drawbacks of continuing to
work under the illusion that those outside the circle of Latin humanist learning
were to be left in a kind of subcultural agrammatical no-man's-land.

As became increasingly clear during the second half of the century, throughout Italy princes and gentlemen and ladies of the court could be expected to
attain the level of competence of the austere humanists in only exceptional
cases. Indeed, the intellectual and linguistic requirements of Latin and Greek
humanism had become only more exigent and rarified as the century progressed.
In the courts one encounters a situation like that Dante had described as operative at the origins of vernacular literature. The reemergence of love as a theme
and vernacular poetry and prose as the means to explore it are exemplified
in this period in a wide variety of contexts: one of the most significant examples is Matteo Maria Boiardo's collection of vernacular lyric, the *Amorum
libri*, written at the Estense court of Ferrara between 1469 and 1476.[29] This
trend received a tremendous ideological-philosophical boost from Florentine
Neoplatonism.

This is not the place to address the philosophical importance of the Florentine Neoplatonism that emerged from the Medici circle and from the mind
and the pen of Marsilio Ficino (1433–99), translator of and commentator on the
works of Plato during the second half of the fifteenth century. For the limited purposes of this discussion of the language question, one might simply observe that
Renaissance Neoplatonism was not restricted to austere philosophical treatises
but broadly influenced the society of the times, in a manner not unlike the way
Freud's psychoanalysis permeated the literary and philosophical culture during
the twentieth century. In this context Ficino's Neoplatonism, according to which
desire of beauty and love were the privileged means through which man might
elevate himself to an apprehension of the supreme perfection of God, stimulated
a renewed appreciation of the philosophical import and resonance of the Trecento
vernacular literary tradition. Ficinian Neoplatonism can be said to have provided
the humanistic cultural-ideological authorization (which had been lacking until
that time) for the revival of the vernacular literary tradition that took place during the last quarter of the century at Lorenzo de' Medici's "court."[30]

From a political perspective, the renewed interest in vernacular literature
in the courts of Italy, both of the major regional states—Venice, Milan, Florence,

Rome and Naples—and of smaller centers like Ferrara and Mantua, emerged during a period of relative peace and stability following the peace of Lodi in 1454. The relative balance of power among the five major states that was achieved around midcentury (thanks largely to the diplomatic efforts of Cosimo de' Medici) permitted a period of relatively undisturbed cultural activity and served as a kind of incubation period for the High Renaissance. Before the first French incursion into the Italian peninsula by Charles VIII in 1494 and the beginning of the Italian wars made familiar by the writings of Machiavelli and Guicciardini, Italy enjoyed a period of relative calm, between 1454 and the death of Lorenzo de' Medici. In fact, according to a commonplace of Italian Renaissance historiography, Lorenzo was known as "l'ago della bilancia" during the later part of this period of relative equilibrium, that is, literally, as the "needle in the balance" or the "man in the middle," the arbiter of politics in the peninsula at this time.[31] Under Lorenzo's leadership, and in the technological, cultural, and political context described above, the late fifteenth century was the period of Florence's greatest reputation as a cultural center. It was under Lorenzo's leadership that Florence then undertook a broad cultural program in favor of the vernacular that enlisted the talents of, besides Lorenzo himself, Florence's leading humanist literary critic, Cristoforo Landino (1424–98), and the greatest poet and humanist philologist of the period, Agnolo Poliziano or Politian (1454–94).

Cristoforo Landino held a professorship in the Florentine university from 1458, and during his tenure, Dante and Petrarch became subjects of university study on the same plane as Virgil and Horace.[32] The focus of Landino's program of linguistic reform, on the other hand, was the transfer from the Latin to the vernacular of those elements of grammar and lexicon lacking to the modern tongue. Translation as a means of strengthening the linguistic structure and lexical resources of the Florentine language (which was particularly weak in scientific vocabulary) accordingly represented a characteristic component of Landino's approach that followed directly from Alberti's precedent. Landino applied in practice the principles of his theory in a landmark and controversial translation into the Florentine vernacular of Pliny's encyclopedic *Naturalis historia* (1472–74), which he dedicated to the king of Naples, Ferdinand I of Aragon. It is at this time that one witnesses a revival of the tradition of translations into the vernacular from the Latin that had been so strong during the Due-Trecento, an activity that had been interrupted during the first half of the Quattrocento, when translating the knowledge and eloquence of the ancients into the vernacular was considered casting pearls to swine.[33]

Landino's appreciation and cultivation of the Florentine vernacular classics meanwhile (which distinguishes him from his predecessor, Alberti) derived in large measure from his keen awareness of the cultural-political advantages of cultivating the Florentine vernacular as a model for the peninsula as a whole. It was an awareness that was shared by the other Laurentians and by Lorenzo himself. Landino's greatest contribution in this regard was his monumental Neoplatonic commentary on Dante's *Commedia,* published in 1481, which will concern us in a moment. But first, a prior illustration of this cultural-political dimension of the Laurentian promotion of the vernacular was the *Raccolta aragonese,* an anthology of ancient and modern vernacular lyric poetry that was dedicated in 1477 to the son of King Ferdinand of Naples, Federigo.[34] The collection recapitulated the entire tradition, beginning with poems of Dante, followed by mainly Tuscan poets of the Due-Trecento and Quattrocento poets, concluding with none other than selected lyrics of Lorenzo de' Medici himself. Lorenzo signed the dedicatory letter also, although Politian is believed to have actually composed it. Politian is credited as well with the philological study of the vernacular tradition that went into the preparation of the anthology. This *Raccolta* therefore has been considered the beginning of Italian vernacular philology accomplished by the greatest scholar of classical Latin and Greek of his age. But beyond its philological importance, the *Raccolta aragonese* expressed an aspiration to Florentine cultural hegemony vis-à-vis the contemporary linguistic scene of Italy. The Tuscan language and literary tradition were presented to Naples in the *Raccolta aragonese* as a prestigious model worthy of imitation. The inclusion of Lorenzo's poetry promotes Lorenzo and his circle as the living inheritors of the leading vernacular tradition in the context of a contemporary vernacular literary scene that was in ferment throughout Italy.

Landino's edition and commentary on Dante in fact, just a few years later (1481), was also conceived in response to that ferment. It represented a counter-offensive to what the Florentines perceived to be the expropriation of their author Dante by other Italian centers that had produced the earliest editions of Dante's poem during the 1470s.[35] One of these, the Milanese edition of 1478, had had the effrontery to present Dante's poem together with the Trecento commentary of the Bolognese Iacopo della Lana and actually to praise the superiority of the Bolognese dialect among all the dialects of Italy. Landino's proem thus included an "apology in which Dante and Florence are defended from false accusers." Landino takes credit for "having liberated our citizen from the barbarisms of many foreign idioms by which he had been corrupted and presented him simple and pure . . . after long exile. . . . not . . . as a romagnolo or a Lombard nor as being any of the idioms that have commented on him but as a mere Florentine." The first vernacular commentary since the Trecento, Landino's 1481 Neoplatonic exegesis, represents a sort of official Laurentian Florentine interpretation of the poem. The edition (which was originally to have been illustrated by engravings based on designs by Botticcelli, only a few of which were executed) became the Dante of the Italian Renaissance, and was reprinted repeatedly for the next one hundred years in various formats throughout the peninsula.

But Lorenzo de' Medici's poetry, and in particular the introductory letter to his *Comento,* or commentary, on a selection of his own lyric poetry (in imitation of Dante's *Vita nuova* and *Convivio*) also from the early 1480s (c. 1482–84), is perhaps the best place to find the explicit articulation of the way in which Florentine political power and ambitions were implicated in the renewed commitment to Florence's vernacular literary tradition toward the end of the Quattrocento. After defending his dedication to love poetry by means of Neoplatonic philosophical commonplaces and appeals to the authority of Dante, Petrarch, and Boccaccio, Lorenzo defended his use of the contemporary Florentine language and expressed the hope that

> perhaps there are yet to be written in this language subtle and important things worthy of being read; especially since until now has represented the adolescence of this language, for it is everyday becoming more elegant and noble. And it could easily happen that in its youthful and adult ages it might come to greater perfection, especially if it were accompanied by some prosperous success and increase of the Florentine empire.[36]

But we know that there was to be no increase of the Florentine "empire" as Lorenzo termed it. He himself would be dead less than ten years later in 1492 at the age of forty-three. Two years after that, in 1494, Charles the VIII of France invaded Italy and the Medici family was driven into exile, thus precipitating the peninsula into a series of foreign invasions and wars, which culminated in the 1527 Sack of Rome and were only concluded by the Peace of Cambrai in 1529, which sealed imperial Hapsburg domination of Italy.

From a linguistic point of view, the Florentine path outlined by Lorenzo and the Laurentians came to represent just one of several positions put forward during the period of the Italian wars in response to the second of the queries posed by the "Questione della lingua," that is, which vernacular was to be the model for modern Italy. This Florentine option, which was eloquently and passionately (as always) argued by Niccolò Machiavelli in his "Dialogo intorno alla nostra lingua,"[37] conceived of the living vernacular language of Florence as a living legacy. This position depended on the "prosperous increase of the Florentine empire," to use Lorenzo's words, in the peninsula for its success. (In this sense, Machiavelli's "Dialogo" represented a linguistic program to go along with the political program of *The Prince*.) A second approach, promoted by, among others, the Lombard courtier Baldassare Castiglione in *The Book of the Courtier*, called for a "lingua cortigiana" (courtier language): a hybrid cosmopolitan linguistic model for Italy that would integrate Latin, Tuscan, and foreign elements into a modern spoken and literary vernacular based on the most cultivated language spoken in the courts of Italy.[38] Both Florentine and courtly options were, however, fatally compromised by the political crisis that engulfed Italy during the first decades of the sixteenth century. The response to the "Questione della lingua" that ultimately prevailed was that of "vernacular humanism," championed by the Venetian humanist, poet, and grammarian Pietro Bembo who programmatically outlined his proposal in the *Prose della volgar lingua* (1525). Bembo argued in that work for the imitation of the Tuscan vernacular classics, in particular, Petrarch for poetry and Boccaccio for prose, and the revival of fourteenth-century grammatical and rhetorical norms that could be culled from these authors (handily provided in the grammar contained in Book 3).[39] Ultimately, the success of Bembo's vernacular humanism as a response to the "Questione della lingua" was the result of a confluence of political, cultural, and technological factors. Politically, the Italian wars had brought home the point that culturally and politically divided Italy did not and could not share a common spoken language (before the invention of radio and television) and that therefore no single modern spoken idiom, whether Florentine or "courtly" or Bergamasco, could serve the peninsula as a whole. Culturally, the Latin humanists of the previous century had effectively provided both a fertile national intellectual territory on which to practice a common strategy and a pedagogical model based on the principle of imitation. Humanist educational models were, in fact, ideally suited for a vernacular alphabetization of the peninsula. The process of teaching Italians how to read and write (not to speak) Italian, based on the Florentine literary classics, would be little different in its principles from the humanist education of the peninsula that had been based on the works of Virgil and Cicero. The printed book, finally, made possible a dissemination of the written linguistic and literary model of the Trecento throughout the peninsula in such a way that for the first time one could speak of the vernacular of Italy as no longer Florentine but Italian. Indeed, Venetian grammarians like Bembo together with the Venetian printers would play as large or larger a role than the Florentine humanists in the promulgation of the new Italian language and literature during the sixteenth century. But how and why they did is the topic for another essay.

NOTES

1. Dante Alighieri, *Vita nuova*, in *Opere minori*, edited by Domenico De Robertis (Milan: R Ricciardi, 1995), vol. 1, t. 1, 88–90; *Vita nuova*, translated with an introduction by Mark Musa (Oxford: Oxford University Press, 1992), 54.

2. For the notion of Dante as "father of the Italian language," see the chapter dedicated to Dante in Bruno Migliorini, *Storia della lingua italiana* (1960; Florence: Sansoni, 1978), 179–94. For an English version of Migliorini's classic, see *The Italian Language*, abridged and recast by T. Gwynfor Griffith (London: Faber and Faber, 1966).

3. "Questo sarà luce nuova, sole nuovo, lo quale surgerà là dove l'usato tramonterà, e darà lume a coloro che sono in tenebre e in oscuritade per lo usato sole che a loro non luce." Dante Alighieri, *Convivio*, in *Opere minori*, vol. 2, t. 1, 174–75.

4. The classic treatment is Bruno Migliorini's essay "La questione della lingua," in *Questioni e correnti di storia letteraria*, edited by U. Bosco et al. (Milan: Marzorati, 1963), 1–75. For synthetic discussions, see Bortolo Tommaso Sozzi, "La questione della lingua," in *Dizionario critico della letteratura italiana*, directed by Vittore Branca (Torino: UTET, 1986), vol. 2, 620–30; and Robert Hall Anderson, *The Italian Questione della Lingua, an Interpretative Essay* (Chapel Hill: University of North Carolina Press, 1942).

5. The son of Florentine exile Petrarch's vernacular was memorably described as "transcendental Florentine" by Gianfranco Contini in a classic essay "Preliminari sulla lingua di Petrarca," in *Francesco Petrarca Canzoniere*, critical text and introduction by Gianfranco Contini (Turin: Einaudi, 1980), xv.

6. For these texts, see *Tutte le opere di Giovanni Boccaccio*, edited by Vittore Branca (Milan: Mondadori, 1964–98), including *Carmina*, edited by Giuseppe Velli (vol. 5, t. 1); *Genealogie deorum gentilium: De Montibus, Silvis, Fontibus, Lacubus, Fluminibus, Stagnis Seu Paludibus, De Diversis Nominibus Maris*, edited by Vittore Branca (vols. 7–8, t. 1–2); *De casibus virorum illustrium*, edtied by P. G. Ricci e V. Zaccaria (vol. 9); and *De mulieribus claris*, edited by V. Zaccaria (vol. 10).

7. Following Boccaccio's (and Petrarch's) tentative encounters with Greek through Leontius Pilatus, who made a Latin translation of Homer in the 1360s (Petrarch himself had no Greek), Manuele Crisolora (1350–1415) brought Greek to Italy and began teaching the language in the Florentine *Studio* in 1397 thanks to the sponsorship of Coluccio Salutati and of the Florentine republic.

8. See Benedetto Croce, "Il secolo senza poesia," in *Poesia popolare e poesia d'arte: Studi sulla poesia italiana dal Tre al Cinquecento,* edited by Piero Cudini (Naples: Bibliopolis, 1991), 191–216.

9. Bruni instead makes a point of emphasizing Dante's civility in taking a wife and having children. This is in contrast to Boccaccio's "Life of Dante" in which Beatrice had figured prominently, as did a discourse on why men dedicated to literature and study should never marry. See Leonardo Bruni, *Opere letterarie e politiche* (Turin: UTET, 1996), 541–42.

10. Platina, a member of the so-called Roman academy under the leadership of Julius Pomponius Laetus, director of the Vatican Library after 1475, is perhaps best known for his history of the popes (*Liber de vita Christi ac omnium pontificium*) and other Latin treatises, including *De principe, De optimo cive, De falso et vero bono,* and *De vera nobilitate.* See *Bartolomeo Sacchi il Platina (Piadena 1421–Roma 1481): Atti del Convegno internazionale di studi per il V centenario (Cremona, 14–15 Novembre 1981),* edited by Augusto Campana and Paola Medioli Masotti (Padua: Antenore, 1986).

11. Cited by Eugenio Garin, "La letteratura degli umanisti," in *Storia della letteratura italiana,* edited by E. Cecchi and N. Sapegno (Milan: Garzanti, 1965–69), vol. 3, *Il Quattrocento e l'Ariosto* (1969), 16 n 1.

12. Bruni, *Opere letterarie e politiche,* 550–51.

13. Citations are from Eugenio Garin, ed., *Prosatori latini del Quattrocento* (Milan: R. Ricciardi, 1952), 41–99.

14. Vittorio Formentin, "La 'crisi' linguistica del quattrocento," in *Storia della letteratura italiana,* edited by Enrico Malato, vol. 3: *Il Quattrocento* (Rome: Salerno, 1996), 162.

15. Migliorini, *Storia della lingua italiana,* 262.

16. Paolo Trovato, "Dai 'Dialogi ad Petrum Histrum' alle 'Vite di Dante e del Petrarca,' Appunti su Leonardo Bruni e la tradizione trecentesca," *Studi petrarcheschi* 2 (1985): 263–84.

17. See Dante Alighieri, *De vulgari eloquentia,* in *Opere minori* (bk. 1, ix, 8–11, 1, x, 2), edited by Pier Vincenzo Mengaldo (Milan-Naples: R. Ricciardi, 1996), vol. 3, t. 1, 78–83. For an English-language translation and commentary, see *De vulgari eloquentia,* edited and translated by Steven Botterill (Cambridge: Cambridge University Press, 1996).

18. Bruni's thesis was misrepresented in the debate by Biondo Flavio who attributed to him the view that the popular Latin spoken in ancient Rome corresponded to the modern vernacular. See Mirko Tavoni, *Latino, grammatica, volgare: Storia di una questione umanistica* (Padua: Antenore, 1984), 5–10; for the debate in general, see also Mirko Tavoni, "The Language Spoken by the Ancient Romans," *Historiographica Linguistica* 9.3 (1982): 237–64. Bruni's notion of a popular spoken Latin language from which the modern vernacular developed in fact corresponds, broadly speaking, to the modern concept that the modern vernaculars developed from "Vulgar Latin." See Claudio Marazzini, *La lingua italiana: Profilo storico* (Bologna: Il Mulino, 1994), 15.

19. Biondo Flavio, "De verbis romanae locutionis Blondi ad Leonardum Aretinum," in Tavoni, *Latino, grammatica, volgare,* 214–15.

20. For a recent biographical treatment, see Anthony Grafton, *Leon Battista Alberti: Master Builder of the Italian Renaissance* (New York: Hill and Wang, 2000).

21. Mirko Tavoni, *Il Quattrocento* (Milan: Il Mulino, 1992), 63.

22. Formentin, "La 'crisi' linguistica," 173.

23. See Antonio de Nebrija, *Gramática de la lengua Castellana y estudios nebrisenses: 1492–1992* (Madrid: Ediciones de Cultura Hispánica, Instituto de Cooperación Ibero-americana, 1992), 3 vols. (including a facsimile of the 1492 edition of the *Gramática de la lengua castellana*, a critical edition of the grammar by Antonio Quilis, and a volume of studies edited by Manuel Alvar).

24. Citation from Leon Battista Alberti, *Grammatichetta e altri scritti sul volgare*, edited by Giuseppe Patota (Rome: Salerno, 1996), 15. For Alberti and the language question, see the studies of Cecil Grayson, *Studi su Leon Battista Alberti*, edited by Paolo Claut (Florence: Olschki, 1998).

25. For the original, see Leon Battista Alberti, *I libri della famiglia*, edited by Ruggiero Romano and Alberto Tenenti (Torino: Einaudi, 1969), 185–89. The translation is from *The Albertis of Florence: Leon Battista Alberti's Della famiglia*, translated and with an introduction and notes by Guido A. Guarino (Lewisburg: Bucknell University Press, 1971), 160–61.

26. These texts together with commentary are available in *De vera amicitia: I testi del primo Certame coronario*, edited by Lucia Bertolini (Modena: Panini, 1993).

27. For the entire episode, see Guglielmo Gorni, "Storia del Certame coronario," *Rinascimento* 2.12 (1972): 135–81, where the "Protesta" is characterized as one of the most efficacious polemical prose pieces of the tradition. For the text, see Alberti, *Grammatichetta e altri scritti sulla lingua*, 42–52.

28. On printing in Italy and its impact on the literary system, see two recent books by Brian Richardson: *Printing, Writers, and Readers in Renaissance Italy* (Cambridge: Cambridge University Press, 1999) and *Print Culture in Renaissance Italy: The Editor and the Vernacular Text, 1470–1600* (Cambridge: Cambridge University Press, 1994).

29. For Boiardo and the language question, see Pier Vincenzo Mengaldo's classic study, *La lingua del Boiardo lirico* (Florence: Olschki, 1963); and for an English-language version, *Amorum libri: The Lyric Poems of Matteo Maria Boiardo*, translated with an introduction and notes by Andrea di Tommaso (Binghamton, N.Y.: Medieval and Renaissance Texts and Studies; Ottawa: Dovehouse Editions, 1993). The other major non-Tuscan center for lyric poetry in this period was the Aragonese court of Naples, which fostered its own Renaissance masterpiece in the bucolic genre, Jacopo Sannazaro's *Arcadia*. See Tavoni, *Storia della lingua italiana: Il Quattrocento*, 99–104, for a synthetic characterization of this literature and a bibliography.

30. See the classic works of Paul Oskar Kristeller on this topic, including *The Philosophy of Marsilio Ficino*, translated by Virginia Conant (New York: Columbia University Press, 1943); as well as the several studies of Michael J. B. Allen, including *The Platonism of Marsilio Ficino: A Study of His Phaedrus Commentary, Its Sources and Genesis* (Berkeley: University of California Press, 1984); and a book by Arthur Field, *The Origins of the Platonic Academy of Florence* (Princeton: Princeton University Press, 1988). See also *Ficino and Renaissance Neoplatonism*, edited by Konrad Eisenbichler and Olga Zorzi Pugliese (Ottawa:

Dovehouse Editions, 1986); and for an older study that presents some of the more popular repercussions of Renaissance Italian Neoplatonism, see Adeline Nesca Robb, *Neoplatonism of the Italian Renaissance* (London: Allen & Unwin, 1935).

31. Among a spate of recent publications on Lorenzo deriving from the celebrations of five hundred years since his death in 1492, see *Lorenzo the Magnificent: Culture and Politics,* edited by Michael Mallett and Nicholas Mann (London: Warburg Institute, University of London, 1996); Melissa Meriam Bullard, *Lorenzo il Magnifico: Image and Anxiety, Politics and Finance* (Florence: Olschki, 1994); and *Lorenzo il Magnifico e il suo mondo: Convegno internazionale di studi (Florence, 9–13 giugno 1992),* edited by Gian Carlo Garfagnini (Florence: Olschki, 1994).

32. See C. Landino, *Scritti critici e teorici,* edited by R. Cardini, 2 vols. (Rome: Bulzoni, 1974). For Landino and the language question, see Marco Santoro, "Cristoforo Landino e il volgare," *Giornale storico della letteratura italiana* 131 (1954): 501–47.

33. Carlo Dionisotti has suggested in fact that the reason Boccaccio's "volgarizzamento" of Livy was handed down unattributed to him was because Boccaccio was already loathe to be associated with the translation from Latin to the vernacular after he had come under the strong influence of Petrarch's Latin humanism. See "Tradizione classica e volgarizzamenti," in *Geografia e storia della letteratura italiana* (Turin: Einaudi, 1971), 125–78.

34. See the classic essay by Michele Barbi, "La Raccolta aragonese," in *Studi sul Canzoniere di Dante* (Florence: Sansoni, 1915 [rpt. 1965]), 217–326. For more recent discussion, see Domenico De Robertis, "La Raccolta aragonese primogenita," in *Editi e rari: Studi sulla tradizione letteraria tra Tre e Cinquecento* (Milan: Feltrinelli, 1978), 50–65; and Corrado Bologna, *Tradizione dei classici italiani* (Turin: G. Einaudi, 1986, 1993), 201–19.

35. See Paolo Procaccioli, *Filologia ed esegesi dantesca nel quattrocento: l'Inferno nel Comento sopra La comedia di Cristoforo Landino,* introduction by Giorgio Petrocchi (Florence: Olschki, 1989).

36. Lorenzo de' Medici, "Comento ad alcuni sonetti d'amore (proemio)," in *Lorenzo de' Medici, scritti scelti,* edited by Emilio Bigi (Torino: UTET, 1965), 293–313. For an English-language version of the *Comento,* see *The Autobiography of Lorenzo de' Medici the Magnificent: A commentary on my sonnets together with the text of Il comento in the critical edition of Tiziano Zanato,* translated with an introduction by James Wyatt Cook (Binghamton, N.Y.: Medieval and Renaissance Texts and Studies, 1995).

37. Niccolò Machiavelli, *Discorso o Dialogo intorno alla nostra lingua,* edited by Paolo Trovato (Padua: Antenore, 1982). See Carlo Dionisotti, "Machiavelli e la lingua fiorentina," in *Machiavellerie* (Turin: Einaudi, 1900), 267–363.

38. See Baldassare Castiglione, *Il libro del Cortegiano,* edited by Bruno Maier (Turin: UTET, 1981), "La lettera a Don Michel de Silva" (69–80) and bk. 1, XXVIII–XLI (131–61). A convenient English-language version is Baldassare Castiglione, *The Book of The Courtier,* translated by George Bull (New York: Penguin USA, 1976).

39. Pietro Bembo, *Prose e rime,* edited by Carlo Dionisotti, 2d ed. (Turin: UTET, 1966).

BIBLIOGRAPHY

Alberti, Leon Battista. *Grammatichetta e altri scritti sul volgare.* Edited by Giuseppe Patota. Rome: Salerno, 1996.

———. *I libri della famiglia.* Edited by Ruggiero Romano and Alberto Tenenti. Turin: Einaudi, 1969.

———. *The Albertis of Florence: Leon Battista Alberti's Della famiglia.* Translated by Guido A. Guarino. Lewisburg: Bucknell University Press, 1971.

Alighieri, Dante. *Il convivio.* In *Opere minori,* edited by Cesare Vasoli and Domenico De Robertis. Milan: R. Ricciardi, 1995.

———. *De vulgari eloquentia.* In *Opere minori,* edited by Pier Vincenzo Mengaldo. Milan-Naples: Ricciardi, 1996.

———. *De vulgari eloquentia.* Edited and translated by Steven Botterill. Cambridge: Cambridge University Press, 1996.

———. *Vita nuova.* In *Opere minori,* edited by Domenico De Robertis. Milan-Naples: R. Ricciardi, 1995.

———. *Vita nuova.* Translated with an introduction by Mark Musa. Oxford: Oxford University Press, 1992.

Allen, Michael J. B. *The Platonism of Marsilio Ficino: A Study of His Phaedrus Commentary, Its Sources and Genesis.* Berkeley: University of California Press, 1984.

Barbi, Michele. "La Raccolta aragonese." In *Studi sul Canzoniere di Dante.* Florence: Sansoni, 1915 [rpt. 1965], 217–326.

Bembo, Pietro. *Prose e rime.* 2d ed. Edited by Carlo Dionisotti. Turin: UTET, 1966.

Bertolini, Lucia. Editor. *De vera amicitia: I testi del primo Certame coronario.* Modena: Panini, 1993.

Boccaccio, Giovanni. *Tutte le opere di Giovanni Boccaccio.* Edited by Vittore Branca. Milan: Mondadori, 1964–98.

Bologna, Corrado. *Tradizione dei classici italiani.* Turin: Einaudi, 1986, 1993.

Bruni, Leonardo. *Opere letterarie e politiche.* Turin: UTET, 1996.

Bullard, Melissa Meriam. *Lorenzo il Magnifico: Image and Anxiety, Politics and Finance.* Florence: Olschki, 1994.

Castiglione, Baldassare. *Il libro del Cortegiano.* Edited by Bruno Maier. Turin: UTET, 1900.

———. *The Book of The Courtier.* Translated by George Bull. New York: Penguin USA, 1976.

Contini, Gianfranco. "Preliminari sulla lingua di Petrarca." In *Francesco Petrarca Canzoniere,* critical text and introduction by Gianfranco Contini. Turin: Einaudi, 1980.

Croce, Benedetto. "Il secolo senza poesia." In *Poesia popolare e poesia d'arte: studi sulla poesia italiana dal Tre al Cinquecento,* edited by Piero Cudini. Naples: Bibliopolis, 1991.

De Robertis, Domenico. "La Raccolta aragonese primogenita." In *Editi e rari: Studi sulla tradizione letteraria tra Tre e Cinquecento,* 50–65. Milan: Feltrinelli, 1978.

Dionisotti, Carlo. "Tradizione classica e volgarizzamenti." *Geografia e storia della letteratura italiana,* 125–78. Turin: Einaudi, 1971.

————. "Machiavelli e la lingua fiorentina." In *Machiavellerie,* 267–363. Turin: Einaudi, 1980.

Eisenbichler, Konrad, and Olga Zorzi Pugliese, eds. *Ficino and Renaissance Neoplatonism.* Ottowa: Dovehouse Editions, 1986.

Field, Arthur. *The Origins of the Platonic Academy of Florence.* Princeton: Princeton University Press, 1988.

Formentin, Vittorio. "La 'crisi' linguistica del quattrocento." In *Storia della letteratura italiana,* edited by Enrico Malato. Vol. 3: *Il Quattrocento.* Rome: Salerno, 1996.

Garfagnini, Gian Carlo, ed. *Lorenzo il Magnifico e il suo mundo: Convegno internazionale di studi (Firenze, 9–13 giugno 1992).* Florence: Olschki, 1994.

Garin, Eugenio. "La letteratura degli umanisti." In *Storia della letteratura italiana.* Edited by E. Cecchi and N. Sapegno. Vol. 3: *Il Quattrocento e l'Ariosto* (1969). Milan: Garzanti, 1965–1969.

————, ed. *Prosatori latini del Quattrocento.* Milan: Ricciardi, 1952.

Gorni, Guglielmo. "Storia del Certame coronario." *Rinascimento* 2.12 (1972): 135–81.

Grafton, Anthony. *Leon Battista Alberti: Master Builder of the Italian Renaissance.* New York: Hill and Wang, 2000.

Grayson, Cecil. *Studi su Leon Battista Alberti.* Edited by Paolo Claut. Florence: Olschki, 1998.

Hall, Robert Anderson. *The Italian Questione della Lingua, an Interpretative Essay.* Chapel Hill: University of North Carolina Press, 1942.

Kristeller, Paul Oskar. *The Philosophy of Marsilio Ficino.* Translated by Virginia Conant. New York: Columbia University Press, 1943.

Landino, Cristoforo. *Scritti critici e teorici.* 2 vols. Edited by R. Cardini. Rome: Bulzoni, 1974.

Mallet, Michael, and Nicolas Mann, eds. *Lorenzo the Magnificent: Culture and Politics.* London: Warburg Institute, 1996.

Marazzini, Claudio. *La lingua italiana: Profilo storico.* Bologna: Il Mulino, 1994.

Mengaldo, Pier Vincenzo. *La lingua del Boiardo lirico.* Florence: Olschki, 1963.

Migliorini, Bruno. *Storia della lingua italiana.* Florence: Sansoni, [1960] 1978.

————. *The Italian Language.* Abridged and recast by T. Gwynfor Griffith. London: Faber and Faber, 1966.

————. "La questione della lingua." In *Questioni e correnti di storia letteraria,* edited by U. Bosco et al., 1–75. Milan: Marzorati, 1963.

Nebrija, Antonio de. *Gramática de la lengua Castellana y estudios nebrisenses: 1492–1992.* 3 vols. Madrid: Ediciones de Cultura Hispánica, Instituto de Cooperación Iberoamericana, 1992.

Machiavelli, Niccolò. *Discorso o Dialogo intorno alla nostra lingua.* Edited by Paolo Trovato. Padua: Antenore, 1982.

Medici, Lorenzo de'. "Comento ad alcuni sonetti d'amore (proemio)." In *Lorenzo de' Medici, scritti scelti,* edited by Emilio Bigi. Torino: UTET, 1965.

Procaccioli, Paolo. *Filologia ed esegesi dantesca nel quattrocento: L'Inferno nel Comento sopra La comedia di Cristoforo Landino.* Introduction by Giorgio Petrocchi. Florence: Olschki, 1989.

Richardson, Brian. *Printing, Writers, and Readers in Renaissance Italy.* Cambridge: Cambridge University Press, 1999.

———. *Print Culture in Renaissance Italy: The Editor and the Vernacular Text, 1470–1600.* Cambridge: Cambridge University Press, 1994.

Robb, Adeline Nesca. *Neoplatonism of the Italian Renaissance.* London: Allen & Unwin, 1935.

Santoro, Marco. "Cristoforo Landino e il volgare." *Giornale storico della letteratura italiana* 131 (1954): 501–47.

Sozzi, Tommaso Bortolo. "La questione della lingua." In *Dizionario critico della letteratura italiana,* edited by Vittore Branca, vol. 2, 620–30. Torino: UTET, 1986.

Tavoni, Mirko. *Latino, grammatica, volgare: Storia di una questione umanistica.* Padua: Antenore, 1984.

———. "The Language Spoken by the Ancient Romans." *Historiographica Linguistica* 9.3 (1982): 237–64.

———. *Il Quattrocento.* Milan: Il Mulino, 1992.

Trovato, Paolo. "Dai 'Dialogi ad Petrum Histrum' alle 'Vite di Dante e del Petrarca.' Appunti su Leonardo Bruni e la tradizione trecentesca." *Studi petrarcheschi* 2 (1985): 263–84.

2   The Persistence of Syriac

JOSEPH P. AMAR

Scholarly interest in Syriac in the West is a relatively recent phenomenon. It has been only in the past three or four decades that Syriac has emerged from the realm of the rare solitary scholar to become an important area of research for disciplines ranging from early Christianity[1] to the origins of Islam and Qur'ānic studies.[2] This essay is offered as an orientation, not to the vast field of Syriac studies, a subject that has been ably addressed,[3] but rather to the interactions of Syriac, a late Aramaic dialect, with the languages and cultures that swept across western Asia during the past two millennia. Since the complex interplay of languages and cultures in modern Lebanon is strikingly evocative of the interrelationships that I discuss here, it seems appropriate to begin with an anecdote that originates from that country.

There is a repertoire of humorous stories that gained a certain cultural currency in Lebanon following World War I and the establishment of the French Mandate. Typical of the genre is the story of a *fellāh,* or peasant, who, while on a visit to the city, decides to treat himself to a proper meal in a restaurant. One look at the menu, which he cannot read because it is in French, and he realizes that he is reduced to ordering the only thing he knows, a dish of lentils and rice called *mujaddarah,* a staple of village life. As he sits sheepishly eating his peasant fare, he has one eye on a table near his own where a gentleman dressed in suit and tie is finishing a meal of "bifteck aux pommes de terre frites." The waiter approaches the man, who points to his plate and says, "Encore!" Minutes later, the waiter emerges from the kitchen with another plate of steak and French fries. At this, the peasant summons the waiter, and announces enthusiastically, "Encore!" When the waiter returns with another plate of lentils, the astonished peasant asks in his mountain dialect of Arabic, "Laysh encory mish mitil encoru"—"Why isn't my 'encore' the same as his 'encore'?"

The Middle East has been an emporium of cultures and languages for as far back as history records. Babylonians and Akkadians vied over issues of cultural supremacy in literary debates known as "dispute poems," which weighed the advantages of one set of rhetorical and linguistic standards against another.[4] The genre survived into the late Aramaic period, roughly 200–700 C.E.,[5] and flourished again among Syriac authors who applied the ancient form to specifically Christian themes, and produced the forerunner of the medieval morality play.[6] The socioreligious and linguistic similarities between Syriac dispute poems and their ancient Mesopotamian models are examples of what Han J. W. Drijvers has identified with regard to the nature of culture and religion in western Asia in the Greco-Roman period, namely, that indigenous religious patterns were influenced by, and assimilated, earlier Mesopotamian, native Semitic, and Hellenistic traditions.[7] The principle would hold true through the Arab period as well.

Well before Alexander introduced the Greek language and the institutions associated with Hellenism to the region, the Levant belonged to what ethnographers identify as an eclectic mix of Greco-Egyptian-Asiatic culture that extended from the Nile Delta to Cilicia. Phoenicia, in particular, due both to its geographic proximity to Greece and to its early maritime activity throughout the Mediterranean, interacted with Hellenistic culture on a grand scale. Beginning in the fourth century B.C.E., Phoenicia maintained links with both Ptolemaic Egypt and Seleucid Syria.[8] Even after Greek had established itself as the language of law and politics in the eastern Mediterranean, the Phoenician language continued to be used on a large scale. The ongoing use of the Phoenician language, as well as what seems to be a deliberate attempt at continuity with earlier Phoenician cultural and religious institutions, is evidence of a conscious conservatism that contributed to the preservation of indigenous Phoenician cultural identity despite the growing influence of Greek.[9]

The interaction of Hellenism with native Semitic cultures east of the Lebanon Mountain Range represents a no less complex situation. Hellenistic Syria was thoroughly bilingual, with Greek assuming the role of the superstrate language, while Aramaic continued as the everyday language of the majority of the native population. Aramaic had established itself as the language of administration and commerce throughout western Asia during the Neo-Babylonian period (627–538 B.C.E.). With the rise of Achaemenid Persia (538–331 B.C.E.), the influence of Aramaic became even more widespread. The vast corpus of texts that have survived from the Indus River to the second cataract of the Nile attests to the dominance of the language over an immense region. Although Aramaic began to displace Hebrew as the vernacular language of the Jewish people after the fall of Jerusalem in 586 B.C.E. during the period known as the Babylonian Captivity, Hebrew by no means disappeared, although evidence for its use is greatly diminished. As early as the middle of the second century B.C.E., Aramaic had become an important spoken and literary language for Jews.[10]

With the waning of Seleucid hegemony in western Asia, new centers of power began to assert themselves, and with them, evidence of regional dialects of Aramaic emerge. The emerging Aramaic-speaking populations took advantage of the vacuum left after the breakup of the Seleucid hold on the region to reaffirm their Aramaic cultural and linguistic identity. The Hasmoneans of Judea are a well-known example of a widespread process that also included the kingdoms of Nabataea (Greek, Petra), Tadmor (Greek, Palmyra), Homs (Greek, Emessa), Urhai (Greek, Edessa), and Houtra (Greek, Hatra). The Aramaic dialects associated with these regions developed related forms of writing that represented local variations on the standard twenty-two-letter Aramaic alphabet in use during the Seleucid period.[11]

While Aramaic served as the everyday language of these Princely States, as they are sometimes called, their rulers were ethnic Arabs who had settled throughout Syria and Mesopotamia following their migration from the north of the Arabian Peninsula at the end of the first millennium B.C.E.[12] By the time these now-sedentary populations entered the sphere of Greco-Roman influence, few indications of their Arab origins survived. Ethnic, cultural, and administrative ties were reinforced among them through politically motivated marriages, but evidence of Arabic survived only in personal and dynastic names and in the names of certain deities.[13] The kingdom of Edessa, the region associated with the Syriac dialect of Aramaic, was ruled by a line of kings known as Abgarids, a name derived from their eponymous ancestor, Abgar. The name, which is actually "Akbar," meaning "Greatest" or "Supreme," is patently Arabic but underwent a metathesis that obscured the Arab identity of the dynasty and its founder.

Worship of the goddess 'Allāt, the pre-Islamic female consort of 'Allāh, was widespread throughout the region. Kings of Tadmor often bore the honorific title 'Abd-'Allāt "servant of 'Allāt," a name clearly related to the later Islamic "'Abd-'Allāh."[14] But apart from rare survivals from Arabic, localized forms of Aramaic served as the everyday language of these kingdoms. Pastoral nomads such as the Lakhmids and the Ghassanids who patrolled the northern fringes of the Arabian Peninsula on behalf of the Persian and Roman Empires respectively generally did a better job of preserving Arabic as the primary language of communication than did their settled relatives to the north.[15]

It is important to keep in mind that our knowledge of late Aramaic dialects is derived entirely from written texts; scholars can only speculate concerning their spoken forms. What is known is that local variations in pronunciation and vocabulary seem not to have constituted an impediment to the dialect of one region being understood by speakers of a neighboring region.[16] These were, after all, essentially merchant populations who did business, shared trade routes, wrote bills of sale, concluded contracts, and implemented treaties with each other on a daily basis. The people who lived up the road may have had their own distinct pronunciation and lexical preferences, but none of this constituted an impediment to doing business with them.

Decline in the use of regional Aramaic dialects is generally traced to the period of Roman consolidation during which these Princely States changed status from client kingdoms to *coloniae* and ultimately to *provinciae* under complete Roman control. During this period, the Aramaic dialects exhibit increased influence from Greek, especially in the profusion of Greek words related to public administration and civic matters.[17]

The exceptionally complex linguistic situation is exemplified in the case of Nabataea.[18] Roman tariffs imposed on the kingdom are typically given first in Greek and then repeated word for word in the Nabataean dialect of Aramaic. Following the incorporation of the kingdom into the Roman Empire as Provincia Arabia in 106 C.E., the number of Greek inscriptions increases while translations of them into Nabataean Aramaic decrease. This in itself is not exceptional. However, though identification in Greek of the people as "Nabataeans" significantly decreases after 106 C.E.,[19] the transition from kingdom to Roman province is not accompanied by any break in indigenous Nabataean, nonclassical architecture.[20] The use of Nabataean Aramaic likewise declined as Greek and the municipal institutions associated with it came to dominate. All indications point to the fact that under the Romans the use of Greek brought with it a certain cultural capital that it had not known before.[21]

The extraordinarily well documented case of Nabataea demonstrates how incorporation of the Aramaic-speaking kingdoms into the empire signaled the eventual demise of the local Aramaic dialect. This was, in fact, the case throughout the region, with one notable exception, the kingdom of Osrhoene whose capital was Edessa, where the local dialect of Aramaic was Syriac. Instead of going out of use or even diminishing, Syriac spread well beyond the confines of the area initially controlled by Edessa, where it originated. Beginning around 200 C.E., two main branches of Aramaic can be distinguished: a western branch consisting of Christian Palestinian, Galilean, and Samaritan Aramaic; and an eastern branch consisting of Babylonian Jewish, Mandaic, and Syriac.[22] Of these dialects,

Syriac represents not simply an exception to the pattern of decline and extinction as a living language but, in fact, a reversal of it.

The exceptional linguistic and cultural influence exercised by Edessa was unique among the Aramaic-speaking capitals of the region. This fact is nowhere better demonstrated than in the emergence of Syriac as the vehicle of a distinct Semitic expression of Christianity.[23] The golden age of Syriac-speaking Christianity is the unique phenomenon of a Christian tradition that conducted its worship, did its thinking, and articulated its theology entirely in a dialect of the same language that served as the vernacular of first-century Palestine.[24]

Because of its strategic location in the shadow of the Roman and Parthian Empires, Edessa engaged in an ongoing balancing act between these two superpowers in order to maintain its political independence. Its geographic location and its awareness from an early date of its ethnically distinct character are key to an understanding of the survival of its cultural and linguistic identity long after it had lost political independence.

Inscriptions in its native dialect of Syriac prevailed until the time Edessa was made a Roman *colonia* in 213 C.E. It is only after this time that Greek inscriptions and papyri begin to proliferate. Coins with bilingual inscriptions in Syriac and Greek begin to appear for the first time during this same period. These are inscribed on the face side in Syriac *rōhem rōmayê,* "Pro-Roman," which is then repeated in Greek on the reverse, *philoi-romanoi.*[25] Local Edessene kings who had a history of affiliation with Persians and Parthians now ruled at the discretion of the Roman Caesar. Advertising this fact on their coins was one way to guarantee their continued survival.[26]

Klaas Dijkstra has identified an important element in the survival of the cultural and linguistic identity of Edessa. As he has recently noted: "Due to [Edessa's] position on the fringe of the Syrian-Mesopotamian steppe, a variety of cultural strands synthesized in an almost inextricable mix of Semitic, Roman, Greek and Arabic traditions."[27] In other words, Edessene society demonstrates ongoing interaction and association between city dwellers and pastoral nomads who occupied the area known as the *'arab* that immediately surrounded the city. The term is used to designate the steppe or desert in general.

Of course, the feature that would come most to distinguish Edessa was its history of Christianity that local legend traced to the first century C.E. The kingdom of Adiabene (Syriac, *Hadyab*) and the city of Nisibis to the east of Edessa had prominent Jewish communities that maintained schools that were in regular contact with Jewish populations in Palestine. At the same time, the

Jewish presence in this area made eastern Syria a natural destination for Jewish-Christian missionaries from Palestine, a pattern that is duplicated throughout apostolic times. Although the sources that record the Christianizing of Edessa in the first century C.E. must be read through layers of accumulated legendary material, they nonetheless preserve significant details concerning aspects of life in Edessa, including the prominence of the Jewish community at the court of King Abgar, nicknamed "the Black," its ongoing connections with Palestine, and the role played by Edessene Jews in welcoming the first Christian missionaries from Palestine.[28]

The distinctive Semitic cultural identification of Christian Edessa is demonstrated by two prominent early literary figures with ties to the city, Tatian and Bardaisan. Both authors were steeped in the traditions of Greek *paideia,* and both were well traveled throughout the Greco-Roman world. Yet at the very time when Hellenism was at the height of its influence in Syria and Mesopotamia, these authors deliberately chose to write in Syriac and not in Greek.[29]

Tatian (d. c. 175), a native Mesopotamian and a student of the Roman Justin Martyr, was the compiler of an immensely influential Syriac Gospel harmony commonly referred to by its Greek name, Diatessaron, but known in Syriac as *'ewangelîôn damhaltê,* "the mixed gospels." Tatian was not only bilingual but bicultural as well. The composition that is commonly referred to as *Oratio ad Graecos* was written around the middle of the second century and attacks all aspects of Hellenistic culture. Tatian argues for the superiority of Aramaic culture in all its manifestations, and expresses in particular his preference for Aramaic thought and learning.

Known by the people of his day as "the Aramaic philosopher," Bardaisan (154–222) wrote on broad cultural issues from the perspective of an insider. His *Book of the Customs of the Countries* shows firsthand knowledge of contemporary cultural and philosophical trends in the Greek-speaking world and beyond.[30] It is from Bardaisan that we first learn of the conversion to Christianity of King Abgar of Edessa. There are solid grounds for questioning the conversion.[31] Yet Bardaisan's point seems to be that Abgar recognized the stabilizing influence of Christianity in Edessa's balancing act between Rome and Persia, and he did so fully one century before Constantine.[32]

The choice by Tatian and Bardaisan to write in Syriac when Greek was equally available to them is an indication that Syriac, a "provincial language," enjoyed a level of prestige that rivaled Greek, the language of power and political preferment. Greek may well have been the undisputed language of political power in the region, but Tatian and Bardaisan are two early witnesses to the fact that Syriac occupied the place of cultural prestige. This is not to understate the complexity of the linguistic situation but simply to underscore the emerging role of Syriac among early witnesses to literacy in one language or the other.[33]

The expanding role of Syriac in the region is further exemplified in a valuable archive of documents from Dura-Europos dating from the first half of the third century. The archive preserves a deed of sale identified as Dura Parchment 28 that was executed in Edessa on May 9, 243.[34] The document is written and signed in Syriac by all parties involved. All but two witnesses also sign in Syriac, the exceptions notably being the administrative officials of the *colonia* who sign in Greek, although their status as *strategoi* is repeated in Syriac. Interestingly, though the document was written at Edessa, it records that the buyer was a native of Harran (Greek, Carrhae), not an Edessan city at all, but one that fell within the Persian sphere of control in the Parthian Empire. Even contracts written in Greek from throughout northern Mesopotamia are frequently signed in Syriac and often contain lengthy Syriac subscriptions. No less significant, however, is the fact that legal documents that do not involve people from Mesopotamia at all have signatures and subscriptions in Syriac.[35]

The examples cited above give a sense of the presence of literacy in Syriac well beyond the traditional boundaries of the area generally understood to have been controlled by Edessa. In addition, documentary evidence such as this requires one to reconsider the once commonly held view that Greek was dominant in cities and the use of Aramaic was restricted to peasants in the countryside, in other words, the traditional demarcation between *polis* and *chora*. It is now obvious that such a distinction never adequately represented the complexity of the interactions between Syriac and Greek where the choice of the use of one language over the other, at least among those who were capable of making the choice, seems to have had as much to do with *what* one was doing as *where* one was doing it.[36] The interrelated urban, rural, and pastoral components that made up Syrian Mesopotamian society worked against any strict separation of substrate and superstrate languages. This extent of the diffusion of Syriac, as well as its religious and cultural affiliations, becomes clearer as we move into the fourth century, when Greek had firmly established itself as the language of the Church of the Byzantine Empire.

The third century presents the student of Syriac with a puzzling phenomenon, namely, the absence of substantial works by known authors. This relative silence is broken by the two major fourth-century authors with whom substantial bodies of writing are identified: Aphrahat (c. 270–c. 345),[37] the first major prose writer in the language; and the towering figure of Ephrem (c. 306–373),[38] whose poetic genius forever transformed and left its imprint on the language. So thoroughgoing was the impact of these two authors on Syriac letters that it very likely accounts for the absence of any evidence of writers who preceded them. Together, Aphrahat and Ephrem inaugurate what has come to be viewed as the golden age of Syriac literature.

By the middle of the fourth century, the use of Syriac had become so widespread that the Byzantine historiographer Theodoret refers to it broadly as "the language of Syria" and ascribes its use to, among others, Palestinians and Phoenicians.[39] The borders of the Syriac-speaking province of Osrhoene were not rigidly fixed. It is generally believed that the Euphrates marked the eastern perimeter, while the Roman crossing point at Zeugma/Seleucia was less than seventy kilometers to the southwest of Edessa. No Syriac inscriptions are found west of the Euphrates prior to the fourth century, and it is not until the early fifth century that we know of any Syriac authors who emerge west of the Euphrates.[40]

There is anecdotal corroboration of Theodoret's observation regarding the extent of the use of Syriac in the fourth century, as well as its identification as the language of Aramaic-speaking Christians both inside and outside the Roman Empire. When the famous pilgrim Egeria visited Jerusalem late in the fourth or early in the fifth century, she made the following observation:

> A portion of the population in this province knows both Greek and Syriac; another segment knows only Greek; and still another, only Syriac. Even though the bishop may know Syriac, he always speaks Greek and never Syriac; therefore, there is always present a priest who, while the bishop speaks in Greek, translates into Syriac so that all may understand what is being preached. Since whatever scripture texts are read must be read in Greek, there is always someone present to translate the readings into Syriac for the people, so that they will understand. [In addition] so that those here who are Latins and who know neither Greek nor Syriac, will not be bored, everything is explained to them, for there are brothers and sisters who are bilingual in Greek and Latin, and who explain everything to them in Latin.[41]

Two points need to be made here. First, it is no surprise, of course, that in hagiopolit Jerusalem the liturgy of the Great Church was conducted in Greek despite the fact that the native population was Aramaic-speaking and would have had difficulty understanding it. Second, by the early fifth century, when most authorities believe Egeria wrote, Syriac had become so well established as the language of Aramaic-speaking Christianity that Egeria used the term "Syriac" as a generic designation for the dialect of Aramaic in use among Palestinian Christians. In fact, they spoke a different, though related, form of Aramaic more properly identified as Palestinian Christian Aramaic.[42] What is at once clear is the high incidence of Christians who spoke only their native dialect of Aramaic after centuries of domination compared to the much smaller number who knew only Greek.[43]

The question of translation from one language to another sheds further light on the status of Syriac in the Byzantine period. In the case of so-called provincial languages (e.g., Coptic, Punic, and Celtic, along with Syriac), translation for the most part was limited—the provincial language most often serving as the receptor of the Greek original. However, beginning in the fourth and fifth centuries, works by Syriac authors increasingly began to be translated into Greek. A notable example is the previously cited work by Bardaisan, *Book of the Customs of the Countries.*[44] The large number of copies of this work that have survived in Greek from late antiquity attests to its popularity throughout the Greek-speaking world. The irony is that Bardaisan's book is a work of protest, asserting the persistence of distinct cultures and languages among un-Hellenized commoners.

In the ecclesiastical realm, the question of translation from one language to another is likewise illuminating. An offhand remark by the Syrian theologian and exegete Theodore of Mopsuestia (d. 428) relates that Flavian, bishop of Antioch, and Diodore, bishop of Tarsus, employed a staff of translators to render Syriac antiphonal poetry into Greek.[45] This is not an insignificant point, since there is sufficient evidence to suggest that, by the fifth century, the growing prestige of Syriac liturgical poetry posed a source of embarrassment to Greek cultural chauvinism.[46] It is now well documented that Syriac contributed to the formation of Greek ecclesiastical literature in other significant ways. In a study that remains unequaled in the field, the eminent Bollandist scholar Paul Peeters demonstrated the direct dependence of Greek hagiographic literature on Syriac models.[47]

The Arab Islamic conquests of the seventh century brought with them a whole new set of cultural and linguistic considerations to the Middle East. The new Islamic polity adapted gradually to life in the areas formerly held by the Byzantine Empire. Initially, at least, Christians who had held administrative positions in the Byzantine Empire found a place in the new Islamic administration, and continued to collect revenues and keep records in Greek side by side with their Arabic-speaking counterparts.[48] In time, Arabic, which was the *lingua sacra* of Islam, became the *lingua franca* and the exclusive language of administration within *dar 'al-'Islām*.[49] However, assimilation into Arab culture and adoption of the Arabic language did not proceed at the same rate among native Christian populations that found themselves under Islamic control. Use of Arabic was adopted first by the so-called Melkites, or "royalists," who, by their acceptance of the Christological definitions of the Council of Chalcedon (451 C.E.), were considered "orthodox" by the Church of the Byzantine Empire. As early as the first half of the eighth century, these Melkites, whose primary language had been Greek, were now under the rule of the Caliphate of Damascus, and adopted Arabic as the new medium of life and worship. They were to become the most Arabized of the Christian communities under Arab rule, and they were responsible for generating the bulk of what is today known as Christian Arabic literature.[50]

The contribution of Syriac-speaking Christianity to Arabic intellectual life in the areas of philosophy, history, literature, and the sciences is well documented and need not be rehearsed here.[51] Through their translations of Greek classical authors, first into Syriac and then into Arabic, Syriac Christian scholars served as the bridge linking the classical world of Greco-Roman antiquity to the efflorescence of Arabic letters associated with ninth-century Baghdad. At the same time, unlike the predominantly Greek-speaking Melkites of Jerusalem and Palestine, Syriac-speaking Christianity remained deeply aware of its distinct Semitic cultural and linguistic identity. Thus, while contributing to the development of Arabic literature, Christians of the Syriac-speaking, non-Byzantine churches vigorously resisted attempts at Arabization. This is seen nowhere more strikingly than in the development of the phenomenon known as *garshūnī*, a word that refers to Arabic that is transliterated into Syriac letters.[52] The earliest, and to date fullest, explanation of the term is given by the Maronite scholar Faustus (Murhij) Nairon. Writing in the preface to his 1703 edition of the Peshitta version of the Syriac New Testament, which was accompanied by such an Arabic *garshūnī* translation, Nairon supplied a lengthy note in which he discussed the origin of the practice.[53] The point to be made here is that *garshūnī* preserves a witness to the ongoing identification with the cultural heritage of the Aramaic language well after Arabic had replaced Syriac as the common vernacular of Syriac-speaking churches.

Discoveries of Syriac archives in the Middle East over the past half century have yielded new evidence for the diffusion and use of Syriac. In 1989 the Lebanese Group for Subterranean Study and Research, known by the French acronym GERSL (Groupe d'Études et de Recherche souterraines du Liban) was excavating in the region of Wadi Qadisha, "the Holy Valley," in northern Lebanon. Near the site of ʿĀṣi-l-Ḥadaṭ the group discovered a cave containing naturally preserved human mummies, everyday artifacts, and manuscripts dating from the late thirteenth century C.E.[54] Political turmoil resulting from Syrian presence in Lebanon prevented public announcement of the discovery until 1994. It was only then that the full extent of the discoveries was made known. But even then, again as a result of Syrian political influence, the texts that were discovered with the mummies received less publicity than the eleven petrified mummies themselves. The cave's geographic location and physical characteristics (constant temperature, absence of humidity, and fine silt soil) inhibited the growth of bacteria and allowed the bodies to be naturally preserved.

The almost inaccessible mountain caves that dot the landscape of this region of Lebanon have a long history of being used for shelter during periods of turmoil. The thirteenth century was just such a period. Mamluke Egypt ruled much of the eastern coast of the Mediterranean. Local Christian militiamen would secure their families and possessions in the caves of the region before going out to do battle. Among the items discovered in the cave of ʿĀṣi-l-Ḥadaṭ are twenty Arabic, Syriac, and *garshūnī* manuscripts. The Syriac and *garshūnī* texts vary widely in content and include liturgical compositions, a decree of divorce, and documents of a religious or pseudoreligious nature.[55] Typical of this last category are a group of texts identified as talismans, which, though written in Syriac, are known popularly in Arabic as *kitāb al-ḥijāb*, or "The Book of Amulets." These discoveries constitute important additions to a body of evidence that has been expanding over the past several decades, and which has given scholars a better sense of the continued use of Syriac in the Middle East well into the Islamic era.

The use of Aramaic dialects in the Middle East is greatly diminished today. A remnant of speakers may be found in the Syrian Christian villages of Maʿlula and Jubbadīn near Damascus. Until recently, modern Aramaic dialects were spoken by both Jews and Christians in an area that extends from Jezīrah in northeastern Syria, through the Lake Van region of eastern Turkey, Azerbaijan, northern Iraq, and Iran. The villages of Zakho and Dahok had significant Syriac-speaking Jewish and Christian populations. As a result of ongoing Kurdish violence, most of the Christians have emigrated to other countries, particularly Germany and Sweden. The Aramaic dialect known as Nash Didan, which is spoken in Israel today, is closely related to Syriac and was imported with immigrants from a region near the Azerbaijani, Turkish, Iranian, and Iraqi borders. Syriac remains the official liturgical language of the Syriac-speaking churches.

Although its use as a spoken language is greatly diminished in modern times, Syriac remains an indispensable tool for scholarship in theology, philosophy, linguistics, and history. Syriac literary tradition represents a form of Christianity that remained culturally and linguistically rooted in the very wellsprings of the Semitic world from which the New Testament emerged. The earliest Syriac fathers are largely untouched by Greek- or Latin-speaking Christian traditions of the Mediterranean world. Syriac translations of the Greek fathers often antedate the earliest Greek manuscripts. In many cases, Syriac translations preserve works of authors that have not survived in the original Greek.[56] In some cases, Syriac sources preserve valuable historical data relating to the Seleucid and post-Seleucid periods that are not recorded in any known Greek source.[57]

As is well known to scripture scholars, Syriac is essential to the field of biblical studies. Every aspect of Syriac-speaking Christianity reflects an abiding interest and focus on the scriptures. In the words of Eberhard Nestle, "No branch of the early Church has done more for the translation of the Bible into their vernacular than the Syriac-speaking."[58] The Old Testament was translated into Syriac directly from Hebrew, and most biblical scholars agree that a direct literary relationship exists between the Pentateuch, in particular, and Aramaic paraphrases known as *targumim* that were in use in synagogues.[59]

The long history enjoyed by Syriac allows scholars the rare opportunity to observe the development and diffusion of a language that has survived from ancient times through political, religious, and ethnic upheavals in the lands of its origin. Syriac survived Hellenism and the Greek-speaking institutions of the Roman and Byzantine Empires. It was strengthened by its contact with Greek, and contributed to Byzantine literary culture. It did not yield to imperial Greek-speaking Christianity; rather, it became the vehicle of an expression of Christianity that is Aramaic in context and language, and which preserves the original Semitic thought-world of the Gospel. Syriac likewise survived Islam and became a bridge linking the intellectual traditions of classical Greece and Rome to the flowering of Abbasid Baghdad, which, in turn, contributed to the emergence of Scholasticism and, ultimately, the Renaissance.

NOTES

1. For a comprehensive introduction to the thought-world of early Syriac-speaking Christianity, see Robert Murray, *Symbols of Church and Kingdom.*

2. See now, Christoph Luxenberg, *Die syro-aramäische Lesart des Koran.*

3. For the current state of the question, see Sebastian Brock, "Syriac Studies in the Last Three Decades."

4. The "debate" or "precedence" poem, also known as *altercatio* or *tenson,* is widely attested in the literatures of many cultures. Its literary and cultural heritage in the ancient Middle East is exhaustively documented in G. J. Reinink et al., eds., *Dispute Poems and Dialogues in the Ancient and Mediaeval Near East.*

5. On the periods of Aramaic, see Joseph Fitzmeyer, S.J., "The Phases of the Aramaic Language," in *A Wandering Aramean,* 57–84.

6. Sebastian Brock is the acknowledged master of the topic. See his "Syriac Dispute Poems: The Various Types," in *Dispute Poems and Dialogues,* 109–19; idem, "A Dispute of the Months and Some Related Syriac Texts," 181–211; both reprinted in idem, *From Ephrem to Romanos.* See also Robert Murray, "Aramaic and Syriac Dispute-Poems and Their Connections," 157–87.

7. H. J. W. Drijvers, *Cults and Beliefs at Edessa,* 16 f.

8. See E. J. Bickerman, *From Ezra to the Last of the Maccabees,* 15 ff. On Phoenician interaction with other native Semitic populations in the region, see now Brian Peckham, "Phoenicians and Aramaeans: The Literary and Epigraphic Evidence," 19–44.

9. The point is most recently made by S. Freyne, "Galileans, Phoenicians, and Itureans," 184–88.

10. On the importance of Aramaic as a Jewish language, see J. C. Greenfield, "Aramaic and the Jews," 1–18.

11. H. J. W. Drijvers, "Hatra, Palmyra und Edessa," 799–906. An up-to-date survey of early Edessan inscriptions and their relationship to related Aramaic dialects may be found now in H. J. W. Drijvers and J. Healey, *The Old Syriac Inscriptions of Edessa and Osrhoene,* esp. 1–41.

12. Klaas Dijkstra, *Life and Loyalty,* 10–11.

13. Persian names likewise occur with some frequency. See Drijvers and Healey, *The Old Syriac Inscriptions,* 265–80.

14. See M. Gawlikowski, "Les Arabs de Syrie dans l'antiquité," 85–92; also H. J. W. Drijvers, "De matre inter leones sedente," 331–51.

15. On the role played by Bedouin Arabs in this period, see F. Donner, "The Role of Nomads in the Near East in Late Antiquity," 73–85. Evidence of retaining Arab ethnic and linguistic identification is especially strong in the case of the Nabataens, as G. W. Bowersock has amply demonstrated. A comprehensive and excellently written orientation to the subject may be found in G. W. Bowersock, *Roman Arabia.*

16. The Aramaic-speaking Princely States maintained ongoing administrative and familial connections that linked regions as far north as Edessa to the southern kingdoms

of Nabataea and Tadmor/Palmyra. Inscriptions in the distinctive Palmyrene script have been discovered in Edessa itself! See W. Ball, *Rome in the East*, 87–89. The dynastic links between Edessa and Nabataea are delineated in J. B. Segal, *Edessa: "The Blessed City,"* 15–21.

17. H. J. W. Drijvers, "Greek and Aramaic in Palmyrene Inscriptions," 31–42. The author points to the tendency toward Hellenization of Palmyrene in bilingual inscriptions.

18. Bowersock, *Roman Arabia*. See especially Appendixes I–IV and the plates that follow for recent archaeological and numismatic evidence, 148–86.

19. Bowersock notes the changes in status that accompanied the shift from client kingdom to province. Ibid., "The New Province," 76–89.

20. The material is well synthesized in Warwick Ball, *Rome in the East*, 60–73.

21. Fergus Millar, *The Roman Near East 31* B.C.–A.D. *337*, 414–36.

22. Fitzmeyer, "The Phases of the Aramaic Language," 60 f.

23. On the emergence and growth of Syriac as a standard Christian language, see L. van Rompay, "Some Preliminary Remarks on the Origins of Classical Syriac as a Standard Language," 70–89. Millar consistently downplays the Semitic character of Edessa in favor of Greek superstrate culture. See, for example, his *The Roman Near East*, 472–88. Recent scholarship has made the claim that Millar distorted and even misrepresented earlier research to support his denial of the role played by Semitic culture in Edessa. See Ball, *Rome in the East*, 94–96, 464 n. 238. Millar's account of the emergence of Syriac scripts, specifically that Syriac first employed the script identified as "estrangelo," which was later replaced by the more cursive "serta" style of writing (ibid., 457) repeats a common misunderstanding. On this point, see Drijvers and Healey, *The Old Syriac Inscriptions*, 2.

24. It is sometimes implied, even by those who have every reason to know better, that Syriac was the language spoken by Jesus. The earliest evidence for the existence of Syriac as a distinct dialect of Aramaic dates to c. 100 C.E. and comes from the region of Gaziantep in southern Turkey. See, for example, K. Beyer, *The Aramaic Language: Its Distribution and Subdivisions*. It is indeed puzzling that so little evidence of Jewish Palestinian Aramaic, the dialect known in first-century Palestine, has survived. On this point, see Fitzmeyer, *A Wandering Aramean*, 10–11.

25. Edessan coins were often indicators of shifting political allegiances. Coins struck during the reign of the pro-Parthian King Wa'el bar Sahru bore the likeness of the king of Parthia. For the numismatic evidence, see Segal, *Edessa*, 13–15, 30, 40, 50; also E. Babelon, "Numismatiques d'Édesse en Mésopotamie," 209, as noted in Millar, *The Roman Near East*, 556.

26. For a detailed study of the early development of Syriac, its epigraphy, and its relation to Palmyrene and other forms of Aramaic, see now Drijvers and Healey, *The Old Syriac Inscriptions*.

27. Dijkstra, *Life and Loyalty*, 251–52.

28. For a detailed study of the documents relating to the foundation of Christianity in Edessa, see Sebastian Brock, "Eusebius and Syriac Christianity," 212–34.

29. The point is made in Sebastian Brock, "Greek and Syriac in Late Antique Syria," 154–55; reprinted in *From Ephrem to Romanos: Interactions between Syriac and Greek.*

30. For a comprehensive assessment of the figure of Bardaisan, see H. J. W Drijvers, *Bardaisan of Edessa.*

31. The chronological inconsistencies in the story are noted in Brock, "Eusebius and Syriac Christianity," 221–27.

32. See Drijvers, *Cults and Beliefs at Edessa,* 14 ff.

33. Brock offers a balanced perspective on the relation between Greek and Syriac. See Brock, "Greek and Syriac in Late Antique Syria," 149–60.

34. J. Teixidor, "Deux documents syriaques," 144–66. See the discussion in Millar, *The Roman Near East,* 472–81.

35. Teixidor, "Deux documents syriaques," 156–66.

36. See Dijkstra, *Life and Loyalty,* 8–10.

37. What is known of the life of Aphrahat and his writings is summarized in Ignatius Ortiz de Urbina, *Patrologia Syriaca,* 46–51; and Anton Baumstark, *Geschichte der syrischen Literatur,* 30–31.

38. Even a basic bibliography on Ephrem would be immense. For fuller treatments of the life and works of Ephrem, see Ortiz de Urbina, *Patrologia Syriaca,* 56–83; Baumstark, *Geschichte,* 31–53. English translations of Ephrem's works have become increasingly available. Selections of poetry are now available in, Sebastian Brock, *The Luminous Eye;* idem, *St. Ephrem the Syrian: Hymns on Paradise;* and Kathleen McVey, *Ephrem the Syrian: Hymns.* For Ephrem's prose works, see Edward Mathews and Joseph Amar, *St. Ephrem the Syrian: Selected Prose Works;* and Carmel McCarthy, *Saint Ephrem's Commentary on Tatian's Diatessaron.*

39. Theodoret, *Questiones in Librum Judicum,* 19; cited in Brock, "Greek and Syriac in Late Antique Syria," 149.

40. Millar is characteristically circumspect in his conclusions. See Millar, *The Roman Near East,* 241–42.

41. George E. Gingras, ed. and trans., *Egeria: Diary of a Pilgrimage,* 125–26.

42. On the distinction between this dialect of Aramaic and Syriac, see M. Bar-Asher, "Le syro-palestinien," 27–59; and now C. Müller-Kessler, "Die Überlieferungsstufen des christlich-palästinischen Aramäisch," 55–60.

43. Examples of people speaking only Syriac abound in the works of major Christian authors of the period, including Jerome, Chrysostom, and Theodoret of Cyr; see George Haddad, *Aspects of Social Life in Antioch,* 89, 101–3, 106–7, 115, on the mixture of Greek and Syriac that was in use.

44. See note 30 above.

45. Theodore of Mopsuestia *apud* Niketas Akominatos, *Patrologia Graeca* 139, col. 1390C, cited in Brock, "Greek and Syriac in Late Antique Syria," 152.

46. See Joseph Amar, "Byzantine Ascetic Monachism and Greek Bias," 123–56. On the claim that Syriac poetry is based on Greek forms of composition, see 137–42.

47. See Paul Peeters, *Tréfonds orientale de l'hagiographie byzantine,* 14–17.

48. See the evidence drawn from the relations between caliphs and their secretaries in Bernard Lewis, ed. and trans., *Islam and the Prophet Muhammad,* 191–201.

49. See now Sidney H. Griffith, "'Melkites,' 'Jacobites' and the Christological Controversies in Arabic," 9–53.

50. For a full account of the development of Christian Arabic literature, see the collected essays of S. H. Griffith, *Arabic Christianity;* also Joseph P. Amar, "Arabic Christian Literature," 98–99.

51. See "The Syriac Impact on Arabic Literature," in *Arabic Literature to the End of the Umayyad Period,* ed. A. F. L. Beeston et al., 497–501; also Peter Brown, *The Rise of Western Christendom,* 184–97.

52. The etymology of the term is disputed. See R. Payne Smith, *Thesaurus Syriacus,* vol. 1 (1879), col. 790.

53. To my knowledge, the note has never been cited in a modern text. It reads in full: "Quod autem pertinet ad Textum *Arabico-Carsciunicum,* qui prima vice in praesenti Editione in lucem emittitur, notandum est hunc esse Textum Arabicum sed Syrorum caracteribus conscriptum, Syri etenim cum ediscere, ac legere cuperent linguam Arabicam a Saracenis in Syriam invectam, quae uti vernacula usque adhuc retinetur, Syrus quidam ex Mesopotamia, ut fert traditio, nomine Carsciun ut facilius ab illis Populis ea perciperetur Patriis caepit caracteribus, hoc est Syriacis, illam conscribere; ex quo factum est ut omnes libri Arabici sic conscripti, hoc nomine Carsciuni appellari, sortiti fuerint." Faustus Nairon, ed., *Novum Testamentum syriacum et arabicum,* Tome I: *Sacrosancta Jesu Christi Evangelica jussu Congregationis de Propaganda Fide ad usum Ecclesiae Nationis Maronitarum;* Tome II: *Acta Apostolorum Epistolae Catholicae et divi Pauli . . . cum Apocalypsi D. Ioannis.* See Tome I, the last page of the unpaginated Latin preface.

54. The report of the discovery, as well as the description of artifacts and manuscripts, appears in *Momies du Liban. Rapport,* 1994; also *Liban Souterrain. Bulletin du GERSL.*

55. *Momies du Liban,* 153 ff.

56. A detailed treatment of the question, including a listing of Greek works preserved in Syriac, may be found in Brock, "Syriac," 1–6.

57. See now L. Van Rompay, "Jacob of Edessa and the Early History of Edessa," 269–85.

58. Cited in Bruce Metzger, *The Early Versions of the New Testament,* 3.

59. See the defining work of Michael P. Weitzman, "Lexical Clues to the Composition of the Old Testament Peshitta," 217–46.

BIBLIOGRAPHY

Amar, Joseph P. "Byzantine Ascetic Monachism and Greek Bias in the Vita Tradition of Ephrem the Syrian." *Orientalia Christiana Periodica* 58 (1992): 123–56.

————. "Arabic Christian Literature." In *Encyclopedia of Early Christianity,* 2d ed., L. Everett Ferguson, 98–99. New York: Garland Publishing, 1997.

Babelon, E. "Numismatiques d'Édesse en Mésopotamie." *Mélanges Numismatiques 2* (1893): 189–220.

Ball, Warwick. *Rome in the East: The Transformation of an Empire.* London: Routledge, 2000.

Bar-Asher, M. "Le syro-palestinien: Études grammaticales." *Journal Asiatique* 276 (1988): 27–59.

Bar Salibi, Dionysius. *A Response to the Arabs.* Ed. and trans. Joseph P. Amar. Forthcoming in *Corpus Scriptorum Christianorum Orientalium.*

Baumstark, Anton. *Geschichte der syrischen Literatur.* Bonn, 1922.

Beeston, A. F. L., T. M. Johnstone, R. B. Serjeant, and G. R. Smith, eds. *Arabic Literature to the End of the Umayyad Period.* Cambridge History of Arabic Literature. Cambridge: Cambridge University Press, 1983.

Beyer, K. *The Aramaic Language: Its Distribution and Subdivisions.* Göttingen: Vandenhoeck & Ruprecht, 1986.

Bickerman, E. J. *From Ezra to the Last of the Maccabees.* New York: Schocken Books, 1962.

Bowersock, G. W. *Roman Arabia.* Cambridge, Mass.: Harvard University Press, 1983.

Brock, Sebastian. "Syriac." In *Horizons in Semitic Studies,* ed. J. H. Eaton, 1–36. Birmingham: University of Birmingham, 1980.

———. "A Dispute of the Months and Some Related Syriac Texts." *Journal of Semitic Studies* 30.2 (1985): 181–211.

———. *St. Ephrem the Syrian: Hymns on Paradise.* Crestwood, N.Y.: St. Vladimir's Seminary Press, 1990.

———. "Syriac Dispute Poems: The Various Types." In *Dispute Poems and Dialogues,* 109–19. Orientalia Lovaniensia Analecta 42. Leuven: Peeters, 1991.

———. "Eusebius and Syriac Christianity." In *Eusebius, Christianity, and Judaism,* ed. Harold W. Attridge and Gohei Hata, 212–34. Detroit: Wayne State University Press, 1992.

———. *The Luminous Eye: the Spiritual World Vision of St. Ephrem the Syrian.* Cistercian Studies 124. Kalamazoo, Mich.: Cistercian Publications, 1992.

———. "Greek and Syriac in Late Antique Syria." In *Literacy and Power in the Ancient World,* ed. A. K. Bowman and G. Woolf, 149–60. Cambridge: Cambridge University Press, 1994.

———. "Syriac Studies in the Last Three Decades: Some Reflections." In *VI Symposium Syriacum 1992,* 13–29. Orientalia Christiana Analecta 247. Rome: Pontificio Istituto Orientale, 1994.

———. *From Ephrem to Romanos: Interactions between Syriac and Greek in Late Antiquity.* Variorum Collected Studies. Brookfield, Vt.: Ashgate, 1999.

Brown, Peter. *The Rise of Western Christendom.* Oxford: Blackwell, 1996.

Dijkstra, Klaas. *Life and Loyalty: A Study in the Socio-Religious Culture of Syria and Mesopotamia in the Graeco-Roman Period Based on Epigraphical Evidence.* Leiden: Brill, 1995.

Donner, F. "The Role of Nomads in the Near East in Late Antiquity." In *Tradition and Innovation in Late Antiquity,* ed. F. M. Clover and R. S. Humphreys, 73–85. Madison: University of Wisconsin Press, 1989.

Drijvers, H. J. W. *Bardaisan of Edessa*. Studia Semitica Neerlandica. Assen: Van Gorcum, 1966.

———. "Hatra, Palmyra und Edessa: Die Städt der syrisch-mesopotamischen Wüste in politischer, kulturgeschichtlicher und religionsgeschichtlicher Beleuchtung." In *Aufstieg und Niedergang der römischen Welt: Principat II, 8,* ed. H. Temporini, 799–906. Berlin: Gruyter, 1977.

———. "De matre inter leones sedente: Iconography and character of the Arab goddess Allat." In *Hommages à Maarten J. Vermaserren* I, 331–51. Leiden: Brill, 1978.

———. *Cults and Beliefs at Edessa*. Études Préliminaires aux Religions Orientales dans l'Empire Romain 82. Leiden: Brill, 1980.

———. "Greek and Aramaic in Palmyrene Inscriptions." In *Studia Aramaica*. Journal of Semitic Studies Supplement 4, ed. M. J. Geller, J. C. Greenfield, and M. P. Weitzman (1995): 31–42.

Drijvers, H. J. W. and John F. Healey. *The Old Syriac Inscriptions of Edessa and Osrhoene: Texts, Translations and Commentary*. Leiden: Brill, 1999.

Fitzmeyer, Joseph, S.J. *A Wandering Aramean: Collected Aramaic Essays*. Society of Biblical Literature Monograph Series 25. Missoula, Mont.: Scholars Press, 1979.

Freyne, Sean. "Galileans, Phoenicians, and Itureans: A Study of Regional Contrasts in the Hellenistic Age." In *Hellenism in the Land of Israel*, ed. John J. Collins and Gregory E. Sterling, 182–215. Notre Dame, Ind.: University of Notre Dame Press, 2001.

Gawlikowski, M. "Les Arabs de Syrie dans l'antiquité." In *Immigration and Emigration within the Ancient Near East: Feschrift E. Lipinski,* ed. K. Van Lerberghe and A. Schoors, 85–92. Orientalia Lovaniensia Analecta 65. Leuven: Peeters, 1995.

Gingras, George E., ed. and trans. *Egeria: Diary of a Pilgrimage*. Ancient Christian Writers 38. New York: Newman Press, 1970.

Grainger, John D. *Hellenistic Phoenicia*. Oxford: Clarendon Press, 1991.

Greenfield, Jonas C. "Aramaic and the Jews." In *Studia Aramaica*. Journal of Semitic Studies Supplement 4, ed. M. J. Geller, J. C. Greenfield, and M. P. Weitzman (1995): 1–18.

Griffith, Sidney H. *Arabic Christianity in the Monasteries of Ninth-Century Palestine*. Variorum Collected Studies. Brookfield, Vt.: Ashgate, 1992.

———. "'Melkites,' 'Jacobites' and the Christological Controversies in Arabic in Third–Ninth-Century Syria." In *Syrian Christians under Islam: The First Thousand Years,* ed. David Thomas, 9–55. Leiden: Brill, 2001.

Groupe d'Études et de Recherches souterraines du Liban. *Momies du Liban: Rapport préliminaire sur la découverte archéologique de 'Āṣi-l-Ḥadaṭ (XIIIᵉ siècle)*. Liban, 1994.

———. *Liban Souterrain*. Bulletin du GERSL. Beirut, Lebanon, no. 5. 1998.

Haddad, George. *Aspects of Social Life in Antioch in the Hellenistic-Roman Period*. New York: Hafner, 1949.

Izre'el, Shlomo, and Rina Drory, eds. *Language and Culture in the Near East*. Israel Oriental Studies 15. Leiden: Brill, 1996.

Lewis, Bernard, ed. and trans. *Islam and the Prophet Muhammad to the Capture of Constantinople*. Vol. 1: *Politics and War*. New York: Oxford University Press, 1987.

Luxenberg, Christoph. *Die syro-aramäische Lesart des Koran: Ein Beitrag zur Entschlüsselung der Koransprache.* Berlin: Das Arabische Buch, 2000.

Mathews, Edward, and Joseph Amar. *St. Ephrem the Syrian: Selected Prose Works; Commentary on Genesis, Commentary on Exodus, Homily On Our Lord, Letter to Publius.* Ed. Kathleen McVey. The Fathers of the Church 19. Washington, D.C.: Catholic University of America Press, 1994.

McCarthy, Carmel. *Saint Ephrem's Commentary on Tatian's Diatessaron, an English Translation of Chester Beatty Syriac MS 709 with Introduction and Notes.* Journal of Semitic Studies Supplement 2. Oxford: Oxford University Press on Behalf of the University of Manchester, 1993.

McVey, Kathleen. *Ephrem the Syrian: Hymns.* Classics of Western Spirituality. New York: Paulist Press, 1989.

Metzger, Bruce. *The Early Versions of the New Testament.* Oxford: Clarendon Press, 1977.

Millar, Fergus. *The Roman Near East 31 B.C.–A.D. 337.* Cambridge, Mass.: Harvard University Press, 1993.

Müller-Kessler, C. "Die Überlieferungsstufen des christlich-palästinischen Aramäisch." In *XXIV. deutscher Orientalistentag, vom 26 bis 30 September 1988 in Köln: ausgewählte Vorträge,* ed. W. Diem and A. Falaturi. *Zeitschrift der Deutschen morgenlandischen Gesellschaft,* suppl. 8. Stuttgart, 1990.

Murray, Robert. *Symbols of Church and Kingdom: A Study in Early Syriac Tradition.* Cambridge: Cambridge University Press, 1975.

———. "Aramaic and Syriac Dispute-Poems and Their Connections." In *Studia Aramaica.* Journal of Semitic Studies Supplement 4, ed. M. J. Geller, J. C. Greenfield, and M. P. Weitzman (1995): 157–87.

Nairon, Faustus, ed. *Novum Testamentum syriacum et arabicum.* Tome I: *Sacrosancta Jesu Christi Evangelica jussu Congregationis de Propaganda Fide ad usum Ecclesiae Nationis Maronitarum.* Tome II: *Acta Apostolorum Epistolae Catholicae et divi Pauli . . . cum Apocalypsi D. Ioannis.* Rome, 1703.

Ortiz de Urbina, Ignatius. *Patrologia Syriaca.* Rome: Pontificium Institutum Orientalium Studiorum, 1965.

Payne Smith, R. *Thesaurus Syriacus.* Oxford: Clarendon Press, 1879–1901.

Peckham, Brian. "Phoenicians and Aramaeans: The Literary and Epigraphic Evidence." In *The World of The Aramaeans II: Studies in History and Archaeology in Honour of Paul-Eugène Dion,* ed. P. M. Michèle Daviau, John W. Wevers, and Michael Weigl, 19–44. Journal for the Study of the Old Testament Supplement Series 325. Sheffield: Sheffield Academic Press, 2001.

Peeters, Paul. *Tréfonds orientale de l'hagiographie byzantine.* Subsidia hagiographica 26. Bruxelles: Société des Bollandistes, 1950.

Reinink, G. J., and H. L. J. Vannstiphout, eds. *Dispute Poems and Dialogues in the Ancient and Mediaeval Near East.* Orientalia Lovaniensia Analecta 42. Louvain: Peeters, 1991.

van Rompay, L. "Some Preliminary Remarks on the Origins of Classical Syriac as a Standard Language: The Syriac Version of Eusebius of Caesarea's Ecclesiastical History." In *Semitic and Cushite Studies,* ed. G. Goldenberg and S. Raz, 70–89. Wiesbaden: Harrassowitz, 1994.

———. "Jacob of Edessa and the Early History of Edessa." In *After Bardaisan: Studies on Continuity and Change in Syriac Christianity in Honour of Professor Han J. W. Drijvers,* ed. G. J. Reinink and A. C. Klugkist, 269–85. Orientalia Lovaniensia Analecta 89. Leuven: Uitgeverij Peeters en Department Oosterse Studies, 1999.

Segal, J. B. *Edessa: "The Blessed City."* Oxford: Clarendon, 1970.

Teixidor, J. "Deux documents syriaques du troisième siècle après J.-C., provenants du Moyen Euphrate." In *Académie des Inscriptions et Belles-Lettres: Comptes rendus des séances de l'année 1990,* 144–66. Paris: 1991.

Weitzman, Michael P. "Lexical Clues to the Composition of the Old Testament Peshitta." In *Studia Aramaica.* Journal of Semitic Studies Supplement 4, ed. M. J. Geller, J. C. Greenfield, and M. P. Weitzman (1995): 217–46.

3 *Dúthaigh* and *Dúchas* in Sixteenth-Century Ireland

PETER McQUILLAN

My purpose is to take a close look at two related words of the Irish lexicon, *dúthaigh* (with the alternative form *dúiche*) and *dúchas,* during one of the formative periods of modern Irish history, the late sixteenth and early seventeenth centuries. Both terms refer variously to the idea of native land, of hereditary right or inheritance in general. To provide a framework for the discussion, I will anticipate at this point my main conclusions:

(i)   The first point concerns aspects of linguistic theory itself. To examine the use of these two words, I will be stressing the pragmatic aspects of meaning. I understand "pragmatics" here as a functional perspective on all aspects of language use in both its cognitive and communicative dimensions. Such an approach naturally emphasizes the role of context in the negotiation of meaning (Verschueren 2001, 242). Specifically, within a linguistic-anthropological framework, I shall be drawing on the work of Silverstein (1976, [1981] 1997) on the context-bound (indexical) nature of linguistic forms like *dúchas.*

(ii) The second point applies the theory to a particular historical context. Both *dúthaigh* and *dúchas* "index" key areas of Irish political, cultural, and social experience. During the period under discussion here, the scope of these terms is extended to include ethnic traditions other than the dominant Gaelic one in order to forge a new Irish national identity. This is reminiscent of the paradigm advanced by Anthony D. Smith for the formation of "premodern" nationalisms that are based on important symbolic cultural attributes.[1]

1. The Concepts of *Dúthaigh* and *Dúchas*

To give some idea of the semantic range of the items involved, I present here the definitions given in Ó Dónaill (1977) of these two words, highlighting those aspects on which I wish to concentrate the discussion (for *dúiche / dúthaigh* and *dúchas* I give the more historical spellings in parentheses):

(i) dúiche (dúthaigh)
1. Hereditary land
2. Native land, native place, home country
3. Land, estate
4. Region, territory; district, locality, countryside

(ii) dúchas (dúthchas)
1. Hereditary right or claim; birthright, heritage; ancestral estate, patrimony
2. Native place or country, ancestral home; traditional connection
3. Kindred affection, natural affinity
4. Heredity, innate quality, natural bent
5. Natural wild state; wildness, madness
6. (*genitive case as adjective*) Inherited, inherent, innate, native

A distinctly "fluid" (Daniel 1984) or shifting range of meanings characterizes *dúchas* in particular. It is in the semantic range of native or hereditary land highlighted above that *dúthaigh* and *dúchas* are contiguous, and this range of meaning is the focus of the present discussion.

Sapir (2000) highlights the importance of language, in particular of vocabulary, as an index to culture. What I want to consider here is the possibility of analyzing the words *dúthaigh* and *dúchas* as indexes of historical developments in early modern Ireland. To do this, a brief consideration of the nature of linguistic signs is appropriate. In the semiotic theory of Peirce, signs are divided into "icons," "indexes," and "symbols."[2] An icon is a sign that bears some kind of graphic or diagrammatic resemblance to its referent. A symbol is a sign whose signification is a matter of convention. Words are symbols in this sense. An index relates a sign to an object in terms of contiguity, concurrence, or causation — a simple nonlinguistic example would be smoke as an index of fire. Of particular interest in the present context is Jakobson's (1971b) insight that many linguistic forms are "shifters." As he puts it (1971b, 131), "the general meaning of a shifter cannot be defined without reference to the message": in semiotic terms, a shifter is both a symbol and an index. Silverstein (1976) and Daniel (1984) have applied this idea to the analysis of cultural contexts, and both stress the indispensable nature of context for the interpretation of signs. In Duranti's (1997, 37) formulation indexicality is "a sign-activated connection between an on-going situation and other situations."

This is the pragmatic aspect of meaning, and it is in such terms that I will argue that the conventional linguistic signs *dúthaigh* and *dúchas* are best understood as "shifters," or context-dependent signs that index various cultural and historical domains. It is precisely in this pragmatic area of dependence on context that contestability arises. This dependence can often have a chronological dimension. Consider one example given by Dinneen for *dúchas* in his dictionary (1927) and the translation that he gives with it:

is fearr **dúthchas** ná gach aon nídh

_____

inherited qualities are best (lit. '*dúchas* is better than everything')

For a speaker of Modern Irish this translation is unexceptionable. However, look at the phrase in its fifteenth-century context. The context is the "Deirdre" story (*Oidheadh Chloinne Uisnigh;* henceforth *OCU*) where Fearghus, Naoise, and his brothers find themselves in exile in Scotland:

"Is fearr **dúthchas** iná gach ní," ar Fearghus, "uair ní haoibhinn do neoch maitheas dá mhéad muna fhaice a **dhúthchas**" "Is fíor sin," ar Naoise, "dóigh is annsa leam péin Éire iná Alba, gé madh mó do mhaith Alban do-ghéabhainn." (*OCU* 169)

_____

"A native land is better than anything," said Fearghus, "for no excellence, however great, is delightful to one unless one sees one's native land." "That is true," said Naoise, "for Ireland is dearer to me than Scotland, though I should get more of Scotland's goods."

In context we can see that the modern default interpretation cannot apply in a purely referential sense. This is clinched by Fearghus talking about "seeing" his *dúchas* (here Ireland, his native land, as opposed to Scotland, the land of his exile) as a material entity. Yet it is a material entity invested with some emotive symbolic force, as the context makes clear. The following text gives us a further example of the shifting, symbolic nature of this term *dúchas,* even where its frame of reference is apparently the native land or patrimony.

2. "Báidh nádúrtha an dúthchais": Ireland's Spanish Connection

The text is a letter from Domhnall Ó Súilleabháin Béirre to the king of Spain, written in Kinsale in December 1601, just before its Irish and Spanish garrison surrendered to the besieging English army. In the first passage, *dú(th)chas* translates naturally as "native land" or "patrimony," which is how Ó Cuív renders it in his 1997 edition. The English translations given below are more or less contemporary with the original and appear in Stafford (1633, 228–29). In addition, I will deal presently with a contemporary Spanish translation. In this first passage (a), Ó Súilleabháin Béirre is appealing for aid:

(a) a n-aghuidh ar n-eascarad atá ag múchadh an chreideimh Chatoilica go diabhluidhe, ag básughadh ar n-uaisle go díbhfheargach, 7 ag sanntughadh ar **ndúthchais** go haindlightheach

---

against our Enemies that seek to overwhelme and extinguish the Catholike faith diabolically, put to death our Chieftaines tyrannously, coveting our **Lands and Livings** unlawfully

At the beginning of the letter, there is a revealing passage that I will give first in (b) its shorter and (c) its longer contexts:

(b) Atá riamh . . . go follas dá hshíordhearbhadh eadrainne na hÉireannaigh nách fuil aonní amháin as neartmhuire oibrigheas inar ccroidhthibh do thuar 7 do bhreith ar ngrádha 7 ar n-inmhuine iná báidh nádúrtha an **dúthchais** 7 cuimhniughadh an charadraidh bhíos do g[h]náth ar ar n-aire . . .

It hath beene ever . . . manifestly proued by daily experience among us the Irish, that there is nothing that worketh more forcibly in our hearts,

to winne, and to draw our loue and affection, then (= than) naturall incli-
nation to **our Progeny and Offspring** and the memoriall of the friendship
which sticketh still in our minds . . .

Here Ó Cuív again takes *dúthchas* as "patrimony," translating *báidh nádúrtha an
dúthchais* as "the natural fondness for our patrimony," which is again unobjec-
tionable as far as it goes. However, the translation "native land" or "patrimony"
may turn out in fact to bear further contextualization. Let us take the wider
context:

(c)   . . . Ar mbheith dúinne, príomhGhaoighuil na hÉireann, cían ó hshoin ar
ttarr[a]ng ar bphréimhe 7 ar **mbunadhuis** ó threibh ord[h]ruic fhíorúasal
na nEasbáinneach .i. ó Mhíleadh . . . do réir fhiadhnuise ar seinleabhur
seanchuis, ar ngég ngeinealuigh, ar starthuidh 7 ar ccroiniceadh

----

Wee the meere Irish (the chief Gaelic people of Ireland) long sithence
deriving our roote and **originall** from the famous and noble race of the
Spaniards: *Viz.* from Milecius . . . from the testimony of our old ancient
bookes of antiquities, our Petigrees, our Histories and our Cronicles

The overall thrust of the passage is the idea of the common origin of the Gaelic
Irish from their ancestor Míl of Spain, an ancestry that of course indicates a
shared ethnic origin with the Spanish themselves.[3] The connection that I want
to highlight here is that between *dúchas* and *bunadhus* "origin," which Ó Cuív
translates here as "foundation." To investigate this relation further I present the
following excerpt from a twelfth-century account of the war of the Irish against
the Vikings, *Cogad Gaedel re Gallaibh* (henceforth *Cog.*). Here Brian and Mathghamhain, leaders of the Irish Dál gCais dynasty, are debating the wisdom of
engaging the enemy in battle. Eventually they agree that they should fight the
foreigners at Cashel, the center of the high kingship of Munster, to which the Dál
gCais feel they have special claim, because

Ba he dna a **mbunadus** ocus a **senducus** badein. (*Cog.*, 68)

It was their place of origin (*bunadhus*) and their own ancestral home
(*senducus*).

This passage indicates a close relation between the ideas of *bunadhus* and *dúchas* as representing points of ethnic and ancestral origins. One interesting feature of Ó Súilleabháin Béirre's letter is the treatment of the phrase *báidh nádúrtha an dúthchais* in the respective English and Spanish translations. The contemporary English translation "progeny and offspring" is a curious one and appears to show some misunderstanding: the genetic associations of *dúchas* are with ancestry rather than with progeny. What is also curious is that in the contemporary Spanish translation *dúchas* is left untranslated and the phrase *báidh nádúrtha an dúthchais* is simply rendered "amor natural." This somewhat erratic treatment suggests that the original phrase is not a simple matter, especially when it is compared to the relative ease of translating the phrase *ag sanntughadh ar ndúthchais* later in the text, where *dúchas* is rendered in the English "lands and livings," in the Spanish "bienas y rentas."

It seems to me that the "difficulty" in this passage from Ó Súilleabháin Béirre's letter lies precisely in the indexical nature of *dúchas*, the way the word points to particular aspects of a present context and links it to other contexts — again in Duranti's (1997, 37) formulation "a sign-activated connection between an on-going situation and other situations." Inevitably, such contexts, as here, tend to be both culturally specific and historically contingent, which makes for certain problems of translation across cultures. What Ó Súilleabháin Béirre does here is to use these indexical properties as a pointer towards a contextually relevant cultural focus of ethnicity: here the "Milesian" connection of a shared ethnic origin (*bunadhus*) between the Irish and the Spanish that is of course highly appropriate in the context of his appeal to Spain for military assistance. This is the performative aspect of indexicality in the creation and formulation of identity. However, such a creative act requires what Gumperz (1996) calls "contextualization cues." I am arguing here that *dúchas* in the above passage is such a "cue" that implies and requires culture-specific knowledge for its interpretation, which is why both the English and Spanish translators "fail" in this instance.

3. The Symbolic Center in Irish Ideology

We now turn to a second focal point of Gaelic Irish unity. In the twelfth-century passage discussed above, a further justification for the decision of the Dál gCais to fight at Cashel is as follows ba he Temair Lethi Moga

———

it was the Tara of southern Ireland

This reference indexes another aspect of the Irish concept of unity: the idea of a symbolic center of power. As is well known, Ireland in the modern period is divided into four provinces (Connacht, Leinster, Munster, and Ulster). However, the Irish word for a "province" is *cúige* (Old Irish *cóiced*), which etymologically means a "fifth." Where, therefore, is the "missing" province? According to Céitinn's account in his history of Ireland (*FFÉ* ii 247 ff.), a "middle" province was created out of the other four. This middle province called *Midhe* (present-day "Meath") was established by the Gaelic king Tuathal Téchtmar by taking a portion of land from each of the four existing provinces. It is worth noting that the name *Midhe* etymologically means "middle" (< *Medion* "middle," cognate with Latin *medium*). Furthermore, within this middle province Tuathal built four fortresses, each one associated with one of the other existing provinces: Tailtiu with Ulster, Teamhair (Tara) with Leinster, Uisneach with Connacht, and Tlachtga with Munster. As Rees and Rees (1961, 148) point out, the division of the world into four quarters with a central fifth is also attested in Indian and Chinese cosmographies. A fraction implies, of course, the existence of a whole entity, one fifth means that there are five fifths, and the middle fifth thus symbolizes in microcosm the underlying unity of the other four. Each of the other four provinces had its own capital, such as Cruachain in Connacht and Cashel in Munster. Assemblies were held at these centers, and participation in such assemblies guaranteed the well-being and prosperity of the kingdom. Mac Cana (1985) speaks here of the "cult of the centre" in Irish, and indeed in Celtic ideology and, as we shall see presently, references to Tara and Tailtiu, to Cashel and Cruachain are used to evoke this cult of the center in the poetry discussed below.

Therefore, though the historical record suggests that the notion of a de facto political high-kingship is a relatively late one in Ireland, nevertheless the idea of a "fifth" presupposes an underlying unity, the reflex, perhaps, of an old cosmological schema. Indeed, as Mac Cana points out, the propaganda associated with the high-kingship depends for any effect that it might have on the persistence and pervasiveness of this *idea* of an underlying unity that receives reinforcement at various junctures in the medieval period. For example, at the time of the Viking invasions in the ninth and tenth centuries, the obstinate resistance staged by the Uí Néill dynasties invoked precisely the idea of the Tara high-kingship as its focal point (Ó Corráin 1978, 8). In addition, Ó Corráin argues (1978, 4 ff.) that the Irish learned classes were preoccupied through the medieval period with the consciousness of themselves as a larger "natio." The earliest efforts to articulate this common consciousness are found in the seventh century when the idea of the common origin of the Gaels from Míl of Spain first takes shape (see section 2 above and, further, section 5 below). This represents an attempt to integrate native Irish traditions of their own origin within the overall framework of Christianity as the origin legend of humankind in general (Ó Corráin 1978, 5; Carney 1971, 73). As Ó Corráin observes, this consciousness based on the same origin legend informs the main corpus of genealogies and aspects of the legal corpus (6–7) from an early period, and we have already considered above its continuing relevance in an early-seventeenth-century context.

What we have here is a classic disparity between political and cultural-symbolic realities; indeed, scholars of premodern societies have stressed the inverse relation that often seems to obtain between the two. Thus cultural homogeneity may render centralized political structures irrelevant and otiose. Fortes and Evans-Pritchard (1940, 23) argue that "bonds of utilitarian interest between individuals and between groups are not as strong as the bonds implied in common attachment to mystical symbols." As Mac Cana (1985, 74 ff.) points out, the main harbingers of this idea of Irish unity in the medieval period were the hereditary, professional poets, attached to a local patron but with unrivaled freedom of movement throughout Ireland. The trope of unity is frequently used as a rather conventional device in the medieval period, but, as Mac Cana and others more recently have pointed out, it acquires a more urgent relevance after the mid-sixteenth century. Political disunity was tolerable as long as shared cultural values and ideology were paramount — it is when these latter come under threat in the late sixteenth and early seventeenth centuries that the "cult of the center," the symbolic center, acquires added cogency.

Perhaps the most dramatic evocation of the symbolic center occurs in one of Tadhg Dall Ó hUiginn's (c. 1550–91) most highly charged political poems, addressed to Brian na Múrtha Ó Ruairc (Knott 1922, 108–19). The poem's basic message is contained in its title: "D'fhior chogaidh comhailtear síothcháin" (To the man of war peace is observed), the implication being that only bellicosity can secure peace and respect from the English. It was likely composed around 1588 after Ó Ruairc had incurred the displeasure of Sir Richard Bingham, English official and president of Connacht, for assisting survivors of the Spanish Armada in the northwest of Ireland (Caball 1998, 48). This poem is a full-blooded appeal to a Gaelic racial pride born of a long historical and cultural awareness. At the heart of Tadhg Dall's appeal to Ó Ruairc is the fact that the English hold the symbolic centre of Ireland while the Irish are banished to the periphery:

> Siad dá gcur i gciomhsaibh Banbha
> buidhne Ghall 'na glémheadhón

> ———

> They are being thrust onto the outskirts of Ireland
> whilst regiments of foreigners are in the centre

Mac Cana (1985, 76) has identified the significance of these lines in terms of traditional Gaelic ideology: "the foreigner has established himself at the sacred spot which symbolizes the unity of the country." Here the apocalyptic struggle will have to be fought, and all traces of the foreign presence obliterated before the Gaels emerge triumphant. In the following excerpts, references pertaining to the symbolic middle are highlighted in bold. (Note that the overriding concern is not at all with the English administrative center of Dublin.)

> Déantar leision láimh re **Tailltin**
> túir mhóra do mhionchuma;
> sgriostar leis go bruinne mbrátha
> a muille a n-átha a n-iothlunna

> Foileóchthar leó learga **Midhe**
> ré méid na gcreach gcathardha
> budh iomdha slighe um **Bóinn** mbreacgloin
> 'gon bhróin neartmhair nathardha

> Líonfaidhear do linntibh corcra
> clár **Midhe** ón dá mhearghasraidh,
> go n-éirghe fuil ós na formnaibh
> san mhuigh thonnghloin **Teamhrach-sain**

> ———

Beside **Tailte** let great towers
be pulverized by him
let him sweep utterly away
their mills, their kilns, their granaries

The slopes of **Meath** will be covered by them
with the vastness of the spoils from the cities
the powerful cunning host will make many a road
about the bright-trouted **Boyne**

The land of **Meath** will be flooded
with ruddy pools from the two vigorous bands
until the blood rises above the shoulders
on that bright-surfaced plain of **Tara**

The poet then delivers his final apocalyptic message of national deliverance:

Muidhfidh ainnséin ar fhóir Saxan
ré síol Ghaoidhil ghéirreannaigh,
nách bia do shíor ón ágh d'fhógra
ós chlár Fhódla acht Éireannaigh

———

Then will the Saxon tribe be vanquished
by the seed of the keen-weaponed Gaels
so that there will be from proclamation of war
none save Irishmen over the land of Ireland

Although the poem is addressed to Ó Ruairc of west Bréifne, the argument is presented in all-Ireland terms—as the poet says, all Ireland will embark on war under his leadership. In any case, quite apart from the various references to "Ireland" and "Irish" in various guises, the fact that the poet centers (literally) his argument on the old symbolic and cultural unity of Ireland clinches, in my view, the argument for a national dimension to this poetry.

4. "Dia libh a laochruidh Gaoidhiol": Gaelic Nationalism in the 1580s

In this section, I want to pursue the association of *dúchas* with the symbolic center in political poetry of the late sixteenth and early seventeenth centuries. The first example is the poem "Dia libh a laochruidh Gaoidhiol" (God with you, warriors of the Gaels!; Mac Airt 1944, 142–44) dating from the 1580s or 1590s. This poem is found in the poem book (*duanaire*) of Feagh McHugh O'Byrne, who joined Viscount Baltinglass in rebellion in 1580 at the time of the second Desmond rebellion in Munster. The growth of English colonialist aggression in South Leinster after the 1550s and 1560s, coupled with the defeat of the Kildare Fitzgeralds, had led to the rise of the O'Byrnes as a political power in the region (Bradshaw 1978). According to Bradshaw, some of the poems in Feagh's poem book give evidence of new concerns among the poets: the traditional medieval theme of the glorification of the local dynast is now set in a national, not a local, context. It is no longer the aggrandizement of the dynasty itself but rather its role in rejuvenating the national cause, the Gaelic race and nation that is in the forefront. Bradshaw identifies this as a type of pan-Gaelic nationalism that asserts the claim of the native Irish to the land of Ireland (*puirt úrghoirt innsi Gaoidhiol*) as their native land (*bhar bhfearuinn dúthchais* "of your native land," where *dúthchais* is the genitive form governed by the preceding noun *fearuinn*, literally, "of your land of *dúchas*"):

> Déntar libh coinghleic calma
> a bhuidhion armghlan fhaoiltioch
> fá cheann **bhar bhfearuinn dúthchais**
> puirt úrghoirt innsi Gaoidhiol

> ———

> Wage war like valorous wolves
> you blessed band of the shining arms
> on behalf of your native land,
> the fresh fields of the island of the Gaels.

The poet then evokes a series of symbolic sites to which the Irish have been slow to press their claim (*agra*): reminiscent of Tadhg Dall's poem above, we have the evocation of Tara (*Lios Teamhra*) and Tailte (here in the genitive form *Tailtean*). According to Céitinn (*FFÉ* ii 247 ff. and see above), in the configuration of Meath as the symbolic central "fifth" or province, these sites are associated with the provinces of Leinster (east) and Ulster (north) respectively. Cashel (Caisiol), the seat of the high-kingship of Munster in the south, and Cruachain, the royal center of the western province of Connacht (here in the genitive *Cruachna*), represent the remaining two provinces:

> Mó as mall gur hagradh libh-si
> Magh Life ná **Lios Teamhra**
> ná **Caisiol** na sreabh nuaghlan
> ná **míonchlár Cruachna Meadhbha**
>
> Is díoth cuimhne, a chlann Míleadh . . .
> tug oirbh gan agra **Tailtean**

> ———

> You seem the more slow to claim
> the plain of the Liffey or the fort of Tara
> or Cashel of the ever clear streams
> or the smooth plain of Maeve's Cruachain.
>
> It is loss of memory, o children of Míl . . .
> that has made you relinquish your claim to Tailte

By evoking these sites, the poet delivers a national message. The O'Byrnes wage war on the English on behalf of the five fifths of Ireland. The symbolism of the center enables the poem's message to transcend the purely local and dynastic.

There is a further significant use of the term *dúchas* in this poem in opposition to the idea of *eachtruinn* "foreigners" and to the idea of outlawry or banditry:

> Crádh liom eachtruinn dá bhfógra
> ríoghradh Fhódla 's a n-oireacht
> 's nách goirthior dhíobh **'na ndúthchus**
> acht ceithearn chúthail choilleadh

> ———

> It kills me that foreigners have outlawed
> the kings of Fódla and their assemblies,

and that all they are now called in their
homeland are shifty woodland bandits.

There is further evidence of this opposition between *dúchas* and banditry in a
proverbial expression that appears in an early-seventeenth-century poem of
Scottish provenance—a cautionary poem that counsels prudence to a High-
land chief after his sons have been taken captive by the Lowland Privy Council
(Black 1974, 199):

> An senfhocal, a chúl chas:
> "cothuigh go dian fad **dhúthchas**"
> a thobar fial na bhfileadh,
> "'s ná hiarr cogadh coillidheadh"

> The maxim, curly-haired one:
> "take good care of your inheritance,"
> —generous fountain of poets—
> "and do not seek the warfare of outlaws"

Thus, *dúchas* is identified with the center of the social order as opposed to out-
law elements of the periphery.

In a poem composed in response to the Plantation of Ulster (1610), "Mo
thruaighe mar táid Gaoidhil" (Alas how the Gaels are; O'Rahilly [1927] 1977,
144–47), Fear Flatha Ó Gnímh (1602–c. 1640) gives considerable attention to
the violation of the physical aspects of the Irish landscape attendant on the
plantation. The English and Scottish planters have destroyed the land's material balance and thus its fundamental symbolic rationale. A remarkable feature
of Ó Gnímh's poem is its focus on the cultural dislocation that has occurred because of the plantation. The planters have replaced the old houses with lime-
washed towers (*túir aolta*), and they have destroyed the symbolic significance
of the landscape by the introduction of agriculture and commerce. Accordingly,
mother Ireland fails to distinguish her own children from the brood of foreigners,
and the Irish are consequently exiles in their own land (*'na ndroing dheórata*):

> Ní aithneann aicme Ghaoidheal
> Banbha, buime a maccdhaoineadh

's ní aithneann Éire iad soin;
tiad re chéile as a gcrothaibh

Is í an drong dhligheas d'aithne
d'inis Chuinn is comhaithghe;
ní Goill is aoighidh aca,
Gaoidhil 'na ndroing dheórata

———

The tribe of the Gaels do not recognize
Banbha, their own foster-mother
and Ireland does not recognize them:
they are mutual strangers.

To the island of Conn, it's the people
that it should recognize who are foreigners;
it is not the English they consider strangers
the Irish are as an exiled troop.

The plight of the Irish as exiles in their own land is compared to the predicament of both the Trojans and the Chosen People of Israel. Note again the references to symbolic sites already considered above—Tara, Tailte, and the River Boyne, historically one of the divisions between the north and south of Ireland:

Mar lucht na Traoi ar n-a toghail
dá ndíchleith i ndíothrabhaibh,
**fian Teamhra a-táid ó Thailtin
a bhfáid sealbha seachaintir**

Cosmhail re Cloinn Isra-hél
thoir san Éighipt ar éidréan
Mic Mhíleadh um Bhóinn a-bhus
ag síneadh dhóibh ó **a ndúthchas**

———

Like the people of Troy after its destruction
hiding in the wilderness

Tara's army is gone from Tailte
their native lands are given up.

Like the children of Israel
in the east in feeble exile in Egypt,
are the sons of Míl here about the Boyne,
wandering away from their **dúthchas**

Thus, the loss of *dúchas* here is the retreat from the cultural center of the Boyne, the loss of the symbolic sites of Tara and Tailte. The Irish have shunned their patrimony and are wandering as feeble exiles like the Israelites in Egypt. We will see another instance below of the idea of *dúchas* situated in and contrasted with a context of exile. Earlier in the poem Ó Gnímh speaks of the Irish as under the oppression of a foreign army, and he makes reference to the dire possibility that Ireland will become another England.

The alleged national scope or "protonationalist" nature of such poetry has been contested, for example, by Dunne (1980), who rejects any analysis in terms of a historiography that would seek antecedents for the Irish nationalism of the nineteenth and twentieth centuries in this earlier material. In discussing Dunne's views, Gibbons (1996, 137–39) makes the point that the amorphous and decentralized nature of Gaelic society was actually its strength against Tudor expansionism, the paradigm being one of native resistance to the concentration of power in the center. Significantly, Gibbons entitles his discussion "identity without a centre." Yet the texts that we have been considering show a marked preoccupation with a symbolic or ideological center that we can perhaps situate in the context of what Cohn (1966), in a discussion of regionalism in India, calls a "symbol pool" of associations. This symbolic pool can consist of various types of cultural and historical artifact, from literature, on the one hand, to religious shrines and important landmarks, on the other. A significant concomitant of this symbolism is that the integrity of territorial units is defined in terms of their centers rather than their boundaries or peripheries.

5. "Fearann cloidhimh críoch Bhanbha": Redefining "Irishness" in the Late Sixteenth Century

The most important development in Irish political ideology in the sixteenth and seventeenth centuries is the emergence of a new nationalism founded on a common allegiance to Catholicism and opposed to Protestant English expansion in Ireland (Morgan 1995; Ó Buachalla 1993). This nationalism represents an accommodation between the two ethnic traditions of later medieval Ireland: the aboriginal Gaelic or "native" Irish (*Gaoidhil* "Gaels") and the so-called Old English (*Gaill* "foreigners" or *Sean-ghaill* "old foreigners"), the descendants of the first English or Anglo-Norman colonists of the twelfth and subsequent centuries. The members of this emergent Irish nation are referred to collectively as *Éireannaigh* ("Irish," plural of *Éireannach*, derived from *Éire* "Ireland") and are opposed to the Protestant New English presence in Ireland (*Nua-ghaill* "new foreigners"). According to Ó Buachalla (1990, 410), the terms *Éireannach* and *Gaedheal* (Gael) were originally used synonymously. In the later medieval period, the term *Éireannach* was inclusive of all the inhabitants of the island of Ireland, and this is its semantic range in the annals of the fifteenth and sixteenth centuries. By the seventeenth century, however, the term *Éireannach* acquires an exclusive element whereby those outside the Catholic faith are not admitted. In the 1630s, Seathrún Céitinn's (anglicized Geoffrey Keating) *Foras Feasa ar Éirinn* (The basis of knowledge on Ireland) becomes the foundational history of this new Irish nation.

Although this development does not receive consistent literary expression until the seventeenth century, Caball (1998, 45 ff.) argues that an early example of this new ethnic understanding is a poem by Tadhg Dall Ó hUiginn — "Fearann cloidhimh críoch Bhanbha" (The land of Ireland is sword land; Knott 1922, 120–31) — addressed to Mac William Burke in the 1570s. For Leerssen (1996, 177) this poem is an example of "cultural fraternization" between the descendants of what he calls the "Hiberno-Normans" and the native or Gaelic Irish, both equally threatened by the growing aggressiveness of the Tudor monarchy in Ireland.[4] Similarly, Caball (1998, 45) sees the poem as evidence of the tension afflicting the Gaelic literati in face of English expansionism in the 1570s and an effort on Ó hUiginn's part to formulate a sense of shared ethnicity between the two groups. This involved rehabilitating the Gaelicized descendants of the Anglo-Normans, bringing them in from the margins of the formalized medieval Gaelic worldview (Caball 1998, 47).

In the light of the potential significance of this poem, it is worth noting the following excerpt from Lughaidh Ó Cléirigh's biography of Red Hugh O'Donnell written in the first years of the seventeenth century (*Beatha Aodha Ruaidh Uí Dhomhnuill* "The Life of Red Hugh O'Donnell") concerning Gaelic attitudes to the ethnicity and legitimacy of the Mac William Burkes. Referring to the Burkes' patrimony of Tyrawley, Co. Mayo (*Tír nAmhalgadha*), the author informs us (Walsh 1957, 114.3):

Ba sain ceinél ro aitreibh í an ionbhaidh sin 7 na tuatha diarbho toich ó
chéin mháir. Búrcaigh slondadh an cheneoil rotus-n-aitreb an tan sin. Ba
do Fhrancaibh a **mbunadh**chenél 7 a críochaibh Saxan ro chedghabhsat
an chrioch.

———

The race who inhabited it then was different from the races whose property it was from remote time. Burke was the name of the family inhab-
iting it then. Their original stock was French, and they had come from
English territory to that place and it was by the power of the English that
they first got possession of the territory.

Note in particular the association of the Burkes with a "French" (or Norman) as
opposed to a "Spanish" (i.e., Gaelic) origin and the characterization of this connection in terms of their *bunadh* (origin, source; stock, race), the same term that
underlies *bunadhus* "origin," as discussed in section 2 above.

Before considering Ó hUiginn's poem in detail, let us return briefly to the
twelfth-century text on the war between the Irish and the Vikings. We have already seen how the Dál gCais had resolved to fight the foreigners at Cashel because they regarded it as their native place and the symbolic center of Munster.
Their rationalization of this decision continues as follows:

ba fearr a **fír catha** ocus comlaind sin inna **nduthaig** . . . innas im **an
ferand forgabala ocus claidim**

———

their cause was more just in their **native land** . . . than regarding land
that had been conquered by the sword

The importance of this passage is that a just cause for the waging of war (*fír catha*,
lit. "truth of battle") is guaranteed when defending the native land (*dúthaig*) but
not where conquered land or "sword land" (*ferand claidim*) is concerned.

The same language is being used in sixteenth-century Ireland in the cause
of "faith and fatherland" against the heretic Queen Elizabeth I. Three letters have
survived in Irish by the leader of the Desmond resistance of the 1570s, James
Fitzmaurice Fitzgerald, written to various mercenary leaders in Munster, as in
the following dated July 18th, 1579 (O'Donovan 1858–59, 362–64):

Agus is coruide dho theacht, is maith an **fíor gcatha** atá aguinn hi n-
aghaidh ár námhud .i. sinne ag cosnamh ár gcreidimh 7 **ár ndúthaighe**,
agus iad-san ag cur an chreidimh ar gcúl 7 ar tí **ár nduthuidhe féin** do
bhuain dínne; sinne ar an bhfírinne 7 iad-san ar an mbréig

———

And it is the more right for you to come, because we have a just cause
of war against our enemies, viz., we are defending our religion and our
country, and they are abolishing the religion and about to take our country from us; we are on the side of truth, they are on the side of falsehood

Here a just cause (*fíor gcatha*) is again associated with the defense of the native
land (*dúthaigh*), as in the twelfth-century passage above. The more significant ideological development that takes place in the sixteenth century, however, concerns
the perceived relationship between the ideas of native land (*dúthaigh*) and conquered land (*fearann cloidhimh*), and for this we turn to Ó hUiginn's poem,
which is roughly contemporary with the letters of Fitzmaurice Fitzgerald.

Ó hUiginn begins his poem by saying that Ireland is sword land, thus ac-
knowledging the claim of the strongest to its territory (Caball 1998, 46). Noteworthy is the way in which Ó hUiginn hammers on the ideas of *ceart* and *cóir*,
both meaning "right" or "just claim," and elaborates on their relationship to the
use of force (*foirneart, neart, éigean*):

Fearann cloidhimh críoch Bhanbha
bíoth slán cháich fá chomhardha
go bhfuil d'oighreacht ar Fhiadh bhFáil
acht *foirneart* gliadh dá gabháil

Ní fhuil *cóir* uirre ag aoinfhear —
críoch shuaitheanta sheanGhaoidheal,
bheith fa *neart* an té is treise —
is é *ceart* na críchese

Ní fhuil do *cheart* ar chrích bhFáil
ag Macaibh Míleadh Easbáin,
's ní bhí ag gach gabháil dár gheabh,
acht sí d'fhagháil ar *éigean*

The land of Banbha is but sword land
let all be defied to show
that any can inherit the Land of Fál
save by conquest by force of battle

No one man has any claim to
the shining land of the ancient Gaels
to be under the power of the strongest
is the law of this country

There is no right to the land of Fál
on the part of the sons of Míl of Spain
nor on the part of any other conquest
except to take her by force

Frequent use of the verbs *gabh-* and *bean-*, both meaning "take," generally forcibly, enhances this rhetoric of right and might. Tadhg Dall then recounts how Ireland was conquered by various waves of invaders. In so doing, he centers the discussion in the canonical tradition of the *Lebor Gabála Érenn,* or *Book of the Taking of Ireland.*[5] In the scheme of this origin legend of the Gaelic Irish, Ireland is peopled by five successive invasions, the fifth and culminating occupation being that of the Gaels themselves ("the sons of Míl of Spain" above). This is of course the same tradition that underlies Ó Súilleabháin Béirre's evocation of the Spanish connection in his letter of 1602 (see section 2 above). In a significant anticipation of Céitinn's *Foras Feasa* of the 1630s, however, the poet extends the scheme to include the Anglo-Norman Burkes and their descendants and issues a refutation to those who impute foreignness to them (Caball 1998, 46):

Gi bé adéaradh gur deóraidh
Búrcaigh na mbeart n-inleóghain —
faghar d'fhuil Ghaoidhil nó Ghoill
nách bhfuil 'na aoighidh agoinn

Gé adeirdís sliocht Ghaoidhil Ghlais
coimhighthe le cloinn Séarlais —

clocha toinighthe bheann **mBreagh**—
coimhighthe an dream adeireadh

———

Whoever says that they are foreigners
the Burkes of the lion-like deeds
let one be found of the blood of Gael or Gall
who is not a guest among us

Though the descendants of Gaoidheal Glas
used to call the children of Charles foreigners
(set stones of Banbha's hills)
they were foreigners who used to say that

In other words, the Burkes and their peers represent in fact a sixth wave of invaders to be accommodated to the Milesian schema. The climax of this argument
revolves around the use of the word *dúthaigh* and its association with the symbolic centers of Tara, the Boyne, and "Bregia" (*Breagha*). The poem continues:

Dul uatha ag Éirinn ní fhuil
deich mbliadhna ar cheithre chéadaibh
atá an tír thiormarsaidh thais
fa fhionnghasraidh shíl Shéarlais

Is siad féin is uaisle d'fhuil;
iad is fhearr fhuair an **dúthaigh;**
díobh is doibheanta **Bóinn Bhreagh**
oireachta dan cóir creideamh

Ní thiocfa 's ní tháinig riamh—
an chlann do chin ó Uilliam—
fine ar chumhachtaibh na gcruth
cumhachtaigh **Thighe Teamhrach**

———

Ireland cannot escape from them
for four centuries and ten years

has the warm, ancient, humid land
been under the fair warriors of the seed of Charles

It is they who are noblest in blood
they who have best won the heritage
from them the **Bregian Boyne** cannot be taken
nobles to whom homage is fitting

There will not be, nor has there ever been,
a line equal in power to the race
that sprang from William
rulers of the **Dwelling of Tara**

The references to the ideological center of the Irish high-kingship (Bregia and Tara) index the scope of the concept *dúthaigh* here. Ó hUiginn makes the most telling use of these associations to bring his argument full circle. Ireland is of course the native land (*dúthaigh*) of the Gaelic Irish, but, as the poet is at pains to point out, their own canonical origin legend tells them that it is also sword land (*fearann cloidhimh*), in which case the only rightful claim to the land is that based on conquest.

I believe that it is possible to place these arguments in a wider European perspective. Based on both the Burkes' nobility and the longevity of their tenure in Ireland, Ó hUiginn's poem argues for an acknowledgment of the right of those inhabitants of Ireland, historically marginal to the Gaelic polity, who have remained in long and successful occupation of the land of Ireland. This is reminiscent of the *praescriptio longi temporis* of natural law (Pagden 1995, 89), which in effect turns a dominion that is de facto into one that is de jure. The continuing successful existence of a claim constitutes its own retrospective legitimacy, and this is the basis of Burke's entitlement (*ceart*) to the native land (*dúthaigh*). Furthermore, there is at least an implicit anticipation here of Céitinn's distinction between the idea of a pagan conquest (*gabháltas págánta*) and a Christian conquest (*gabháltas Críostamhail*). The pagan conquest obliterates native tradition and language as part of the act of appropriation, while the Christian conquest is content to accept the submission of the original inhabitants and to introduce new settlers from the metropolis to coexist peacefully alongside them (*FFÉ* i, 34). As Bradshaw (1993, 189) points out, Céitinn's ideological position is reminiscent of contemporary debates in Spain about the legitimacy of conquest in the Americas (Skinner 1978, 168–72). Céitinn's notion of the pagan conquest accords with the views of Sepúlveda, for example, that the indigenous inhabitants might legitimately be conquered and enslaved, while his notion of the Christian conquest squares with the ideas of de las Casas that native inhabitants have certain rights of dominion (*dominium*) based on natural law.[6]

It is worth considering a passage in Céitinn's *Foras Feasa* that expands on the overall relationship between *ceart* and *dúchas* given the emphasis placed by Ó hUiginn on the former term as an agent of legitimization.[7] The context is given by the events of the first English (Anglo-Norman) invasion of 1169 in which Diarmaid Mac Murchadha, king of Leinster, and his Anglo-Norman ally, Robert Fitzstephen, face the advancing king of Connacht and aspiring high king of Ireland, Ruaidhrí Ó Conchobhair, and are reluctant to engage him in battle. When Ruaidhrí observes this reticence, he orders Fitzstephen to leave Ireland because:

> nach raibhe **ceart ná dúthchas** aige ar bheith innte . . . Is amhlaidh do
> críochnuigheadh an tsíoth soin eatorra .i. Cúigeadh Laighin do léigeadh
> do Dhiarmaid amhail fá **dúthchas** dó (*FFÉ* iii, 5102–13)

> as he had neither right nor *dúthchus* (birthright) to be there. . . . This is
> how that peace was concluded between them: Diarmaid was left the prov-
> ince of Leinster as was his birthright.

Here *dúchas* occurs disjunctively with the more general term *ceart,* and the relevant point of contrast appears to revolve around the issue of indigenousness as opposed to foreignness: Diarmaid's birthright gives him the kingship of Leinster as his *dúchas.* Fitzstephen, however, is on all counts excluded from any kind of right or claim, and it is thus worthwhile to examine further Céitinn's attitude to Fitzstephen as expressed elsewhere in his history. Céitinn characterizes Fitzstephen as one of five evil leaders of the Norman conquest who had visited more destruction and violence on Ireland than in the previous two centuries combined (*FFÉ* iii, 358). He expressly contrasts this treachery and tyranny with those other leaders of the Norman invasion (*gabháltas Gall*) who did much good in Ireland by respecting native traditions and by becoming acculturated to them over time (369). The former group significantly left no heirs or descendants; the latter, on the other hand, prospered in Ireland, and Céitinn expressly includes the Burkes among their number. Fitzstephen thus personifies the pagan conquest, while Burke epitomizes the Christian one.

6. "Fada i n-éagmais inse Fáil": The European Revival of Patriotism
in the Sixteenth Century

Among Céitinn's catalog of the Norman leaders who did good in Ireland
and whose descendants, known by the sixteenth century as the Old English, had
therefore continued to thrive are also the Nugents, or *Nuinnsionnaigh.* Two poems
of exile have come down to us from Uilliam Nuinseann (William Nugent, son
of the Baron of Delvin in Co. Westmeath) written after 1571 when he had gone
to study at Oxford. In the poem "Fada i n-éagmais inse Fáil" (A long time absent
from the island of Fál) the poet talks longingly of the physical beauty of Ireland
and its cultural integrity. This he contrasts with the misery he feels at being in
England (Murphy 1948, 8–15). The poem gives a fine sense of Bradshaw's (1981,
241) characterization of sixteenth-century patriotism as "inward-looking and
protective" rather than "aggressively expansionist." I begin consideration of this
poem by giving the first and last stanzas, since the occurrence of *dúchas* in each
of them serves to frame the poem's content:

Fada i n-éagmais inse Fáil
i Saxaibh dia do dhiombáidh:
sia an bhliadhain ó Bhanbha a-bhus
's labhra dhiamhuir **ar ndúthchus**

Gibé uaibh do bheath a-bhus
dá roiche a-rís **dá dhúthchus**
fearr ós chách do-chím a chor
go bráth ó' thír ní thiogfadh

———

A long time absent from Ireland
in England enough cause for dejection
away from Ireland the year seems longer here
it's a mysterious saying: "our native land/heritage" (*dúchas*)

Whoever of you who happens to be here
if he reaches again his native land (*dúchas*)
I see his state as better than anyone's
never would he leave his land

In the final stanza *dúchas* can reasonably be translated as "homeland," "native land," but note in the first stanza Nuinseann's recognition of the shifting indexical quality of *dúchas* in the phrase "it's a mysterious saying our *dúchas*"—it is a quality that makes the time seem longer when he is absent from it. Significantly, in the current context, by focusing on the native land itself, Nuinseann engenders what Bradshaw (1981, 241) describes as "a common bond that made for internal unity and a value that could be shared with members of other racial groups and nationalities." Thus, the poet devotes considerable attention to describing the beauty and prosperity of Ireland (*tír na gcúan gcubhrach* "land of foaming bays"; *d'eangaibh Banbha braonaighe* "to the fields of dew-dropped Ireland"; *Fódla chrannard chorrubhlach* "Fódla of the high trees and round apples"; *trom le cnoibh a claoinghéaga* "her bowed branches are heavy with nuts"). Then he refers to the poets of Ireland as *filidh cláir Ghall a's Ghaoidheal* "the poets of that land where Gaill and Gaoidhil live," which formulation represents precisely the ethnic accommodation between Gaelic Irish and Old English that was adumbrated in Ó hUiginn's poem above and developed subsequently by Céitinn:

A haifrinn, a húird chrábhaidh
a haos ciúil, mo chompánuigh
filidh cláir Ghall a's Ghaoidheal
ann is cáir do chommaoidheamh

———

Her masses, her religious orders
her musicians who were my companions
and the poets of that land where Gaill and Gaoidhil live
all should be included in our remuneration

Finally, Nuinseann contrasts the warmth of the feeling engendered by his *dúchas* with the coldness and desolation of England (*goimheach gaoth na bhfearannsa* "bitter is the wind of those regions"):

M'aittreabh sunn is fuar fallsa;
goimheach gaoth na bhfearannsa;
searc m'amna don chloinn chroidhe
do Bhanbha Choinn cathaighe

———

My dwelling here is cold and false
bitter is the wind of those regions
My soul's love goes to the dear race
who live in Conn the Battler's Banbha

Elliott (1969, 47) speaks of "the increasingly confident use in sixteenth century Europe of the words *patria* and *patrie*." In the same vein, Caball (1998, 77) speaks of the "burgeoning sense of patriotism" evident in Nuinseann's poems whereby the author uses his experience of foreign culture to set in relief those aspects of Ireland which he regards as characteristic of identity. Simms (1989, 197) refers to a "new concept of patriotism" in Nuinseann's poems spawned by the Renaissance and Counter-Reformation. Mac Craith (1990, 68) and Caball (1998, 130) also connect the evolution of the exile genre in Irish—a genre that Nuinseann was among the first to cultivate—to the Renaissance rediscovery of the idea of *patria,* which is as much inclusive of people and culture as of territory. In Nuinseann's poem, the idea of *dúchas* forms the pragmatic essence of this patriotism in both its more material and more elusive, emotive, and subjective aspects. However, the impression should not be given that such a version of patriotism was the preserve of the Old English at this period. In a poem composed in Rome in the late sixteenth century, *A fhir théid go Fiadh bhFuinidh,* Maol Mhuire Ó hUiginn, archbishop of Tuam between 1586 and 1590 and brother of the more famous Gaelic poet Tadhg Dall, envies a companion about to set off on a journey home to Ireland (O'Rahilly [1927] 1977, 139–41). After an idealized discussion of the merits and delights of Ireland, the poet chastises the Irish for their sinfulness and arrogance. Note again the apparent equivalence of *dúthaigh* and *dúchas* in the following two stanzas:

Fuilngidh Día **dúthaigh** a sean
tré anuabhar Mac Míleadh
tír ainglidhe fá n-iadh tonn
fá rian ainbhfine eachtrann

Gan fhágbháil oirir Bhanbha
gan anmhain ón athardha
mo-chean lén héidear é a-nois
gan tréigean Dé ná **a dhúthchais**

———

God suffers the **dúthaigh** of their ancestors
through the trumped up pride of the sons of Míl
angelic land around which the wave closes
to be under the rein of foreign oppression

Not to leave the shores of Ireland
not to remain from the fatherland
happy the one who can manage it now
not to forsake his God or his **dúthchas**

There is here a strong "faith and fatherland" dimension, based on a common Catholicism (Morgan 1995), which is also evidenced by the use of the word *athardha* "fatherland" (Irish *athair* "father"; cf. Latin *patria*), which, from Ó hUiginn's vantage point on the Continent, clearly suggests Ireland as a whole. Moreover, both *dúthaigh* and *dúthchas* are again explicitly contrasted with the manifestation of foreignness, here *ainbhfine eachtrann* "the evil race of foreigners."

7. Summary

The words *dúthaigh* and *dúchas* index a particular pragmatic domain of cultural unity in early modern Ireland. This unity is based on the historically "Gaelic" ideas of descent from Míl of Spain and the establishment of a symbolic center of kingship and sovereignty around *Midhe*—"the Middle," or the fifth that represents the unity of Ireland in microcosm. This sense of unity is extended to those historically non-Gaelic elements of Irish society that have the *praescriptio longi temporis* of a successful, "Christian" occupation of the country. This extension has its wider synchronic and international counterpart in the Renaissance rediscovery of the idea of *patria* in sixteenth-century Europe. We can now move to consider a further aspect of *dúchas* that becomes salient in the seventeenth century.

8. "Na bearta as dúthchas duit": Social Change in Early Modern Ireland

The late sixteenth and early seventeenth centuries also witness great social and economic change in Ireland. In particular, the traditional Gaelic lordship and the medieval pattern of familial landownership is increasingly undermined by the cumulative effect of plantation, administrative centralization, the enactment of common law, and the advent of individual proprietors. An invaluable Irish-language source for this period is the satirical text *Pairlement Chloinne Tomáis* (*PCT*), and my final set of examples is based on a consideration of that text. Caball (1993b) argues that the traditional interpretation of *PCT* as an upper-class satire on the rural agricultural class has obscured its true inspiration and focus. Its historical remit is rather the lampooning of an emergent, increasingly anglicized entrepreneurial class of nouveaux riches, an upwardly mobile agrarian "middle class" that the author claims has consolidated its prosperity in the aftermath of the wars of the late sixteenth century (*PCT*, 707 ff.). According to the text, the origins of "Clann Tomáis" lay in the fact that St. Patrick had permitted the diabolical Tomás to remain in Ireland because he was human on his mother's side. He then laid down strict ordinances to govern the demeanor of Clann Tomáis towards the nobility (*PCT*, 110 ff.). By the seventeenth century, however, Clann Tomáis were sending their children to school (*PCT*, 725), espousing English common law (*PCT*, 797 ff.; 1171 ff.), embracing the English language (*PCT*, 1250 ff.), being irreligious (*PCT* 45 ff.; 1165 ff.), and making matches beyond their station (*PCT*, 713 ff.). The first section of the text includes a speech by their leader, Murchadh Ó Multuaiscirt (ll. 377 ff.), that lays down the code of conduct prescribed for Clann Tomáis—to unite against the aristocracy in a policy of careful social and economic advancement and to abandon their uncultivated ways:

> Léigidh dhíbh a bhráithreacha . . . bhur gcótuidhe croicinn . . . léigidh dhíbh fós bhur mbéasa brocacha brúideamhla (*PCT* 373)

> ———

> Leave off, brothers, your leather coats. . . . Leave off also your filthy brutish ways

The last third of *PCT* is concerned with the "pairlement" convened by the Clann Tomáis in Co. Kerry in 1632. The session has just commenced when it is interrupted by the approach of Labhrás Ó Lándornáin from Co. Limerick who informs the parliament that countless members of Clann Tomáis have been sentenced to hanging by various courts of law throughout the south of Ireland for offenses of theft and robbery (*déanamh gada agas foghla*). This only surprises them to the extent that, although they steal land because it is expensive, blame for such depredations has traditionally been assigned to the "idle nobility, the minor nobility, and scroungers among the tail-end of noble families" (*uaisle díomhaoine, leathdhaoine uaisle 7 sgramuiridhe d'iarmhur folanna uaisle*). When one of their number advances this opinion, Labhrás informs him that the game is up and advises Clann Tomáis to renounce the violence and theft that are second nature to them. Note how the phraseology echoes that of the citation given immediately above (except now it is singular *léig díot a bhráthair* for plural *léigidh dhíbh a bhráithreacha*):

> léig díot, a bhráthair, na bearta as **dúthchus** duit do theacht tríot, óir do-chuadar cách amach orainn, 7 do fríth fiaghnuise 7 fionnachomharthuighe ar n-uilc (*PCT* 848)

> ⎯⎯⎯⎯⎯

> Give up, brother, the tricks that are come naturally (lit., "are *dúchas*") to you, for everyone has got wise to us, and evidence and certain proof of our wrongdoing have been found

One thing worth drawing attention to here is the phrase *do theacht tríot* "to come through you"—literally, the entire sentence reads "give up the tricks are natural to you *to come through you*," that is, stop allowing them to come (out) through you, which presupposes that the same traits are internal to the individual. Compare the very current contemporary proverb:

> Briseann an dúchas **trí shúile an chait**

> ⎯⎯⎯⎯⎯

> *Dúchas* breaks out through the cat's eyes

This is unlike any of the other examples previously considered: *dúchas* here stands for inherited personal characteristics that are manifested by "breaking through" from the "inside." This is a sense that becomes salient in the modern period. To resume the argument from *PCT*: after two more visitors have taken their leave of the parliament and urged Clann Tomáis to wind up its business, the "prophet of the Clan Thomas" (*fáidh Chloinne Tomáis*) Brian Brúideamhail states the fact that it is simply not in their nature to do so. Significant again here is the depiction of *dúchas* in terms of character traits (*tréighthe*):

Ní dual dóibh críoch mhath do chor orra . . . óir broid agas goid agas
bréaga, tunáth, tnúth agas tuaisgiort, míchreidiomh, mírún 7 míchráb-
hadh, éitheach, imirt agas ól as *tréighthe* do chlannuibh lábánach san
aimsir si. . . . Tugabhuir **bhur gceárda dúthchais** ar mhalairt .i. ionnra-
cus ar ghuid agus ar ól cannuighe, umhlacht agus lábántacht ar mhórd-
háil agus ar stámur, bhur gcríochnumhlacht agus bhur bfhuadar ar ól
píopuidhe tobaca (*PCT* 914)

It isn't natural for them to complete it . . . for harshness, lying, secret
murder, envy, coarseness, irreligion, malice, impiety, perjury, gambling
and drunkenness are the characteristics of the progeny of churls these
days. . . . You have exchanged your native crafts: honesty for robbery
and the drinking of galley-pots, humility and serfdom for swaggering
and insolence, your thoroughness and energy for the smoking of tobacco pipes

Brian concludes by urging the Clann Tomáis to return to its former honest and
servile demeanor, in other words, to return to their *cearda dúthchais*. This phrase
also occurs among the poetic elite at this period. By the beginning of the seventeenth century, the impending downfall of the hereditary bardic order is one of
the main themes of the poetry. One of the most famous Ulster practitioners of
his time, Fear Flatha Ó Gnímh, addresses the following poem to one of the Ma-
gennises of Down (*IBP,* 120, §§1–2) where the issue is very much the demise of
what was part of hereditary right for the poets:

Mairg do-chuaidh **re ceird ndúthchais:**
rug ar Bhanbha mbarrúrthais
nach dualghas athar is fhearr
i n-achadh fhuarghlas Éireann

Alas for him who has followed his family profession
it has befallen Banbha of the fresh soft surface
that in Ireland's cool green field
one's father's natural calling is not the best

In the same way Ó Gnímh's contemporary Mathghamhain Ó hIfearnáin laments the change in artistic fashion—the craft of the poets' ancestors no longer has what is *dual* (proper, natural, due) to it:

> A mhic ná mebhraig éigsi
> cerd do shen rót ró-thréig-si
> tús anóra gér dual di
> fa tuar ansógha in éigsi

> ———

> Son don't even think about poetry
> abandon the craft of your ancestors before you
> though it really should have pride of place
> poetry has been a cause of misery

Note the equivalence here of *cerd do shen* "the craft of your ancestors" and Ó Gnímh's *re ceird ndúthchais* "hereditary profession" and the equivalence of both to *dualghas athar* "a father's natural calling." Thus, the phrase *ceird dhúthchais / cearda dúthchais* becomes in a sense a crystallization of social and economic change in early-seventeenth-century Ireland, viewed both with regret by the poets themselves and as the subject of cutting satire on the part of their apologists.

In his discussion of the relation between semantic and social change in English, Hughes (1988, 6) sees the dissolution of feudalism and the concomitant rise of capitalist exchange and ideas of a new equality as one of the decisive transformations—a manifestation of growing bourgeois pragmatism whereby erstwhile terms of privilege become the new vocabulary of self-advancement. Hughes (1988, 60) speaks here of the "democraticization of status words." In a related vein, C. S. Lewis (1967, 22) talks of the moralization of status words whereby terms associated with status and qualifications based on birthright have a tendency to become generalized as descriptions of character. This process ultimately internalizes such concepts in the individual and means that they are within the attainment of everyone. We can locate the increased salience of this use of *dúchas* in the seventeenth century to analogous processes in the community of Irish speakers, in particular an increase in the relative social flexibility of an *arriviste* entrepreneurial middle class, which profits from the demise of the traditional Gaelic aristocratic order.

9. Conclusion

Both *dúthaigh* and *dúchas* are "shifters" that pragmatically reference key areas of the domain of Irish cultural and social identity, such as those of origin (*buna-dhus*) and the symbolic center (*Midhe* "the fifth fifth" and *Teamhair* "Tara"). We found that these are already present in the twelfth century. During the period under discussion here, this pragmatic essence has both the centripetal dimension of the extension of these concepts to make them inclusive of a wider Irish ethnicity and the centrifugal one of reflecting the democratization and internalization of meaning that accompanies the demise of the Gaelic aristocracy and the rise of individualism in the seventeenth century. Because class, social, or cultural grouping is generally not coterminous with the speech or sign community as a whole, we have here what Voloshinov ([1929] 1973, 23) calls "the social multi-accentuality of the sign" whereby the same word is spoken with different social, cultural, and political accents.

In the course of this discussion, I have repeatedly emphasized the pragmatic aspects of the words *dúchas* and *dúthaigh*. Verschueren's definition of pragmatics, alluded to at the start of this essay, integrates the study of language use into the study of human behavior in general (Hanks 1993). Pragmatics is

> a general functional (i.e. cognitive, social and cultural) perspective on language and language use aimed at the investigation of dynamic and negotiated meaning generation in interaction. Language use is then viewed as a form of action with real-world consequences and firmly embedded in a context. (Verschueren 2001, 242)

Our own study has repeatedly emphasized the importance of context—here the social, cultural, and political changes affecting Irish-speaking society in the sixteenth and seventeenth centuries—and the ways in which language in its dynamic and interactive aspects both shapes and reflects responses to those developments. In the case of *dúthaigh* and *dúchas,* we have seen how meaning is in fact socially and interculturally negotiable, and how the indexical function of language presupposes certain contexts in addition to creating new ones. My aim has been to show how their semiotic structure makes them inherently "contestable." In this way, the "contest of language" can be intrinsic to language itself as well as reflective of nonlinguistic developments.

NOTES

1. For a discussion of the importance of the ethnic past in the formation of nationalisms, see Smith 1995, [1986] 1998.

2. Charles Sanders Peirce (1839–1914) was one of the founders of modern semiotics. Since his concerns were more epistemological and metaphysical than linguistic, his work remained largely peripheral to the study of linguistics until rehabilitated by Roman Jakobson. See Jakobson 1971a, 1980.

3. For a discussion of the origin of the Irish-Spanish connection, see Baumgarten 1984. He argues that the connection arose from the teaching of Isidore of Seville that Spain was the part of Europe closest to Ireland. This association was enhanced by the similarity between the Latin names for Ireland and Spain, respectively *Hibernia* and *(H)iberia*.

4. For a more recent discussion that similarly emphasizes the failure of the native literati to formulate a positive response to conquest and colonization, see O Riordan 1990. For an opposing view that stresses the dynamism of the Gaelic reaction, see Caball 1998, as well as two reviews of O Riordan: Ó Buachalla 1992 and Caball 1993a.

5. This text was compiled in its final form in the eleventh century but was the work of several preceding centuries. For a brief discussion of some seventh-century antecedents, see Carney 1971, 73. See also Ó Corráin 1978, 5. For a detailed discussion of the growth of the text and the tradition, see Scowcroft 1982, 1987, 1988. For a synopsis of the position of the Gaelic origin legend within the overall evolution of the text, see Carey 1993.

6. More recently Carroll (2001, 124–34) has shown that the arguments deployed by Pilib Ó Súilleabháin Béirre in his *Historiae Catolicae Hiberniae Compendium* (Lisbon, 1621) are based on a Suárezian interpretation of such natural law concepts as *dominium* and *consuetudo* or "custom" (Pagden 1987, 80–81).

7. For a discussion of the Renaissance humanist context of Céitinn's history, see Ó Buachalla 1982–83, Bradshaw 1993.

BIBLIOGRAPHY

Baumgarten, Rolf. 1984. "The Geographical Orientation of Ireland in the Time of Isidore and Orosius." *Peritia* 3: 189–203.

Black, Ronald, ed. 1974. "A Manuscript of Cathal Mac Muireadhaigh." *Celtica* 10: 193–209.

Bradshaw, Brendan. 1978. "Native Reaction to the Westward Enterprise: A Case Study in Gaelic Ideology." In *The Westward Enterprise: English Activities in Ireland, the Atlantic and America, 1480–1560,* edited by K. R. Andrews, N. P. Canny, and P. E. H. Hair, 65–80. Liverpool: Liverpool University Press.

———. 1981. "The Elizabethans and the Irish: A Muddled Model." *Studies* 70: 233–44.

———. 1993. "Geoffrey Keating: Apologist of Gaelic Ireland." In *Representing Ireland: Literature and the Origins of Conflict, 1534–1660,* edited by Brendan Bradshaw, Andrew Hadfield, and Willie Maley, 166–90. Cambridge: Cambridge University Press.

Caball, Mark. 1993a. "'The Gaelic Mind and the Collapse of the Gaelic World': An Appraisal." *Cambridge Medieval Celtic Studies* 25 (Summer): 87–96.

———. 1993b. "'Pairlement Chloinne Tomáis': A Reassessment." *Éigse* 27: 47–57.

———. 1998. *Poetry and Politics: Reaction and Continuity in Irish Poetry, 1558–1625.* Cork: Cork University Press.

Carey, John. 1993. *A New Introduction to Lebor Gabála Érenn.* London: Irish Texts Society.

Carney, James. 1971. "Three Old Irish accentual poems." *Ériu* 22: 23–80.

Carroll, Clare. 2001. *Circe's Cup: Cultural Transformations in Early Modern Writing about Ireland.* Cork: Cork University Press, 2001.

Cog.: Todd, James H., ed. 1867. *Cogadh Gaedhel re Gallaibh.* London: Longmans.

Cohn, Bernard. 1966. "Regions, Subjective and Objective: Their Relation to the Study of Modern Indian History and Society." In *Symposium on Regions and Regionalism in South Asian Studies: an Exploratory Study,* edited by Robert Crane, 5–37. Durham: Duke University Press.

Culler, Jonathan. 1986. *Ferdinand de Saussure.* Ithaca: Cornell University Press.

Daniel, E. Valentine. 1984. *Fluid Signs: Being a Person the Tamil Way.* Berkeley: University of California Press.

Dinneen, Patrick S. 1927. *Foclóir Gaedhilge agus Béarla.* Dublin: Irish Texts Society.

Dunne, T. J. 1980. "The Gaelic Response to Conquest and Colonization: The Evidence of the Poetry." *Studia Hibernica* 20: 7–30.

Duranti, Alessandro. 1997. *Linguistic Anthropology.* Cambridge: Cambridge University Press.

Elliott, J. H. 1969. "Revolution and Continuity in Early Modern Europe." *Past and Present* 42: 35–56.

FFÉ. Comyn, David, and Patrick S. Dinneen, eds. 1902–14. *Foras Feasa ar Éirinn.* 4 vols. London: Irish Texts Society.

Fl. Earls: Walsh, Paul, ed. 1916. *The Flight of the Earls.* Dublin: Gill and Son.

Fortes, Meyer, and E. E. Evans-Pritchard, eds. 1940. *African Political Systems.* Oxford: Oxford University Press.

Gibbons, Luke. 1996. *Transformations in Irish Culture.* Cork: Cork University Press.

Gumperz, John J. 1996. "The Linguistic and Cultural Relativity of Conversational Inference." In *Rethinking Linguistic Relativity,* edited by John J. Gumperz and Stephen Levinson, 374–406. Cambridge: Cambridge University Press.

Hanks, William F. 1993. "Notes on Semantics in Linguistic Practice." In *Bourdieu: Critical Perspectives,* edited by Craig Calhoun, Edward LiPuma, and Moishe Postone, 139–55. Chicago: University of Chicago Press.

Hughes, Geoffrey. 1988. *Words in Time: A Social History of the English Vocabulary.* Oxford: Blackwell.

IBP: Bergin, Osborn, ed. 1970. *Irish Bardic Poetry.* Dublin: Dublin Institute for Advanced Studies.

Jakobson, Roman. 1971a. "Quest for the Essence of Language." In *Roman Jakobson: Selected Writings II,* 345–59. The Hague: Mouton.

————. 1971b. "Shifters, Verbal Categories and the Russian Verb." In *Selected Writings* II, 130–47. The Hague: Mouton.

————. 1980. "A Few Remarks on Peirce, Pathfinder in the Science of Language." In *The Framework of Language,* 31–39. Michigan Studies in the Humanities.

Knott, Eleanor, ed. 1922. *The Bardic Poems of Tadhg Dall Ó hUiginn.* 2 vols. London: Irish Texts Society.

Leerssen, Joep. 1996. *Mere Irish and Fíor-Ghael: Studies in the Idea of Irish Nationality, Its Development and Literary Expression Prior to the Nineteenth Century.* Cork: Cork University Press.

Lewis, C. S. 1967. *Studies in Words.* Cambridge: Cambridge University Press.

Mac Airt, Seán. 1944. *An Leabhar Branach.* Dublin: Dublin Institute for Advanced Studies.

Mac Cana, Proinsias. 1985. "Early Irish Ideology and the Concept of Unity." In *The Irish Mind: Exploring Intellectual Traditions,* edited by Richard Kearney, 56–78. Dublin: Wolfhound Press.

Mac Craith, Mícheál. 1990. "Ireland and the Renaissance." In *The Celts and the Renaissance: Tradition and Innovation: Proceedings of the Eighth International Congress of Celtic Studies 1987,* edited by Glanmor Williams and Robert Owen Jones, 57–89. Cardiff: University of Wales Press.

————. 1996. "Creideamh agus athartha. Idé-eolaíocht pholaitíochta agus aos léinn na Gaeilge i dtús an seachtú haois déag." In *Nua-Léamha. Gnéithe de chultúr, stair agus polaitíocht na hÉireann, c. 1600–c. 1900,* edited by Máirín Ní Dhonnchadha, 7–19. Baile Átha Cliath: An Clóchomhar.

Matthews, Peter. 2001. *A Short History of Structural Linguistics.* Cambridge: Cambridge University Press.

Morgan, Hiram. 1995. "Faith and Fatherland Ideology in Sixteenth-Century Ireland." *History Ireland* 3.2 (Summer): 13–20.

Murphy, Gerard. 1948. "Poems of Exile by Uilliam Nuinseann mac Barúin Dealbhna." *Éigse* 6: 8–15.

Ó Buachalla, Breandán. 1982–83. "Annála Ríoghachta Éireann agus Foras Feasa ar Éirinn: an comhthéacs comhaimseartha." *Studia Hibernica* 22–23: 59–105.

————. 1990. "Cúlra is tábhacht an dáin 'A leabhráin ainmnighthear d'Aodh." *Celtica* 21: 402–16.

————. 1992. "Poetry and Politics in Early Modern Ireland." *Eighteenth-Century Ireland. Iris an dá Chultúr* 7: 149–75.

————. 1993. "James Our True King: The Ideology of Irish Royalism in the Seventeenth Century." In *Political Thought in Ireland since the Seventeenth Century,* edited by D. G. Boyce et al., 7–35. London: Routledge.

Ó Corráin, Donnchadh. 1978. "Nationality and Kingship in Pre-Norman Ireland." In *Nationality and the Pursuit of National Independence,* edited by T. W. Moody, 1–35. Historical Studies 11. Belfast: Appletreee Press.

OCU: Mac Giolla Léith, Caoimhín, ed. 1993. *Oidheadh Chloinne hUisneach.* London: Irish Texts Society.

Ó Cuív, Brian. 1997. "An Appeal to Philip III of Spain by Ó Súilleabháin Béirre, December 1601." *Éigse* 30: 18–26.

Ó Dónaill, Niall. 1977. *Foclóir Gaeilge-Béarla*. Baile Átha Cliath: Oifig an tSoláthair.

O'Donovan, John, ed. 1858–59. "The Irish Correspondence of James Fitzmaurice Fitzgerald of Desmond." *Journal of the Kilkenny and South-east of Ireland Archaeological Society* 2: 354–68.

O'Rahilly, Thomas F. [1927] 1977. *Measgra dánta* II. Cork: Cork University Press.

O Riordan, Michelle. 1990. *The Gaelic Mind and the Collapse of the Gaelic World*. Cork: Cork University Press.

Ó Ruairc, Maolmhaodhóg. 1996. *Díolaim d'abairtí dúchasacha*. Baile Átha Cliath: Coiscéim, 1996.

Pagden, Anthony. 1987. "Dispossessing the Barbarian: The Language of Spanish Thomism and the Debate over the Property Rights of the American Indians." In *The Languages of Political Theory in Early-Modern Europe,* edited by Anthony Pagden, 79–98. Cambridge: Cambridge University Press.

———. 1995. *Lords of All the World: Ideologies of Empire in Spain, Britain and France, c. 1500–c. 1800*. New Haven: Yale University Press.

PCT: Williams, N. J. A., ed. 1981. *Pairlement Chloinne Tomáis*. Dublin: Dublin Institute for Advanced Studies.

Rees, Alwyn, and Brinley Rees. 1961. *Celtic Heritage: Ancient Tradition in Ireland and Wales*. London: Thames and Hudson.

Sapir, Edward. 2000. "The Status of Linguistics as a Science." In *The Routledge Language and Cultural Theory Reader,* edited by Lucy Burke, Tony Crowley, and Alan Girvin, 395–400. London: Routledge.

Scowcroft, Mark. 1982. "Miotas na gabhála i *Leabhar Gabhála*." *Léachtaí Cholm Cille* 13: 41–75.

———. 1987. "*Leabhar Gabhála*—Part I: The Growth of the Text." *Ériu* 38: 81–140.

———. 1988. "*Leabhar Gabhála*—Part II: The Growth of the Tradition." *Ériu* 39: 1–66.

Silverstein, Michael. 1976. "Shifters, Linguistics Categories and Cultural Description." In *Meaning in Anthropology,* edited by K. Basso and H. Selby, 11–56. Albuquerque: University of New Mexico Press.

———. [1981] 1997. "The Limits of Awareness." Reprinted in *Linguistic Anthropology: A Reader,* edited by Alessandro Duranti, 382–401. Oxford: Blackwell.

Simms, Katharine. 1989. "Bards and Barons: The Anglo-Irish Aristocracy and the Native Culture." In *Medieval Frontier Societies,* edited by Robert Bartlett and Angus MacKay, 177–97. Oxford: Clarendon Press.

Skinner, Quentin. 1978. *The Foundations of Modern Political Thought*. Vol. 2. Cambridge: Cambridge University Press.

Smith, Anthony D. 1995. "Gastronomy or Geology? The Role of Nationalism in the Reconstruction of Nations." *Nations and Nationalism* 1: 3–23.

———. [1986] 1998. *The Ethnic Origins of Nations*. Oxford: Blackwell.

SSA: Ó Maonaigh, Cainneach, ed. 1952. *Scáthán Shacramuinte na hAithridhe.* Dublin: Dublin Institute for Advanced Studies.

Stafford, Thomas. 1633. *Pacata Hibernia.* London.

Verschueren, Jef. 2001. "Pragmatics." In *The Routledge Companion to Semiotics and Linguistics,* edited by Paul Cobley. London: Routledge.

Voloshinov, V. N. [1929] 1973. *Marxism and the Philosophy of Language.* Translated by Ladislav Matejka and I. R. Titunik. Cambridge, Mass.: Harvard University Press.

Walsh, Paul, ed. 1957. *Beatha Aodha Ruaidh Uí Dhomhnaill.* 2 vols. Dublin: Irish Texts Society.

STUDIES IN SPEECH POLITICS

4 Language and Imperial Ideology in Late Antiquity and Early Islam

DIMITRI GUTAS

As language frequently plays a significant role in the historical process, it is one of the elements in historical hermeneutics that needs to be considered. My main subject is the Arabic language in its relation to power and politics during the two centuries after the rise of Islam—roughly, from the middle of the seventh century to the middle of the ninth. In particular I wish to look at the Arabic language as it related to Greek and Persian, for these were the two major languages of culture that it supplanted in the vast geographic area from Egypt to central Asia. The events that took place during this period, namely, the rise of Islam and the conquest by Arab armies of almost all the civilized world west of India—I say "almost" because Constantinople, though twice besieged (in 672 and 716), was not taken—have been much analyzed in scholarly literature, but they have not been investigated from the standpoint of language politics and its consequences, or of how events fashioned language policies, which in turn were instrumental in determining certain historical developments. It need hardly be stressed that this is a preliminary discussion that aspires only to stimulate more basic research.

The cataclysmic but all too brief career of Alexander the Great set the stage for historical developments that were to be fully realized only a millennium later with the advent of Islam: this was the unification of East and West, the unification of the Indo-Iranian world east of the Euphrates with the Greek world to its west. Alexander accomplished this in his lifetime, but his successors were not able to hold on to the East; and though the seed for later developments was inevitably sown, the Indo-Iranian world reasserted its independence, including its cultural and linguistic independence, after Alexander's death. The Fertile Crescent and Egypt, however, under the domination of Alexander's successors for the next three centuries, gradually became Hellenized, in culture as well as in language. The native languages in the lands of the successor states—Coptic in Egypt, Aramaic in the Fertile Crescent, and Arabic in Palestine and the Sinai— continued naturally as the languages of the local populations, but Greek, in addition to having been imposed as the language of administration, gradually also became the language of culture and eventually of commerce. In the case of Coptic, the penetration of Greek went so far as to determine the very alphabet in which this latest phase of ancient Egyptian was written: the Greek alphabet replaced the Hieratic and Demotic forms of traditional Egyptian writing, to say nothing of the substantial influence of Greek on the vocabulary and some syntactical forms of Coptic.

The modalities of this process of Hellenization in terms of the interplay between language and empire are just now beginning to be investigated in the contemporary secondary literature.[1] Nevertheless, the paradoxical fact remains that Greek remained the dominant language of empire in the Near East even when Greek speakers were no longer in control of it, but it had devolved upon the Latin-speaking Romans with Augustus. Christianity, as one factor among many, may have helped. The choice of the Aramaic-speaking disseminators of Christianity, Paul and the Evangelists, to write in Greek merely reflects the cultural state of affairs during the first century of our era. No ideology with universalist claims could have reached its intended audience in any other language at the time. Three centuries later, the situation was reversed. When Constantine decided to make Christianity the religion of the empire, he was in fact ensuring the continued dominance of Greek: the canonized religion by necessity also canonized the language in which were written not only the New Testament but also the foundational literature of the Apologists and the early church fathers. The Eastern Roman Empire, with its new Christian capital, Constantinople, was thus completely Hellenized culturally and linguistically, and gradually even in its administration.

With the introduction of Christianity into the eastern Mediterranean world as another major ideological factor, religious politics began to play a significant historical role with inevitable consequences for language and culture. At first sight, it would appear that after Constantine the dominance of Greek could not be shaken, which in fact was the case. However, the situation that developed then created *two* Greek cultures vying for supremacy, a pagan Greek and a Christian Greek culture. The uneven fight between the two from the fourth to the eighth century, the sordid details of which have been recently discussed, ended with the victory of Christian Greek.[2]

Pagan Greek, however, though defeated, did not disappear, for the very religious politics that ensured the victory of Christian Greek also created the circumstances in which, ironically, pagan Greek could survive. I am referring here to the inter-Christian quarrels, with Chalcedonian Christianity (i.e., Christianity as defined by the Council of Chalcedon of 451) emerging as the chosen version of the imperial court in Constantinople and henceforth styling itself as "Orthodox." The exclusionary theological policies and practices of Chalcedonian "Orthodoxy" that created religious schisms are directly responsible for the secession of the Syriac-speaking churches[3] of the Fertile Crescent and the Coptic-speaking church of Egypt and for the formation of the eastern churches known as the Monophysite and the Nestorian.

The historical consequence of this split was that the Greek-speaking Chalcedonian Christians, through their relentless war against pagan Greek, eventually slid into the barbarism and the dark ages of the iconoclastic controversy in the seventh and eighth centuries. The Syriac-speaking Christians, on the other hand, who were now doctrinally and after the Islamic conquests in the early seventh century also politically separated from the Chalcedonians, were spared these nefarious consequences and developed along different cultural lines. After the fifth century, secular, that is, pagan, Greek learning was "thoroughly assimilated by Syriac speakers"[4] and well entrenched in the major centers of Eastern Christianity throughout the Fertile Crescent, from Edessa and Qinnasrīn in the west, through Nisibis and Mosul in northern Mesopotamia, to Jundīsābūr well into western Persia, to mention only the most famous centers. In these centers, as elsewhere, we witness translation activities from Greek into Syriac of Christian writings, as one might expect, but also of secular Greek works, primarily on logic and medicine and, to a lesser extent, on astronomy, astrology, and popular philosophy. The same atmosphere also existed in Monophysite and Nestorian congregations throughout the area, if we are to judge by scholars who appeared during the early 'Abbāsid period with a solid background in Greek learning; witness Dayr Qunnā south of Baghdad on the Tigris, the site of a large and flourishing Nestorian monastery, where Abū-Bišr Mattā ibn-Yūnus, the founder of the Aristotelian school in Baghdad early in the tenth century, studied and taught. In addition to religious centers, other prominent cities in pre-Islamic times maintained a tradition of pagan Greek learning; an example would be al-Ḥīra close to the Euphrates in southern Iraq, the capital of the Arab Lakhmids, which, despite the waning of its fortunes after the rise of Islam, could still be the hometown of the famous translator Ḥunayn ibn-Isḥāq. To these should be added at least two other major centers of Greek learning at the antipodes of each other and, in a way, embracing the Hellenized world that was to be the birthplace of the ʿAbbāsid Greco-Arabic translation movement, Ḥarrān (Carrhae) in northern Mesopotamia just south of Edessa and Marw in northeasternmost Persia at the gates of central Asia. The former remained obstinately pagan well into the tenth century and kept alive numerous Greek ideas, beliefs, and practices that seem to have been extinguished in most other areas, whereas the latter combined a vigorous Hellenism as exhibited in its brand of Zoroastrianism that was to play a significant role in early ʿAbbāsid times with an equally Hellenized Nestorianism.[5]

Pagan Greek thus survived among these Hellenized Syriac speakers, and it was overwhelmingly they who informed Arab sponsors about the contents of secular Greek learning and eventually executed the Greco-Arabic translations when commissioned by them. The Greco-Arabic translations in turn were influential in reviving interest in classical learning among the Byzantines of the ninth century and I believe directly caused the Photian renaissance.[6] Thus the very policies of Chalcedonian Christians against pagan Greek eventually led, by these very tortuous historical developments, to the revival of secular Greek culture among their descendants three or more centuries down the line.

This is, necessarily very briefly, the account of Greek in the Near East until the first few centuries after the rise of Islam. We can now turn to a similarly brief review of Persian in the same period. The language of Iran during this period is called Pehlevi (Middle Persian) by the historians of the language, and it is the language of the Persian Empire ruled by the Sasanian dynasty, founded by Ardashīr I in 224 A.D. and destroyed by the Arabs in 651.[7] In the case of Persia too the relationship between language and power was affected by the deeds of Alexander the Great, though in quite different ways from those in the Fertile Crescent. It is true that after the death of Alexander his successors were unable to hold on to Iran and as a result it was not Hellenized linguistically. However, because of the state ideology that was subsequently adopted by the Sasanians, Persia was Hellenized culturally to a certain extent, in the following manner.

The Sasanian empire, with its state religion of Zoroastrianism, developed an ideology whereby it presented itself as the heir to the ancient Achaemenid empire of Darius the Great and other glorious emperors.[8] This self-image of the Sasanians has been preserved in the Zoroastrian book known as the Dēnkard, the latest version of which, according to expert opinion, dates to the reign of one of the most celebrated emperors, Chosroes I (Anūshirwān, r. 531–78). The Dēnkard, a treasure house of Sasanian culture and civilization, also contained (in Book 4) an account of the origins of knowledge and the transmission of learning and the sciences in Persia, from the earliest times until the reign of Chosroes I.

According to this account, all knowledge vouchsafed to humans was received by the prophet Zoroaster from Ahura Mazda, the Good God, and was recorded in the texts of the Avesta. When Alexander the Great invaded Persia and put an end to the Achaemenids, he took these Avestan texts and had them translated into Greek and Coptic. In this fashion the rest of the world received its sciences and philosophy from the translated Avestan texts. After the Sasanian empire came into being in the third century A.D., its emperors took it upon themselves to collect from the various places where they had been scattered all these texts—both the texts originally thought to have been translated into other languages and those deriving from them—and "retranslate" them into Persian (Pehlevi).

The main thrust of this account of the alleged loss and recovery of the Avestan texts is first that *all* the sciences derive originally from the Avesta; if this is so, then it follows that any book prior to the Sasanian period that treats any science or philosophical subject—in particular *any Greek book*—is by definition part of the Zoroastrian canon, since it is maintained that the Greeks came to learn about the sciences and philosophy when Alexander conquered Persia and had the Avestan books translated into Greek. Second, and no less important, is the recovery part of the story, which promotes translation as the means to regain the lost ancient Persian knowledge. Translation thus plays a central role in the account and by so doing promotes what can be called a culture of translation as a cultural good: the alleged translations from Avestan to Greek and Coptic brought science and philosophy to the world, while the real translations from Greek into Pehlevi that were made during the Sasanian period helped the Persians to "regain" their lost heritage.

"Zoroastrian imperial ideology thus provided both a corpus of works as the foundation of civilization—in essence, all extant works from antiquity in all languages, since they had been allegedly either translated from the Avesta or derived from it—and a cultural outlook that made their acquisition both possible and desirable, the virtues of translation."[9] By means of translation, therefore, Persian, both in its ancient form, the Avestan, and in its current form in the sixth century, Pehlevi, was made into the most significant language in the world and the depository of all knowledge. This is a fitting linguistic ideology for an empire whose kings saw themselves, like the Achaemenid emperors of the past, as king of kings.

This was the linguistic situation in the two worlds east and west of Mesopotamia when, according to Muslim tradition, the Qur'ān was revealed to the Prophet Muḥammad in Mecca and Medina, beginning around 610 and ending in 632, with his death. The Qur'ān, of course, is the holy book of Islam and its foundation; however, in addition to its many religious functions, it has a linguistic one, which is very important. It quite deliberately identifies itself as an Arabic book in no less than eleven passages.[10]

The question of language is thus built into the new religion from the very beginning, and is one of its inalienable features. The import of these passages is that God has revealed the Qur'ān to Muḥammad in Arabic so that he can warn his fellow Arabs of the day of judgment in their own language. The immediate and obvious implication here — the direct purpose of the Qur'ān's self-identification as an Arabic book — is that God took special measures to ensure two things: first, that the Arabs have their own revealed book that will grant them salvation, much like the Jews have their sacred scripture in Hebrew, the Christians in Greek, and the Zoroastrians in Avestan; and second, that those who have been so warned by God against impiety and sin have in fact understood the message — because it is in plain Arabic — and thus, if they disobey and as a result are cast into the Fire, it would be their own responsibility.[11]

It is obvious that the Qur'ān was revealed in Arabic primarily for religious-salvational reasons. There is, however, also a political aspect to the Arabic Qur'ān that becomes even more obvious if one observes the history of the Muslim community in Muḥammad's time. First, by addressing itself to Arabic speakers, the Qur'ān inevitably separates them off from non-Arabic speakers, whom it excludes from being recipients of its message. It may be anachronistic to speak of Arab nationalism in Muḥammad's time, but clearly there was a sense of linguistic and ethnic unity among the Arabic-speaking tribes; we have the additional corroboration of pre-Islamic Arabic poetry, which was intertribal and a major unifying factor of all Arabs. By the same token, there was just as clearly the sense that non-Arabic speakers were alien to their concerns. Muḥammad's entire career was thus devoted to spreading Islam among the Arab tribes, and when, after

his death, some tribes apostatized (the *ridda*), their revolt was quickly and effectively crushed by his successors. Backsliding by Arabic speakers could not be tol-
erated at all because it negated the very essence of the Arabic Qur'ān and made
a mockery of proselytizing among other unconverted Arabs. Effectively, therefore, the Arabic Qur'ān and Muḥammad's career identified Islam as the religion
of the Arabs, or better yet, if we wish to avoid modern connotations of nationalism,[12] as the religion of Arabic speakers. This perception of Islam, apparently held
by Arabs and non-Arabs alike, dominated the century following Muḥammad's
death and helps us better to understand the historical developments.

Under Muḥammad's initial four successors—the "rightly guided" caliphs
(632–61)—and then the Umayyad dynasty (661–750), the Arab empire spread
far and wide, from the Pyrenees to central Asia and the Indian subcontinent.
Numerous peoples, with a great variety of linguistic backgrounds, became subjects of this empire. What was the ideology behind this expansion? It has been
maintained for centuries, principally in anti-Muslim Christian polemics, as well
as by some modern historians, that it was to spread the religion of Islam. This
does not appear to be historically accurate. In the century following Muḥammad's
death, that is, during the period of the four caliphs and the Umayyad dynasty, the
primary ideology was not the spread of Islam but the spread of the *dominion* of
Islam, with the Muslim Arabs as the beneficiaries in terms of power and wealth.[13]

The existence of an Arabic Qur'ān requires and justifies such an expansionist but not proselytizing ideology. As I just mentioned, Islam is the religion
of the Arabs precisely because it was self-consciously revealed *in Arabic*. This
sets the Arabs apart from other peoples in their relationship to God and gives
them the right to rule over them. This is additionally enhanced by the self-image
of the Qur'ān that it is the final and correct version of the Abrahamic revelation
that was distorted when it was written down by Jews and Christians in languages other than Arabic in the Old and New Testaments. The version revealed
to Muḥammad—the Seal of the Prophets—contains the definitive version. It is
only right that God's truth, as revealed in the Qur'ān, rule the earth, with the
Arab Muslims as its executors.

Conversion to Islam of subjected peoples was not a component of this ideology. This is also evident from the rate of early conversions to Islam, as far as
these can be ascertained,[14] and from the tax policies of the Arab conquerors.
Initial conversion to Islam was very slow and sparse and thus appears to have
been a *consequence* of the Arab conquests and not their purpose. All evidence
that we have suggests that there were no systematic efforts by the Muslim Arab

rulers to proselytize local populations until the end of the Umayyad era. There are, naturally, sporadic exceptions, as for example the Umayyad Caliph 'Umar II (r. 717–20), but it clearly was not official policy and certainly far from being the ideology behind the expansion of Islam. Even further from the truth, of course, is the older notion, already discredited by Arnold in 1914,[15] of coerced conversions. "Virtually all the purported texts of treaties with conquered Persian cities contain guarantees of protection for the existing religious communities and for the free exercise of their customary religions."[16] The same applies to what we know of other conquered cities in the Near East. Conquering armies with a proselytizing ideology could hardly sign such treaties.

Similar conclusions can be drawn from the tax system instituted by the Muslim Arabs among the subjected peoples. In addition to the land tax, the *kharāj*, which was carried over from Byzantine practices, as the Greek derivation of the word itself, *chorēgía* ($\chi o \rho \eta \gamma \acute{\iota} \alpha$), indicates, the Muslim Arabs levied a poll tax (*jizya*) from all non-Muslims. Such a tax policy is clearly incompatible with an ideology of active proselytization, since conversion would have meant the willful and effective reduction in tax revenues. One can hardly imagine the politically astute Arab rulers, who conquered half the civilized world in a century, to have committed such blunders.

There is, finally, the important evidence provided by the language of the administration during the early Umayyad dynasty. After the initial Arab conquests of Syria, Palestine, and Egypt from the Byzantines—lands that were just as important economically as they were administratively, with millennia-long traditions of effective bureaucratic practices—necessity dictated that, for reasons of continuity, the early Umayyads keep both the Greek-speaking functionaries and the Greek language in their imperial administration in Damascus. It was only during the reign of 'Abd-al-Malik or his son, Hishām (r. 685–705 and 724–43) that the administrative apparatus (*dīwān*) was translated into Arabic and presumably Arabic became the official language of the government administration. What this implies, other than the realization on the part of the Umayyads that pragmatic considerations—competence in administration and tax collection—should take precedence over ideological ones, is that the initial aims of their dominion were neither to spread Islam nor to Arabize the subjected peoples.

The political function of the Arabic language during this period was thus to provide cultural cohesion to the ruling element of the new empire and to ensure the uncontested dominance of Islam among its speakers. The subjected peoples who were not born Arabs could provide all sorts of services, generate the wealth, and even run the bureaucracy until after 'Abd-al-Malik, but they were not readily invited to participate in the Arab culture of the imperial rulers. Cultural life under the Umayyads is hardly different from what it was among pre-Islamic Arabs— based on Arabic poetry that maintained the Arab tribal system as its focus for meaning.

But things inevitably changed, and the Umayyad state of affairs, based on pre-Islamic Arab tribalism, however useful it may have been for the initial success of the Arab expansion, had, even before the downfall of the dynasty, grown counterproductive by falling back on its pre-Islamic pattern of tribal factionalism: the last Umayyad caliph Marwān II (r. 744–50), beset by political problems created for him by his political opponents among the Kalb tribe in southern Syria and Palestine, transferred the capital of his dynasty from Damascus to Ḥarrān farther in the north, where he could count on the support of the tribe of the Qays.

Even more serious problems were gathering outside the ruling Umayyad elite and beyond the Arabic speakers. The effect of more than a century of Arab-Islamic domination over the subjected peoples was naturally some Islamization, despite the Umayyads' lack of interest in proselytization, but even more important, it was the spread of Arabization. This was to a large extent cultural, but it was also predominantly linguistic: imperial languages, reflecting military and economic power, as a rule impose themselves on the subject peoples automatically, without intervention by the rulers.

The degree of Arabization is clearly illustrated by the earliest translations into Arabic of Persian materials. Toward the end of the Umayyad period, various groups, whose political aims were apparently the overthrow of the Arab dominion and the revival of the Sasanian empire, were forming in the east of the Islamic world. But it appears that after more than a century of Islam and Arabization, the old high language of the Sasanian empire, Pehlevi, was little understood by the Persians, while the Neo-Persian that was spoken by them was felt not to be the proper means of formal expression. As a result, the revivalist ideology of the various Persian or pro-Persian groups manifested itself through the translation of Zoroastrian material into Arabic. These translations must have acted as propaganda intended to convince those Arabized Persians who would not have known Pehlevi of the inevitability of the Umayyad downfall and of the validity of the Zoroastrian tradition whose revival was envisaged.

The direct threat to the Umayyads came from the 'Abbāsid family, distant cousins of the Umayyads and thus direct descendants from the line of the

Prophet.[17] Their plans to overthrow the Umayyads and gain power for themselves were a long time in the making and culminated in what has been called by historians the 'Abbāsid revolution of 750. Astute politicians, the 'Abbāsids perceived the weaknesses of the Umayyads' rule and by exploiting them, were able to mount a successful revolution. Because the new 'Abbāsid state came into power as a result of a civil war between rival factions of the house of the Prophet, the main concern of the new rulers was twofold. On the one hand, it was essential for the survival of the new regime to follow policies that aimed at the reconciliation not only of the former rivals but also of the different interest groups that participated in the revolution, each for its own purposes, on behalf of their cause. On the other hand, the new regime clearly had to legitimize its rule, after a civil war, in the eyes of all the factions of the empire.

The first aim was achieved through the mastery exhibited by the early 'Abbāsids in building coalitions and playing one rival against the other; the second, by promulgating the view that the 'Abbāsid dynasty was the rightful heir of all the empires that preceded it in Mesopotamia and the Near East, and especially of their immediate predecessors, the Sasanians. In this way they were able to incorporate Sasanian culture, which was still dominant among large masses of the population east of Iraq, into mainstream 'Abbāsid culture. This also entailed the adoption by the 'Abbāsids of the Sasanian culture of translation, as described above. As a result, starting with the founder of Baghdad, the second 'Abbāsid caliph al-Manṣūr (r. 754–75), there was initiated in Baghdad a far-reaching translation movement that lasted for well over two centuries. At the end of this period—by the turn of the first millennium A.D.—almost all nonliterary and nonhistorical secular Greek works that were available in Byzantium and the Near East in late antiquity had been translated into Arabic. This was to be a cultural achievement of tremendous historical consequences for Western civilization— in effect, this was the first Western renaissance.[18]

The support given to the translation movement by the early 'Abbāsid caliphs had its basis in political considerations and reflected their desire to construct and project a transnational ideology in order to legitimize their rule in the eyes of all their subjects, Arab and non-Arab alike. Along with the Umayyads, the 'Abbāsids thus also ousted *Arab* culture as its political and ideological focus: because Arabism excluded by its very nature those not born Arabs, it could not serve the need of the 'Abbāsid dynasty either to form political coalitions with partners of different ethnic backgrounds or to base their legitimacy on their claim to be the inheritors and continuators of a civilization that transcended ethnic boundaries. What they substituted was *Arabic* culture, based on the language, in which everybody could participate. In this manner, the Arabic language, which under Muḥammad and the early caliphs functioned to separate Arabs from non-Arabs, under the 'Abbāsids became the political instrument that united all subjects of the Arab empire in a commonwealth that at the same time produced a brilliant civilization and ensured the longevity of the 'Abbāsid dynasty. Monolingualism, as many others have discovered since, is the pillar on which are erected multi-cultural empires.

NOTES

1. For the linguistic situation in the Hellenistic and Roman Near East, see the surveys by Rüdiger Schmitt, "Die Ostgrenze von Armenien über Mesopotamien, Syrien bis Arabien," in G. Neumann and J. Untermann, eds., *Die Sprachen im Römischen Reich der Kaiserzeit,* Beihefte der Bonner Jahrbücher 40 (Köln-Bonn: Rheinland Verlag, 1980), 187–214, a very important volume overall, and his "Sprachverhältnisse in den östlichen Provinzen," in W. Haase, ed., *Aufstieg und Niedergang der Römischen Welt* (Berlin: W. de Gruyter, 1983), II,29,2, 554–86, here 576–78. The whole question of language contacts in Hellenistic and Roman times was studied in detail by V. Bubenik, *Hellenistic and Roman Greece as a Sociolinguistic Area,* Current Issues in Linguistic Theory 57 (Amsterdam: J. Benjamins, 1989), esp. 264–76, "Hellenistic Koine in contact with Phoenician, Aramaic and Arabic." In this context, speaking foreign languages and multilingualism as social phenomena in antiquity are discussed by J. Werner, "Zur Fremdsprachen Problematik in der griechisch-römischen Antike," in C. W. Müller, K. Sier, and J. Werner, eds., *Zum Umgang mit fremden Sprachen in der griechisch-römischen Antike,* Palingenesia 36 (Stuttgart: F. Steiner, 1992), 1–20. A mine of information for research in this direction is now provided by the numerous articles in the comprehensive and exhaustive history of the Greek language from the earliest times to the end of late antiquity by A.-Ph. Christidis, ed., Ἱστορία τῆς Ἑλληνικῆς Γλώσσας. Ἀπό τις αρχές ἕως την ὑστέρη αρχαιότητα (Thessaloniki: Κέντρο Ἑλληνικῆς Γλώσσας, 2001). These specialized studies have not yet surfaced in the general treatments of the subject. In the recent "Guide to the Postclassical World," as the subtitle of *Late Antiquity* has it, there is no entry either on language or Greek language — though strangely, there is an entry on "Latin"; ed. G. W. Bowersock, Peter Brown, and Oleg Grabar (Cambridge, Mass.: Harvard University Press, 1999).

2. See Ramsay MacMullen, *Christianity and Paganism in the Fourth to Eighth Centuries* (New Haven: Yale University Press, 1997).

3. Syriac is the form of Aramaic in Christian times.

4. See S. Brock, "From Antagonism to Assimilation: Syriac Attitudes to Greek Learning," in N. Garsoian, T. Mathews, and R. Thompson, eds., *East of Byzantium: Syria and Armenia in the Formative Period* (Washington, D.C.: Dumbarton Oaks, 1980), 17–34; and "Syriac Culture in the Seventh Century," *Aram* 1 (1989): 268–80.

5. D. Gutas, *Greek Thought, Arabic Culture* (London: Routledge, 1998), 14, with slight modifications.

6. See the discussion in Gutas, *Greek Thought,* 175–86.

7. See the informative article "Sāsānids" by M. Morony in the *Encyclopaedia of Islam,* 2d ed. (henceforth, *EI²*), vol. 9, 70–83.

8. Incidentally, the last shah of Iran in the twentieth century, Reza Shah Pahlevi, also promoted a similar ideology.

9. Gutas, *Greek Thought,* 45. For a presentation and detailed analysis of all the pertinent texts, see 34–52.

10. See *Sūras* 12:2, 13:37, 16:103, 20:113, 26:195, 39:28, 41:3, 41:44, 42:7, 43:3, 46:12.

11. Cf. the following passage, where both these aspects are evident: "And so We [i.e., God] have revealed to thee [i.e., Muḥammad] an Arabic Koran, that thou mayest warn the Mother of Cities and those who dwell about it, and that thou mayest warn of the Day of Gathering, wherein is no doubt—a party in Paradise, and a party in the Blaze. / If God had willed, He would have made them one nation." *Sūra* 42:7–8, trans. A. J. Arberry, *The Koran Interpreted* (London: George Allen & Unwin, 1955) and later reprints.

12. Cf. the remarks by G. R. Hawting in *EI²* X,840b.

13. Wellhausen's thesis, though in need of fine-tuning in light of the more sophisticated modern approaches to the use of the original sources, is nevertheless still valid in its main outlines. See for a brief overview the article "Umayyads" by G. R. Hawting in *EI²* X,840–41.

14. Cf. R. W. Bulliett, *Conversion to Islam in the Medieval Period* (Cambridge, Mass.: Harvard University Press, 1979).

15. T. W. Arnold, *The Preaching of Islam* (Lahore, 1914).

16. E. L. Daniel in *Encyclopaedia Iranica,* VI,231a.

17. The eponymous founder of the dynasty, al-ʿAbbās, was the prophet's paternal uncle.

18. For the details of the historical circumstances leading to the development of the translation movement by the early ʿAbbāsids, see D. Gutas, *Greek Thought,* esp. chaps. 2–4.

5 "Till Some Person Attain to the Universal Monarchy"

Seventeenth-Century Language Technologies and What They Say

HAUN SAUSSY

1.

It has happened again and again in divers places that certain types, tones, or uses of language become classical, forms that both evidence and transmit authority. The details vary (and the differences matter), but the common pattern is that powerful precedents dig a channel for subsequent speech, directing later flows (as we say that a consequence or right "flows" from an assumption) of certainty, beauty, power, and sense. Ciceronian Latin, the Arabic of the Qur'ān, the French of the age of Louis XIV do not look out on a landscape of linguistic equals but dominate and set standards. In a word, classicism is the central case of the meeting of "language and power"—a vast theme, rediscovered every time a new alignment of idioms prescribes a new rhetoric, or when the faltering of a previous classicism opens it to disparagement and critique.

Manuals for the attainment of classical idioms are legion: most grammar books are their implicit abettors. In the western European canon at least, the critical account of classicism received its most explicit treatments at the hands of Marx and Nietzsche. Both argued against the fallacy of taking language as a neutral or impartial medium that simply reflected the world; language for them is a means of exerting leverage on it. In Marx, and more notoriously for his followers, the denunciation of reflection-theories of language took the form of separating an

111

ideological avant-garde that knew that language was interested and an *arrière-garde* that never thought to question its inherent biases.[1] "Philosophers have heretofore reflected on the world; the point, however, is to change it": Marx's "point" grants the nonreflection school of philosophy all the power of "change." But surely this is rhetorical exaggeration, for reflection-theory changes the world too, only it does to the world the things that a reflection-theory might be expected to do: reportedly, it informs the world with a stable set of categories and instills in the speaker a predisposition to contemplation, a desire to separate the observer from the observed, an anxiety about making speech truthful (as distinguished from effective). Nietzsche saw more clearly that every language practice has a materiality of its own and irreducible consequences: his case is made tacitly by the polemics against the distortions of language and society that he lays at the door of ascetic religion.[2] Both Marx and Nietzsche foresee a new sort of man emerging from the full recognition of language as practice. (Perhaps in the longer perspective this has already happened over and over.)

When we link "language" and "power" we are, then, inevitably making some form of homage to Marx and Nietzsche. These days our homage is likely to fall first on Michel Foucault, who took over and extended many of their notions. My homage will take the form of reusing (though to slightly different purposes) a quotation Foucault once used.

One indication of how thoroughly forgotten the seventeenth-century passion for new, artificial, universal or philosophical languages is the fact that most people know about them only through a short, ironic essay by Jorge Luis Borges, "El idioma analítico de John Wilkins." And that essay, in turn, is mostly known through the frequent citation of one passage that dismisses the whole enterprise of baroque linguistics. After summarizing the systematic vocabulary of the philosophical language invented in the 1660s by Bishop John Wilkins, a member of the Royal Society, Borges points out that its inventory of the contents of the universe does not do a very good job of representing reality.

> These ambiguities, redundancies and deficiencies recall those attributed by Dr. Franz Kuhn to a certain Chinese encyclopedia called the *Heavenly Emporium of Benevolent Knowledge.* In its distant pages it is written that animals are divided into (a) those that belong to the emperor; (b) embalmed ones; (c) those that are trained; (d) suckling pigs; (e) mermaids; (f) fabulous ones; (g) stray dogs; (h) those that are included in the present classification; (i) those that tremble as if they were mad; (j) innumerable ones; (k) those drawn with a very fine camel's-hair brush; (l) etcetera; (m) those

that have just broken the flower vase; (n) those that at a distance resemble flies. . . . I have noted the arbitrariness of Wilkins, the unknown (or apocryphal) Chinese encyclopedist, and the Bibliographical Institute of Brussels; obviously there is no classification of the universe that is not arbitrary or conjectural.[3]

You have probably encountered this passage before, and not necessarily in its original context. It appears, for example, on the first page of Foucault's *Les Mots et les choses* (*The Order of Things*), where he says that the passage indicates "the limits of our own thought," a limit reached as we recognize "the naked impossibility of thinking *that*," that is, of thinking about animals as the encyclopedia's author is supposed to have done.[4] Presumably someone (a Chinese?) situated outside our ("our"?) system of knowledge would have the same disoriented feeling about European classifications.

Foucault's use of the quotation appropriately opens his account of the emergence of a set of naming practices that we know as the human sciences, from roughly 1600 to 1900. A fuller citation history, which I am unable to provide, would show the lessons the passage has been used to teach. The same perennial quotation appears in a recent essay by Umberto Eco on Athanasius Kircher's universal language scheme: there it occupies the position of a decisive refutation, as if nothing more could or needed to be said.[5] What Borges says, that every representation of the universe is arbitrary and conjectural, is a response to what he sees as the error or innocence of Wilkins, the inventor of a philosophical language. Wilkins must then have assumed the possibility of a language that would be both rational and grounded in evidence (if these are the correct opposites of "arbitraria y conjectural"). The correction of the error leads on to the idea that any pattern of knowledge holds up, not because it matches the universe, but because artificial, humanly invented networks and constraints keep it in place. Among these networks, of course, political organizations (the usual referent of the unadorned word "power") are conspicuous. "Arbitrary," as Borges's readers have noticed, is a political as well as a semiotic term.

The idea that there is no pure language (or pure knowledge) that stands apart from social contexts of authority and command is often brought forth as a "postmodern" discovery. Postmoderns, however, need naive moderns to be "post-" in regard to; and just as Borges did with Wilkins, so Eco did with Kircher, and Foucault did with a whole range of thinkers and classifiers in his second major book. Thus the use of the Borges quotation in Foucault and Eco, their restaging of its reversal of Wilkins's touching faith in a reliable language, puts the quoters in the position of people no longer in thrall to the idea of language, but able to see what interests language serves, to deny that it is immovable, and to exert some leverage on it.

Where this account of things falters is in its first, diagnostic moment, the description of baroque language projects. Borges (seconded by Foucault, Eco, and others) brings a theory of language as pure cognition before the bar of a theory of language as power. The awkwardness ("ambiguities, redundancies and deficiencies") of Wilkins's language condemns it on cognitive grounds, and no attempt is made to justify it on pragmatic grounds; the realms of arbitrariness and conjecture are added on as dimensions that Wilkins was simply unable to perceive. Here I think that Borges and company have drawn the line incorrectly, misallocated the teams, and scored an own goal. The "transparency" of philosophical language is by no means the simple assumption that commentators make it out to be; rather, as part of the historical emergence of the issue, moments and situations occurred in which transparency was claimed as possible or needful, but these moments and situations were strategically arranged in the service of a social project. There is an imagination of power throughout the baroque imagination of language. We simply need to notice it.[6] The point *was* to change the world.

2.

The *Polygraphia nova* of Athanasius Kircher offers little that was new in the world of cryptography or language theory in 1663. What retains the attention is rather the packaging, the ways in which several kinds of concerns are brought together and made to mirror one another around a central axis that would be the nature of language. The work's table of contents promises the following:

Section I.
The Reduction of All Languages to One.

Section II.
The Extension of One Language to All.

Section III.
A Techno-logia; or, a universal Steganographic Secret operating
by combinations of things; whereby, through a technique
impenetrable to the human mind, one may transmit one's
secrets to another in nearly a thousand ways.[7]

Section I, "The Reduction," offers an international code in which words will be represented by a two-part symbol, one part referring to the meaning of the word (as recorded in a table of vocabulary items), one part referring to its grammatical function (as represented by the morphology of the Latin language). The earliest version of this nomenclator seems to have been composed by a mute Spanish Jesuit in the 1650s, and another, more refined version was published by Johann Joachim Becher in 1661.[8] Kircher adds to these inventions a polyglot dictionary. Section II, "The Expansion," is another kind of dictionary of equivalences, only the use of this dictionary is to supply a word as the substitute for a letter: what the user copies down is a message in flowing Latin prose, which the reader decodes by checking each word against the columns of a special table and recovering the letter that the word replaces. Section III consists of substitution ciphers and letter keys, a set of cryptographic techniques put into circulation nearly a hundred years earlier by Vigenère.[9]

The *Polygraphia nova* is not the only work in which Kircher discusses codes and communicative devices; as for his interest in language, around half of his vast output is dedicated to the oriental studies (particularly hieroglyphic decipherments) of which he was a renowned exponent. The book thus opens a door on a number of activities. Kircher is one of those baroque polymaths with a word to say about everything, but his obsessions are consistent: Whatever particular domain of nature or art Kircher focuses his attention on, it sooner or later applies to problems of communication. In *Magnes, sive de arte magnetica* (Magnes, or the magnetic art, 1643), the fascinating because unexplained play of forces between magnetized objects even when held at a distance from one another suggests the fabrication of a "Machina Cryptologica," a sort of magnetic telegraph. The Machine consists of a series of bottles, each stoppered by a well-lubricated magnet, the magnets all strong enough and near enough to attract or repel one another. When the stopper on the far left of the series is twisted, causing an attached pointer to indicate a letter of the alphabet, the remaining magnets one by one twist in "sympathy," so that the last of the series, also fitted with an alphabetic label and pointer, will give a readout corresponding to the first. Less a cryptographic device than a semaphoric one, the "machine" is fully plugged into the energetic circuits of Kircher's universe.[10] The attraction and repulsion of magnets is only the plainest evidence for the same forces that account for the surprising cures achieved by application of snake-stone or the playing of tarantella music; the arrangement of the planets and the sun around the earth; the lives and loves of plants, animals, and men. A chapter title in *Magnes* gives the category label for these startling phenomena: we live in a "Mundus magneticus, sive catena magnetica" (a magnetic world, or chain of magnetism). The sole key to nature, says Kircher, is the unity among dispersed things, the "rerum omnium naturalium Magneticus in hoc Universo nexus" (the magnetic tie among all the natural things in this universe).[11] There is distance—always; but there are forces that overcome distance, and we can harness these forces to serve the primary human need to send messages. (Is perhaps the need to send messages simply another form of those forces?) Thus the possibility of communication across spaces of separation is a natural potential that the clever scientist (or natural magician) puts to work. It is like the numerological puzzles and magic squares Kircher borrows from Agrippa of Nettesheim, who had ascribed them to the Egyptians.

> The Egyptians believed that by using these very numbers, they could bind to their service the spirits of this world. . . . This much at least is certain, that beneath all this there lies something analogous to the highest orders of ideas, which, were anyone able to extract it from the confused mixture [*miscella*] of worldly objects by using some artifice [*artificium*] akin to this one, I am sure that nothing in the investigation of natural things would be closed to him.[12]

Nature swarms with hidden connections. Although language as given to us is confusing (like hieroglyphics or encoded messages), ideal communication will be like the magician's view of nature: identification of a "sameness" or "unity" hiding in the mingled disorder of things as they appear to us, and prodigious travel through the universe along the epistemological shortcuts thus revealed. Here is one imagination of language and power in Kircher: powerful language follows nature's magnetic chain, revealing the connection, the nexus, among things; weaker languages merely show nature as a disorganized heap or "miscella."[13]

It was doubtless because of Kircher's gift for expressing the symbolic web of the universe that he received one of his most difficult royal commissions. As Kircher puts it at the beginning of his *Polygraphia nova:*

> Once while the most wise Emperor Ferdinand III was engaged in one of those familiar discussions of literary matters to which he resorted in order to lighten the weight of the world pressing on his shoulders, the question came to him: whether there might exist a universal language by means of which someone might correspond with all the peoples of the world; and as there was no one capable of providing a sure ground for such a

language, it pleased his Holy Roman Majesty to commit to my feeble talents the solution of the problem proposed by him.[14]

A language permitting communication "with all the peoples of the world" would have been particularly handy for a seventeenth-century Hapsburg monarch whose domains covered several dozen distinct linguistic areas (including languages as far apart as Italian, Hungarian, Polish, German, and Croatian) and who had the Turks intermittently at his gates. What sort of idiom might Ferdinand III have had in mind when he issued his command, probably in the early 1650s?

The projects for universal languages that circulated in the first half of the seventeenth century promised, in general, to make language learning easy and universal (one would learn, in a few hours' time, a single system of writing applicable to every language on earth), and, as a prelude to this universal writing, to draw all known languages back to their "original" or to their "primitive" form. Precisely these claims appear, though shorn of their justification, among others in Descartes's famous letter on the relation of a "philosophical language" to "true philosophy."[15] Many authors echo, in this endeavor, Francis Bacon's praise of the Chinese writing system as a set of "Characters Real, which express neither letters nor words in gross, but Things or Notions; insomuch as countries and provinces, which understand not one another's language, can nevertheless read one another's writings."[16] Another avenue to reuniting the dispersed languages of the world was through etymology, as in Pierre Besnier's 1674 announcement of a new universal language, *A Philosophical Essay for the Reunion of the Languages, or, the Art of Knowing All by the Mastery of One.* Besnier holds: "First, there is a certain accord between the several languages, and that therefore they are attainable by comparison. . . . Secondly, that they are unquestionably founded upon reason."[17] Besnier's reason is etymology: in a series such as

cadere > caer > ker > cher > choir > déchoir

one can recognize the continuity between the different stages, though it is not easy to describe their motivation; both sound and meaning differ at every step, so that linguistic history is, for Besnier, an "alembic." A good etymological theory, like the much later Grimm's Law, should work like a cryptoanalytic key: given an input in French, or whichever language, application of the right rules should produce an output in German, or whichever language. Whatever the difficulties of execution, Besnier's project is plain: if you could lead all the words of every language back to a primitive original, then the roots of this historically prior language would become the basis of a recovered universal speech.[18]

It must have been by beginning with something like the expectations that converge in Besnier—universality of application added to comprehensive historical elucidation—that Kircher's response to the emperor's commission eventually took its technical course. For as Kircher tells it, he began by seeking to reduce all existing languages to a set of common roots that would form the core vocabulary of the new language. But he writes,

> the same thing happened to me that might happen to a typesetter who has several pages of type laid out and ready for putting under the press: by some inexplicable chance the bonds dissolve and the letters rain down onto the floor, retaining no trace of their true former meaning and no longer capable of being brought back to their lost prototype. So it is with that near-infinite multitude and diversity of languages which, from the beginning of the world until now, has been exposed to so many changes of empire, so much mixing of diverse populations, and so many historical vicissitudes that I believe it most unlikely that a foundation common to all languages should be discovered.[19]

As a result of contemplating too closely the historical debris of language change, Kircher's mind, normally so attentive to the unifying sympathies and nexuses dispersed through the natural world, lost its power of connection (*dissolutis ligaminibus,* as he puts it in his comparison). That is to say, the encounter with the irregular and capricious history of language causes the natural magician's explanatory framework to shatter. But rather than reply to the imperial command with an admission of failure, Kircher presented to the throne a "linguistic device" (*artificium linguarum*) bearing the proud titles of universal communication and penetration but accomplishing those ends in oddly reduced fashion. Kircher's student Gaspar Schott describes the secrecy surrounding the first "publication" of what was later to be the *Polygraphia nova:*

> Many years ago Kircher thought of a new device, which he called an *artifice of languages;* it enabled anyone to read and understand whatever unfamiliar language he wished, by making various arrangements of rods and combinations of the characters written on them. He demonstrated it once to the most august Kaiser Ferdinand III and to his brother, the most serene archduke Wilhelm Leopold, governor of Belgium at the time. Both

of them were delighted with it, as this new and ingenious invention, worthy of great princes, deserved; and they decreed that it not be made public, but rather be reserved for their own use and that of their most august family. And it is for this reason that at no time, in the three years I spent offering my paltry scribal services to the Author of the device, was I able to obtain from Kircher that he show me, even as if through a crack, anything connected to it, except a great number of bare and uninscribed rods stored in a chest shaped like a pipe-organ.[20]

The chest's shape is the last relic of the language Kircher hoped to speak about language and nature. It echoes another expression of his view of the world as filled with divine forces, the analogy of the cosmos as an immense pipe organ animated by God's breath in *Musurgia universalis.*[21] The organ suggests the unlimited circulation of one force through all particulars. But being an opaque object with an inside, a cover, and a lock, the chest also symbolizes secrecy. These chests were actually made and presented to a few patrons or correspondents of Kircher's. As Nick Wilding has observed, the closed system of circulation into which Kircher introduced his linguistic artifices (the very few patrons of high rank who received wooden chests with inscribed tallies and the several dozen recipients of the *Polygraphia*'s first edition, every copy apparently destined to be presented with the author's compliments) is inseparable from the content of those artifices themselves. Composed in an atmosphere of secrecy, they are meant to facilitate communication not with the world in general, but only among the possessors of the gifts.[22]

The *Polygraphia nova* promises miraculous connectivity—the "expansion" and "reduction" of languages between the poles of oneness and infinite diversity—but on closer inspection, Kircher's linguistic artifice hides an unbridgeable duality, the incommensurability of the meaning and the letter(s). Just as cryptogram and semaphore appear as equivalent—though functionally opposite—terms in *Magnes,* so the *Polygraphia* alternates natural magic and mechanical tricks. Language is a different object according to the different social context in which Kircher imagines and addresses it. This may help us to reformulate the problem of the gap or blank occupying the space of the essence of language, the thing that his artifices "expand" and "reduce." Kircher divides language into two and ascribes part of it to a universal register, primarily semantic, where the purpose of collocating dictionary entries is to make meanings and access to meanings problem-free. This is language in the register of the church: the "arithmetical nomenclator" was in fact devised by a fellow Jesuit for use by a multinational, multilingual brotherhood implanted on five continents and monitored through a steady flow of documents in a standard language (Latin). The "nomenclator" simplifies and speeds up access to what the other person is trying to say (at least that is what it does in principle, whatever the difficulties attached to its execution). A second register is reserved for different modes of communication: this is the register where the writer seeks to keep meaning private, to restrict access to a tiny number of qualified readers equipped with decoding devices. This is language as it is used in courts and diplomatic missions: the language of alphabetic substitutions, where what matters is not transmitting meanings in their immediacy but frustrating the unchosen reader, to the point of composing messages that deny that they are private at all (the word-for-a-letter cipher). Competence in this second language is conferred by the bestowal of an artifact, the steganographic dictionary or "ark." Thus the Kircherian information workshop is divided between two languages, each passing for "language," and the difference between them is (roughly speaking) political. Instead of a linguistics or a theory of communication, we should see in Kircher's *Polygraphia nova* an essay in verbal technology, a set of methods for transmuting messages into new forms. But the reason for transforming a message into this or that form will depend on the purpose of communication. It is as if there were no category of language-as-such.

Kircher saw the communicative landscape as a hostile territory dotted with tiny pockets of qualified readers. The experience of the previous century, with its religious wars cutting kingdoms apart and separating areas of like belief and policy from each other, obviously weighed on his thinking, as it would have in the case of any traveler or letter writer in confessionally divided Europe. But across the hostile spaces or in the magnetic atmosphere above them, communication takes place, as it does between sun and turning sunflower, and Kircher supposes a system of forces or waves that the properly prepared observer will see at work everywhere. In other words, communication is sovereign, though perhaps not just now: for the time being, we talk to each other in the guarded codes of court and diplomacy.

3.

John Wilkins, veteran of one great religious war, saw what was at stake in the "[r]eduction of all languages to one": the imposition of a single universal language, "repairing the curse of Babel," was unlikely "until some person attain to the Universal Monarchy." In Wilkins's *Essay towards a Real Character and a Universal Language,* published under the auspices of the Royal Society in 1668, code writing is alluded to only in passing, although Wilkins had demonstrated his facility in devising codes and semaphoric devices for the royalist party during the English Civil War and subsequently published *Mercury or the Swift and Silent Messenger,* a collection of his techniques. In the *Essay towards a Real Character,* though, it is not unsuspected communication across hostile territory that language is meant to make possible; it is rather unrestricted communication for all across an unlimited territory. Wilkins adopts the vocabulary of disinterested public service: "as things are better than words, as real knowledge is beyond elegancy of speech, as the general good of mankind is beyond that of any particular Country or Nation," so is the formation of the universal language to be preferred to all lesser linguistic studies. So, to map Wilkins's enterprise onto Kircher's, the steganographic arks and their restricted community are not part of this effort; Wilkins's vocabulary serves the same general communicative ends as the "Arithmetic Nomenclator" in the *Polygraphia.* Vocabulary also occupies the place of the magnetic, symbolic interweave of the various things of the world imagined by Kircher in his writings on natural philosophy but with an obvious difference, for Wilkins is no Hermeticist but an Aristotelian or Ramist classifier. The world of things is first broken down into a massive branching system of categories, and then every node in the system—every individual term—is assigned a name, or rather an "address," permitting the location of the term in relation to the whole system. In this way "we should, by learning the Character and the Names of things, be instructed likewise in their Natures, the knowledge of both which ought to be conjoyned."[23] So the power that in Kircher's language belonged to the initiate, the natural magician, the wonderworker who had special insight into the universe, in Wilkins's system is given over to the framer of the perfect language, and (through learning the language) to every speaker of it. Knowledge is power, and Wilkins is putting forth a utopia in which everyone has a share.[24]

Kircher's language, as we saw, is divided between two modes: the church and the court. In both contexts, a prior acquaintance obtains between the speakers, an institution mediates between them, and the distribution of the language follows the reach of the institution. (A necessary exception is made for spies or interceptors of messages, but cryptography promises to keep these out, so that the institution maintains control over access to the language and the content it vehicles.) Wilkins is aware of the model, and argues for a different channel whereby the new language may impose its authority: the self-interest of speakers each pursuing his own ends.

> As men do generally agree in the same Principle of Reason, so do they likewise agree in the same *Internal Notion* or *Apprehension* of things. . . .
>
> That *conceit* which men have in their minds concerning a Horse or Tree, is the Notion or *mental Image* of that Beast, or natural thing, of such a nature, shape and use. The *Names* given to these in several Languages, are such arbitrary sounds or words, as Nations of Men have agreed upon. . . .
>
> So that if men should generally consent upon the same way or manner of *Expression,* as they do agree in the same *Notion,* we should then be freed from that Curse in the Confusion of Tongues, with all the unhappy consequences of it. Now if this can onely be done, either by *enjoyning* some one Language and Character to be universally learnt and practiced, (which is not to be expected, till some person attain to the *Universal Monarchy;* and perhaps would not be done then:) or else by *proposing* some such way as, by its facility and usefulness, (without the imposition of Authority) might *invite* and ingage men to the learning of it; which is the thing here attempted.[25]

Enjoining universal learning (as of a catechism) and practice (as of a liturgy)—this sounds rather like the modes of operating of an established church. But Bishop Wilkins, writing in 1665–68, knew only too well that some people would always refuse to "agree" on a system of names, however arbitrary. The English Revolution and the Restoration had presented for study multiple cases of recalcitrant speakers, shifting meanings, and radical disagreement. So Wilkins will not "enjoin," or wait for the Universal Monarch to do it either. He will simply "propose" and leave the reader to adopt what he finds useful and creditable.[26]

Robert Stillman, in a wonderful recent book, has explained what is behind this attitude. Stillman sees in this a reflection of the new political environment of early Restoration England, in which the returned Charles II quickly discovered that his power to command went no farther than his financial autonomy, and the royal finances being depleted by the ten years of the Commonwealth and his own expensive foreign wars, he had no choice but to become a new kind of sovereign, one who negotiated everything with a powerful Parliament. Instead of commanding, this new model of king had to persuade and cajole, had to convince his subjects that it was in their interest to follow his lead—a routine that would have seemed unnatural and impossible to Louis XIV across the channel, for example. And Stillman shows how the language of negotiation, of interest, of convenience, spread throughout English society of the 1660s and 1670s, becoming the master language held in common by court, Parliament, law bench, scientific societies, merchants, architects, painters, and musicians. The imagination of power here becomes subject to new forms of consent. Wilkins, ever an agile social actor, has figured out what the proper mode of address in this new world will be.

The mode of address does not quite carry over to the performance of the language. The Philosophical Tongue is based on an extensive series of branching classifications, parceling out reality from larger categories to smaller ones: a place for everything and everything in its place. Users of the language have only to locate the meanings they need and express them either graphically or vocally. But this ready-made character is also a liability: what if it became necessary to reclassify an object, to change its name? Wilkins classifies the whale among the fishes (using habitat rather than body type to categorize an animal), which now seems to us an error. How would one fabricate a new distinction not anticipated by Wilkins? The only way to build changes into the language would be to publish new tables of categories and promulgate them, instantly, wherever the language is spoken. Otherwise the universal speech community will be in danger of splitting into sects or dialects, precisely because in "learning the Character and the Names of things, [speakers will] be instructed likewise in their Natures." And science, no less than other human activities, does not stand still.

Imagine, for example, that what you call a "king," I call a "tyrant." That is certainly a statement I could make in the philosophical language, perhaps by referring to an established category, perhaps by adding a modifier to an existing term. But if I belong to a group of radical republicans that always uses the word "king" in the sense of "tyrant" (imagine British North America around the time of the Boston Tea Party), and if we hold that there is no such thing as a legitimate "king" but only "tyrants" decked out in specious verbiage, then the universal language is apt to split into dialects merely by usage and habitual meaning.[27] A republican and a monarchist would not be applying the same categories or using the same words. In such a way, "negotiation" and "interest" make the appeal for the initial adoption of the philosophical language, but thereafter they endanger (or are endangered by) its consistency.

Just such a possibility of dissent emerges in a book written at the same time as Wilkins's and published, like his, under the patronage of the Royal Society. Robert Hooke's *Micrographia* delights in confounding the certainties of language by altering perception. Hooke starts his investigation of the world as seen through a microscope by nearly parodying the methodical order of Wilkins.

> We will begin these our Inquiries therefore with the Observations of Bodies of the most simple nature first, and so gradually proceed to those of a more compounded one, to prosecution of which method, we shall begin with a Physical point; of which kind the Point of a Needle is commonly reckon'd for one; and is indeed, for the most part, made so sharp, that the naked eye cannot distinguish any parts of it. . . . But if view'd with a very good microscope, we may find that the top of a Needle (though as to the sense very *sharp*) appears a *broad, blunt,* and very *irregular* end; not resembling a Cone, as is imagin'd, but onely a piece of a tapering body, with a great part of the top remov'd, or deficient. . . .
>
> Now though this point be commonly accounted the sharpest (whence when we would express the sharpness of a point the most *superlatively,* we say, As sharp as a Needle) yet the *Microscope* can afford us hundreds of Instances of Points many thousand times sharper: such as those of the *hairs,* and *bristles,* and *claws* of multitudes of *Insects;* the *thorns,* or *crooks,* or *hairs* of *leaves,* and other small vegetables; nay, the ends of the *stiriae* or small *parallelipipeds* of *Amianthus,* and *alumen plumosum;* of many of which, though the Points are so sharp as not to be visible, though view'd with a *Microscope* (which magnifies the Object, in bulk, above a million of times) yet I doubt not, but were we able *practically* to make *Microscopes* according to the *theory* of them, we might find hills, and dales, and pores, and a sufficient bredth, or expansion, to give all those parts elbow-room, even in the blunt top of the very Point of any of these so very sharp bodies.[28]

Hooke does something to language by changing the conditions of perception: "small," "large," "as sharp as a needle," the geometrical "point," and so forth, all lose their previous meanings and become strange haunted spaces full of "hills, and dales, and pores." (Gulliver's voyage to Brobdignag is in the offing.) Geometry, that science of certainty from first principles, now has a harder time making its case: "how much therefore can be built upon demonstrations made onely by the productions of the Ruler and Compasses, he will be better able to consider that shall but view those *points* and *lines* with a *Microscope*." Hooke is the anti-Wilkins, unmaking what his senior colleague has made. He exposes an incompatibility between the procedures of scientific investigation and the ideal of a settled, ambiguity-free language based on nature: for our terminologies are based not on nature itself but on ideas about nature, and those ideas, like their margins of error, are always changing.

4.

Leibniz too began his investigation into language with the ideal of a "real character." The systems proposed by Kircher, Wilkins, Dalgarno, and others failed to meet Leibniz's demands, however, because his goal was a symbol set that would serve to represent concepts and to indicate their regular (i.e., logically permissible) transformations, *autonomously*—without intervention by the users of the language.[29] (The inflexibility of Wilkins's language could be seen as a form of autonomy but not a very encouraging one.) The idea would be to start with a set of initial terms and derive all other terms, potential or actual, from them. A language constructed in that fashion always eluded Leibniz, in part because he was unable to work out the set of logical "primes" that would generate all possible human thoughts and in part because he raised but could not solve the problem of representing relations within the intensional logic inherited from Aristotle.[30] That he could not attain it himself does not take away from the fact that he could formulate the ideal and diagnose its absence in, for example, ordinary language or what he was able to learn of the Chinese character. The first obstacle to linguistic autonomy was simply the nature of meaning. Meanings are attached to signs by speakers and speech communities; they are *heteronomous* to the features of articulation, grammar, inscription, and so on, that organize the level of the signifier. How to make meaning and inference inhere in the signs themselves? Leibniz tried various ways of making semantic relations accessible to the senses:

> If I could choose any kind of characters at all, vocal or otherwise, by far the easiest means would be to connect the parts of the characters with various little lines which would be simultaneously visible on the page. For as sounds vanish, that is why a prior sound is unable to refer to a later one unless it has in it something *similar to the prior one* corresponding to that which has gone before.[31]

The most convincing glimpse of the perfect language was afforded him by his discovery of binary arithmetic notation.

> The aim of our Characteristic is to stick to words so constructed that all possible consequences may be immediately derived from the words or character themselves, e.g. "David is the father of John" [*sic;* read "Solomon"], therefore "Solomon is the son of David." This conclusion cannot be demonstrated from the Latin words unless they are broken down into other, equivalent words; but in the general language it ought to be demonstrable from analysis of the words into their letters. . . .
>
> And it should be known that characters are more perfect in measure that they are more self-sufficient [*autarkeis*], so that all consequences can be produced from them. For example, the binary numerical character is more perfect than the decimal one or any other, because in the binary [system] everything that is asserted about numbers can be demonstrated from the characters, which is not the case with the decimal [system]. For there is no way to prove from the characters 3 and 9 that nine is three times three, which can however be done with binary characters. The binary figure for 3 is 11 and that for 9, 1001. And 11 times 11 is [in binary notation] 1001:

$$\begin{array}{r} 11 \\ 11 \\ \underline{11} \\ 1001 \end{array}$$

So three times three is nine.[32]

The great advantage of binary notation is that it permits all the arithmetical operations to be carried out on formal, visual grounds alone, with no need of memorizing multiplication tables or other rules. The periodicity of the binary sequence gives rise to automatic patterns that are infinitely, and also mechanically, extensible: to construct the series of the binary integers (1, 10, 11, 100, 101, 110, 111, 1000, 1001, 1010, 1011, 1100, 1101, 1110, 1111, 10000, etc.), "there is no need of calculation, since one need only observe that each column is periodic and in it the same periods recur on to infinity. The first [i.e., rightmost] column contains 010101, etc.; the second 00110011, etc., the third 0000111100001111. . . . In this way one can construct the table of all natural numbers with no calculation at all."[33] The binary mathematician, having penetrated to "the innermost ground and origin of numbers," discovers an order of self-evident signs that disclose their relations to the most casual onlooker, "exactly as if one had never learned to count."[34] The fact is striking enough for Leibniz to repeat it: one will henceforth calculate "without doing any calculation at all, merely by continuing to write."

The signs, in other words, are self-sufficient, and transcribing the signs amounts to doing the thinking that in a less perfect sign system, the signs would be signs "for." What binary notation does for the realm of integers is precisely what the "characteristica universalis" was supposed to have done for the wider domain of words, meanings, and utterances. How simple, that is, how mechanical, and yet how extensive, that use is, we in the electronic age know better than any eighteenth-century sage could imagine. We see features of Leibniz's sign system, though oddly permuted, now at work in our electronic environment. The translation of information into binary signals has entered every imaginable domain, like a universal but minimally signifying language, and the automated factoring of enormously large numbers into primes has become the basis for open-key cryptography.

Leibniz is often accused of naive faith in human reason and the neutrality of language. The famous argument in his notes, that all disputes in religion or politics can be resolved by working out the terms with pen and paper, is held to exhibit this simplicity. "Let us calculate (*Calculemus*)!" he imagines people saying to each other, instead of launching pamphlets or wars. But the outcome of submitting everything to calculation would, perhaps, be more likely to lead people to question the relevance of the calculations, as happens when people discuss economics or social policy: what is at issue is usually not the arithmetic but the ends to which it is applied. The neutrality of a philosophical language would thus seem to most of us an illusion. But to be fair to Leibniz, neutrality or impersonality in language means first taking language away from those who have it. If the locus of proof were to be removed from the battlefield or the law court and put in a language that anyone could learn, the leveling effects of Leibniz's reform would be enormous. Unlike the systems of Kircher and Wilkins, which depend on the distribution of a printed codebook to all users, the factoring system can be worked out by anybody relying on simple mathematics and the light of nature — a do-it-yourself formula that circumvents institutions. Even Leibniz's faith in the cognitive abilities of impartial observers — a faith that, as we see today, is apt to be discredited by the view that language is always involved in power structures — encloses a certain imagination of power. To look at Leibniz's logical language as a social formation, self-evident truths are truths that do not need a particular social structure to preserve them. They are robust or indifferent to situations. Their *autarkeia* would be both semiotic and political. That makes them the model for an ancient type of person—the contemplative philosopher—and a new type of self-organizing community.

5.

These four examples—Kircher, Wilkins, Hooke, and Leibniz—show that to invent a language is always to invent a form of social life; it is not just a matter of grammar and semantics; and conversely, that the social forms languages produce are more reliably connected to their structure than to the intentions of their makers. Conventional accounts of utopian or imaginary languages see them as nothing more than more or less ingenious arrangements of rules and meanings, but this is to scant their importance. They are really imaginings of communicative networks, of justification procedures for establishing the truth of statements, and of the bases of authority.

Kircher's communicative devices take their power from an act of foundation (distributing copies of the codebook to the members of a restricted fraternity) and from arbitrary decisions taken in order to keep communication from becoming general (decisions such as which key to use, which Latin word to correlate with which letter in the book cipher, etc.). At another level, his imagined language of nature, the great concatenation of things, would have been powered by physical forces (magnetism, stellar energy flows, flesh calling to flesh, etc.). As unlike as these two forms of language are, in both cases the power of speech derives from and is wholly in the gift of an originator. Kircher's understanding of language makes it an initiatory medium: there are those who possess the secret or the codebook, and then there are the others. The only way to get into the group of speakers is to have the book. No other process of education is set forth. Wilkins addresses the whole human race as a group with common interests and desires. For Wilkins, the "Universal Empire" exists already but in the subtler form of a marketplace; the king's name is Interest. But in its actual workings Wilkins's language would have resembled Kircher's: speech is still a grant from an originator, and has to be led back to its source in a multiply produced object (a book). Speakers come into language always by the same door, possession of the codebook, and it is an open question whether they can modify the language's preexisting pattern of meanings. Both Kircher's and Wilkins's languages are scriptural in the sense that the codebook, the source of meanings, is given at the out-set by the language maker and thereafter only *cited* by the speakers, who are within the language's communicative space only so long as they continue to cite the codebook. Hooke, more a critic than a framer, sets the codebook of ordinary language and the observations made with a microscope side by side, and lets the latter pull apart the former: microscope vision unsettles consensus, puts doubt in its place, and demands ever more powerful lenses. Leibniz's unfinished project suggests that the best language is one in which linguistic power leaves the speakers, the previously given social world and even the codebook to become inherent in the terms themselves. The language giver supplies the prime terms and their initial relations, but speakers can thereafter combine them or analyze them to get legitimate results. What all speakers will share is a foundational scripture of some kind, though greatly reduced (a table of primes), and mostly a habit of rule following. Because you and I are following the same rules in composing and decomposing signs, and because these rules are unambiguous and manifest to everyone, our communication can be problem-free. Obedience to the law of the philosophical language takes precedence over the usual social institutions: whoever can show that a consequence follows from an assumption is authorized by the language to pronounce truthful conclusions. And since this rule-based activity is open to everyone who, aided by the light of nature, can master some basic principles of arithmetic, the speech community is to a great degree open. The agreement to follow it resembles the rules of professional training, a know-how that forms a community of competence (like those of medicine, the law, or academic disciplines) and issues in practical results.

To classify these philosophical languages according to the social formations they found, Kircher's is a language of the courtier, where legitimacy flows from what we nowadays call "access"; Wilkins, that of a politician who has to persuade people that their interests are identical with his (but the deal once done can go back to consulting no interest but his own); Leibniz, that of a jurist, for whom process and mastery of a professional technique assure legitimacy. In the light of the sociologies of professionalization and the "public sphere" that we associate with the names of Weber and Habermas, Leibniz is the language reformer who comes closest to founding a new social ethic. His notes on universal language, fittingly, came to light only in the last years of the nineteenth century, when "autarchy" and "self-organization" began to bear a different meaning, and international organizations that recruited their memberships through competency (philosophical societies, professional organizations, labor unions, reform bodies, the Red Cross, etc.) seemed poised to limit the authority of nation-states.[35] Among these international organizations was, inevitably, the revived movement for a universal language, in which the logician and Leibniz scholar Louis Couturat played a major part. Such projects as theirs seek to fashion, through language, a "universal empire" as the empire of universality. But it will not belong to "some person"; rather it will exist in and by collectivities of those whose professional training equip them to deal in more than merely local networks of authority. Couturat's appropriation of Leibniz's semiotic autarchy to project the self-governing character of professions beyond their specific fields of competence and toward the universal horizon of communication brings out the many forms of utopia lurking in what appears to be a merely technical calculus.

NOTES

1. Marx, "Theses on Feuerbach," in Marx and Engels, *Selected Works,* 28–30. A stimulating recent work on Marx's ideology-criticism is Brudney, *Marx's Attempt to Leave Philosophy.*

2. Nietzsche, *On the Genealogy of Morals,* in *Sämtliche Werke* 5:247–412.

3. Borges, "John Wilkins' Analytical Language," in *Selected Non-Fictions,* 231. I have slightly modified the wording of the translation. The German sinologist Franz Kuhn (translator of a shortened version of *Dream of the Red Chamber*) really existed; the encyclopedia, probably not.

4. Foucault, *Les Mots et les Choses,* 7.

5. "The same fatal incongruity of every list is the secret flaw affecting even the more philosophically grounded projects of *a priori* philosophical languages. This was later noticed by Jorge Luis Borges"—whereupon follows the quotation. Eco, "Kircher tra steganografia e poligrafia," 213.

6. Toward this endeavor, we should keep in mind the "capillary" picture of power developed by Foucault in his last years (see e.g., "Clarifications on the Question of Power," in *Foucault Live,* 179–92). Power, in this account, does not have a location, a center, or an opposite: it courses through society and knows no other limit than society's.

7. Kircher, *Polygraphia nova,* 2. On this supreme Baroque savant, see Findlen, *Athanasius Kircher: The Last Man Who Knew Everything.* The following sections condense material from my chapter in that volume.

8. For descriptions of the Spaniard's and Becher's inventions, see Schott, *Technica curiosa,* 483–503. Schott was a student of Kircher's. Becher's work was previously published as *Character pro notitia linguarum universali.* On invented languages generally, see Albani and Buonarroti, *Dictionnaire des langues imaginaires.*

9. Vigenère, *Traicté des chiffres.* For a description of Kircher's artifices, see Wilding, "'If You Have a Secret.'"

10. Kircher, *Magnes,* 333–46. See also "Appendix Apologetica," in *Polygraphia nova,* 18. Kircher's *Ars magna lucis et umbrae,* 907–8, applies similar reasonings to telescopes and mirrors.

11. Kircher, *Magnes,* 463, 469. For scoffing at "old wives' tales" about flesh grafts and other cases of "like calling to like," see p. 334. But contrast the credence accorded quite similar tales in Book 3 of the same work.

12. Kircher, *Arithmologia,* 144–45.

13. Kircher, *Sphinx mystagoga,* 20.

14. Kircher, *Polygraphia nova,* 6. On the *Polygraphia* and its history, see Wilding, "'If You Have a Secret.'"

15. Descartes to Mersenne, 20 November 1629, in *Œuvres philosophiques,* 227–32.

16. Bacon, *Of the Advancement of Learning,* in *Works,* 3:399–400.

17. Besnier, *A Philosophical Essay,* 3. Besnier's 1674 essay is introduced here simply as an example of a type, not as the specific inspiration for Descartes or Kircher (that would be impossible, as Descartes's letter dates from 1629 and Kircher must have received his commission from Ferdinand III around 1655).

18. Also in this current of ideas is Webb, *An Historical Essay Endeavoring a Probability That the Language of the Empire of China Is the Primitive Language* (1669), on which see Porter, *Ideographia,* 42–49. On Grimm's Law as originally formulated, see Robins, *A Short History of Linguistics,* 170–72.

19. Kircher, *Turris Babel sive Archontologia,* 218.

20. Schott, *Technica curiosa,* 479–80.

21. See the illustration and description (chapter title: "In quo mundus organo comparatur") in Kircher, *Musurgia universalis,* 2:366.

22. Thus the 1663 *Polygraphia nova* was "a printed book paradoxically circulat[ing] in a manuscript economy": Wilding, "'If You Have a Secret,'" 100.

23. Wilkins, *An Essay Towards a Real Character and a Philosophical Language,* 21.

24. For a portrait of Wilkins as utopian, see Hogben, *Dangerous Thoughts,* 25–43. Hogben's chapter is one of Borges's sources (it always pays to verify their existence!), providing both evidence and conclusion for the verdict of arbitrariness and confusion.

25. Wilkins, *Essay,* 20.

26. On the changing meanings of "interest," see Stillman, *The New Philosophy and Universal Languages in Seventeenth-Century England,* 193–227.

27. "Bilingualism," "incommensurability," and "divergence of dialects" are analogies for problems in the development of science described by Kuhn in *The Structure of Scientific Revolutions.* The growth of an originally philosophical language would instantiate the analogy both literally and figuratively.

28. Hooke, *Micrographia,* 2–3.

29. Leibniz, *Opuscules et fragments inédits,* 284–85. See also p. 280, where Leibniz draws courage from Kircher's invention of a set of tokens that allowed anyone, by drawing and combining them at random, to compose "original" music (an idea later adapted or independently discovered by Mozart). See Kircher, *Musurgia universalis,* 2:184.

30. See Russell, *The Philosophy of Leibniz;* Ishiguro, *Leibniz's Philosophy of Logic and Language.*

31. Leibniz, *Opuscules et fragments,* 284–85.

32. Leibniz, *Opuscules et fragments,* 284–85.

33. Leibniz, "Lettre sur la philosophie chinoise, à Nicolas de Rémond," in *Zwei Briefe,* 130–31.

34. "Neujahrsbrief an den Herzog Rudolf August von Braunschweig-Lüneburg-Wolfenbüttel," in *Zwei Briefe,* 20. See also Zacher, *Hauptschriften zur Dyadik,* 233.

35. See Leibniz, *Opuscules et fragments,* for Couturat's resurrection and editorial ordering of these papers from the Hanover Leibniz-Archiv. Couturat also organized the first International Philosophic Congress (Paris, 1900) and founded, with Léopold Leau, the "Delegation for the adoption of an international auxiliary language." See Couturat, *Histoire de la langue universelle.*

BIBLIOGRAPHY

Albani, Piero, and Berlinghiero Buonarroti. *Dictionnaire des langues imaginaires.* Trans. Egidio Festa. Paris: Les Belles Lettres, 2001.

Bacon, Francis. *The Works of Francis Bacon.* Ed. James Spedding, Robert Ellis, and Douglas Heath. London: Longmans, 1872.

Becher, Johann Joachim. *Character pro notitia linguarum universali, inventum steganographicum hactenus inauditum.* Frankfurt, 1661.

Besnier, Pierre. *A Philosophical Essay for the Reunion of the Languages, or, the Art of Knowing All by the Mastery of One.* Trans. Henry Rose. Oxford, 1675.

Borges, Jorge Luis. *Selected Non-Fictions.* Ed. Eliot Weinberger. New York: Viking, 1999.

Brudney, Daniel. *Marx's Attempt to Leave Philosophy.* Cambridge, Mass.: Harvard University Press, 1998.

Couturat, Louis. *Histoire de la langue universelle.* Paris: Hachette, 1903.

Descartes, René. *Œuvres philosophiques.* Ed. Ferdinand Alquié. Paris: Garnier, 1963.

Eco, Umberto. "Kircher tra steganografia e poligrafia." Pp. 209–13 in Lo Sardo, ed., *Athanasius Kircher: Il museo del mondo.*

Findlen, Paula, ed. *Athanasius Kircher: The Last Man Who Knew Everything.* New York: Routledge, 2004.

Foucault, Michel. *Les Mots et les Choses.* Paris: Gallimard, 1966.

———. *Foucault Live.* Ed. Sylvère Lotringer. New York: Semiotexte, 1989.

Hogben, Lancelot. *Dangerous Thoughts.* New York: Norton, 1940.

Hooke, Robert. *Micrographia.* London, 1665. Republished on CD-ROM, Palo Alto: Octavo, 1998.

Ishiguro, Hidé. *Leibniz's Philosophy of Logic and Language.* London: Duckworth, 1972.

Kircher, Athanasius. *Magnes, sive de arte magnetica.* Cologne, 1643.

———. *Musurgia universalis.* Rome, 1650.

————. *Polygraphia nova et universalis.* Rome, 1663.

————. *Arithmologia.* Rome, 1665.

————. *Ars magna lucis et umbrae.* Rome, 1666.

————. *Sphinx mystagoga.* Amsterdam, 1676.

————. *Turris Babel sive Archontologia.* Amsterdam, 1679.

Kuhn, Thomas. *The Structure of Scientific Revolutions.* Chicago: University of Chicago Press, 1962.

Leibniz, Gottfried Wilhelm von. *Opuscules et fragments inédits de Leibniz.* Ed. Louis Couturat. Paris: Alcan, 1903.

————. *Zwei Briefe über das Binäre Zahlensystem und die chinesische Philosophie.* Ed. Renate Loosen and Franz Vonessen. Stuttgart: Belser, 1968.

Lo Sardo, Eugenio, ed. *Athanasius Kircher: Il museo del mondo.* Rome: Edizioni de Luca, 2001.

Marx, Karl, and Friedrich Engels. *Selected Works.* New York: International Publishers, 1968.

Nietzsche, Friedrich. *Sämtliche Werke.* 10 vols. Ed. Giorgio Colli and Mazzino Montinari. Berlin: de Gruyter, 1988.

Porter, David. *Ideographia: The Chinese Cipher in Early Modern Europe.* Stanford: Stanford University Press, 2001.

Robins, R. H. *A Short History of Linguistics.* Bloomington: Indiana University Press, 1967.

Russell, Bertrand. *A Critical Exposition of the Philosophy of Leibniz.* 1899. 2d ed. London: Allen & Unwin, 1937.

Schott, Caspar. *Technica curiosa, sive mirabilia artis.* Würzburg, 1664.

Stillman, Robert. *The New Philosophy and Universal Languages in Seventeenth-Century England: Bacon, Hobbes, and Wilkins.* Lewisburg: Bucknell University Press, 1995.

Stolzenberg, Daniel, ed. *The Great Art of Knowing: The Baroque Encyclopedia of Athanasius Kircher.* Stanford: Stanford University Libraries, 2001.

Vigenère, Blaise de. *Traicté des chiffres.* Paris, 1586.

Webb, John. *An Historical Essay Endeavoring a Probability That the Language of the Empire of China Is the Primitive Language.* London, 1669.

Wilding, Nick. "'If You Have a Secret, Either Keep It, or Reveal It': Cryptography and Universal Language." Pp. 93–103 in Stolzenberg, *The Great Art of Knowing.*

Wilkins, John. *An Essay Towards a Real Character and a Philosophical Language.* London, 1668.

Zacher, Hans Joachim. *Die Hauptschriften zur Dyadik von Leibniz.* Frankfurt am Main: Klostermann, 1973.

6 Nationalism without Linguism

Tolerating Chinese Variants

SUSAN D. BLUM

Linguism—for some yet to be adequately explained reasons—is
particularly intense in the Indian subcontinent, has been something
of an issue in Malaya, and has appeared sporadically elsewhere.
But as language has sometimes been held to be the altogether essential
axis of nationality conflicts, it is worth stressing that linguism is not
an inevitable outcome of linguistic diversity. As indeed kinship, race,
and the other facts . . . , language differences need not in themselves
be particularly divisive: they have not been so for the most part in
Tanganyika, Iran[,] . . . , the Philippines, or even in Indonesia, where
despite a great confusion of tongues linguistic conflict seems to be the
one social problem the country has somehow omitted to demonstrate
in extreme form. Furthermore, primordial conflicts can occur where
no marked linguistic differences are involved, as in Lebanon, among
the various sorts of Batak-speakers in Indonesia, and to a lesser extent
perhaps between the Fulani and Hausa in northern Nigeria.

—Clifford Geertz, "The Integrative Revolution"

It has come to seem quite natural for scholars as well as citizens to
equate nations and languages; when boundaries between them do not coincide,
it has become natural to expect struggles over linguistic differences. The world
of the twentieth and twenty-first centuries, of 185 or so nations, each with official

languages, has made linguistic questions our questions. The "Questione della lingua," the question of which language is to predominate in which setting, has filled volumes of scholarly inquiry and hours of public debate—often acrimonious and occasionally deadly. I suggest an alternative to contestation over language, a lack of debate, a nonfit between nation and language. I show how the situation in China with regard to linguistic diversity gives rise to tolerance of multilingualism despite the existence of an official language and of nationalistic sentiment.

Most societies everywhere are multilingual.[1] This claim may strike Americans, with our "monoglot standard" view (in Michael Silverstein's terms), as impossible, dangerous, inefficient, somehow unnatural.[2] The United States has considerable difficulty struggling over English-only laws, bilingual education, and foreign language requirements in high school and college—the last in some cases dispensable with a doctor's testimony.[3] Given this background, Americans can also sympathize with the linguistic contests fought in such places as Montreal and Belgium, where the notion of the rightful dominance of a single language makes sense. Tamil struggles over language, which in some cases have resulted in death, may go a little far. But the basic principle that societies should have a single language resonates with American views of how the world should work.

At the same time, the claims of, first, Latin, later French, and now perhaps English as *the* world language resonate with the American (and sometimes European) ideology of monolingualism. The details may be disputed, but we would scarcely question the principle. Other chapters in this book describe arguments about Latinity, conceived as a pure, changeless language, or claims about the spirit of Ireland as embodied in the Irish language.

This chapter presents a different version of how the world might work linguistically. This is the multilingual reality described by John Edwards in *Multilingualism,* as it is seen in present-day China. It shows a type of society that is common in the world at present—even more common in the past—but that is quite different from the contemporary linguistic view of monolingualism that accompanies nationalism. In this contrasting type of society, visible in pre-twentieth-century Italy, in Indonesia, in India, and in many parts of the Arabic world, there may be an official language that has claims to represent the elite and the polity; but in reality many people do not speak this language, and there is little official concern about their lack of competence.

The first, familiar type of society I call "boundary contesting." We can see expression of such a society in a poem by the Tamil poet Bharatidasan (1938) about the beauty of the Tamil language:

Our bodies, our wealth, our very breath,
We will surrender to our sweet Tamil!
Even the pleasures woman alone gives do not compare to our great Tamil,
We will declare . . . !

In her fascinating book *Passions of the Tongue,* on what she calls "language devotion in Tamil India," Sumathi Ramaswamy quotes another person who says, "The battle for Tamil is the battle of my life."[4] She discusses the motives and methods by which Tamil devotees are willing to sacrifice everything, including their lives, for their language. This is the extreme end of boundary-contesting societies.

The second type of society, "boundary shrugging," is the focus of this chapter. There is a third type, described by Suzanne Romaine, which I call "boundary celebrating," as may be found in Papua New Guinea (PNG). People in PNG exaggerate differences among linguistic varieties because they think they are interesting. Romaine writes that in attempting to understand how nine hundred languages could be spoken in that country, one must take into consideration the fact that "diversity is cultivated in Melanesia as a badge of identification and is largely a conscious reaction . . . [and] that none of the pressures towards convergence found for a long time in Europe and elsewhere, such as literacy, standardization, centralized administrative control, schooling, media, was present to any great degree in pre-colonial days."[5] Indeed, she claims—and I agree—that "the very concept of discrete languages is probably a European cultural artifact fostered by processes such as literacy and standardization. Any attempt to count distinct languages will be an artifact of classificatory procedures rather than a reflection of communicative practices."[6] This suggestion is strikingly at odds with the way language and its differences have been naturalized in scholarship and popular ideas about language, so that it may be difficult at first to believe that people would exaggerate differences in order to make life interesting. I cannot pursue the matter of boundary celebration here, but it is worth keeping in mind as yet another way human societies make sense of their complexity.

Returning to the focus here, China is a boundary-shrugging society for the following reasons:

1. Linguistic difficulties are rarely mentioned in Chinese contexts where familiarity with other (mostly Indo-European) societies would lead one to expect them: definitions of the nation, war, or political struggles.

2. Most attention in China has been paid to the written form of the language, and most people are scarcely aware of the characteristics of speech. Though there has been concern with literacy, it has not led to suppression of variation.
3. Many people acquire multiple varieties of language easily and often, leading to a disposition that tolerates rather than rebuffs linguistic differences. A description of contemporary linguistic pluralism will demonstrate the vibrancy of multilingualism in China.

For the most part, China's linguistic complexity has not led to contentious disputes. In effect, I am making an argument from silence. A good sleuth may turn up an example that contradicts my thesis, but I am more interested here in the general discourse regarding the relationship between nationalism and language in China, not in individual views.

Nationalism

The list of struggles over language in the context of nationalism is a long one, especially in the twentieth century. In Sri Lanka "Tamil Tigers" fight with Sinhala nationalists about the language of education (Tamil vs. Sinhala).[7] In Montreal there has been a several-decades-long, intense struggle over the signs and visual markers of language, in addition to the rules for children of English-educated parents, culminating in several recently defeated referenda on Quebecois independence.[8] In Ireland English has dominated politically, culturally, and linguistically for a century, though poignant counterefforts have tried to revive the language.[9] The struggles between the Flemish and Wallon (French-speaking) parts of Belgium have resulted in the Linguistic Divide, separating Flanders and Wallonia across the middle of the country.[10] At the height of its acculturation policies, the United States forbade Native American children from speaking their mother tongues in boarding schools.[11] In the U.S. for the past several decades there has been discussion of whether we need a de jure in addition to a de facto national language, to stem the tide of increasingly visible multilingualism in the face of Spanish-speaking immigration.[12] In Spain the Catalan speakers of Barcelona have fought the dominance of Castilian.[13] The Académie Française has mandated the use of native French terms rather than English cognates in an attempt to reverse the process of Anglicization.[14] All these cases, which could of course be multiplied, suggest the centrality of language for a national identity. National-ism and linguism—the notion that a single language embodies the spirit of the nation—have been intertwined in Europe especially since Herder voiced the sentiment that a nation, though not a state, should ideally coincide with a people and a language (*Eine Nation, ein Volk, eine Sprache*).[15] But as Eric Hobs-bawm and others have pointed out, the development of a linguistic definition of nationalism—certainly central in contemporary definitions—is very recent.[16]

In the case of China, we find little real concern with language in contem-porary or historical discussions of the polity. Here is what Sun Yatsen, popularly regarded as the "father" of Chinese nationhood, wrote about a century ago in appealing to his fellow subjects:

> For the most part the four hundred million people of China can be spoken of as completely Han Chinese [*sic*]. With common customs and habits, we are completely of one race. But in the world today what position do we occupy? Compared to the other peoples of the world we have the great-est population and our civilization is four thousand years old; we should therefore be advancing in the front rank with the nations of Europe and America. But the Chinese people have only family and clan solidarity; they do not have national spirit. Therefore even though we have four hundred million people gathered together in one China, in reality they are just a heap of loose sand. Today we are the poorest and weakest nation in the world, and occupy the lowest position in international affairs. Other men are the carving knife and serving dish; we are the fish and the meat. Our position at this time is most perilous. If we do not earnestly espouse na-tionalism and weld together our four hundred million people into a strong nation, there is danger of China's being lost and our people being de-stroyed. If we wish to avert this catastrophe, we must espouse national-ism and bring this national spirit to the salvation of the country.[17]

In the context of China's need to modernize in the face of Western incursions, weapons, education, and technology, we might easily sympathize with the call for nationalism. Most of the Chinese nationalist rhetoric at the beginning of the twentieth century appealed to science, modernization, unity, obedience, and mo-rality. What is not seen here is reference to language, especially spoken language. Sun Yatsen's appeal resembles that of Renan, who urged *volonté*, "will," as the pri-mary unifying factor of the nation.[18] In very few of the myriad tirades against China's backwardness can one find reference to language—and then it involves the script. No one inveighs against the decline of proper usage of particles; no one mocks the accents of those from other regions, though they may mock their marriage practices; no one laments the fact that government leaders have loyalty to their own regions. (It should not be overlooked that Sun Yatsen, like many revolutionary leaders, was from Guangdong, southern China, and that he spoke Cantonese. He made no appeal to linguistic unification.)

When China's imperial system fell in 1911, the Nationalist party (KMT or GMD) came into power. It similarly focused—as much as this disarray can be said to have had a focus—on economy and power, science, industry, and modernization but not on language. Prasenjit Duara describes "cultural nationalism" in the Republican period (1911–49), including fights between federalists and centrists, who mobilized provincial armies against those of other provinces, but never mentions language.[19] Only when the KMT was forced to move to Taiwan with the Communist victory in 1949 did spoken language come into the equation, and then began the ruthless suppression of Taiwanese (also known as Hokkien, or Southern Min) in favor of official Mandarin (called, polemically, *guoyu,* the national language).

Taiwan's recent history begins with a wave of Chinese migration from the mainland, mostly from nearby Fujian Province, during the Qing dynasty (1644–1911). Descendants of these people are called "natives," *benshengren,* even though there was also a small aboriginal population, Malayo-Polynesian speakers, who had been on the island for thousands of years. Taiwan was a Japanese colony for fifty years, from 1895 to 1945, during which time suppression of Chinese language and religion was common. A second wave of Chinese migrants, now called *waishengren,* "outsiders," arrived in 1949; they had a population of approximately 2 million, compared to the "native" population of 10 million. Yet because of their superior political and military force, they were able to suppress the natives. Children were forbidden from speaking Taiwanese, and all official interactions were to take place in Mandarin. Still, once the suppression relaxed in the mid-1980s, Taiwanese resurfaced and began to overtake Mandarin in some functions. Even children of mainlanders have begun to learn Taiwanese. Commerce in much of Southeast Asia, in which Taiwan is a significant participant, is now conducted in Hokkien.[20] Interestingly, the only part of China—if indeed it is a part of China—in which one can currently find activism on behalf of a linguistic variety is Taiwan.[21]

Once the Chinese Communist Party established itself in 1949 in mainland China, language played some role in its educational policies, but unlike many other newly defined nations, China did not use its considerable power to enforce those policies. Many constitutions, whether of new nations such as Slovenia or India or older nations such as France, specify the official or state language, sometimes making explicit provision for speakers of other languages. By contrast, China's constitution (1982 version) mentions language only once and only in the context of ethnic minorities: "All nationalities have the freedom to use and develop their own spoken and written languages and to preserve or reform their own folkways and customs."[22]

The "nationalities" are understood to have their own languages; nonethnic minorities' languages are irrelevant (more on this below).[23] Linguistic differences in speech and linguistic differences among the Chinese topolects (languages and dialects) are not worthy of notice.

We do find struggles in China over language used by national minorities with coethnic counterparts across international borders, such as the Uighurs (Muslims who speak a Turkic language) in the restive northwest province (autonomous region) of Xinjiang and Dai speakers in southern Yunnan, whose Thai language is similar to that spoken in Thailand.[24] Interestingly, both Uighurs and Dai have rock songs that invoke the use of the minority language rather than that of the dominant Han—much in the spirit of Tamil poetry described by Ramaswamy. I would not be surprised to find this in Tibet as well.

In so-called Greater China, such as Southeast Asia, ethnic Chinese battle to use Chinese (Mandarin) in school. In Malaysia and Indonesia the national languages include the newly defined Malay and Bahasa Indonesia, Chinese, and English. In Singapore the use of Chinese varieties endures, though there is increasing support for acquisition of Mandarin and English.[25] However, in the interesting and multifaceted recent treatment of diaspora Chinese in Southeast Asia, one finds few mentions of linguistic issues.[26] This suggests to me that such issues, which I am arguing were not significant in China, are still not especially noteworthy.

Historical Disposition toward Multilingualism

If we trace the idea of a standard back in history, we run into the problem that we must first identify a "Chinese" language. Like the nation itself, this is more easily said than done. The contemporary "Chinese" language is, of course, multiple, consisting of at least seven or eight major subdivisions, all mutually unintelligible.[27] When we read works of early China, such as the *Zuo zhuan,* an account of political life in the Warring States period (479–221 B.C.E.), we find evidence of what appear to be cultural or ethnic differences, but language is rarely discussed. Jerry Norman writes of the scant notice given the regional dialects. "There is very little information to be found concerning Chinese dialects right up to modern times. . . . The lack of dialectal texts in earlier times indicates that, throughout most of her history, China has had a standard language; this is clearly the case for the written language, but there are numerous indications that it was also the case for the spoken language as well."[28] I think it might mean something different: it might mean that the dialects were beneath notice.

There are at least three possible explanations for this absence. First, there were no linguistic differences among the people from various states (*guo*). Second, there were differences, but they did not lead to difficulty in communication. Third, there were differences, and people were quite tolerant of the difficulties, adjusting and accommodating just as people in PNG are said to now. In many ways the third explanation accords most with the situation in contemporary China, where there are substantial linguistic differences, but they are often not remarked. Well-defined linguistic varieties accord with Western ideologies of linguistic kinds,[29] but on the ground one often finds a continuum of difference that is adjusted to but is without real import. I once came upon two young women reading a book out loud together. One, from Kunming, wanted to learn the Shanghai dialect, so she asked the other to read the book aloud in Shanghai-hua. Despite the fact that a small proportion of the language might not be representable in ideographs, both felt that this was a very useful way to pick up a new variety. After hearing the Shanghai pronunciation for a time, the Kunming native believed that she would automatically adjust and know the correspondences of sounds and sound categories.

Virtually the only sources for recovering linguistic difference in the past come from the rhyme books *Qieyun* of the Nanbeichao (601) and the *Guangyun* (1011) and the rhyme tables of the Song (960–1229). Historical philologists have combed these works for evidence regarding the sound system of Middle Chinese. But we can also read the introductions of these rhyme books for what they suggest in terms of the social and cultural and multilingual context: they were aiming to "regularize the sounds of north and south" so that people could agree about the perfect rhymes for poetry. This would be useful or necessary only if there were significant differences already in existence. The writers of these works did not state that they had trouble understanding one another, only that they did not agree about the rhymes. This may be akin to arguments about ending English with prepositions — a matter of authority over niceties that indicate prestige and knowledge in elites but that also show how much diversity in usage exists.

Much has been made of the notion that *guanhua*, an administrative vernacular, existed for the purpose of officials communicating with one another. How widespread this was, who learned or used it, and how it was learned are all important questions that have not yet been answered.[30] Chinese linguists[31] commonly make the peculiar claim that in the so-called *Analects* of Confucius, references to the "elegant language" (*ya yan*) of the master were essentially to a shared vernacular. Yet the situation at the turn of the twentieth century, when such matters as defining a national standard became truly pressing, indicates that there was profound disagreement about which variety should prevail. This carries with it the implication that *guanhua* had no automatic legitimacy as a standard.

In Charles Ferguson's terms, what characterized China's linguistic situation right up to the present might be thought of as diglossia (though I think not in the present),[32] where a literary and elite standard coexisted with a multiplicity of vernaculars that were so beneath notice that people might not even acknowledge that they were speaking them. Arabic is the prototypical case of diglossia, since there is a high language with certain associated functions coexisting with a set of colloquial languages with wider functions. The Chinese case differs from that of Arabic, however, in that there are some people in China who speak only Putonghua, whereas there are no Arabic speakers who do not also speak a colloquial language.[33] Still, only Putonghua has, in some ways, official existence. When I tried to find someone to teach me the Kunming dialect, a version of southwestern Mandarin spoken in Kunming and very similar to the other topolects spoken in Yunnan and Sichuan Provinces, there were no resources. Only the national standard, and a few of the minority languages, had pedagogical support. Indeed, Chinese topolects and even the actual speech of Putonghua speakers are only beginning to be fully described by linguists. Linguists in China have until recently focused on the grammar of literature and minority languages.[34]

Language Policy

China's language policy is usually divided into three related issues: script reform, romanization, and standardization of the spoken language. In general linguistic and anthropological circles, dominated by the understanding of European languages and other languages represented by alphabets, the focus has been language planning, which means standardization and promulgation of a national or official language.[35] In contrast, when people in China, including linguists, mention "language reform" they usually mean simply reform of the script, the writing system. One of the main concerns in discussion since the 1920s was whether to substitute phonetic symbols for the traditional ideographs, which in turn required agreement on which pronunciation would replace the symbol. For instance, the symbol for 'person' 人 is pronounced *ren* in standard Mandarin, *yaan* in Cantonese, and *nin* in Shanghai dialect. Speakers of these three varieties could look at the ideograph and pronounce it accordingly. But if the ideograph were to be replaced by a phonetic representation, which would it be?[36] Abolishing the script has essentially been abandoned as an option.

In the 1920s and 1930s, following the May Fourth movement initiated in 1919 that urged that writing match speech more closely than did classical Chinese, many scholars argued about how to modernize. Language reform took many forms. A romanization scheme was proposed, simplification or elimination of the Chinese script was implemented, and standardization of the spoken language was initiated.[37] Debates arose about the proper variety to serve as standard: Cantonese, Southern Min (the family to which Taiwanese belongs), Shanghainese, or Mandarin? Though we often assume a natural dominance for a variety such as Mandarin, it is important to recall that as recently as eighty years ago it had serious rivals. Southern Min's (Minnan's) claim was that it more accurately reflected the characteristics of earlier forms of Chinese and would be better for preserving the literary qualities of the classics. The rhymes would work out better if poetry were read in Min rather than in Mandarin. (This is still claimed by Southern Min speakers, in Taiwan for example. I once had a teacher who said he liked to read Tang poetry aloud in Taiwanese.) Cantonese (the Yue dialects) has the virtue of preserving from earlier forms of Chinese a series of final stop consonants that had disappeared in Mandarin, the entering, *rusheng*, tones (final *-m, -p, -t*, and *-k*, which either merged with other nasals in Mandarin or changed the tone class of the words); many of the leaders of the Revolution spoke this form. Shanghai was seen as the most advanced and cosmopolitan city in China. The Wu dialects preserve voiced stops, which no longer exist in any other Chinese topolects. Mandarin was known to have some compromise in its origins; it had absorbed features of the Altaic languages spoken by Mongols and Manchus, because of its proximity to the north, and hence was not a very pure form of Chinese. What it had on its side, however, was numbers. Since Mandarin prevailed as the target of standardization, the question of alternatives has been dropped.

In the 1950s language issues had practical as well as ideological and nationalistic consequences. China's new Communist regime had many real and important challenges, and one of its considerable concerns was literacy. Pre-1949 literacy has been assessed in different ways,[38] but all figures suggest that there was widespread rudimentary literacy but very little full literacy.[39] China's leaders had to address the issue of universal, compulsory education, in part because of concerns about modernization and international status. Language was one of the crucial items in this field.

A standard was chosen that continued the tradition begun under the preceding Nationalist regime: the language of northern China. This was to be called *Putonghua*, "common speech" (borrowing the term from Japanese).[40] The name was important. Other names suggest more limited usage. *Zhongguohua* is the language of China (Zhongguo)—but what about the other languages spoken in China? *Hanyu* is the language of the Han—but what about the other languages spoken by Han, and what about the non-Han who also speak it? Putonghua, by its very name makes clear that it is to serve as a lingua franca, no matter what other varieties continue to coexist with it. Others argue that it should be called *guoyu*, the national language, which would elevate its status to an official rather than merely widespread variety. During the Qing period, the language referred to as *guoyu*, the national language, was Manchu, whereas *guanhua*, the administrative lingua franca, was the language of Beijing.

A standard, *biaozhun*, pronunciation for Putonghua was defined in 1955. It was to be northern pronunciation without the peculiarities of the Beijing variety of northern Chinese. Much as New York English is identified in the popular imagination by its *r*-less quality, *biaozhun* Putonghua has a beautiful series of retroflex consonants (*zh, ch, sh*) that contrast with an alveolar series (*z, c, s*), in contrast to the local versions, especially in the south, with only the alveolars. Most speakers of Putonghua lack the northern contrasts, and virtually all Mandarin speakers outside the People's Republic also lack them. (Most of the topolectal differences in China's languages lie in consonants rather than in vowels as in the United States.) Still, the fact that most speakers could be understood did not mean there were no jokes made of the poor southerners who mixed up *laoshi* 'teacher' and *laoshu* 'rat', terming both *laosu*. This is also a matter of social class.

Education is to be conducted entirely in Putonghua—but one must recognize that like much propagandistic work in China, it is understood to be an ideal rather than an immediately attainable reality. Implementation of language policy is only one goal. The statement of the policy embodies a wish, but the reception depends on shared assumptions about how language functions. In China people know that local varieties are not stigmatized, so the unitary ideal will continue to coexist with multilingual reality.

The children who enter school in areas where Putonghua is not spoken must be taught it, which means that their teachers must speak it. Teacher training was thus one of the important foundations of this program. Teachers from northern, metropolitan areas might be reluctant to move to remote, poor, southern, or minority areas. Hence, a de facto compromise was reached. The teachers from their own areas might return home from teachers' colleges, and they would do their best to teach their students Putonghua. When I did fieldwork in southwestern China and asked students what languages their teachers actually spoke, most reported that at all levels, from elementary through university, their language teachers (Chinese teachers) used Putonghua, but most of their other teachers did not. My adviser Li Zhaotong, a linguist, told me that most classrooms in Kunming, including university classrooms, conduct their work in the local dialect rather than in Putonghua. (When I observed, I was usually assigned to the teachers who used primarily Mandarin. In fact, in an amusing contradiction, I was told at one school that they had me look at a particular class because if I went to another I would not understand the Kunming dialect. They were being thoughtful and considerate. The same person, on being asked what varieties are in use in the classrooms, reported that Putonghua was used in all classes.) An official in charge of language work in Yunnan told me proudly that one minority area had begun to succeed in attracting qualified teachers because they had decided to pay them well. Before this new approach, they had had very few teachers able to speak the national standard—and willing to go to this remote area.

China's Contemporary Linguistic Diversity

Despite the existence of a national standard language, China is still a vibrantly multilingual country. At least for languages historically related to Mandarin—local dialects and other Chinese languages—there is no stigma attached. Languages spoken by ethnic minorities, in contrast, are relatively more disdained.

In linguistic usage, "dialects" are usually taken to be mutually intelligible and "languages" mutually unintelligible. This apparently clear-cut distinction is, however, impossible to apply consistently. There are cases in which it is impossible to decide whether or not the forms are mutually intelligible, such as varieties of French and Italian. In some cases, there is asymmetry in mutual understanding: Swedes do not understand Danes, but Danes understand Swedes.

Languages such as Hindi and Urdu are linguistically essentially the same but belong to different nations, are written with different scripts, and are spoken by practitioners of different religions; they are regarded as separate and distinct. Sociolinguists prefer the term "linguistic variety," to avoid the task of deciding what is really a social and political question of identifying distinct languages.[41] Chinese has its own way of describing local varieties: *fangyan*, the language (*yan*) of a particular place ([*di*]*fang*). Victor Mair has proposed "topolect" as the translation, and this has recently been acknowledged by the *American Heritage Dictionary.*[42] Though China's linguistic diversity has been compared to Europe's, it is clear that the Chinese context does not include economic, political, and literary divisions corresponding to language. Despite lack of intelligibility of the Chinese varieties, they are *felt* as somehow sharing a language. The way they share a language is through being inconsequential. What has weight is writing, and there is only one variety of writing.

Local Varieties

Local varieties, such as that spoken in my field site of Kunming, capital of Yunnan Province in southwestern China, may vary considerably in pronunciation and vocabulary — and even grammar — from the standard. They have been little studied until recently, so actual knowledge of common people's, in contrast to educated people's, local speech is rudimentary and speculative.[43] Linguists can reconstruct histories for them and can show correspondences among tonal categories — using elicited word lists, usually of the regional standard — but speakers of the standard are often at a considerable disadvantage when they have to understand the local variants. It would be comparable to a speaker of Bostonian, upper-class English moving to rural Texas and speaking to working-class people, but more so. Some have compared the Mandarin varieties to English and German. People in China have always moved, just as all humans have migrated to a greater or lesser extent, with the understanding that higher social status brings with it the right to ask others to accommodate. At the same time, there is usually little stigma attached to local varieties, and a good deal of flexibility in understanding, so communication seems to be little hindered.[44]

A survey I conducted — subject to all the errors that reports, as opposed to observation, might yield — showed an astonishing richness of linguistic varieties in use in various settings. I was especially interested in the ways my respondents conceived linguistic varieties, so I did not present a neat set of choices but rather gave them a blank line. Of thirty-three students from Yunnan Province at

Yunnan University (in 1991), only one reported using Putonghua at home, though four said they used Putonghua "usually." Some respondents used the term *fang-yan* (topolect), some said they used Yunnanhua, the language of Yunnan, and others said they used Hanhua, the language of the Han, in contrast to the languages of ethnic minorities. All the others named either a place or an ethnic group, so there were responses such as "Wudinghua," the language of Wuding, or "Jianshuihua," the language of Jianshui, or "Bai hua," the language of the Bai people. Workers at a metal factory, whether from Kunming or Yunnan in general, used Putonghua only "in class" or "traveling," though one person said he or she used "local Putonghua" both usually and at home. Local Putonghua is a devalued approximation of Putonghua, scorned because it falls short of the standard.[45]

In another study, I asked listeners to respond to taped voices speaking a range of varieties, in a variant of the matched-guise test developed by Lambert and colleagues.[46] An overwhelming number found the affective characteristics of local varieties much higher, though the prestige of speakers speaking the national language, in its standard form, was greater. From the matched-guise test, I ascertained that people felt great solidarity and little stigma in speaking local varieties. As has been repeated throughout the world, tension between power and solidarity is revealed in attitudes toward nonstandard varieties: standard Mandarin might be recognized as the language of the educated class, but that does not make its speakers likely friends or family. People are drawn to speakers of their own varieties. Sociolinguists have often remarked on the solidarity, or covert prestige, that attaches to local varieties.

Other Chinese Languages

Chinese has often been divided into seven or eight distinct language groups: Mandarin, Yue, Wu, Hakka, Gan, Xiang, Minnan, and Minbei. Each of these has many varieties as well. Some version of Mandarin is the native language of perhaps 70 percent of China's residents, leaving 30 percent of 1.3 billion people, or 390 million, who have a different native variety. Indeed, according to one source, of the world's top twenty languages by number of native speakers, Mandarin was first, but Wu and Yue were also listed.[47] Each of these varieties has a regional standard along with other forms. In the case of the Yue dialects, for instance, spoken in the cities of Hong Kong and Canton and generally in the province of Guangdong, the language of Canton is often regarded as most prestigious.

I have already mentioned Southern Min, spoken in Fujian province and Taiwan. Hong Kong was largely populated by southern Chinese who spoke variants of Cantonese (Yue); under the British, success depended on the use of English. In contemporary Hong Kong, Putonghua is increasingly favored and required. Although most Chinese in Singapore were speakers of southern varieties, the official languages of Singapore were declared to be English and Mandarin. Multilingualism endures.

Mary Erbaugh writes that the southern dialects Cantonese and Hokkien (Taiwanese) have grown in power and prestige in the past decade because the economic and political power of the regions in which those varieties are spoken have as well—Hong Kong and Taiwan and the mainland areas facing them.[48] It was never the case that public officials were required or expected to speak the standard. National elections have never been held; if they were, I expect that standard Mandarin would provide only limited prestige. Solidarity among southerners would also prevail. Many of China's twentieth-century leaders have been southerners (Deng Xiaoping, Mao Zedong, Jiang Jieshi) who might give public addresses in very heavily accented and barely intelligible Mandarin, or even in their native dialects. But their linguistic affiliation is scarcely remarked.

Shanghaihua, or Shanghainese, has always had a certain cachet ("always" meaning in recent memory). The Wu dialects, of which it is the best-known exemplar, are considered beautiful and cultivated, with the greatest preference given to the language spoken by Suzhou's beautiful women.

What Y. R. Chao wrote in 1961 still obtains: "A command of Mandarin during the imperial days was regarded rather as a convenience than a matter of prestige and having a southern accent was more of an inconvenience than anything to be ashamed of."[49]

Minority Languages

China is not only multilingual; it is also multiethnic. Following an exercise at classification of the diverse peoples within its borders, the contemporary People's Republic recognizes fifty-five ethnic minorities as well as the majority group, termed the Han. These ethnic groups speak languages classified—not especially confidently—as belonging to at least six linguistic families: Sino-Tibetan (including Tibeto-Burman languages), Indo-European, Altaic, Mon-Khmer, Tai (Zhuang-Dong), and Hmong-Mien (Miao-Yao).[50] Unlike variation among Chinese topolects, these differences are seen as significant. They are recognized in the constitution and are giving rise to lingua-nationalism in places such as Xinjiang.

Minority languages have been especially targeted in policies that alternate between preservation and annihilation. The language of higher education is Putonghua, and there are few schools above the primary level that include the use of minority languages. The Minorities Institutes (Minzu Xueyuan)—institutions of higher education that study ethnic minorities and also train representatives of minority groups—do not use minority languages in their instruction. Publication and broadcasting in minority languages have ebbed and flowed in the fifty-odd years of the People's Republic. The stated goal, however, has always been the teaching of Putonghua, using whatever means are most effective.[51]

At present, most minorities who live in marginal areas but aspire to move to metropolitan areas attempt to learn Putonghua. Their accent, however, sometimes gives them away. While educated speakers of local varieties encounter little prejudice, anyone perceived to be a rural bumpkin faces quite a lot. The accents of minorities who attempt Putonghua are sometimes laughed at and scorned.

Many individuals are able to speak a number of varieties. A close friend who is a member of the Yi minority group in Yunnan speaks this variety as her native language, but she also loved school and studying and is quite happy to speak Putonghua. However, her Putonghua clearly falls short of the standard (this is called Mapu, or Street Putonghua). She also speaks the local version of Yunnan's Mandarin, which is different again from Putonghua. Finally, she learned English. She has a different name in each of these languages; and although it was evident that she identifies as a Yi from her village, she functions easily and comfortably in this great assortment of linguistic varieties. She has a somewhat more adventurous personality than some people yet is essentially a poor minority person from a remote village with a junior high school education. Her linguistic disposition is replicated millions of times in China.

Language, Power, and Identity

Language standardization and the relationship between language and power have been studied largely from two directions: in European languages the focus has been on competition between varieties, often as a surrogate for general struggles between the speakers of these varieties,[52] and in Asian languages the focus has been on policy. Here I have discussed attitudes toward and ideologies about linguistic difference, showing that in China there is no inevitable social advantage to possession of the standard in the same way as has become familiar in Anglo-European societies.

During the nearly three-century rule of the Manchus in China's last dynasty, nationalistic Chinese deplored the exclusion of Chinese from power. During the medieval period, poets claimed their own linguistic form as most like that of the ancients and hence most suitable for rhyming. Yet during the early years of the twentieth century, the need for a common national language — a spoken language — was suggested for the first time, as Chinese nationalism modeling itself on other nations such as Japan and Germany was born. But for all the autocratic power held by earlier Chinese regimes as well as by the current one, tolerance for linguistic diversity, and indeed full-fledged multilingualism, has been the rule. Policies that call for standardization nonetheless presuppose the endurance of linguistic diversity; political policies regarding language can be understood only if we have a greater sense of how linguistic diversity is understood in China. What we find is lack of concern for boundaries between varieties, as well as expectations that communication may prevail notwithstanding speakers speaking their own, different, varieties. Unlike in North America, the United Kingdom, and Europe, where most research on language variation has been carried out, the *fangyan* are not stigmatized. There is no overwhelming linguistic insecurity about *fangyan*, only about Mapu, the inferior form of attempted Putonghua. There are no language mavens. There is no railing against *fangyan*. Ethnic minorities are forced by the realities of the Chinese situation to abandon their native languages in favor of the dominant variety, but this is not done with a sense of betrayal of their native place but rather with a sense of the pull of the center. In interviews and conversations, students of minority background failed to understand my question, Do you feel you lose anything of your own culture when you function entirely in the majority language for your education? Incomprehension was consistent. There was no linguism.[53] Some of the policies regarding minority languages, especially Thai and Uighur, have been harsh and deliberately created to disrupt potential continuities with their literary and religious past as well as with similar peoples across international borders, but none of this is found in the Chinese spoken languages.

Still, though there is little political concern about topolects, people in private conversations may make fun of other Chinese dialects. Northern dialects are seen by southerners as stiff; southern dialects are seen as sly. But these are the makings of idle conversation, not movements or policies.

My basic thesis is that we may not assume that the idea of "language" is the same everywhere, or that the contests over language are always of the same degree of import. I have suggested that we think of a classification by means of which linguistic differences are celebrated in one set of cultures, deplored and testily fought in a second set of cultures, and taken in stride in a third set of cultures. The first set, rare and little documented, is boundary celebrating. The second set, usually taken for granted as the norm as they exist principally in Indo-European societies, including the United States, I have called boundary-disputing societies. They fight, often viciously, over which variety deserves dominance. The third set, often found in situations of diglossia as in Arabic-speaking and some other Asian societies, I have called boundary-shrugging societies. Taking for granted that all societies are to some but varying degree multilingual, however defined, we must still examine how people within them think of the varieties contained within and alongside them, how they think of prestige versus nonprestige varieties, and how they conceptualize the entities of language.

This helps to explain the lack of concern for local speech. The literary tradition is the focus of political and educational attention. All students who learn to read and write learn something about the national language, but it is what is technically called additive bilingualism or multilingualism. No one expects or even desires that the primary home variety will be replaced by knowledge of the standard.[54]

We well know all the struggles and contests played out by European nationalists, in what Steinberg calls the *questione della lingua*, meaning different things at different times but ultimately culminating in the question of "imposing uniformity of speech in order to make what had been a patchwork of peoples into a national community."[55] In Italy as recently as the 1860s it was not obvious which linguistic variety would predominate in a nation newly forming.

Nationalism in many places in the world is bound up with language. We cannot imagine German or French nationalism without the unification of the standard languages. In the past century or two, the separation of empire and nation has led to a feeling that nations, peoples, territories, cultures, and languages should overlap (Mazzini, Herder, and others). Anderson describes how this was worked out in the Americas, Europe, and Southeast Asia, as nationalism seemed to require a national language.[56] He explains the abandonment of local varieties of language, such as Javanese in favor of Indonesian, as political and economic but also as stemming from ideas within Javanese tradition. Such ideas are likely alive and well in many parts of Europe, as Jan Blommaert and Jef Verschueren point out.[57]

The Idea of a Standard

It is well known that languages derive their importance and power through the power of their speakers rather than from any intrinsic quality of the linguistic variety itself. Many works on language and power describe contests for legitimacy or survival among competing varieties, especially named entities called "languages." These are often life-and-death contests for the languages, and it is clear that the modern world is not kind to languages spoken by small numbers of people.[58]

Some of the contests we see involve issues of education, literacy, governmental recognition, and many other issues of practical as well as psychological and cultural concern. The claim is often made that speakers must be connected to the past of their society through maintenance of a particular variety. Irish is clung to for many reasons, but the literary tradition and the flavor of the world assessed through the language are among them.[59] In the United States advocates of bilingual education often insist that ties to the speakers' heritage will be lost, as well as a feeling of connection to that culture, if they are forced to function entirely in English. (Advocates of English-only have rather different arguments—a topic for another time.)

Disputes over standardization and the actual implementation of policies reflect deeply held ideas of what language is and how it varies; the prevalent view of language standardization and its victims derives primarily from European languages and their wars. A rather different notion of the stretch of standardization may be seen if we include consideration of other traditions. China provides a fruitful contrast.[60]

China's countervailing ideology of what linguistic varieties mean is a useful foil for our broader understanding of how standardization works. Linguistic diversity is not lamented or deplored with quite the fervor it is in the West. Though efforts have been made to promulgate a standard, along with the increasing national integration of China in the twentieth century, tolerance of linguistic diversity has been the rule in all but the most autocratic of KMT regimes. In fact, much of what we see in the West, whether in the varieties of standardization with academies and jealous guarding of the official line (as in France and Spain) or in the snobbishness of the middle class as it maintains its unique privilege in keeping the standard, stems from certain unique and peculiar notions of how language works. Many places in the world might better be understood if we examine the case of China, where ideas of the standard are limited, circumscribed, and not especially powerful.

Indeed, modern Chinese efforts to promote a national standard presuppose the continuation of multilingualism. Variation is and has ever been part of the Chinese linguistic scene. It is not to be deplored but rather understood. A standard has a role as a symbol of modern nationhood, especially in certain domains, most notably writing. Spoken language is not seen as significant or threatening, so most efforts to promote a standard ignore actual speech in everyday life. This is significant because of the lessons drawn about how language is conceptualized. In the United States and Europe spoken language, with its closer relationship to writing, is the target of standardization efforts. The linguistic tolerance of China also shows that political regimes may be autocratic in some domains yet remarkably lax in others.

Finally, this heuristic taxonomy of three approaches to the variety present in all languages may provide a scaffold for the comparative study of linguistic differences, in societies that contest linguistic dominance as well as in those that accept or even celebrate the coexistence of multiple varieties. Sorting out factors that accompany these approaches would be a worthwhile future project but would at minimum require consideration of population size, the relationship between script and spoken language, national and ethnic relations, and notions of verbal beauty. I find a kind of liberation, at least, in the knowledge that acceptance of linguistic diversity has characterized much of human life on earth. This says something about the nature of identity and heterogeneity that can be processed by creatures as complex as human beings.

NOTES

Some of the research for this chapter was supported by the Committee on Scholarly Communication with China, for which I am continually grateful. I would also like to thank Martin Bloomer for inviting me to participate in both the conference and this volume. My fellow contributors helped to sharpen my thinking—though shortcomings belong solely to me.

1. John Edwards, *Multilingualism.*

2. Michael Silverstein, "Monoglot 'Standard' in America: Standardization and Metaphors of Linguistic Hegemony."

3. This is true. My husband was on a university committee the main activity of which was releasing students from the modest three-semester language requirement, usually because of psychological or psychiatric tests showing their inability to learn a foreign language or the trauma caused by trying.

4. Ilakuvanar, quoted in Sumathi Ramaswamy, *Passions of the Tongue: Language Devotion in Tamil India, 1891–1970.*

5. Suzanne Romaine, *Language in Society: An Introduction to Sociolinguistics,* 9.

6. Ibid., 10. In discussing a tradition in which there was literacy but not necessarily standardization, I attempt to investigate the "classificatory procedures," or what Harold F. Schiffman, in his *Linguistic Culture and Language Policy,* means by "linguistic culture," and others by "language ideology" in China, tracing ideas about linguistic difference.

7. Ramaswamy, *Passions of the Tongue;* E. Valentine Daniel, *Charred Lullabies: Chapters in an Anthropography of Violence.*

8. Edwards, *Multilingualism,* 87–88, 134–36, 181–87; Jean A. Laponce, *Languages and Their Territories.*

9. Tony Crowley, *Standard English and the Politics of Language;* and Crowley, ed., *The Politics of Language in Ireland, 1366–1922: A Sourcebook.*

10. Edwards, *Multilingualism,* 137.

11. Nancy Bonvillain, *Language, Culture, and Communication: The Meaning of Messages,* 324.

12. James Crawford, ed., *Language Loyalties: A Source Book on the Official English Controversy;* Edwards, *Multilingualism,* 166–70.

13. Kathryn A. Woolard, *Double Talk: Bilingualism and the Politics of Ethnicity in Catalonia;* José del Valle, "Monoglossic Policies for a Heteroglossic Culture: Misinterpreted Multilingualism in Modern Galicia."

14. Edwards, *Multilingualism,* 156.

15. Isaiah Berlin has a very nuanced discussion of Herder's views about nationhood and its location in culture rather than "race" or blood. Though he believed in universalism to some degree, he opposed the French views on this, which essentially imposed the French language on all. See Berlin, *Vico and Herder: Two Studies in the History of Ideas.*

16. E. J. Hobsbawm, *Nations and Nationalism since 1780: Programme, Myth, Reality.*

17. Sun Yatsen, *The Three People's Principles: Zhongshan Quanshu,* 106–7.

18. Ernest Renan, "Qu'est-ce qu'une nation?" 17–18.

19. Prasenjit Duara, "Provincial Narratives of the Nation: Centralism and Federalism in Republican China."

20. Despite recognition that many people in Taiwan spoke Hokkien, many social scientists working in Taiwan have for decades employed Mandarin in their writing. Stephen O. Murray and Keelung Hong (*Taiwanese Culture, Taiwanese Society: A Critical Review of Social Science Research Done on Taiwan*) present a devastating critique of this body of work. Hong writes that when he began to read works on Taiwan, as a native: "It was very odd to see what are supposed to be native terms not in Holo [Taiwanese], the language of the people who use them, but in Beijinghua, the language of the people who dismiss our religion and customs. I know that when anthropologists write in English about groups numbering in the hundreds in Amazonia, they do not present native terms in Portuguese or in Spanish. Similarly, concepts from African tribes embedded in English texts are not translated into French or Afrikaans first. They are represented in the native language, not in the language of the government, even when—unlike Taiwan—

the language of the government is the language of the majority of the country's population" (4). Murray says bluntly, "I can think of nowhere other than Taiwan where the solution to writing 'native terms' has been to translate them into the language of the colonial government" (7).

21. See Jean DeBernardi, "Linguistic Nationalism: The Case of Southern Min."

22. 1982 Chinese constitution, Article 4, concerning equality of ethnic minorities, or nationalities (http://www.insidechina.com/constit/chcons02.php3). The Slovenian constitution says the following (Article 11): "The official language of Slovenia shall be Slovenian. In those areas where autochthonous Italian or Hungarian ethnic communities reside, the official language shall also be Italian or Hungarian" (http://www.uni-wuerzburg.de:80/law/si20000_.html). The Indian constitution, Part XVII, is on Official Language, with four subparts dealing with the details, down to provisions made for children whose mother tongue is not Hindi (http://alfa.nic.in/const/p17343.html). The writing system — since there are several options — is specified in the constitution as well. The French constitution, Title I, Article 2, says simply, "The language of the Republic is French" (http://www.chanrobles.com/france.htm). The Polish, Slovak, and Russian constitutions also specify the official or state language (http://www.uni-wuerzburg.de:80/law/pl00000_.html; http://www.uni-wuerzburg.de:80/law/lo00000_.html; http://www.chanrobles.com/russia.htm, Article 68), while the Czech, Hungarian, and Japanese constitutions say nothing about language (http%3a//www.uni%2dwuerzburg.de/law/ez00000%5f.html&pskip=&skip=10&se=0,0,0,1000&index=2; http://www.uni-wuerzburg.de:80/law/hu00000_.html; http://www.chanrobles.com/japan.htm).

23. This occurs as well in the Mexican constitution, which in many respects shows similarities with China in its explicit multiculturalism. See http://www.fortunecity.com/victorian/wooton/34/mexico/constitution.html.

24. Jay Dautcher, "Reading Out-of-Print: Popular Culture and Protest on China's Western Frontier"; Sara L. M. Davis, "Singers of Sipsongbanna: Folklore and Authenticity in Contemporary China."

25. S. Gopinathan, "Language Policy Changes, 1979–1997: Politics and Pedagogy"; Tan Su Hwi, "Theoretical Ideals and Ideologized Reality in Language Planning"; Xu Daming, Chew Cheng Hai, and Chen Songcen, "Language Use and Language Attitudes in the Singapore Chinese Community."

A recent study of language in Singapore shows that by a large margin, people reported that it was much easier to learn alternate forms of Chinese than to learn English, even though English had a degree of prestige (if not beauty) (Xu et al., "Language Use"). Singapore is quite different from China because of the inclusion of English in the repertoire of linguistic varieties. Xu et al. classify the languages of Singapore as "English, Mandarin, and Dialects" and say that they find "a clear trend of shifting from Dialects to English and Mandarin, although Dialects still dominate the home domain of language use" (139). Hugo Baetens Beardsmore, "Language Shift and Cultural Implications in Singapore," 92, questions a comparison between the situation of bilingual education in Wales and Singapore: "Bryam . . . warns that to live, a language needs an economic basis and that if the Welsh language has no market value it will in time decay, in spite of bilingual education. If Welsh is merely the language of the school and English the language of the screen, street and shop, then even the best bilingual programme cannot guarantee its survival. A parallel between the Welsh situation and that of Singapore can be drawn if one assumes, as some do, that the link between language and culture is central to the preservation of Asian cultural values. This link is not self-evident, however, since there may be other factors at play." Even if Singapore has different characteristics from China, some of the attitudes toward language are similar.

26. It might seem obvious, in looking for areas of linguistic awareness, to pursue works on literature, transnationalism, and nationalism. This would turn up a plethora of material in the case of Ireland, Quebec, India, and France, among many other places. Yet in the Chinese case little turns up. Either the scholars discussing these matters are uniquely oblivious to language questions or there is no evidence of concern to be found. One writer from Canton, Kong Jiesheng (the name is given in Mandarin), was said to use Cantonese expressions in his fiction—also reported in romanization for their Mandarin pronunciation (Laifong Leung, *Morning Sun: Interviews with Chinese Writers of the Lost Generation,* 65)—but that was the extent of the discussion. This might be akin to a regional American writer using local colorful idioms embedded in otherwise standard prose. Kong spent time on the then-remote island of Hainan but mentions nothing about linguistic difficulties or opportunities. Another interview, with Lu Tianming, a writer originally from Shanghai, discusses Lu's time in the border region on China's northwest, Xinjiang, and again has no mention of language, although food, economics, hygiene, and other differences are discussed.

There was little mention of language in the material on Chinese transnationalism that I examined. An entire book, *Transnational Chinese Cinemas: Identity, Nationhood, Gender* (edited by Sheldon Hsiao-peng Lu), disregards the topic of language, with a few exceptions. An article by Yingjin Zhang titled "From 'Minority Film' to 'Minority Discourse': Questions of Nationhood and Ethnicity in Chinese Cinema," in *Transnational Chinese Cinemas,* 81–104, did mention that some effort had been made to fight the hegemony of Mandarin-language films and their dominance over Cantonese-language films, but in subsequent discussions of nationalism and minority usage in the films, the actual linguistic variety employed in the films, the words spoken by minorities, were unnoticed. Another article, "Constructing a Nation: Taiwanese History and the Films of Hou Hsiao-hsien," by June Yip (139–68) makes much of the filmic techniques in Hou's film *City of Sadness* that privilege language over image, yet does not always specify which language was used. Yip gives both Taiwanese and Mandarin names for the film's characters, explaining in a footnote that the Taiwanese was derived from what she heard in the film. In one short section she discusses the "babel of mutually incomprehensible tongues—Japanese, Taiwanese, Cantonese, Mandarin, Shanghainese, and Hakka—spoken by the characters" (147). In another, she describes a radio broadcast "in Shanghai-accented Mandarin" (149) when the violent incident of February 28, 1947, is reported. Still, all the films' titles are reported in Mandarin.

Many overseas Chinese are speakers of southern varieties, especially Southern Min, Hakka, and Yue (Cantonese), as well as, increasingly, Mandarin. Yet the comfort people feel with linguistic difference is reflected in lack of reference to it. Aihwa Ong and Donald Nonini's *Ungrounded Empires: The Cultural Politics of Modern Chinese Transnationalism* contains ten important articles, plus an introduction and an afterword, on the global economic and political factors in the lives of people of Chinese descent—in contrast to prevailing essentialized views of unchanging "Chineseness"—yet language is mentioned only once in the introduction (Nonini and Ong, "Chinese Transnationalism as an Alternative Modernity"), and then only in a footnote (27 n. 2), to explain why all Chinese terms are cited in transliterated Mandarin, with the exception of the article by Carl A. Trocki ("Boundaries and Transgressions: Chinese Enterprise in Eighteenth- and Nineteenth-Century Southeast Asia," 61–85). He similarly discusses his use of topolectal terms in a footnote (82 n. 1). He does mention that the area around the southeastern provinces of Guangdong and Fujian "has one of the highest degrees of linguistic diversity in China" and that in "Singapore and Malaysia, it is common to speak of the 'five kinds of Chinese' as a generality" (64), but there the matter rests.

Prasenjit Duara, "Nationalists among Transnationals: Overseas Chinese and the Idea of China, 1900–1911" (39–60), suggests that diasporic Chinese often organized themselves in a variety of groupings, including linguistic ones (40) but does not elaborate. He states, "The establishment of a republican administration in China after 1911 and especially after 1927 deepened support for republicanism, particularly as a result of the proliferation of (Mandarin) Chinese schools across Southeast Asia" (54), but does not discuss what it might signify. He mentions "transnational communities pulled in multiple directions by foreign political authorities, dispersed economic networks, and English-language-based career possibilities for their children" (57). This would be an issue in many other contexts but seems casually accepted here.

A handful of other mentions of language can be found in that collection, including one longer meditation on Chinese Malaysians who contest the preeminence of Bahasa Malaysia for education (Nonini, "Shifting Identities, Positioned Imaginaries: Transnational Traversals and Reversals by Malaysian Chinese," 206–9). Most mentions of language in discussions of transnationalism are relegated to footnotes (other exceptions are a sentence or paragraph each in Christina Blanc Szanton, "The Thoroughly Modern 'Asian': Capital, Culture, and Nation in Thailand and the Philippines," 278–79; You-tien Hsing, "Building *Guanxi* across the Straits: Taiwanese Capital and Local Chinese Bureaucrats," 156–57; Xin Liu, "Space, Mobility, and Flexibility: Chinese Villagers and Scholars Negotiate Power at Home and Abroad," 91; Mayfair Mei-hui Yang, "Mass Media and Transnational Subjectivity in Shanghai: Notes on (Re)Cosmopolitanism in a Chinese Metropolis," 301).

27. Jerry Norman, *Chinese,* follows most Chinese scholars since Li Fanggui proposed these divisions in 1937. See Li Fang Kuei [Fanggui], "Languages and Dialects," *Chinese Year Book 59–65;* and Zhou Youguang, *Zhongguo Yuwende Shidai Yanjin (The Evolution of China's Language),* 9–10. John DeFrancis, in *The Chinese Language: Fact and Fantasy,* identifies eight varieties. The difference lies in whether Southern and Northern Min are considered separate or unitary. See also Zhang Kun, "Hanyu Fangyan de Fenlei (Classification of Chinese Topolects)," in *Zhongguo Jingnei Yuyan ji Yuyanxue, I. Hanyu Fangyan (Chinese*

Languages and Linguistics, I. Chinese Topolects), 1–21, for discussion of the complexities of classification.

28. Norman, *Chinese,* 5.

29. Ideologies are discussed, e.g., in Bambi B. Schieffelin, Kathryn A. Woolard, and Paul V. Kroskrity, eds., *Language Ideologies: Practice and Theory,* 189–210. I suggest the use of the idea of linguistic kinds, on analogy to that of human kinds, or natural kinds. At issue here is the matter of how "natives" conceptualize the components of their world in given domains. A prominent line of thinking in cognitive science and psychology suggests that many domains are innate, part of the biologically given structure of the mind. I strongly question this biological deterministic view and see much of what passes as "science" as merely confirmation of the researchers' own assumptions, derived from the categories of their own society. See, e.g., Emile Benveniste, "Categories of Thought and Language," in *Problems in General Linguistics,* 55–64; R. C. Lewontin, Steven Rose, and Leon J. Kamin, *Not in Our Genes: Biology, Ideology, and Human Nature;* and Susan D. Blum, *Portraits of "Primitives": Ordering Human Kinds in the Chinese Nation.*

30. It is discussed with confidence in Zhang Yuquan, ed., *Yuwen Xiandaihua Gailun (On Linguistic Modernization),* 26, as originating in the Ming and Qing periods (1368–1644, 1644–1911), but some of this strikes me as overly clear-cut. See Tan Su Hwi, "Theoretical Ideals and Ideologized Reality in Language Planning" for a discussion of "ideologized reality."

31. Zhang Yuquan, *Yuwen Xiandaihua Gailun,* 22; and Zhou Youguang, *Zhongguo Yuwende Shidai Yanjin,* 2–3.

32. Charles A. Ferguson, "Diglossia."

33. Asma Afsaruddin, pers.com.

34. See, e.g., Zhou Youguang, *Zhongguo Yuwende Shidai Yanjin.*

35. Benedict Anderson, *Language and Power: Exploring Political Cultures in Indonesia;* Joshua A. Fishman, Charles A. Ferguson, and Jyotirindra Das Gupta, eds., *Language Problems of Developing Nations;* John Earl Joseph, *Eloquence and Power: The Rise of Language Standards and Standard Languages;* Crowley, *Standard English;* Schiffman, *Linguistic Culture.*

36. The practice of simplifying characters and making them simpler to write often makes them harder to read because they are then more similar to one another. There is also the danger of cutting off earlier Chinese writing from the contemporary people; but during the 1950s when this strategy was solidified, this was regarded as beneficial in the construction of a new China. In Hong Kong and Taiwan, where the Chinese literary past was more carefully guarded, the traditional characters were also preserved.

37. See, e.g., DeFrancis, *Nationalism and Language Reform in China;* Guojia Yuyan Wenzi Gongzuo Weiyuanhui Bangongshi, comp. [Office of the National Language and Writing Committee], *Wenzi Gaige he Xiandai Hanyu Guifanhua (Script Reform and Standardization of Contemporary Chinese);* Paul Kratochvíl, *The Chinese Language Today: Features of an Emerging Standard;* Winifred P. Lehmann, ed., *Language and Linguistics in the People's Republic of China;* Norman, *Chinese;* S. Robert Ramsey, *The Languages of China;* Zhang Yuquan, *Yuwen Xiandaihua Gailun;* Zhou Youguang, *Zhongguo Yuwende Shidai Yan-*

jin; Chu Yu-kuang, in collaboration with Koji Nishimoto, *A Comparative Study of Language Reforms in China and Japan;* and Paul L.-M. Serruys, *Survey of the Chinese Language Reform and the Anti-Illiteracy Movement in Communist China.*

38. Evelyn Sakakida Rawski, *Education and Popular Literacy in Ch'ing China;* or James Hayes, "Specialists and Written Materials in the Village World."

39. DeFrancis, *The Chinese Language,* especially takes all these estimates to task, based on his view of what writing is and how little a person knowing only five hundred characters could actually write. This is related to his claim that it would be best to eliminate the traditional script and replace it with romanization.

40. Zhang Yuquan, *Yuwen Xiandaihua Gailun,* 25.

41. Romaine, *Language in Society,* 1–31.

42. Victor H. Mair, "What Is a Chinese 'Dialect/Topolect'?"; *American Heritage Dictionary of the English Language.*

43. The Yuen Ren Society, a collection of formal linguists inspired by the late Chao Yuen Ren and led by David Prager Branner, is devoted to description and analysis of the lesser-known varieties of Chinese. See, e.g., Y. R. Chao, "Languages and Dialects in China." See also the Web site of the Yuen Ren Society, http://www.geocities.com/Athens/Forum/8351/.

44. This is not always the case. A woman in Kunming, who had moved thirty years earlier from Northeast China, claimed to know nothing of the local dialect. She is a university professor and hence can occupy the superior position of forcing her interlocutors to accommodate to her variety.

45. See Blum, *Portraits of "Primitives,"* 31–36, for more details.

46. Wallace Lambert, R. C. Hodgson, R. C. Gardner, and S. Fillenbaum, "Evaluational Reactions to Spoken Languages."

47. Terralingua, http://www.sil.org/ethnologue/top100.html, accessed April 9, 2001.

48. Mary S. Erbaugh, "Southern Chinese Dialects as a Medium for Reconciliation within Greater China."

49. Chao, "What Is Correct Chinese?" 73.

50. See Ramsey, *The Languages of China,* 230–91.

51. For a dazzling discussion of the realities of multilingualism in a single ethnic group, the Yi, see David Bradley, "Language Policy for the Yi."

52. See Joseph, *Eloquence and Power.*

53. Martin Schoenhals found the same thing when he probed for evidence of linguistic identification and did not find it. See his "Education and Ethnicity among the Liangshan Yi."

54. It is not necessarily the case that there is no language shift occurring. Some young people are replacing local varieties with a prestigious form of language—perhaps the regional standard—but I do not think this entails a complete convergence to monolingualism. Silverstein, "Monoglot 'Standard,'" writes of ideas of a standard stemming from a "culture of monoglot standardization" (1)—something that I think cannot be found in China.

55. Jonathan Steinberg, "The Historian and the *Questione della Lingua*," 204.

56. Benedict Anderson, *Imagined Communities: Reflections on the Origin and Spread of Nationalism;* and his *Language and Power.*

57. Jan Blommaert and Jef Verschueren, "The Role of Language in European Nationalist Ideologies."

58. See, e.g., Nancy Dorian, *Language Death;* and Daniel Nettle and Suzanne Romaine, *Vanishing Voices.*

59. See, e.g., Crowley, *Politics of Language.*

60. Even in the same language, English, different ideologies of standard may hold. See Lesley Milroy, "Britain and the United States: Two Nations Divided by the Same Language (and Different Language Ideologies)."

BIBLIOGRAPHY

American Heritage Dictionary of the English Language. 4th ed. Boston: Houghton Mifflin, 2000.

Anderson, Benedict. *Imagined Communities: Reflections on the Origin and Spread of Nationalism.* Rev. ed. London: Verso, [1982] 1991.

————. *Language and Power: Exploring Political Cultures in Indonesia.* Ithaca: Cornell University Press, 1990.

Beardsmore, Hugo Baetens. "Language Shift and Cultural Implications in Singapore." In *Language, Society and Education in Singapore: Issues and Trends,* 2d ed., edited by S. Gopinathan, Anne Pakir, Ho Wah Kam, and Vanithamani Saravanan, 85–98. Singapore: Times Academic Press, 1998.

Benveniste, Emile. "Categories of Thought and Language." In *Problems in General Linguistics,* translated by Mary Elizabeth Meek, 55–64. Coral Gables, Fla.: University of Miami Press, [1958] 1971.

Berlin, Isaiah. *Vico and Herder: Two Studies in the History of Ideas.* New York: Vintage, 1976.

Blanc Szanton, Christina. "The Thoroughly Modern 'Asian': Capital, Culture, and Nation in Thailand and the Philippines." In *Ungrounded Empires: The Cultural Politics of Modern Chinese Transnationalism,* edited by Aihwa Ong and Donald Nonini, 261–86. New York: Routledge, 1997.

Blommaert, Jan, and Jef Verschueren. "The Role of Language in European Nationalist Ideologies." In *Language Ideologies: Practice and Theory,* edited by Bambi B. Schieffelin, Kathryn A. Woolard, and Paul V. Kroskrity, 189–210. New York: Oxford University Press, 1998.

Blum, Susan D. *Portraits of "Primitives": Ordering Human Kinds in the Chinese Nation.* Lanham, Md.: Rowman & Littlefield, 2001.

Bonvillain, Nancy. *Language, Culture, and Communication: The Meaning of Messages,* 4th ed. Upper Saddle River, N.J.: Prentice Hall, 2003.

Bradley, David. "Language Policy for the Yi." In *Perspectives on the Yi of Southwest China,* edited by Stevan Harrell, 195–213. Berkeley: University of California Press, 2001.

Chao, Y. R. "Languages and Dialects in China." In *Aspects of Chinese Sociolinguistics: Essays by Yuen Ren Chao,* selected and introduced by Anwar S. Dil, 21–25. Stanford: Stanford University Press, 1976.

———. "What Is Correct Chinese?" In *Aspects of Chinese Sociolinguistics: Essays by Yuen Ren Chao,* selected and introduced by Anwar S. Dil, 72–83. Stanford: Stanford University Press, 1976.

Chu Yu-kuang, in collaboration with Koji Nishimoto. *A Comparative Study of Language Reforms in China and Japan.* Saratoga Springs, N.Y.: Skidmore College Faculty Research Lecture, 1969.

Crawford, James, ed. *Language Loyalties: A Source Book on the Official English Controversy.* Chicago: University of Chicago Press, 1992.

Crowley, Tony. *Standard English and the Politics of Language.* Urbana: University of Illinois Press, 1989.

———, ed. *The Politics of Language in Ireland, 1366–1922: A Sourcebook.* London: Routledge, 2000.

Daniel, E. Valentine. *Charred Lullabies: Chapters in an Anthropography of Violence.* Princeton: Princeton University Press, 1996.

Dautcher, Jay. "Reading Out-of-Print: Popular Culture and Protest on China's Western Frontier." In *China beyond the Headlines,* edited by Timothy B. Weston and Lionel M. Jensen, 273–94. Lanham, Md.: Rowman & Littlefield, 2000.

Davis, Sara L. M. "Singers of Sipsongbanna: Folklore and Authenticity in Contemporary China." Ph.D. dissertation, University of Pennsylvania, 1999.

DeBernardi, Jean. "Linguistic Nationalism: The Case of Southern Min." *Sino-Platonic Papers,* no. 25. (Philadelphia, 1991).

DeFrancis, John. *The Chinese Language: Fact and Fantasy.* Honolulu: University of Hawai'i Press, 1984.

———. *Nationalism and Language Reform in China.* Princeton: Princeton University Press, 1950.

del Valle, José. "Monoglossic Policies for a Heteroglossic Culture: Misinterpreted Multilingualism in Modern Galicia." *Language & Communication* 20 (2000): 105–32.

Dorian, Nancy. *Language Death: The Life Cycle of a Scottish Gaelic Dialect.* Philadelphia: University of Pennsylvania Press, 1981.

Duara, Prasenjit. "Nationalists among Transnationals: Overseas Chinese and the Idea of China, 1900–1911." In *Ungrounded Empires: The Cultural Politics of Modern Chinese Transnationalism,* edited by Aihwa Ong and Donald Nonini, 39–60. New York: Routledge, 1997.

———. "Provincial Narratives of the Nation: Centralism and Federalism in Republican China." In *Cultural Nationalism in East Asia: Representation and Identity,* edited by Harumi Befu, 9–35. Berkeley: Institute of East Asian Studies, University of California, 1993.

Edwards, John. *Multilingualism.* Harmondsworth: Penguin, 1994.

Erbaugh, Mary S. "Southern Chinese Dialects as a Medium for Reconciliation within Greater China." *Language in Society* 24 (1995): 79–94.

Ferguson, Charles A. "Diglossia." *Word* 15 (1959): 325–40.

Fishman, Joshua A., Charles A. Ferguson, and Jyotirindra Das Gupta, eds. *Language Problems of Developing Nations.* New York: Wiley, 1968.

Geertz, Clifford. "The Integrative Revolution: Primordial Sentiments and Civil Politics in the New States." In *Old Societies and New States: The Quest for Modernity in Asia and Africa,* edited by Clifford Geertz, 105–57. New York: Free Press, 1963.

Gopinathan, S. "Language Policy Changes, 1979–1997: Politics and Pedagogy." In *Language, Society and Education in Singapore: Issues and Trends,* 2d ed., edited by S. Gopinathan, Anne Pakir, Ho Wah Kam, and Vanithamani Saravanan, 19–44. Singapore: Times Academic Press, 1998.

Guojia Yuyan Wenzi Gongzuo Weiyuanhui Bangongshi, comp. [Office of the National Language and Writing Committee]. *Wenzi Gaige he Xiandai Hanyu Guifanhua* (Script Reform and Standardization of Contemporary Chinese). Beijing: Yuwen Chubanshe, 1996.

Hayes, James. "Specialists and Written Materials in the Village World." In *Popular Culture in Late Imperial China,* edited by David Johnson, Andrew J. Nathan, and Evelyn S. Rawski, 75–111. Berkeley: University of California Press, 1985.

Hobsbawm, E. J. *Nations and Nationalism since 1780: Programme, Myth, Reality.* Cambridge: Cambridge University Press, 1992.

Hsing, You-tien. "Building *Guanxi* across the Straits: Taiwanese Capital and Local Chinese Bureaucrats." In *Ungrounded Empires: The Cultural Politics of Modern Chinese Transnationalism,* edited by Aihwa Ong and Donald Nonini, 143–64. New York: Routledge, 1997.

Joseph, John Earl. *Eloquence and Power: The Rise of Language Standards and Standard Languages.* New York: Basil Blackwell, 1987.

Kratochvíl, Paul. *The Chinese Language Today: Features of an Emerging Standard.* London: Hutchinson University Library, 1968.

Lambert, Wallace, R. C. Hodgson, R. C. Gardner, and S. Fillenbaum. "Evaluational Reactions to Spoken Languages." In *Language, Psychology, and Culture: Essays by Wallace E. Lambert,* 80–96. Stanford: Stanford University Press, 1972. Originally published in *Journal of Abnormal and Social Psychology* 60.1 (1960): 44–51.

Laponce, Jean A. *Languages and Their Territories.* Translated by Anthony Martin-Sperry. Toronto: University of Toronto Press, 1987.

Lehmann, Winifred P., ed. *Language and Linguistics in the People's Republic of China.* Austin: University of Texas Press, 1975.

Leung, Laifong. *Morning Sun: Interviews with Chinese Writers of the Lost Generation.* Armonk, N.Y.: M. E. Sharpe, 1994.

Lewontin, R. C., Steven Rose, and Leon J. Kamin. *Not in Our Genes: Biology, Ideology, and Human Nature.* New York: Pantheon, 1985.

Li Fang Kuei [Fanggui]. "Languages and Dialects." In *Chinese Year Book,* 59–65. Shanghai: Shangwu Yinshuguan, 1937.

Liu, Xin. "Space, Mobility, and Flexibility: Chinese Villagers and Scholars Negotiate Power at Home and Abroad." In *Ungrounded Empires: The Cultural Politics of Modern Chinese*

Transnationalism, edited by Aihwa Ong and Donald Nonini, 91–114. New York: Routledge, 1997.

Lu, Sheldon Hsiao-peng. *Transnational Chinese Cinemas: Identity, Nationhood, Gender.* Honolulu: University of Hawai'i Press, 1997.

Mair, Victor H. "What Is a Chinese 'Dialect / Topolect'? Reflections on Some Key Sino-English Linguistic Terms." *Sino-Platonic Papers,* no. 29. Philadelphia, 1991.

Milroy, Lesley. "Britain and the United States: Two Nations Divided by the Same Language (and Different Language Ideologies)." *Journal of Linguistic Anthropology* 10 (2000): 56–89.

Murray, Stephen O., and Keelung Hong. *Taiwanese Culture, Taiwanese Society: A Critical Review of Social Science Research Done on Taiwan.* Lanham, Md.: University Press of America, 1994.

Nettle, Daniel, and Suzanne Romaine. *Vanishing Voices: The Extinction of the World's Languages.* Oxford: Oxford University Press, 2000.

Nonini, Donald M. "Shifting Identities, Positioned Imaginaries: Transnational Traversals and Reversals by Malaysian Chinese." In *Ungrounded Empires: The Cultural Politics of Modern Chinese Transnationalism,* edited by Aihwa Ong and Donald Nonini, 203–27. New York: Routledge, 1997.

Nonini, Donald M., and Aihwa Ong. "Chinese Transnationalism as an Alternative Modernity." In *Ungrounded Empires: The Cultural Politics of Modern Chinese Transnationalism,* edited by Aihwa Ong and Donald Nonini, 3–33. New York: Routledge, 1997.

Norman, Jerry. *Chinese.* Cambridge: Cambridge University Press, 1988.

Ong, Aihwa, and Donald Nonini, eds. *Ungrounded Empires: The Cultural Politics of Modern Chinese Transnationalism.* New York: Routledge, 1997.

Ramaswamy, Sumathi. *Passions of the Tongue: Language Devotion in Tamil India, 1891–1970.* Berkeley: University of California Press, 1997.

Ramsey, S. Robert. *The Languages of China.* Princeton: Princeton University Press, 1987.

Rawski, Evelyn Sakakida. *Education and Popular Literacy in Ch'ing China.* Ann Arbor: University of Michigan Press, 1979.

Renan, Ernest. "Qu'est-ce qu'une nation?" (1882). Reprinted in *Nationalism,* edited by John Hutchinson and Anthony D. Smith, 17–18. Oxford: Oxford University Press, 1994.

Romaine, Suzanne. *Language in Society: An Introduction to Sociolinguistics.* 2d ed. Oxford: Oxford University Press, 2000.

Schieffelin, Bambi B., Kathryn A. Woolard, and Paul V. Kroskrity, eds. *Language Ideologies: Practice and Theory.* New York: Oxford University Press, 1998.

Schiffman, Harold F. *Linguistic Culture and Language Policy.* London: Routledge, 1996.

Schoenhals, Martin. "Education and Ethnicity among the Liangshan Yi." In *Perspectives on the Yi of Southwest China,* edited by Stevan Harrell, 238–55. Berkeley: University of California Press, 2001.

Serruys, Paul L.-M. *Survey of the Chinese Language Reform and the Anti-Illiteracy Movement in Communist China.* Berkeley: Center for Chinese Studies, 1962.

Silverstein, Michael. "Monoglot 'Standard' in America: Standardization and Metaphors of Linguistic Hegemony." *Working Papers and Proceedings of the Center for Psychosocial*

Studies. Chicago, 1987. Reprinted in *The Matrix of Language: Contemporary Linguistic Anthropology,* edited by Donald Brenneis and Ronald K. S. Macaulay, 284–306. Boulder, Colo.: Westview Press, 1996.

Steinberg, Jonathan. "The Historian and the *Questione della Lingua.*" In *The Social History of Language,* edited by Peter Burke and Roy Porter, 198–209. Cambridge: Cambridge University Press, 1987.

Sun Yatsen. *The Three People's Principles: Zhongshan Quanshu,* I, 4–5. Lecture I, excerpted in *Sources of Chinese Tradition,* Vol. 2, compiled by William Theodore de Bary, Wing-tsit Chan, and Chester Tan, 106–7. New York: Columbia University Press, [1960] 1964.

Tan Su Hwi. "Theoretical Ideals and Ideologized Reality in Language Planning." In *Language, Society and Education in Singapore: Issues and Trends,* 2d ed., edited by S. Gopinathan, Anne Pakir, Ho Wah Kam, and Vanithamani Saravanan, 45–64. Singapore: Times Academic Press, 1998.

Trocki, Carl A. "Boundaries and Transgressions: Chinese Enterprise in Eighteenth- and Nineteenth-Century Southeast Asia." In *Ungrounded Empires: The Cultural Politics of Modern Chinese Transnationalism,* edited by Aihwa Ong and Donald Nonini, 61–85. New York: Routledge, 1997.

Woolard, Kathryn A. *Double Talk: Bilingualism and the Politics of Ethnicity in Catalonia.* Stanford: Stanford University Press, 1985.

Xu Daming, Chew Cheng Hai, and Chen Songcen. "Language Use and Language Attitudes in the Singapore Chinese Community." In *Language, Society and Education in Singapore: Issues and Trends,* 2d ed., edited by S. Gopinathan, Anne Pakir, Ho Wah Kam, and Vanithamani Saravanan, 133–54. Singapore: Times Academic Press, 1998.

Yang, Mayfair Mei-hui. "Mass Media and Transnational Subjectivity in Shanghai: Notes on (Re)Cosmopolitanism in a Chinese Metropolis." In *Ungrounded Empires: The Cultural Politics of Modern Chinese Transnationalism,* edited by Aihwa Ong and Donald Nonini, 287–319. New York: Routledge, 1997.

Yip, June. "Constructing a Nation: Taiwanese History and the Films of Hou Hsiao-hsien." In *Transnational Chinese Cinemas: Identity, Nationhood, Gender,* edited by Sheldon Hsiao-peng Lu, 139–68. Honolulu: University of Hawai'i Press, 1997.

Zhang Kun. "Hanyu Fangyan de Fenlei (Classification of Chinese Topolects)." In *Zhongguo Jingnei Yuyan ji Yuyanxue, I. Hanyu Fangyan* (Chinese Languages and Linguistics, I. Chinese Topolects), 1–21. Taipei: Academia Sinica, 1992.

Zhang, Yingjin. "From 'Minority Film' to 'Minority Discourse': Questions of Nationhood and Ethnicity in Chinese Cinema." In *Transnational Chinese Cinemas: Identity, Nationhood, Gender,* edited by Sheldon Hsiao-peng Lu, 81–104. Honolulu: University of Hawai'i Press, 1997.

Zhang Yuquan, ed. *Yuwen Xiandaihua Gailun* (On Linguistic Modernization). Beijing: Shoudu Shifan Daxue chubanshe, 1995.

Zhou Youguang, ed. *Zhongguo Yuwende Shidai Yanjin* (The Evolution of China's Language). Beijing: Qinghua Daxue chubanshe, 1997.

7 Whose Language Is It Anyway?

The Irish and the English Language

TONY CROWLEY

In *Topographia Hibernica* (1188) Giraldus Cambrensis (Gerald of Wales) (1146–1223) described the Irish as "so barbarous that they cannot be said to have any culture." "A wild and inhospitable people" who "live like beasts," they are, he said, "devoted to laziness," barbarian (though "incomparably skilled" in music), treacherous, and vicious. Their coronation ritual, outlined in detail by Giraldus, stood as a cipher of their civilization: the king copulates with a white mare, which is then slaughtered and boiled; the king bathes in that water, and he and his people eat the horseflesh and drink the broth. "When this unrighteous rite has been carried out," Giraldus informed his readership, "his kingship and dominion have been conferred" (Giraldus Cambrensis 1982: 110). The *Topographia* was an influential account, greatly resented by later native historians, and marked the beginning of a long tradition of colonial observation of Ireland. The range and depth of the prejudice of that tradition has been revealed over the past twenty years or so: from the description of the Irish made by Edmund Spenser (1552–99) that they suffered from ignorance "in matters of learning and deep judgment" to Victorian *Punch*'s simian cartoons of the Irish and the "thick paddy" jokes of recent times, the profundity of anti-Irish sentiment in British culture has been demonstrated.[1] One aspect of this part of the colonizing and decolonizing process, of which we have also recently been made aware, is the complex of attitudes of the colonizers towards the Gaelic language of the native inhabitants of Ireland. Henry the Eighth's *Act for the English Order, Habit, and Language* (1537), for example, blamed Gaelic, among other cultural factors, for keeping "many of [the king's] subjects of this his said land, in a certain savage and wild kind and manner of living" (*Stat. Ire.* 1786: 28 H8. c.xv). A little later the Tudor Chronicles took on many of the details of the account of Irish history given by Giraldus but added their own specifics with regard to the indigenous language. Edmund Campion's *Historie of Ireland* (1571) described Irish as being "sharp and sententious," a language that "offereth great occasion to quick apothegms and proper allusions" (Campion [1571] 1633: 12). And in his *Treatise Containing a Plain and Perfect Description of Ireland* (1577), Richard Stanihurst (1547–1618) reported on a woman at Rome who was possessed. She babbled and could speak any language except Irish; the reason, he observed, is that "it was so difficult, as the very devil was gravelled therewith" (Stanihurst [1577] 1587: 7). This set the tone for later attitudes: though often the subject of curiosity, and sometimes supported for proselytizing purposes, Gaelic was commonly seen as the language of a heathen, barbarian population in need of civilization. In the early eighteenth century, the Reverend E. Nicolson, in a letter to the Society for Promoting Christian Knowledge, described Irish as a "barbarous language (so intimately fraught with cursing and swearing and all vile profaneness)." Popery and "the superstition of their language," he said, will "but keep up the distinction of [the Irish] people from ours" and prevent the creation of "one people and of one religion, which would have but one language" (*Analecta Hibernica* 1931: 27). This gradually became the dominant view: to consolidate and guarantee colonial rule Ireland would have to be Anglicized. Among other things, it was asserted, the Irish needed the English language (though of course this might be more accurately phrased: the colonizers wanted the Irish to need the English language).

Yet if we have started to gain an understanding of the viewpoint of the linguistic colonizers, what of those who were the subjects of this process? What did the Irish make of the attempt to impose a new language on them? What in short were Irish attitudes to the colonial language? Was there a sustained wholescale rejection? Was there organized resistance? Did they accept such a change? Did they welcome it even? Did they have pragmatic views of the issue? Were "they" to be distinguished in their attitudes with regard to social status, gender, geographic location? Did the question develop and change over time? It is my contention here that we do not as yet know the answer to these questions and that we should, since this is a significant gap in our understanding of the colonizing and decolonizing process in Ireland. It is also potentially revealing with regard to the contestation of languages in a wider context. It is therefore the aim of this essay to begin, necessarily briefly and sketchily, to examine some of the evidence and to suggest answers to some of the questions posed.

It may be useful to start at the end, so to speak, with an essay by Seamus Heaney from the mid-1970s. In "The Interesting Case of John Alphonsus Mulrennan" Heaney refers to "the breaking point of Gaelic civilisation" and notes that whether the moment of that rupture be identified as the Battle of Kinsale (1601), or the Flight of the Earls (1607), or the defeat of Jacobitism (1691) and the migration of the Wild Geese, the effect was catastrophic. "There is no doubt," he asserts, "that the social, cultural and linguistic life of the country [was] radically altered" at that point and that the change was psychologically damaging: "the alteration is felt by the majority of Irish people as a kind of loss, an exile from an original, whole and good place or state" (Heaney 1978: 35). The sense of loss and the radical psychological hurt that come from colonial imposition and dispossession are not to be underestimated, and expressions of that feeling are cited later. But it is worth commenting in passing on the romanticized way in which Heaney presents this process. It is a manner typical of cultural nationalist movements, be they Irish, English, German, Italian, Hungarian, or Kenyan: a sense of nostalgia for a past golden age, a feeling of removal from origins "whole and good." In response to which, one question, an important question, must be asked: when was this Ireland, this England, this Germany, this Italy, this Hungary, this Kenya?

Heaney's standpoint in the essay leads him to a particular view of the English language in England, its speakers, and Englishness. With an implicit reference to Joyce, Heaney argues that "words like 'ale' and 'manor' and 'sheepfold' and 'pew' and 'soldier' have a charge of fidelity and implication for an English person that is indigenous and uncontested and almost imperturbable. They are to an extent exclusive words. All of us whose language is English are familiar with them, but unless we are English by birth and nurture, I suspect that these words and words like them do not possess us and we do not possess them fully" (1978: 35). This alienation from a language that had been a colonial imposition is a reminder to us of Joyce's *Portrait,* in which English is described as at once "so familiar and so foreign" by the young Stephen Dedalus. Heaney ascribes this feeling to the impact of colonial history, which has "rent the fabric of Irish life" and "effected a breach between its past and its present, and an alienation between the speaker and his speech." He contrasts this with the situation in England, where "history . . . has woven the fabric of English life and landscape and language into a seamless garment" (Heaney 1978: 35). Again it is possible to agree with this statement of the cultural and psychological damage produced by colonialism; but there are other things to say. It is possible to begin simply by raising the question of whether Heaney's view of the English language and Englishness is accurate, or whether in fact it is a simplified, romanticized, and conservative view. Whether in reality "*the* English language" was ever such a vehicle for the transmission of a continuous and assured Englishness. Or whether English in fact was always riven by the marks of internal difference, social, cultural, political; to use Bakhtin's term, whether English was a heteroglot language, always escaping the grasp of those who would make it serve a narrow and exclusive definition of Englishness. Whether, that is to say, the English language itself was open to contestation from within. Was the delineation of a particular form of the language in the Renaissance period, that spoken by the elite of the court and the powerful, as the privileged and best form of the language, a definition of the linguistic and cultural inclusiveness which resembles that given in Heaney's account? Or was the emergence of the idea of a spoken form of the language—Standard spoken English—and the accent that went along with it—Received Pronunciation—as the language of the civilized and educated in the late nineteenth and early twentieth century—was that not a cause of alienation between some English speakers and their speech?[2] And what might the words "ale," "manor," "sheepfold," "pew," and "soldier" mean, for example, to someone born into working-class Liverpool in the 1960s. As someone who falls into that category, if it is permissible to write personally for a moment, those words do not feel indigenous, uncontested, imperturbable; they sound exclusive to me, and whatever it might mean to possess a word fully, I don't feel that I have these words secure. This is asserted not so much to pick an argument with Seamus Heaney but simply to raise a problem that is at least worth noting: Irish cultural nationalist attitudes towards the English and their language can be dangerously oversimplified. The history, for better or worse, is much more complex and difficult.

The story of the English language in Ireland is often made much less complex than it should be, and a couple of examples can demonstrate the point. Spenser's famous comment in *A View of the Present State of Ireland* (1596) that "it hath ever beene the use of the Conquerour, to despise the language of the conquered, and to force him by all meanes to learne his" (1633: 47) is often cited as a summary of colonial language policy. An early example of such policy is contained in Henry VIII's "Address to the Town of Galway" in 1536 in which he ordered "that every inhabitant within the said town endeavour themselves to speak English, and to use themselves after the English fashion" and "do put forth your child to school, to learn to speak English" (Crowley 2000: 20). Yet though Spenser's assertion describes the policy that was carried out in many colonial situations and though it partly accounts for English practice in Ireland, Spenser's claim is ironic in its historical context. For in linguistic terms what Spenser described in his text was not a successful policy of linguistic imposition, contempt for a native language and its displacement by the language of the conquerors, but exactly the opposite. What Spenser detailed in his *View* was not the Anglicization of the Irish under colonial rule but the Gaelicization of the English; not the triumph of the English language but the gradual encroachment of Gaelic and the threat to cultural and political Englishness that this process brought with it. Spenser's fearful summary made clear that as a result of this process, some of the English "are degenerated and growne almost meere Irish, yea, and more malitious to the *English* then the *Irish* themselves" (1633: 34). What Douglas Hyde (1860–1949) was later, in the seminal essay "The Necessity of De-Anglicising Ireland" (1893), to praise as Ireland's capacity to assimilate the invaders, Spenser, echoing Gerald of Wales, saw as its capacity to corrupt them.

Despite legislation against the Gaelic language, the extremely limited impact of the English language on Irish life in the sixteenth and early seventeenth century is revealed in the numerous references in state papers to the problems caused by this for the colonists. In the very year of Henry's *Act for English Order, Habit and Language* an "abstract of the misorders and evil rule within the land of Ireland" observed simply that "all the English March borderers use the Irish apparel and the Irish tongue, as well in peace as in war, and for the most part use the same in the English Pale, unless they come to Parliament or Council" (*Cal. S. P. Ire.* 1509–73: 32). Henry's declaration of himself as king of Ireland in 1541, after it had been read in English, had then to be translated into Gaelic for the Irish lords who would not have understood it. In 1562 we hear the plaintive cry of Alexander Craik, bishop of Kildare, pleading with Lord Cecil to be disburdened of his bishopric as he cannot understand Irish (*Cal. S. P. Ire.* 1509–73: 208). In 1578 Her Majesty's Commissioners reported that "all English, and the most part with delight, even in Dublin, speak Irish, and are greatly spotted in manners, habit and conditions with Irish stains" (Crowley 2000: 37). And even as late as 1657, the Calendar of Ancient Records of Dublin noted that "in open contempt" of the law, even in the capital, "there is Irish commonly and usually spoken, and the Irish habit worn not only in the streets, and by such as live in the country and come into this city on market days, but also by and in several families in this city, to the great discontentment of the right honourable his high council for the affairs of Ireland, [and] the scandalising of the inhabitants and magistrates of the City" (Walsh 1920: 248).

The dominance of Gaelic as the language of the Irish posed one obvious problem for the Tudor monarchs and forced a development of colonial policy. For as part of the general protest against centralized authority, one of the central tenets of the Reformation had been the promotion of access to the Bible in the vernacular language. Various colonial servants addressed the problem. Sir William Herbert, referring to the "waste and desolate parts" of Cork, reported that he had been "careful those parts wherein I am, to have them taught the truth in their natural tongue, to have the Lord's Prayer, the Articles of the Creed, the Ten Commandments, translated into the Irish tongue; public prayers in that language, with the administration of the sacraments and other ecclesiastical rites, which in a strange tongue could be to them but altogether unprofitable" (*Cal. S. P. Ire.* 1586–88: 331). Henry Sidney urged Elizabeth to appoint Irish-speaking ministers "for the remote places where the English tongue is not understood," recommending that she look to Scotland for potential candidates (*Cal. S. P. Ire.* 1574–85: 93). It was left to the monarch herself, however, to rectify the main difficulty: Elizabeth sent a Gaelic font to Ireland for the translation of the Bible, and William Daniel's *Tiomna Nuadh* (New Testament) appeared in 1602. On the grounds of her apparent interest in Gaelic, Christopher Nugent, Lord Delvin, sent Elizabeth a primer of the Irish language in 1585; there is no record in the state papers of any letter of thanks from Elizabeth in return.

Two themes appear during this period that were to dominate the politics of language in Ireland for the next three hundred fifty years. The first was Irish resistance to the English language, articulated for various reasons, expressed in various ways. The second, an opposed tendency, was that of the benefits to be gained from the use of English. Irish reluctance to use English is not recorded in great detail in the Tudor period, probably because there was no widespread need to use the language, despite legislative efforts. Stanihurst, however, reported in 1577 that "the English pale is more given to learn the Irish, than the Irishman is willing to learn English"; why, he asked rhetorically, "must [we] embrace their language and they detest ours?" Significantly, he cites one Irishman asking another why the recently defeated leader of the Irish rebels, O'Neill, "would not frame himself to speak English?" The indignant response was: "Thinkest thou that it standeth with O'Neill's honour to writhe his mouth in clattering English?" (Stanihurst 1587: 6). A little later, in his *Itinerary* (1617), Fynes Moryson (1566–1630) noted that not only "the mere Irish disdained to learn or speak the English," but the "English Irish" of Waterford and Cork, "having wives that could speak English as well as we, bitterly . . . chide with them when they speak English with us" (Moryson [1617] 1903: 213). Yet despite this early evidence of a rejection of English, there are signs that the language already accrued benefits to its speakers. The Lord Deputy and Council appealed to Cromwell in 1539, for example, to spare six monasteries from the general suppression in part because they educated children in the English language. In a property dispute in 1587, Sir Owen O'Sullivan charged his opponent that the people of the disputed land were barbarous and uncivil and followed Irish custom under his leadership. The opponent, Donnell O'Sullivan, responded that the people of the territory were "always brought up in learning and civility, and could speak the English and Latin tongues." In fact, he argues, Sir Owen O'Sullivan's charges were simply "to excuse his own ignorance and want of bringing up, being not able to speak the English language" (Crowley 2000: 39). English was already a prestige language; it was also the language of law, and this also brought pressure to bear on Irish speakers. Sir John Davies (1569–1626), the attorney general, noted that "civil assemblies at assizes and sessions" had reformed Irish hairstyles and fashion; they had also made clear the benefit of speaking English to Irish litigants: "because they find a great inconvenience in moving their suits by an interpreter, they do for the most part send their children to schools, especially to learn the English language; so as we may conceive an hope that the next generation will be in tongue and heart and every way else become English" (Davies [1612] 1890: 335–36).

Yet if, as these two examples suggest, English was recognized as requisite for legal or financial success, the Gaelic response was at least in part one of ridicule. *Pairlement Chloinne Tomás* (1615) satirized those among the Irish who took advantage of the cultural reordering that was taking place in the early seventeenth century by exploiting English. One episode mocked the hybridized English spoken by this new group in a meeting between the clan and Roibín an Tobaca. Selected because he has "swallowed the best of English," Tomás is made to bargain with the English tobacco dealer. He asks: *"What the bigg greate órdlach for the what so penny for is the la yourselfe for me?"* Roibín, presumably on the grounds of previous experience of macaronic English, is able to translate this: "I know Thomas, you aske how many enches is worth the penny" (Williams 1981: 40, 97). It is arguable that what the satire demonstrates is the relative lack of perceived threat to the Gaelic language at this point, and this is borne out by the testimony of the Jesuit Richard Conway in 1615. Against Davies's point about the Irish sending their children to schools to learn English, Conway argued that education was largely in the hands of the colonists and that they have "taken singular care that all children be taught English, and they chastise them if they hear them speak their own native tongue." Yet, he adds, these "efforts did not have the desired effect, and the natives did not only not go to England, but rather preferred to remain in ignorance, than run the risk of their faith and religion," either that or they went to Europe, to stop "the ravages these [English] colleges were committing" (McDonald 1874: 204). The threat, as can be seen from the texts published in Irish in the seventeenth century, was evidently considered to be directed primarily against Catholicism and Irish historiography rather than the language.

The first stirrings of a recognition that a momentous linguistic shift was starting to take place, with all that implied for the old Gaelic order, came predictably from those most directly affected by it in terms of their livelihood; after the Flight of the Earls and the waning of patronage, the bardic poets were soon to confront the economic realities of cultural change. The writings of Dáibhí Ó Bruadair (?1625–98) addressed the transformations that were taking place in the seventeenth century, stressing the difficulties of the Gaelic aristocracy and heaping contempt on the usurpers who were taking their place. In an early poem, "Nach ait an nós" (How queer this mode), he observes, partly in wonder perhaps, mostly in anger:

Nach an ait an nós so ag mórchuid d'fhearaibh Éireann,
d'at go nó le mórtus maingléiseach,
giodh tais a dtreoir ar chódaibh gallachléire,
ni chanaid glór acht gósta garbhbhéarla.

How queer this mode assumed by many men of Erin,
With haughty, upstart ostentation lately swollen,
Though codes of foreign clerks they fondly strive to master,
They utter nothing but the ghost of strident English.
(Ó Bruadair 1910: 18–19)

Elsewhere the poet regrets having to pass up the chance of good beer because of "the difficulty which I experience in endeavouring to fetter my tongue for fluent speech in the language of the foreigner" (Ó Bruadair 1910: 113). And in a poem celebrating the expected triumph of James II, Ó Bruadair describes the language of the colonists as "béarla breaganta beoiltirim" (the lip-dry and sim-

pering English tongue) (Ó Bruadair 1917: 88–89). Ó Bruadair's poetic successor, and an observer even more acutely aware of the death of the Gaelic order,
Aodhagán Ó Rathaille (?1670–1729), also composed a poem foretelling the victory of the Jacobites in which he foresaw:

> Beidh Éire go súgach 's a dúnta go haerach
> Is Gaedhilg 'gá scrúdadh n-a múraibh ag éigsibh;
> Béarla na mbúr ndubh go cúthail fá néaltaibh,
> Is Séamus n-a chúirt ghil ag tabhairt chongata do Ghaedhealaibh.

> Erin will be joyful, and her strongholds will be merry;
> And the learned will cultivate Gaelic in their schools;
> The language of the black boors will be humbled and put beneath a cloud,
> And James in his bright court will lend his aid to the Gaels.
> (Ó Rathaille 1911: 166–67)

The Williamite victories and the imposition of the Penal Code led to the situation in which Ó Rathaille bitterly describes Ireland as "Tír do briseadh le fut-
rinn an Bhéarla!" (A land broken by the English-prating band!). The Penal Code
itself, with its harsh measures against the native population, and the development
of English economic and bureaucratic influence, initiated a process of gradual,
if slow, erosion of Gaelic culture and of course language. There was a response
to this movement. At a larger cultural level there was the growing interest in
Irish antiquity and Gaelic language; Edward Lhuyd's (?1660–1709) *Archaeolo-
gia Britannica* in 1707 contained the first printed Irish-English dictionary, and
Aodh Mac Cruitín (?1680–1755) published a massive Irish grammar in 1728
and, with Conor Begly, the first English-Irish dictionary in 1732; the first arguments for reviving the Irish language were heard in the 1740s. An incidental
feature of the philological interest in Gaelic was the frequent invocation of its
purity (taken to be one of the redeeming features of Ireland's historical isolation
and refusal to take on the language of the colonizers) over against the hybrid nature of English, a language described by one commentator as "compounded of
all the barbarous dialects which imperfectly communicated the thoughts of sav-
ages to each other" (*Analecta Hibernica* 1931: 27). At the cultural ground level
the same pattern that we saw earlier continued: Irish antipathy to English opposed by the persuasive force of the material benefits that were on offer to its

users. John Richardson (1664–1747), a Protestant proselytizer in the early eighteenth century, made a general and acute observation:

> Difference of Language being generally a Sign of Difference of Nation, an Attempt against a Language, will look like a Design against the Nation that speaks it: And all the Nations, or distinct Societies of People, having a natural inclination to favour their own Community, and being apt to glory in their Antiquity, and to boast of the great Merit and Renown of their Ancestors, they will be very loth to part With their Native Language, and apt to give any Design against it all the Opposition they can. (Richardson 1712: 111)

Such opposition, he warned, would be severe, and any attempted eradication of Gaelic "will very much provoke and exasperate [the Irish], and consequently prejudice them against our Instructions, and render them more averse to our Communion. If we shall endeavour to rob them of their Tongue, we shall be sure to lose their Hearts; without which, I doubt, we shall never be able to convert them" (Richardson 1712: 111–12). Forcing Irish speakers to listen to prayers and services in English rather than their own language "made few or no sincere Converts, and only provoked them to rebel on the first Opportunity."

Against these feelings, however, was pitted the brute reality of economic necessity. Sir William Petty (1623–87), one of the first political economists, argued in *The Political Anatomy of Ireland* that it was sensible for the Irish "to decline their language" for economic reasons: "It is their Interest to deal with the *English*, for Leases, for Time, and upon clear Conditions . . . rather than to stand always liable to the humour and caprice of their Landlords, and to have every thing taken from them, which he pleases to fancy" (Petty 1691: 101). Whatever Petty's naïveté about the relations between tenant and landlord, the general point holds: in a diglossic situation in which one language is that of commerce, law, and power, not to know that language is to exacerbate dispossession. This was not a lesson lost on any of the Irish who needed to relate to the English on terms. Richardson's great opponent in the Protestant proselytizing debates of the early eighteenth century, the Reverend Nicolson, argued that a generational shift had taken place: the old "will not learn [English], or do scorn to speak it," whereas "there is hardly a boy of 16 years old in Ireland but can understand and speak English. Their parents encourage them to it for their own trading and dealing with English landlords" (*Analecta Hibernica* 1931: 27). Nicolson's claim about the use of English at the time is simply inaccurate through exaggeration; and it would be a long time before the claim became true, though it was eventually realized, but as an observation on what was happening it was perceptive. English was becoming increasingly necessary even to compete on uneven terms in the economic market. A comment in Arthur Young's (1741–1820) *A Tour in Ireland* at the century's end made the situation clear: "Lord Shannon's bounties to labourers amount to 50l a year. He gives it to them by way of encouragement; but only to such as can speak English, and do something more than fill a cart" (Young 1780: 2:50).

One sign of the increasing use and status of English in Ireland was the interesting set of debates over the propriety of the language. Of course, it is important not to divorce this from the debates that were taking place in England; eighteenth-century debates over linguistic correctness demonstrate that English itself was suffering from a crisis. Jonathan Swift's (1667–1745) *Proposal for Correcting, Improving and Ascertaining the English Language* (1712) and the Plan (1747) and Preface of Samuel Johnson's *Dictionary* (1755) bear witness to that. But in Ireland there were early signs of a development that has taken hold only with the emergence of postcolonial Anglophone states around the world: that is, the idea that the English used elsewhere is at least as good as the English of the imperial center. Swift, of course, would have had none of it and satirized Hiberno-English, particularly the English of the Planters, in his "Dialogue in Hibernian Style" (1735). He also commented on the "brogue" (a term first used in 1702) as compared with English accents: "None of these defects derive contempt to the speaker; whereas, what we call the Irish brogue is no sooner discovered, than it makes the deliverer, in the last degree, ridiculous and despised; and from such a mouth, an Englishman expects nothing but bulls, blunders and follies. Neither does it avail whether the censure be reasonable or not, since the fact is always so" (Swift [?1740] 1973: 281). Swift's apology for English linguistic prejudice, on the familiar conservative ground that it is not a question of justice but one of just is, did not hold muster with his opponents. In his *Vindication of the Antiquities of Ireland* (1748), John Keogh admitted that the English disparage the Irish "because they have a kind of Tone, or Accent, in their Discourse, (which they are pleased to call a Brogue)." But he turns this charge against the English and notes that in England speech variation is so great "that oftentimes one Shire cannot understand another." That, he argues, is culpable, whereas for the Irish, the so-called brogue "ought to be no Disgrace to them, but rather an Honour, because they distinguish themselves by retaining the Tone of their Country Language, which shows, that they have a Knowledge of it" (Keogh 1748: 75). The contention regarding variation in England was repeated by Maria Edgeworth (1767–1849) in her *Essay on Irish Bulls* (1802). She argued that all counties "have peculiar vulgarisms, dialects, and brogues, unintelligible to their neighbours"; London, she adds, is the worst: "the language peculiar to the metropolis, or the *cockney* dialect, is proverbially ridiculous." In comparison, she asserts, and this is one of the earliest and boldest expressions of confidence in the use of English in Ireland, "we are only going candidly to suggest, that we think the Irish, in general, speak *better English* than is commonly spoken by the natives of England." It is a remarkable claim and one that she feels the need to temper: "We allude," she says, "to the lower classes of the people in both countries." The argument follows thus:

> In some counties in Ireland, a few of the poorest labourers and cottagers do not understand English, they speak only Irish . . . but amongst those who speak English [there] we find fewer vulgarisms than amongst the same rank of persons in England. The English which they speak is chiefly such has been traditional in their families from the time of the early settlers in the island. During the reign of Queen Elizabeth and the reign of Shakespeare, numbers of English migrated to Ireland; and whoever attends to the phraseology of the lower Irish, may, at this day, hear many of the phrases and expressions used by Shakespeare. (Edgeworth and Edgeworth 1802: 199–200)

If, as Swift had argued in the *Proposal*, the golden age of the English language spanned the period of Elizabeth's reign to 1641, then Edgeworth's argument is that the easiest route back is by way of rural Ireland.

The story of the disaster that befell the Irish language in the nineteenth century is a familiar one. The decision of Maynooth to choose English as the language of instruction, the developing need for English as the language of socioeconomic advancement, the prestige given to English as the language of national politics after the Act of Union, the calamities of the various famines and the consequent population shift to the towns as well as the massive emigration, the introduction of the National Schools — all were factors in the decline of Gaelic. And while this was happening, the same structures of feeling noted earlier were appearing again. There were many reports of widespread reluctance to use English, usually on predictable grounds: Daniel Dewar noted that for many in the rural areas, the understanding of English is "the characteristic of Protestantism[,] . . .

the Irish tongue is the mark of Catholicism[, and] . . . the Catholic considers English as allied to protestantism and damnable error" (1812: 99–100). Another Protestant proselytizer, Henry Monck Mason (1778–1858), pointed out that "the two inveterate prejudices in the Irish peasant's mind, are that against the Saxon language, and that against the creed of the Protestant"; he came up with a novel solution: "by employing the scriptures in the much loved native tongue, you neutralise the second prejudice with the first." And he argued that nothing could prevent "the gradual progress of the English tongue, which is the commercial, the legal, the political, the fashionable medium of communication, towards its finally becoming the universal language of the country" (Mason 1829: 5). Although economics may have supported his argument, it did not mean that the process was universally welcomed. In fact, numerous reports of the early nineteenth century cite the distinction made by bilingual speakers between the two languages and the functions they served. Christopher Anderson (1782–1852) asserted that in the western seaboard districts, Irish was cherished by the populace as the "language of their fathers": "Irish is to them the language of social intercourse, of family communion; every feeling connected with moral duty is closely interwoven with that language. . . . Can the same be said of English? It is to them the language of barter, of worldly occupations; taken up solely at the market, laid aside when he returns home, a very confined vocabulary" (Anderson 1818: 54). Another writer put it more succinctly: for the Irish speaker, English "is the language of his commerce — the Irish the language of his heart" (Coneys 1842: 73).

Such sentiments, however, were pitted against the tide of history. Though it is perhaps too clear a line to draw, it is still in general accurate to say that nineteenth-century political nationalism saw the question of language very differently from the adherents of cultural nationalism. In a letter to the secretary of education in 1812, Henry Grattan (1746–1820) had argued that though he "should be very sorry that the Irish language should be forgotten," on the grounds of unity, he would be "glad that the English language should be generally understood" (Grattan 1812: 336). His lead was followed by the most successful political leader of the nineteenth century, Daniel O'Connell (1775–1847). Responding to a question in 1833, two years after the introduction of the first National Schools, as to whether Gaelic was declining among the peasantry, O'Connell confirmed that he thought that it was, and, he said, "I am sufficiently utilitarian not to regret its gradual abandonment. . . . [A]lthough the Irish language is connected with many recollections that twine around the hearts of

Irishmen, yet the superior utility of the English tongue, as the medium of modern communication, is so great, that I can witness without a sigh the gradual disuse of the Irish" (Daunt 1848: 14). O'Connell was followed in turn by the Catholic church hierarchy in this line of argument, at least until the appearance of Archbishop MacHale as a figure of national importance. In an essay, "The Ruin of Education in Ireland and the Irish Fanar," written at the end of the century, Peadar O'Donnell asserted simply that "Priests kill the Irish language and Irish studies. . . . [F]rom the beginning of the century, if not earlier, increasing multitudes of the Irish priests addressed their Irish-speaking congregations in the finest Maynooth English." And the results, he wrote, were "calamitous for the race and the religion" (O'Donnell 1902: 177). The case was exaggerated, of course, but the sentiment was not unusual.

Economic realities, allied with the advocacy of the use of English (though this was fiercely contested in the midcentury, not least by Thomas Davis in *The Nation,* the organ of the Young Irelanders), had a severe impact on native attitudes towards the language in the latter half of the nineteenth century. Patrick Keenan, an influential inspector of education, summarized the situation of islanders:

> They see, whenever a stranger visits their islands, that prosperity has its peculiar tongue as well as its fine coat; they see that whilst the traffickers who occasionally approach them to deal in fish, or in kelp, or in food, display the yellow gold, they count it out in English, and if they ever cross over to the mainland for the "law," as they call any legal process, they see that the solemn words of judgment have to come second to them, through the offices of an interpreter. . . . [A]nd whilst they may love the cadences, and mellowness, and homeliness of the language which their fathers gave them, they yet see that obscurity and poverty distinguish their lot from the English-speaking people; and accordingly, no matter what the sacrifice to their feelings, they long for the acquisition of the "new tongue," with all its prizes and social privileges. The keystone of fortune is the power of speaking English, and to possess this power there is a burning longing in their breasts that never varies, never moderates. (Keenan 1857–58: xx)

It is a devastating account, extended only to describe the situation in an island school: "the master adopts a novel mode of procedure to propagate the 'new language'. He makes it a cause of punishment to speak Irish in the school, and he has instituted a sort of police among the parents to see that in their intercourse with one another the children speak nothing but English at home. The parents are so eager for the English, they exhibit no reluctance to inform the master of every detected breach of the school law" (Keenan 1857–58: xxi). Synge reported the same attitude, if not the same practices, among the older generation on Aran in 1907. Perhaps the most destructive aspect of this process was the development of shame about the Gaelic language. Again, it is a commonplace of late-nineteenth-century texts. Keenan cited a Tory islander's description of his monolingual Irish companions: "he said he 'was ashamed of them; they stood like dummies; the cattle go on as well as them.'" The Society for the Preservation of the Irish Language (1884: 60) reported on the need "to remove the prejudices of the unenlightened *shoneen* who is said to be ashamed to speak his mother's tongue." It was an attitude that was seen by the Gaelic revivalists as one of the greatest threats to their project.

One response of the revivalists to this threat was to insist, as the title of Douglas Hyde's enormously influential lecture put it, on the "necessity for deanglicising Ireland"; the lecture was to become the founding manifesto of the Gaelic League. For Hyde what was at stake was nothing less than "the end of the Gaelicism of the Gaelic race" (Ó Conaire 1986: 158). One Gaelic League writer described "the language war" as "a war to the death between Irish ideas and British sordid soulessness" (Butler 1900: 2). Patrick Dinneen (1860–1934), author of what was to become the standard Gaelic dictionary, declared that "the struggle between the languages, is a deeper, a more far-reaching struggle than appears on the surface; it is a struggle between the civilisations which these languages represent." Defeat for Irish in the struggle would lead to the destruction of Irishness itself and the predominance of "foreign civilisation, of foreign ideals, of foreign customs, foreign vices" (Dinneen 1904: 28). For "an enslaved nation can call nothing its own but its mind," and thus Ireland's defense could only be her language (Kavanagh ?1902: 2). Without the language Irish nationality, culture, and ethnicity would be lost, and Anglicization would lead to horrible miscegenation: "Should we lose our national identity, we shall become at best but a mongrel race—neither Celts or Saxons. . . . [A]nything at all would seem preferable to a mongrel, colourless, nondescript racial monstrosity evolved somewhere in the bosom of the twentieth century. . . . [W]e are compelled to choose between retaining our national identity and becoming a mongrel race—without a history and without a future" (O'Hickey 1900: 4). This belief was closely tied to the doctrine of "Irish Ireland," popularized by the journalist D. P. Moran. It was used by Patrick Pearse (1879–1916), one of the 1916 revolutionaries, in an attack on Yeats and the "heresy" of the Irish Literary Theatre project: "the heresy is that there can be an Irish literature, an Irish social life, whilst the language of Ireland is English" (Crowley 2000: 189). If *Timon of Athens* is not Greek literature, nor *Romeo and Juliet* Italian, then how, Pearse asked, could Yeats's *The Countess Cathleen* be described as Irish? "Literature written in English cannot be Irish"; with that Pearse dismissed Yeats as "a mere English poet."[3]

Irish nationalism won its war of independence against the British, though its victory was spoiled by the nature of the eventual political settlement. Likewise the Gaelic revivalists won "the language war," at least in terms of constitutionality and legality. Hyde had confidently predicted that if Home Rule was gained, "we *shall* insist, that in those baronies where the children speak Irish, Irish shall be taught, and that Irish-speaking schoolmasters, petty-sessions clerks, and even magistrates be appointed in Irish-speaking districts" (Ó Conaire 1986: 161). And so, after independence, it happened: the Irish Constitution of 1937 declared clearly in favor of Gaelic, making it both the national language and the first official language (English was given the status of the second official language); in the case of any textual disputes with regard to the constitution itself, the text in the national language was given precedence. Gaelic also became compulsory for entrance into the Civil Service and a mandatory subject for all schoolchildren. Yet though one of the executed leaders of the 1916 revolution had proclaimed the necessary victory of Gaelic in the struggle between the languages, another had noted a different outcome to the linguistic conflict that had lasted for centuries. Thomas MacDonagh (1878–1916), in the posthumously published *Literature in Ireland*, described the result of that curious and complex history of conflict and contact, intermingling and alienation, that had characterized the relations between colonial English and native Irish. What had emerged, MacDonagh (1920: 41) asserted, was a new form of language, "an English that had to be knit into a different complication from the modern complication of the central English language." Rather than Gaelic or English as victor, what had been produced as a dialectical historical fact was a form of the English language in Ireland that had "an individuality of its own, and the rhythm of speech a distinct character"; a new language "at its best is more vigorous, fresh and simple than either of the two languages between which it stands" (MacDonagh 1920: 48). In America Noah Webster had attempted to forge a new form of English consciously on the grounds that "as an independent nation, our honour requires us to have a system of our own, in language as well as government" (Webster 1789: 20). In Ireland, in contrast, a new language had evolved from linguistic and cultural conflict and contact rather than direct intervention. Hiberno-English (Anglo-Irish as it used inaccurately to be called) bore testimony to its roots in a very specific history. It is worth noting in this respect that at a particular historical moment at the beginning of the twentieth century in Ireland, a period of war and violence, the first notable attempts were made to record this new language: Lady Gregory's creation of the language of the rural village of Kiltartan (Kiltartanese) and of course the more famous representation of the Hiberno-English of the Aran islanders in the work of Synge. Around the same time too, Sean O'Casey was attempting to portray the language of working-class Dubliners; if it wasn't quite Synge's Hiberno-English, it was certainly a distinct form of Irish-English.

Gaelic then won the war de jure, but English won it de facto. For despite a recent revival in its fortunes, Gaelic has been shrinking since the inception of independent Ireland, and its enshrined, compulsory status has been considered by many to have hastened its decline. Attitudes towards Irish remain ambivalent, as the Bord na Gaeilge report *The Irish Language in a Changing Society* (1988) made clear:

> Public attitudes place a high value on the language as a marker of Irish cultural distinctiveness, and there is widespread reluctance to see it disappear from public life or from the experience of future generations. The central problem, however, is that popular use of the language has remained at a low level, and current indications are that this is contracting further in some important respects. (Bord na Gaeilge 1988: x)

In the 2002 census in the Irish Republic some 1,570,894 respondents categorized themselves as Irish speakers (42.8% of the population), which was an encouraging figure. But despite the fact that more people claimed to be able to speak Irish in 2002 than did in 1851, it is clear that patterns of use (as opposed to ability) do not bode well for the future and consist largely of passive bilingualism.[4] English, if not the national or first official language of the country, is clearly the practical everyday language of the people. Yet it is an altered English, a postcolonial English, probably the first postcolonial English. In a beautifully nuanced depiction of a colonial linguistic encounter, Stephen Dedalus, after his dispute with the English dean of studies in *A Portrait of the Artist as a Young Man* over the word "tundish" (the dean insists on the word "funnel" instead), reflects, "The language in which we are speaking is his before it is mine . . . His language, so familiar and so foreign, will always be for me an acquired speech." Acquired it might have been, but mastered and turned to distinct purposes it was too; Stephen later discovers that "tundish" is in fact an English word (a late Middle English coinage) that still happens to be used in Dublin. It leads Stephen to exclaim angrily: "Damn the dean of studies and his funnel! What did he come here for to teach us his own language or to learn it from us? Damn him one way or the other!" (Joyce [1916] 1992: 274). Stephen, echoing Caliban in his use of the colonial language to curse the colonial language master, poses an interesting postcolonial question: whose language is it anyway?

NOTES

1. See, for example L. P. Curtis, *Apes and Angels: The Irishman in Victorian Caricature* (Washington, D.C.: Smithsonian Institution, 1971); and Liz Curtis, *Nothing But the Same Old Story: The Roots of Anti-Irish Racism* (London: Information on Ireland, 1984).

2. This topic is explored in chapter 4, "The Standard Language: The Language of the Literate," in Tony Crowley, *Standard English and the Politics of Language* (Houndmills: Palgrave, 2003).

3. Pearse was nineteen at the time and can be forgiven the rhetorical excess; in 1905 he praised *Cathleen Ni Houlihan* as "the most beautiful piece of prose that has been produced by an Irishman in our day" and asserted that Yeats "has never ceased to work for Ireland" (O'Leary 1994: 333).

4. In the 1851 census 1,524,286 Irish speakers were recorded out of a population of 6,552,365 (23.25%), though this may have been an underrecording; the 2002 census figures show 1,570,894 Irish speakers from a population of 3,750,995 (42.8%); in 1851 there were 319,602 Irish monoglots, today there are none. The 2002 figures do not of course include Northern Ireland. The 2002 census attempted to measure use as well as ability. Of the recorded Irish speakers, 21.6 percent use the language daily (76.8% in the 5–19 school age group), but almost two-thirds do not use the language at all or use it less than weekly. In the Gaeltacht areas, out of a population of 86,517, 62,157 were recorded as Irish speakers (72.6%), a slight drop from 1996; the proportion of Irish speakers declined in all areas except the Meath Gaeltacht. Usage figures were as follows: daily 33,789 (54.3%), weekly 6,704 (10.8%), less often 15,811 (25.4%), never 4,515 (7.2%), not stated 1,338.

BIBLIOGRAPHY

Analecta Hibernica, including the Reports of the Irish Historical Manuscripts Commission. 1930– . Dublin: Irish Historical Manuscripts Commission.

Anderson, Christopher. 1818. *A Brief Sketch of Various Attempts which Have Been Made to Diffuse a Knowledge of the Holy Scriptures through the Medium of the Irish Language.* Dublin.

Bord na Gaeilge. 1988. *The Irish Language in a Changing Society: Shaping the Future*. Dublin: Bord na Gaeilge.

Butler, Mary E. L.? 1900. *Irishwomen and the Home Language*. Dublin: Gaelic League.

Calendar of the State Papers Relating to Ireland, 1509–1573. 1860–1912. 24 vols. London.

Campion, Edmund. [1571] 1633. *A Historie of Ireland*. In *The Historie of Ireland Collected by Three Learned Authors*, ed. James Ware. Dublin.

Coneys, Rev. 1842. "The Irish Language." *The Nation*, no. 5. Dublin.

Crowley, Tony. 2000. *The Politics of Language in Ireland, 1366–1922: A Sourcebook*. London: Routledge.

Daunt, W. J. O'Neill. 1848. *Personal Recollections of the Late Daniel O'Connell, M. P.* Dublin.

Davies, Sir John. [1612] 1890. "A Discovery of the True Causes Why Ireland Was Never Entirely Subdued." In *Ireland under Elizabeth and James I*, ed. J. Morley. London: Routledge.

Dewar, D. 1812. *Observations on the Character, Customs and Superstitions of the Irish*. London.

Dinneen, Rev. P. S. 1904. *Lectures on the Irish Language Movement*. Dublin: Gill.

Edgeworth, Maria, and Richard Edgeworth. 1802. *Essay on Irish Bulls*. London.

Giraldus Cambrensis (Gerald of Wales). [1188] 1982. *The History and Topography of Ireland*. Trans. J. J. O'Meara. Dublin: Dolmen.

Grattan, Henry. 1812. "Letter to the Secretary of the Board of Education." 14th Report, Commission of the Board of Education, Ireland, October 1812, appendix 3, 336. *House of Commons Papers*.

Heaney, Seamus. 1978. "The Interesting Case of John Alphonsus Mulrennan." *Planet* 4.1: 34–40.

Hyde, Douglas. [1892] 1986. "The Necessity for De-Anglicising Ireland." In *Language, Lore and Lyrics: Essays and Lectures of Douglas Hyde*, ed. B. Ó Conaire. Dublin: Irish Academic Press.

Joyce, James. [1916] 1992. *A Portrait of the Artist as a Young Man*. Ed. Seamus Deane. Harmondsworth: Penguin.

Kavanagh, Rev. P. F. ?1902. *Ireland's Defence—Her Language*. Dublin: Gaelic League.

Keenan, P. J. 1857–58. "Twenty-third Report of the Commissioners of National Education in Ireland," i, 143–44. *House of Commons Papers*. London.

Keogh, John. 1748. *A Vindication of the Antiquities of Ireland*. Dublin.

MacDonagh, Thomas. 1920. *Literature in Ireland*. Dublin: Talbot Press.

Mason, H. M. 1829. *Facts Afforded by the History of the Irish Society*. Dublin.

McDonald, D. W. 1874. "An Account of the Decrees and Acts . . . in the Year 1611 in Dublin." Trans. Richard Conway. *Irish Ecclesiastical Record*, 203–7.

Moryson, Fynes. [1617] 1903. *Shakespeare's Europe: Unpublished Chapters of Fynes Moryson's Itinerary*. Ed. C. Hughes. London: Sherratt and Hughes.

Ó Bruadair, Dáibhí (David O'Bruadair). 1910. *Duanaire Dhábhidh Uí Bhruadair, The Poems of David Ó Bruadair*, pt. 1. Ed. and trans. J. C. MacErlean. London: Irish Texts Society.

———. 1917. *Duanaire Dhábhidh Uí Bhruadair, The Poems of David Ó Bruadair*, pt. 3. Ed. and trans. J. C. MacErlean. London: Irish Texts Society.

Ó Conaire, B., ed. 1986. *Language, Lore and Lyrics: Essays and Lectures of Douglas Hyde*. Dublin: Irish Academic Press.

O'Donnell, F. H. 1902. *The Ruin of Education in Ireland and the Irish Fanar*. 2d ed. London: Nutt.

O' Hickey, Rev. M. P. 1900. *The True National Idea*. Dublin: Gaelic League.

O'Leary, Philip. 1994 *The Prose Literature of the Gaelic Revival, 1881–1921: Ideology and Innovation*. University Park: Pennsylvania State University Press.

Ó Rathaille, Aodhagáin (Egan O'Rahilly). 1911. *Dánta Aodhagáin Uí Rathaille: The Poems of Egan O'Rahilly* 2d ed. Ed. and trans. P. S. Dinneen and T. O'Donoghue. London: Irish Texts Society.

Petty, William. 1691. *The Political Anatomy of Ireland*. London.

Richardson, John. 1712. *A Proposal for the Conversion of the Popish Natives of Ireland to the Established Religion: With the Reasons upon which it is Grounded: And an Answer to the Objections made to it*. 2d ed., corrected and enlarged. London.

Society for the Preservation of the Irish Language. 1884. *Proceedings of the Congress Held in Dublin 1882*. Dublin.

Spenser, Edmund. [1596] 1633. *A View of the State of Ireland*. In Sir James Ware, *The Historie of Ireland Collected by Three Learned Authors*. Dublin.

Stanihurst, Richard. [1577] 1587. "A Treatise Containing a Plain and Perfect Description of Ireland." In R. Holinshed, *The Chronicles of England, Scotland and Ireland*. Ed. John Hooker et al., 3 vols.; ed. Henry Ellis, 6 vols., 1807–8. London.

Swift, Jonathan. [?1740] 1973. "On Barbarous Denominations in Ireland." In *Prose Writings*, vol. 4, ed. Herbert Davis with Louis Landa. Oxford: Blackwell.

The Statutes at Large Passed in the Parliaments Held in Ireland. 1786–1801. 1310–1800, 20 vols. Dublin.

Walsh, Fr. P. 1920. "The Irish Language and the Reformation." *Irish Theological Quarterly* 15: 242–53.

Webster, Noah. 1789. *Dissertation on the English Language*. Boston.

Williams, N. J. A., ed. [1615] 1981. *Pairlement Chloinne Tomáis*. Dublin: Dublin Institute for Advanced Studies.

Young, Arthur. 1780. *A Tour in Ireland, with General Observations on the State of that Kingdom*. 2 vols. Dublin.

LITERATURE AND
THE PRESERVATION
OF NATIVE TONGUES

8 Speaking in *Glossai*

Dialect Choice and Cultural Politics in Hellenistic Poetry

RICHARD HUNTER

Language matters, particularly in periods of change, and the story of the Greek language from the fourth century B.C.E. onwards is the story of the steady spread of a "common language" (the *koinē*), based on the dialect of Athens, accompanied by a corresponding decline in the use of local dialects.[1] The rapidity of this decline is difficult to gauge, as the language of both public and private inscriptions, our principal source of evidence, and that of "real speech" do not necessarily develop at the same speed. Moreover, our ability to track these changes through works of high literature is hampered by a crucial fact about Greek poetry.

The most important determinative factor for poetic dialect was genre: if you wrote epic, you used the "language of Homer," regardless of your own native speech. As Geoffrey Horrocks puts it, "Each genre employs a form of language which exhibits certain distinctive 'markers' of the dialect group to which the spoken and official varieties of its supposed region of origin belonged, but which conventionally eliminates narrow linguistic parochialism in favour of a more stylised diction which conveys its dialectal affiliations in a rather neutral way and which, in varying degrees, reflects authorial ambitions to reach a panhellenic audience. Wherever poetry of a particular kind came to be composed outside its 'traditional' region . . . the associated 'literary' dialect was then routinely adopted as a genre-specific standard by all practitioners, regardless of their native speech."[2] Most famously, perhaps, the dialectal coloring of choral poetry was always lightly Doric, even in the midst of Attic tragedies whose predominant dialect is quite different. It may be worth adding that we do not have evidence for the "translation" of works from one dialect to another when they were performed outside their areas of original composition, and here again we may see the conservative power of genre. In the poetry of the third century B.C.E., however, we do find clear traces of both the political charge that language forms carry and of the changes that Greek was undergoing. In this chapter, I wish to tease out some of these traces.

The *Fifteenth Idyll* of Theocritus of Syracuse (first half of third century B.C.E.) is a hexameter mime in which Gorgo and Praxinoa, two Syracusan women resident in Alexandria, decide to go to the royal palace to see the festival of the eastern god Adonis that is being staged by Arsinoe, the wife and sister of Ptolemy II Philadelphus, in honor of her dead mother, the now deified Berenice; the dramatic date of the poem may reasonably be placed in the late 270s (Arsinoe died in either 270 or 268). When the women reach the palace, their admiring comments about the tapestries celebrating the Adonis story are apparently overheard by another member of the crowd who makes his feelings plain; he, however, then gets more than he bargained for:

> ΠΡ. πότνι' Ἀθαναία, ποῖαί ψ' ἐπόνασαν ἔριθοι,
> ποῖοι ζωογράφοι τἀκριβέα γράμματ' ἔγραψαν.
> ὡς ἔτυμ' ἑστάκαντι καὶ ὡς ἔτυμ' ἐνδινεῦντι,
> ἔμψυχ', οὐκ ἐνυφαντά. σοφόν τι χρῆμ' ἄνθρωπος.
> αὐτὸς δ' ὡς θαητὸς ἐπ' ἀργυρέας κατάκειται
> κλισμῶ, πρᾶτον ἴουλον ἀπὸ κροτάφων καταβάλλων,
> ὁ τριφίλητος Ἄδωνις, ὁ κἠν Ἀχέροντι φιληθείς.
> ΞΕΝΟΣ. παύσασθ', ὦ δύστανοι, ἀνάνυτα κωτίλλοισαι,
> τρυγόνες· ἐκκναισεῦντι πλατειάσδοισαι ἄπαντα.
> ΠΡ. μᾶ, πόθεν ὤνθρωπος; τί δὲ τίν, εἰ κωτίλαι εἰμές;
> πασάμενος ἐπίτασσε· Συρακοσίαις ἐπιτάσσεις.
> ὡς εἰδῆς καὶ τοῦτο, Κορίνθιαι εἰμὲς ἄνωθεν,
> ὡς καὶ ὁ Βελλεροφῶν. Πελοποννασιστὶ λαλεῦμες,
> δωρίσδειν δ' ἔξεστι, δοκῶ, τοῖς Δωριέεσσι.
> μὴ φύη, Μελιτῶδες, ὃς ἁμῶν καρτερὸς εἴη,
> πλὰν ἑνός. οὐκ ἀλέγω. μή μοι κενεὰν ἀπομάξῃς.
> (Theocritus 15.80–95)

PRAXINOA: Lady Athena, what workers they must have been that made them, and what artists that drew the lines so true! The fig-

ures stand and turn so naturally, they're alive not woven.
What a clever thing is man! And look at him; how marvel-
lous he is, lying in his silver chair with the first down spreading from the temples, thrice-loved Adonis, loved even in
death.

STRANGER: My good women, do stop that ceaseless chattering—perfect
turtle-doves, they'll bore one to death with all their broad
vowels.

PRAXINOA: Gracious, where does this gentleman come from? And what
business is it of yours if we do chatter? Give orders where
you're master. It's Syracusans you're ordering about, and let
me tell you we're Corinthians by descent like Bellerophon.
We talk Peloponnesian, and I suppose Dorians may talk
Dorian. Lady Persephone, let us have only the one man in
power over us. I don't care about you—don't waste your
time on me.[3]

This fascinating passage, which dramatizes, inter alia, the coming of Sicilian
mime traditions to Alexandria, raises a host of questions.[4] The annoyed gentleman seems, "unless there has been interference with the transmitted text on a
large scale,"[5] to speak the same kind of Doric-flavored Greek (whose most familiar characteristic is the retention of a long *a* where most dialects had long *e*)
as the women, and thus in calling attention to the possibility of linguistic difference in textual representation, the passage speaks directly (and self-reflexively)
to the kind of literary *mimesis* here offered by the Syracusan poet Theocritus; as
the women admire the lifelike "realism" of the tapestries, we are forced to confront our own interpretive models for dealing with the characters of a "lifelike"
mime.[6] It is, however, not this aspect of the passage, or its detailed implications
(if any) for our knowledge of dialect Greek (all those "broad vowels"), that concern me here.[7] I want rather to consider how the linguistic concerns and the
politics, understood at first rather narrowly, of the passage might overlap, and
then to see how this passage can help us to map the linguistic consciousness
of the early Hellenistic world.

Third-century inscriptions reveal how strongly Doric forms of all types
held on against the "common" tide (see Bubeník 1989), and there is no reason to
doubt that Syracuse in particular and Sicily and Magna Graecia in general were
through the third century B.C.E. the sites of flourishing dialectal culture and
self-conscious pride about the Doric literary heritage.[8] As for Alexandria, it may

be worth noting that inscriptions show a very marked survival of dialect in Cyrene,[9] for important members of the Alexandrian elite, including Callimachus and Eratosthenes, came from this flourishing kingdom to the west, and Willy Clarysse has also pointed to the evidence of census lists and lists of priestly offices for the survival, until a relatively late date, of Doric name forms both among Cyrenean communities and the Alexandrian sociopolitical elite.[10] I shall return both to Cyrene and to the particular place of poetry within these developments presently, but—to anticipate somewhat—it is clear that, in the broad scheme of things, "Doric" is the marked member of the linguistic set; that is, Doric features call attention to themselves amid the ever-rising tide of the *koinē*. This passage of Theocritus's *Fifteenth Idyll,* which seems to bear (a special kind of) witness to a contemporary consciousness of and self-consciousness about linguistic difference, presumably fostered by the growth of the *koinē,* perhaps then also hints at an important phenomenon that is otherwise largely unattested.

We have considerable evidence for scholarly interest in dialectology and its connection to poetry in the third century and even already in the fourth. Thus, for example, Philodemus of Gadara (first century B.C.E.) charges the critic and philosopher Heraclides of Pontus (mid-fourth century B.C.E.) with "strangely burdening the good poet with an accurate and thorough knowledge of dialectal forms of speech, although the one in which a poet chooses to write is sufficient" (*On Poems* 5, col. V.10–16 Mangoni).[11] Nevertheless, we have no explicit witness as early as this to a recognition by language users themselves, however scholarly, of the growth of *koinē* and the concomitant weakening of the local dialects.[12] It is, of course, not difficult to see the flourishing dialectological and glossographical industries of the third century, that is, the scholarly identification and collection of words allegedly peculiar to a particular (usually relatively small) area, as themselves implicit witnesses to such a recognition,[13] but Theocritus 15 perhaps adds a precious piece to our overall picture.

As a spoken language form, dialect was in fact always "local," in a fairly prescribed sense; throughout antiquity, "dialect" was predominantly something individual to a particular city or group of people. Although there is a little evidence as early as the fifth century B.C.E. for a consciousness of the broad categories into which we—following the scholarship of later antiquity—now group the dialects of ancient Greek (Attic, principally associated with Athens and Attica; Ionic, principally associated with the coast of Asia Minor and the Aegean islands; Doric, principally associated with central and northern Greece, the Peloponnese, and southern Italy and Sicily; and the Aeolic of central Greece, Lesbos, and the Asian coast opposite), it is really only in the third century B.C.E. that there is solid evidence for this division as in any way determinative on how linguistic difference was conceived. Until then, there was, as Anna Morpurgo Davies put it, "no such thing as Doric."[14] Both aspects—the sense of "the local" and the new scholarly drive towards the "rescue archaeology" of language—are on view in a passage of Theocritus's *Twelfth Idyll* in which a self-deluding lover wishes that his relationship with a beloved boy were as such things were "in the past":

εἴθ' ὁμαλοὶ πνεύσειαν ἐπ' ἀμφοτέροισιν Ἔρωτες
νῶιν, ἐπεσσομένοις δὲ γενοίμεθα πᾶσιν ἀοιδή·
δίω δή τινε τῶδε μετὰ προτέροισι γενέσθην
φῶθ', ὃ μὲν εἴσπνηλος, φαίη χ' Ὠμυκλαϊάζων,
τὸν δ' ἕτερον πάλιν, ὥς κεν ὁ Θεσσαλὸς εἴποι, ἀίτην.
ἀλλήλους δ' ἐφίλησαν ἴσῳ ζυγῷ. ἦ ῥα τότ' ἦσαν
χρύσειοι πάλιν ἄνδρες, ὅτ' ἀντεφίλησ' ὁ φιληθείς.

Theocritus 12.10–16

Would that the Loves might breathe equally upon both of us, and that we might be a subject of song for all future men. Excellent were these two among former generations, the one Inspirer (*eispnēlos*), as he would be called in the speech of Amyklai, the other Hearer (*aitēs*), as the Thessalian would say. They loved one another under an equal yoke: then indeed were men truly golden, when the loved one returned the love.

There are difficulties of text and interpretation here,[15] but it is clear that the appeal to local glosses goes hand-in-hand with a wistful nostalgia for an idealized (and imaginary) past; it would be dangerous to think that such a literary construction can have had no real resonance in the linguistic consciousness of the educated elite.

The contrast with the position of dialect speech in the late-fifth-century Athenian comedies of Aristophanes, the subject of a recent study by Stephen Colvin, is here instructive.[16] Colvin makes a plausible case for believing that the Megarian and Boeotian characters in *Acharnians* and the Spartans in *Lysistrata* speak a "dialect" that is not comically "marked" per se, except as being appropriate to these particular characters; to put it oversimply, we might say that the fact that a character speaks a non-Attic dialect is not of itself worth remarking on. Spartans speak Laconian. What else would you expect? Colvin also notes (p. 297) that, through the comedies as a whole, the representation of non-Attic speech is, broadly speaking, consistent and reasonably accurate, that "the dialect colouring [of non-Attic speakers] is not Greek literary dialect,"[17] and that (with the interesting exception of slaves) "there is no example . . . of a non-Athenian Greek or barbarian whose speech is not marked as foreign in some way." To move from this world to that of linguistically adventurous Alexandrian poetry is indeed to realize the magnitude of the political and linguistic changes that had come over the Greek world and of the new importance of written circulation as a primary medium for the reception of poetry. The linguistic archaeology of the Hellenistic age is thus fundamentally a textual operation; Thomas Schmitz has argued that the very difficulty of Callimachus's style and lexicon, which demands interpretive energy and cooperation from the reader, who is thus given a sense of belonging to a poetic in-group, is precisely the way an "imagined community" can be created in a world of freely circulating written texts.[18]

In asserting her right to "speak Doric," Praxinoa makes her accent and/or dialect a political issue: "freedom of speech" (*parrhēsia*), one of the most potent ideological banners of classical democratic Athens, that right of any male citizen to say what he thinks and to address the sovereign assembly, is here rewritten as the right, even for women, to keep their own dialect and/or accent under the protective and benevolent absolute rule of Ptolemy (the "one"). The "political" character of Praxinoa's declaration is most easily seen by setting it alongside the speech that, in the late fifth century, Thucydides places in the mouth of the Syracusan politician Hermocrates as he seeks, in the presence of Athenian ambassadors, to rouse resistance to the Athenians in the people of Sicilian Camarina: "[Are we unwilling] to show them that here are not Ionians or Hellespontines or island-dwellers, who are forever swapping one master, Persian or whoever, for another, but Dorians, free men from the independent Peloponnese who live in Sicily?" As so often, however, in Theocritus, Praxinoa's words also have a Homeric subtext. In Book 2 of the *Iliad* Agamemnon's "testing" of the troops backfires spectacularly when they take up with great alacrity his suggestion that everyone should go home. Odysseus, however, saves the day, but only just. Here is how Homer describes Odysseus's intervention with the ordinary troops (*demos*):

ὃν δ' αὖ δήμου τ' ἄνδρα ἴδοι βοόωντά τ' ἐφεύροι,
τὸν σκήπτρωι ἐλάσασκεν ὁμοκλήσασκέ τε μύθωι·
"δαιμόνι', ἀτρέμας ἧσο καὶ ἄλλων μῦθον ἄκουε,
οἳ σέο φέρτεροί εἰσι, σὺ δ' ἀπτόλεμος καὶ ἄναλκις,
οὔτε ποτ' ἐν πολέμωι ἐναρίθμιος οὔτ' ἐνὶ βουλῆι.

οὐ μέν πως πάντες βασιλεύσομεν ἐνθαδ' Ἀχαιοί·
οὐκ ἀγαθὸν πολυκοιρανίη· εἷς κοίρανος ἔστω,
εἷς βασιλεύς, ὧι δῶκε Κρόνου πάις ἀγκυλομήτεω
σκῆπτρόν τ' ἠδὲ θέμιστας, ἵνα σφίσι βουλεύηισι."

Homer, *Iliad* 2.198–206

―――――

But whenever he saw a commoner and found him shouting, he would
strike him with the sceptre and berate him, saying: "Friend, sit quiet and
listen to what others tell you, your superiors—you are a coward and a
weakling, of no account either in war or in counsel. We cannot all be
kings here, every one of the Achaians. Having many masters is a bad
idea; there must be one master, one king, the man endowed by the son
of devious-minded Kronos with the sceptre and the ways of law, to make
judgements for his people." (Trans. M. Hammond, adapted)

In Theocritus it is in the mouth of one of the "ordinary people" (very ordinary
indeed) that this justification of absolute rule resonates; Ptolemy himself could
not have put it better. The direct link that these Homeric verses make between
the power of Zeus and the power of the king picks up one of the most common
ideas of Alexandrian encomiastic poetry (e.g., Theocritus 17 [the *Encomium of
Ptolemy*]; Callimachus's *Hymn to Zeus*; etc.), but does so from the ironized distance of the mime. Finally, we should note that these Homeric verses precede the
most famous ancient scene of the denial of free speech, Odysseus's physical and
verbal attack on the hideously ugly Thersites ("the Reckless One"), who had dared
to criticize Agamemnon; in Theocritus, however, all that "democratic" energy
is turned to the service of the king (*basileus*), in a provocative display of willing
submission.

The obvious humor of Theocritus's Homeric rewriting should not stop us
from asking about the place of language marking at the Ptolemaic court itself;
in doing so, it will be well to acknowledge at the outset that what we might op-
timistically call "evidence" is here pretty thin on the ground. Ptolemaic public
decrees, like those of Alexander and Philip before them, and presumably these
kings themselves, used the *koinē* language. Nevertheless, for a dynasty that traced
its ancestry back to the greatest Dorian hero of them all, Heracles (cf. Theocritus 17.26–7), and (through the supposed settlement of the Argive Temenids
in Macedonia) to the Argive royal house, Dorian traditions were important.

Herodotus in fact records a tradition of early settlement in northern Greece by a "Dorian-Makednan" people of Hellenic race who finally came to rest in the Peloponnese (1.56, 8.43).[19] This is clearly suggestive for the passage discussed here, but whatever ethnographic and patriotic traditions are in fact in play, it is clear that when at 24.137–38 the young Heracles, in whom an increasing number of modern scholars wish to see a reflection of the young Ptolemy Philadelphus himself, dines on "large Dorian bread," more is at stake than merely types of grain. So too, in Theocritus's *Encomium of Ptolemy Philadelphus* the speech of welcome to the royal baby placed in the mouth of the island of his birth, Cos, establishes a link between the future king and the Dorian pentapolis centered on Knidos. The verses are unfortunately obscure and perhaps corrupt, but it is clear that the importance given to this Dorian center in Theocritus's *Encomium* replaces the Ionian festival on Delos that is described in Theocritus's principal model text, the archaic *Homeric Hymn to Apollo*. Just as the Ionian traditions appealed to the Delian "patrons" of the archaic singer, so Theocritus will have judged his audience well in appealing to Dorian traditions, and in fact we find this Dorian heritage of the Ptolemies still appealed to at the end of the third century by Dorian Greek cities needing help.[20]

A new piece for the jigsaw puzzle has recently appeared. One of the poems on the new Milan papyrus of the third-century epigrammatist Posidippus of Pella (P. Mil. Vogl. VIII 309)[21] celebrates the chariot victories of the Ptolemaic house; the epigram is imagined as inscribed upon, and thus spoken by, an image of Philadelphus:

πρῶτο[ι] τρεῖς βασιλῆες Ὀλύμπια καὶ μόνοι ἁμές
  ἅρμασι νικῶμες καὶ γονέες καὶ ἐγώ·
εἷς μὲν ἐγὼ [Π]τολεμαίου ὁμώνυμος, ἐ‹κ› Βερενίκας
  υἱ[ός],˙Ἐορδαία γέννα, δύω δὲ γονεῖς·
πρὸς μέγα πατρὸς ἐμὸν τίθεμαι κλέος, ἀλλ᾽ ὅτι μάτηρ[22]
  εἷλε γυνὰ νίκαν ἅρματ‹ι›, τοῦτο μέγα.

We were the first three kings to win on our own the chariot race at Olympia, my parents and I. I am one of them, Ptolemy's namesake, son of Berenice, of Eordean stock, and my two parents. To my father's great glory I add my own, but that my mother won a chariot victory as a woman, this is something great.

Posidippus 88 A-B, trans. Austin (adapted)

The language of this poem is Doricizing, and strongly so by the standards of contemporary literary epigrams (to which I will return): this Philadelphus speaks with a markedly Doric flavor. We have more than enough poems on the royal house to show that royal themes did not necessarily have to be "Doricized" (the surviving fragment of Theocritus's own poem on Philadelphus's mother, Berenice, shows no Doric color) and that, conversely, Doric coloring does not necessarily mean a Ptolemaic resonance. Moreover, the Doric color of the epigram could be put down to a generic positioning within the tradition of epinician poetry for athletic victories (Pindar, Bacchylides, etc.), where the dominant dialectal color was that of Doric lyric; some surviving epigrams in honor of athletic and chariot victors do indeed seem to echo this Doric tradition,[23] though there is no real evidence that poets of such epigrams outside Doric areas used Doric generic markers with any regularity. We should, moreover, freely admit puzzlement as to why some third-century poems are written in Doric.[24] Nevertheless, the new epigram of Posidippus ought to make us look again at other third-century poems, such as Asclepiades XXXIX G-P and Callimachus XV G-P,[25] two mildly Doricizing epigrams in honor of a "Berenice," and Asclepiades XLIII G-P, in which Alexander the Great speaks a pentameter of mild Doric flavor. Praxinoa's linking of Doric speech and Ptolemaic power, in the setting of the Alexandrian palace, begins to look more complex than previously imagined; her comic "right" to speak the same language as the royal family is itself a result of the blessings of Ptolemaic rule.

We must, however, still ask why and how "Doric" speech is marked in its connection with the Ptolemaic house. In the new epigram, Philadelphus proudly declares himself "nursling of Eordaia" (an important province of central Macedonia), and it is this combination of Doric language and Macedonian heritage that is presumably central to our subject. It is, however, perhaps not quite as simple as Clarysse's observation that Doric was "the 'prestige' dialect which the Macedonian kings spoke among their peers" might suggest.[26]

The Macedonian language — for which we have painfully little evidence — has been much discussed, particularly under the heading "Was it Greek?"[27] Nevertheless, a recently published text — a *defixio*, or curse tablet — from Pella, to be dated in the first half of the fourth century, is indeed in Greek and a kind of Greek which, to both expert and nonexpert eyes, is clearly of West Greek (i.e., "Doric") type.[28] We cannot, of course, be sure that this text or its author was (in any important sense) "Macedonian,"[29] but if we were to speculate for a moment that some memory, if not in fact knowledge, of a believed affinity between the local dialects of Macedonia and Doric speech had survived through to the Ptolemaic court, then, as the language of both Argos and Macedonia, Doric would indeed have been "marked" in a particularly powerful way at the court. Its "otherness" marks it as the preserver of genuine Greek tradition, in particular of the rightful claim of the Ptolemies to be the heirs of Heracles and Alexander. If this analysis is even remotely on the right lines, then we may also see here an act of historical reconstruction, operative at the level of public ideology, which bears a significant resemblance to the recuperative and "historical" operations that dominated the scholarship and literature of third-century Alexandria, as the Greek elite sought to reconstruct and adapt the Greek past. Whereas the Macedonian ruling class had—whatever the nature of their local dialects—for at least a century adopted the Attic *koinē* in their push for international prestige and power, and it was this standard language that Alexander's armies carried throughout the world,[30] when indicators of continuity and "genuineness" were needed, it was to now-fading linguistic markers that they and their poets turned. The use of a Doricizing language is thus a politically and culturally charged act of repetition. It must be stressed (again) that this is not a matter of "writing in Macedonian." Posidippus's Ptolemy speaks a language that subsumes local traditions into a distinctive but (as far as we can tell) not specifically localized linguistic *mimesis* of Greek heroic culture. Praxinoa's claim to share in such a culture may seem inherently absurd, and this would be in keeping with the mimic context in which it is set, but in fact she reflects both Ptolemy's Macedonian heritage and his claims to be the standardbearer of Greek culture.

Praxinoa's exchange with the exasperated bystander thus takes its place within the Alexandrian preoccupation with the loss and recovery of the past. Alexandrian scholarship and the institutionalizing of knowledge in the "Museum" and Library are perhaps the best-known expressions of that preoccupation. "Language" is a further feature of the Greek homeland, uprooted from its "natural context" and reused in new and creative ways in Alexandria.[31] Here the study of language goes hand in hand with the contemporary study of local customs and cults, which makes its most obvious poetic appearance in the third-century fondness for "aetiology." Thus we see already in Aristotle—in this, as in so many ways, a spiritual father of Alexandrianism—that among the ways in which apparent interpretive problems in the Homeric text can be solved are explanations based on the contemporary practices of remote peoples (*Poetics* 1461a3–4, the Illyrians; fr. 389 Gigon, the Thessalians—obviously appropriate for Achilles)[32] or on contemporary dialect usages (*Poetics* 1461a12–14, a Cretan gloss). What is "other" and different is thus constructed as closer to the past than "we" are.

In trying to place Hellenistic poetry within these developments, we may begin again with the idea of the poetic lexicon, and particularly "the gloss." The concern with categories of words, not just from a semantic point of view, but also in terms of stylistic level, is one of the many intellectual themes that the Sophistic movement of the later fifth century B.C.E. bequeathed to subsequent ages. It is, however, in the rhetorical writing of the fourth century that we see the full flowering of these preoccupations, which foreshadow the concerns of the lexical scholarship of the following century. Thus, for example, Isocrates sets the restrictions on prose writers against the freedom enjoyed by the poets as follows:

> To the poets is granted the use of many embellishments of language (κόσμοι), since they can represent the gods as associating with men, conversing with and aiding in battle whomsoever they please, and they can treat of these subjects not only in conventional expressions (τοῖς τεταγμένοις ὀνόμασιν), but in words now exotic (ξένοις), now newly coined, and now in figures of speech (lit. "metaphors," μεταφοραῖς), neglecting none, but using every kind with which to embroider their poetry. Orators (τοῖς δὲ περὶ τοὺς λόγους), on the contrary, are not permitted the use of such devices; they must use with precision only words in current use and only such ideas as bear upon the actual facts (ἀλλ' ἀποτόμως καὶ τῶν ὀνομάτων τοῖς πολιτικοῖς μόνον καὶ τῶν ἐνθυμημάτων τοῖς περὶ αὐτὰς τὰς πράξεις ἀναγκαῖόν ἐστι χρῆσθαι). (Isocrates, *Evagoras* 8–10; trans. Norlin, adapted)

In the Aristotelian tradition, the principal virtue of both poetic and rhetorical verbal style (*lexis*) is "clarity" (*Poetics* 1458a18, *Rhetoric* 2.1404b2), but the two differ in that the former admits more "exotic" elements that do not belong to "ordinary speech," to the "clear" (perhaps suggesting also "true") speech of "ordinary words" (κυρία ὀνόματα). These "exotic" (*xenika*) elements include metaphors, "glosses," and compound adjectives. "Ordinary words are those used by each speech community, whereas 'glosses' are words used by others. The same word can thus be both a gloss and a standard word, but not for the same people: *sigunon* ('spear') is a standard word for the Cypriots, but a gloss for us" (*Poetics* 1457b3–6). Such an eminently fair-minded approach to lexical variety contains within itself, of course, the seeds for a much more radically hierarchized approach to the control of language. Be that as it may, Aristotle also observes (1458a23–34) that an overuse of these "exotic" features will turn a poem into either a riddle (αἴνιγμα), if what is overused is metaphor, or a non-Greek babble (βαρβαρισμός), if the fault lies in too many glosses. Lycophron's linguistically extraordinary *Alexandra,* in which the principal voice is indeed that of a *barbaros,* the Trojan prophetess Cassandra, shows what a Hellenistic poet could do with this intellectual structure.[33]

Meter too is important here. In the bucolic poems and mimes Theocritus married "low" subject matter to a meter, significantly called "heroic" (τὸ ἡρ-ωικόν),[34] which theorists regarded as the most "poetic" measure and the one most removed from the rhythms of ordinary speech (cf. Aristotle, *Poetics* 1449a 27–8, 1459b 34–7 "the hexameter is the stateliest and weightiest [στασιμώ-τατον καὶ ὀγκωδέστατον] of the metres; for this reason it is the most receptive to rare words [γλῶτται] and metaphors").[35] In using in his hexameters words drawn not from the inherited poetic language but the pastoral world of herdsmen or the chatter of Alexandrian housewives, Theocritus exploits and challenges received notions of poetic appropriateness (τὸ πρέπον); elevated meter was supposed to be accompanied by elevated style and subject matter.[36] Here again Hellenistic poetics are importantly shaped by a now-flourishing tradition of stylistic criticism.

A glance through the fourth-century poems, largely epitaphs, which happen to have been preserved on stone,[37] and through the similar material from Hellenistic Egypt[38] reveals relatively few strongly marked Doric features, even in apparently "Doricizing" poems and even from areas where prose inscriptions suggest a tenacious persistence of dialect in the face of the *koinē.* It is the standardizing Ionic language of epic that everywhere predominates. There are, of course, caveats to be entered: we are at the mercy of the random chances of preservation; there are some striking exceptions to which one could point;[39] and the stones largely preserve only one type of poem; but the broad picture is, I think, not to be doubted.

In the Hellenistic period the boundaries between literary/nonliterary and/or elite/nonelite are precarious indeed,[40] but when we turn from poems preserved on stone to the poetry of the Alexandrian elite, the linguistic difference is palpable. Callimachus wrote four hymns in the traditional Ionic epic language and two (both perhaps set in Doric cities) with a strongly marked, but probably generalized, Doric color. So too the same poet's narrative *Hecale,* which is set in Attica and tells the story of how the great Attic hero Theseus was entertained by a peasant woman on his way to fight with the bull of Marathon, shows a marked Attic flavor in its vocabulary, though it is basically composed in a version of the inherited epic language. Philikos's *Hymn to Demeter* (*Supplementum Hellenisticum*

676–80) in choriambic pentameters is written in a version of Attic appropriate to the setting in Eleusis; we know the author was an important cultural figure at the court of Philadelphus. Theocritus's bucolics, on the other hand, are written in strongly marked Doric; in a famous article, C. J. Ruijgh argued that the language of the bucolics, as of Callimachus's Doric hymns, is in essence the language spoken by an expatriate Cyrenean elite resident in Alexandria,[41] but the objections to this interesting hypothesis are too many to ignore.[42] Be that as it may, what I wish to emphasize here is the *relative* thoroughness of the dialectal exercises of the Hellenistic poets, whatever their actual linguistic status. More usually it is the superficiality of the poetic dialect that is highlighted. Thus, for example, in his standard edition of Callimachus's *Hymn to Demeter* Neil Hopkinson (rightly) describes the Doric of Callimachus *h*. 5 and 6 as "merely a cosmetic adaptation of essentially epic diction and phraseology," "a thin veneer," and adduces as evidence of this the "many phonetic and morphological inconsistencies" and the fact that "every line in these poems could be 'translated' into epic dialect without damage to the metre."[43] This may well be so, but what matters here is not so much the linguistic "essence" of such compositions but rather their distinctiveness when set in the broader poetic context.

Particularly strong cases of this phenomenon are the poems of Theocritus (*Idylls* 28–30), which are written in a reconstruction of the archaic Aeolic of the great poets of Lesbos, Sappho, and Alcaeus, and the reconstructions of the language of archaic Ionic iambus by both Herodas in his *Mimiamboi* and Callimachus in the *Iamboi*. We would dearly like to know how these poets wished these poems "to sound," but we can do little better here than speculate. What some of the questions should be, however, is suggested (unintentionally) by the remarks of A. S. F. Gow, the magisterial commentator on Theocritus, concerning the Aeolic poems:

> Theocritus could hope to produce something which would strike his contemporaries as a plausible imitation of Alcaeus, and perhaps to please them here and there with some scrap of recondite knowledge. To produce something which would at all points have satisfied Alcaeus himself was plainly beyond his powers and probably beyond his ambitions. . . . It is however worth remembering that though it would be of interest to know the exact form which Theocritus gave to these imitations, the information would be of much more interest to students of Sappho and Alcaeus than to students of Theocritus himself; and also that if we sometimes replace with a correct Lesbian form one which, though incorrect, was what

Theocritus wrote, he himself would have been likely to welcome the dep-
ravation of his text.[44]

In this breathtaking passage, Gow's assumptions about what kind of poem Theocritus wanted to write entirely prevented him from asking serious questions
about the nature of the Hellenistic poetic enterprise. To go no further, it is worth
reminding ourselves that the "historical reconstruction" of language, particularly
where past linguistic forms carry a cultural and political charge, may be a quite
different activity from "scientific" linguistic archaeology (which was, in any case,
in its very first infancy in antiquity).[45]

For Gow, Theocritus's Aeolic poems were a search—doomed from the
beginning—for "authenticity." Callimachus, however, had provided a better path
to understanding long before.[46] In the *Thirteenth Iambus* he defends himself against
(real or alleged) criticisms that his poems do not preserve authentic dialectal and
generic differences; in versus 11–19 we apparently hear the voice of a critic:

> [. οὔτ'] Ἴωσι συμμείξας
> οὔτ' Ἔφεσον ἐλθών, ἥτις ἐστι αμ. [
> Ἔφεσον, ὅθεν περ οἱ τὰ μέτρα μέλλοντες
> τὰ χωλὰ τίκτειν μὴ ἀμαθῶς ἐναύονται·
> ἀλλ' εἴ τι θυμὸν ἢ 'πὶ γαστέρα πνευσ.[
> εἴτ' οὖν ἐπ...ἀρχαῖον εἴτ' ἀπαι.[
> τοῦτ' ἐμπέπλεκται καὶ λαλευσ[
> Ἰαστὶ καὶ Δωριστὶ καὶ τὸ σύμμικ[τον.
> τεῦ μέχρι τολμᾶις; οἱ φίλοι σε δήσουσι κτλ.
>
> (fr. 203.11–19)

... [N]either having mixed with Ionians nor gone to Ephesus, which
is ..., Ephesus, from where those who wish skilfully to give birth to
limping verses draw the fire of inspiration. But if something [? fires]
spirit or stomach, whether archaic or ..., this is woven in and [?] they
speak ... Ionic and Doric and a mixture. What is the limit of your reck-
lessness? Your friends will bind you up.

The charge seems to be twofold. First, Callimachus has no right to attempt "Hip-
ponactean" choliambics because he has never even been to Ephesos, the home

of Hipponax; second, Callimachus's poems use "Ionic and Doric and a mixture." The link between the two charges is that of "authenticity," and Callimachus's answer is clear: the re-creation of archaic poetic forms should not be, as his "critics" are made to suggest, the search for a "historical authenticity" in which the resulting poems, written in conditions as near as possible to those of the original (i.e., by going to Ephesus to "give birth to lame verses"), would be fit for nothing other than a museum (as opposed to the Museum), but rather a flexible frame in which the various resources of the literary heritage could be used to produce a living poetry (here we should reflect again on the inadequacy of Gow's view of Theocritus's Aeolic poems). The genres, whether defined by meter or subject, are not to be invoked to preclude imaginative composition. It is the genres, not the poems, which are the secondary and subordinate "invention"; whereas the genres are merely the result of scholarly convenience, poetry is the gift of Apollo and the Muses (cf. v. 1).[47] The critics demand a reproduction of the original performative context, a "going to Ephesus," although poetry, as properly understood, is now only possible by a frank exploitation of the absence of that context.

As with genre, so with language. That this absurd demand for "authenticity" is framed in terms of linguistic "purity" takes us straight back to the heart of Alexandrian scholarship. So too does the architecture of the *Iambi,* for in the first poem Hipponax, returned (briefly) from the dead, summons the *philologoi* to tell them an apparently improving tale; in the matching thirteenth poem the modern Hipponax, Callimachus, lectures (?unnamed) critics, who may well be constructed as these same *philologoi.*[48] Some of the ironies of the poem need no explication, but we might dwell for a further moment on the demand for "authenticity," here expressed as a "going to Ephesus." At the heart of the Alexandrian project lies the idea that things, including words and poetic forms, come to Alexandria, not vice versa.[49] The charge that Callimachus's ruinous innovations are the result of insufficient fieldwork — which is what the critics' charge amounts to — is one that many modern theoretical scholars may recognize with a smile. In Callimachus's poem, however, this is the pot calling the kettle black in a big way. The nature of Hipponax's dialect has, of course, itself been established by the scholarly activity of the Museum, not by a "going to Ephesus." "Authenticity," whether of genre, language, or authorship, is itself a second-order concept, a scholarly construction (if that is a better way to put it): the power, however, that this "idea of the authentic" can now be made to carry is a clear sign of what had been lost, and of what we in turn owe to our Alexandrian forebears.

NOTES

Warm thanks to Martin Bloomer for his invitation to the Notre Dame conference and to the participants for their comments on the oral version of this chapter. The discussion of Theocritus 15 now appears also in Fantuzzi and Hunter 2004.

1. For a helpful and brief account, see Horrocks 1997a: 32–70. From a literary point of view, the spread of the *koinē* coincides with the spread of Attic New Comedy, particularly the works of Menander, throughout the Greek world during the late fourth and third century; the two phenomena should more often be considered together.

2. Horrocks 1997b: 193; see also Morpurgo Davies 1987: 10.

3. Praxinoa in fact uses an obscure proverb here; see Gow's note ad loc.

4. There is an acute discussion in Burton 1995: 58–62, though it will become clear that I differ radically from her interpretation (p. 61) of the linguistic "problem." Much recent bibliography on this poem can be traced through Burton 1995; Hunter 1996b: chap. 4; and Reed 2000.

5. Dover 1971: 20.

6. See Hunter 1996b: 117–19.

7. On these matters, see Hunter 1996a: 152–27; 1996b: 120–23. How "silly" Praxinoa's claim that she and her friend speak "in the Peloponnesian manner" is supposed to sound is a difficult question that cannot be pursued at any length here. The Peloponnese may be the spiritual home of all true Dorians, but the dialectal differences between each "Doric-speaking" city there could still be remarked on by Strabo (8.1.2), writing in the time of Augustus. Praxinoa's adverbial form in –ιστιν apes the dialectological classificatory style, but there is perhaps no more reason to grant authority to it than to her equally sweeping, and equally stylized, condemnation of Egyptians as muggers in v.48. Moreover, though Syracuse was indeed originally a Corinthian foundation (see Thucydides 6.3.2, 7.57), it is at best unclear whether anyone in the third century would have observed an important similarity between the language of the two cities (see Buck 1955: 14); our knowledge of the language of Syracuse is, however, exiguous.

8. Cf. the remarks of A. C. Cassio in Cassio 1999: 207.

9. Bubeník 1989: 78 claims that of 17 third-century public and private inscriptions only one shows *koinē* influence, whereas 25 of 44 public inscriptions on Cos, the island where Philadelphus was born and with which Theocritus seems to have had very important links, show some *koinē* features. See also Dobias-Lalou 1987. An interesting case is the Cyrenean epigram published by Chamoux 1958; see Fraser 1972: II 864 n. 433. For Ruijgh's view of the importance of "Cyrenean dialect" at Alexandria, see below.

10. Clarysse 1998. Morpurgo Davies 2000: 24 n. 19 cautions that retention of Doric markers in name forms does not necessarily imply the survival of the dialect: "it would be conceivable that *koinē*-speakers kept the old forms of the personal names."

11. There is a translation of Philodemus, *On Poems*, bk. 5, by David Armstrong in D. Obbink, ed., *Philodemus & Poetry* (New York, 1995), 255–69.

12. The remarks of the Platonic Socrates at *Cratylus* 418b–c on alleged changes within Attic speech illustrate a rather different point but suggest the kind of observations I have in mind.

13. See in general Latte 1968: 649–66.

14. Morpurgo Davies 1987: 18.

15. See Hunter 1996b: 193–94.

16. Colvin 1999.

17. For this concept, see p. 200–201.

18. Schmitz 1999.

19. See Hammond 1972: 272–73.

20. See the decree of Xanthos in *Supplementum Epigraphicum Graecum* xxxviii (1988) 1476 and Hunter 2003: 149–50.

21. See Bastianini and Gallazzi 2001; Austin and Bastianini 2002.

22. For the text, see R. Fuhrer apud H. Bernsdorff, *Göttinger Forum für Altertumswissenschaft* 5 (2002) 39, which slightly modifies M. Gronewald, *Zeitschrift für Papyrologie und Epigraphik* 137 (2001) 5.

23. Cf. Ebert 1972, No. 72 (second-century Rhodes); Kaibel 1878, No. 942 (first-century Thera).

24. Cf. Kerkhecker 1991: 32–34; Sens 2004.

25. References are to the numeration in Gow and Page 1965.

26. Clarysse 1998: 12. Walbank 1996: 129 notes of the Posidippus epigram that "Ptolemy II is represented as taking pride in his origins in Eordaea and his use of the Macedonian tongue"; is this, however, what he is speaking?

27. See Hammond in Hammond and Griffith 1975: 39–54; Brixhe and Panayotou 1997: 207–22; O. Masson in *Oxford Classical Dictionary,* 3d ed., s.v. "Macedonian language"; Horrocks 1997a: 32–33; C. Haebler in *Der Neue Pauly,* vol. 7, s.v. "Makedonisch"; Hatzopoulos 2000: 113–15; Hall 2001: 159–86. Many ancient and Byzantine references to "the Macedonian language" are gathered by Kapetanopoulos 1999: 122–28.

28. See Dubois 1995; Voutiras 1998: 20–34; Brixhe 1999.

29. See Brixhe 1999: 44.

30. See Horrocks 1997a: 33; Brixhe 1999: 66–69.

31. For such decontextualization as an Alexandrian hallmark, see Selden 1998; Too 1998: chap. 4.

32. See Latte 1968: 642–44 on the pan-"Cymaean" interpretation of Ephoros.

33. On the *Alexandra,* see West 2000 and Hunter in Fantuzzi and Hunter 2004 [= 2002: 518–26], both with further bibliography.

34. Cf. Demetrius, *On Style* 5: "The hexameter is called 'heroic verse' because of its length and appropriateness for heroes."

35. Cf. *Rhet.* 3.1404a 34–35, 1408b 32–33; Demetrius, *On Style* 42: "the heroic verse is solemn and not suited to prose, being resounding (σεμνὸς καὶ οὐ λογικός, ἀλλ' ἠχώδης)." γλῶσσαι in this context are largely archaisms, often from Homer, which were often no longer fully understood.

36. Some of the most familiar theoretical statements in this field are, of course, later than Theocritus (e.g., "Longinus" 30.2), but it is hardly to be doubted that there is an academic, as well as a poetic, background to Theocritus's practice.

37. Hansen 1989.

38. Bernard 1969; see also Fraser 1972: I 608 ff.

39. Of particular interest is the first-century Isis hymn from Andros (Totti No. 2), a text that raises issues both of innovation and conservative archaizing in religious texts.

40. The Doric (and Cynic) *meliamboi* of Cercidas of Megalopolis (late third century) are not "Alexandrian" but also raise interesting questions about the development of poetic dialect.

41. Ruijgh 1984.

42. For a brief account and bibliography, see Hunter 1996b: 37.

43. Hopkinson 1984: 44.

44. Gow 1952: I lxxviii, lxxx.

45. The work of Albio Cassio on ancient notions of dialect and conceptions of poetic language is particularly important here, see, e.g., Cassio 1993a–c.

46. For a fuller discussion, see Hunter 1997, from which these remarks borrow.

47. On the "speaker" of v.1, see Kerkhecker 1999: 253.

48. Cf., e.g., Kerkhecker 1999: 258, 269–70.

49. Selden 1998 is particularly important here.

BIBLIOGRAPHY

Austin, C., and G. Bastianini. 2002. *Posidippi Pellaei quae supersunt omnia*. Milan.

Bastianini, G., and C. Gallazzi. 2001. *Posidippo di Pella, Epigrammi (P. Mil. Vogl. VIII 309)*. Milan.

Bernard, E. 1969. *Inscriptions métriques de l'Egypte gréco-romaine*. Paris.

Brixhe, C. 1999. "Un 'nouveau' champ de la dialectologie grecque: Le Macédonien." In Cassio 1999: 41–69.

Brixhe, C., and A. Panayotou. 1997. "Le Macédonien." In F. Bader, ed., *Langues Indo-Européennes*, 207–22. Paris.

Bubeník, V. 1989. *Hellenistic and Roman Greece as a Sociolinguistic Area*. Amsterdam.

Buck, C. D. 1955. *The Greek Dialects*. Chicago.

Burton, J. B. 1995. *Theocritus's Urban Mimes: Mobility, Gender, and Patronage*. Berkeley.

Cassio, A. C. 1993a. "Parlate locali, dialetti delle stirpi e fonti letterarie nei grammatici greci." In *Dialectologica Graeca*, 73–90. Madrid.

———. 1993b. "Alcmane, il dialetto di Cirene e la filologia alessandrina." *Rivista di Filologia e di Istruzione Classica* 121: 24–36.

———. 1993c. "Iperdorismi callimachei e testo antico dei lirici." In R. Pretagostini, ed., *Tradizione e innovazione nella cultura greca da Omero all'età ellenistica*, 903–10. Rome.

Cassio, A. C., ed. 1999. *Κατὰ Διάλεκτον. Atti del III Colloquio Internazionale di Dialettologia Greca*. Naples.

Chamoux, F. 1958. "Épigramme de Cyrène en l'honneur du roi Magas." *Bulletin de Correspondance Hellénique* 82: 571–87.

Clarysse, W. 1998. "Ethnic Diversity and Dialect among the Greeks of Hellenistic Egypt." In A. M. F. W. Verhoogt and S. P. Vleeming, eds., *The Two Faces of Graeco-Roman Egypt,* 1–13. Leiden.

Colvin, S. 1999. *Dialect in Aristophanes: The Politics of Language in Ancient Greek Literature.* Oxford.

Dobias-Lalou, C. 1987. "Dialecte et koine dans les inscriptions de Cyrenaique." *Verbum* 10: 29–50.

Dover, K. J. 1971. *Theocritus: Select Poems.* London.

Dubois, L. 1995. "Une tablette de malédiction de Pella: S'agit-il du premier texte macédonien." *Revue des Études Grecques* 108: 190–97.

Ebert, J. 1972. *Griechische Epigramme auf Sieger an gymnischen und hippischen Agonen.* Berlin.

Fantuzzi, M., and R. Hunter. 2002. *Muse e modelli: La poesia ellenistica da Alessandro Magno ad Augusto.* Rome-Bari.

———. 2004. *Tradition and Innovation in Hellenistic Poetry.* Cambridge.

Fraser, P. M. 1972. *Ptolemaic Alexandria.* Oxford.

Gow, A. S. F. 1952. *Theocritus.* 2d ed. Cambridge.

Gow, A. S. F., and D. L. Page. 1965. *The Greek Anthology: Hellenistic Epigrams.* Cambridge.

Hall, J. M. 2001. "Contested Ethnicities: Perceptions of Macedonia within Evolving Definitions of Greek Identity." In I. Malkin, ed., *Ancient Perceptions of Greek Ethnicity,* 159–86. Cambridge, Mass.

Hammond, N. G. L. 1972. *A History of Macedonia* I. Oxford.

Hammond, N. G. L., and G. T. Griffith. 1975. *A History of Macedonia* II. Oxford.

Hansen, P. A., ed. 1989. *Carmina Epigraphica Graeca* II. Berlin.

Hatzopoulos, M. 2000. "'L'histoire par les noms' in Macedonia." In S. Hornblower and E. Matthews, eds., *Greek Personal Names: Their Value as Evidence,* 99–117. Oxford.

Hopkinson, Neil. 1984. *Callimachus, Hymn to Demeter.* Cambridge.

Horrocks, G. 1997a. *Greek: A History of the Language and Its Speakers.* London.

———. 1997b. "Homer's Dialect." In I. Morris and B. Powell, eds., *A New Companion to Homer,* 193–217. Leiden.

Hunter, R. 1996a. "Mime and Mimesis: Theocritus, *Idyll* 15." In A. Harder et al., eds., *Theocritus,* 149–69. Groningen.

———. 1996b. *Theocritus and the Archaeology of Greek Poetry.* Cambridge.

———. 1997. "(B)ionic Man: Callimachus' Iambic Programme." *Proceedings of the Cambridge Philological Society* 43: 41–52.

———. 2003. *Theocritus: Encomium of Ptolemy Philadelphus.* Berkeley.

Kaibel, G. 1878. *Epigrammata Graeca ex lapidibus conlecta.* Berlin.

Kapetanopoulos, E. 1999. "Alexander's *Patrius Sermo* in the Philotas Affair." *Ancient World* 30: 117–28.

Kerkhecker, A. 1991. "Zum neuen hellenistischen Weihepigramm aus Pergamon." *Zeitschrift für Papyrologie und Epigraphik* 86: 27–34.

———. 1999. *Callimachus' Book of Iambi.* Oxford.

Latte, K. 1968. *Kleine Schriften.* Munich.

Morpurgo Davies, A. 1987. "The Greek Notion of Dialect." *Verbum* 10: 7–28. Reprinted in T. Harrison, ed., *Greeks and Barbarians,* 153–71. Edinburgh, 2002.

———. 2000. "Greek Personal Names and Linguistic Continuity." In S. Hornblower and E. Matthews, eds., *Greek Personal Names: Their Value as Evidence,* 15–39. Oxford.

Reed, J. D. 2000. "Arsinoe's Adonis and the Poetics of Ptolemaic Imperialism." *Transactions of the American Philological Society* 130: 319–51.

Ruijgh, C. J. 1984. "Le dorien de Théocrite: Dialecte cyrénien d'Alexandrie et d'Égypte." *Mnemosyne* 37: 56–88.

Schmitz, T. A. 1999. "'I hate all common things': The Reader's Role in Callimachus' *Aetia* Prologue." *Harvard Studies in Classical Philology* 99: 151–78.

Selden, D. 1998. "Alibis." *Classical Antiquity* 17: 289–412.

Sens, A. 2003. "Doricisms in the New and Old Posidippus." In B. Acosta-Hughes, E. Kosmetatou, and M. Baumbach, eds., *Labored in Papyrus Leaves: Perspectives on an Epigram Collection attributed to Posidippus (P. Mil. Vogl. VIII 309),* 65–83. Cambridge, Mass.

Too, Y. L. 1998. *The Idea of Ancient Literary Criticism.* Oxford.

Voutiras, E. 1998. *ΔΙΟΝΥΣΟΦΩΝΤΟΣ ΓΑΜΟΙ. Marital Life and Magic in Fourth-Century Pella.* Amsterdam.

Walbank, F. 1996. "Two Hellenistic Processions: A Matter of Self-Definition." *Scripta Classica Israelica* 15: 119–30.

West, S. 2000. "Lycophron's *Alexandra*: 'Hindsight as Foresight Makes No Sense'?" In M. Depew and D. Obbink, eds., *Matrices of Genre,* 153–66. Cambridge, Mass.

9 Marble Latin

Encounters with the Timeless Language

W. MARTIN BLOOMER

In recollecting his first hearing of Latin, the poet Seamus Heaney recollects another literary schoolboy's linguistic recollection. Stephen Dedalus is made to feel embarrassed for using a word his professor deems not English. Later Stephen has his revenge, for he learns that *tundish* is not an Irish word for "funnel" but an English word that crossed to Ireland long ago and which the English and the professor, his critic, now do not recognize.[1] The Irish figures, Dedalus and Heaney, embody a memory that the English grammarian slights even as they carry a double memory, of the slight and of their own layered, ancestral language. Their complex ancestral language requires more than recollection, for it is ambivalent and dormant. The identity of this language fluctuates: perhaps it is Irish (revived or ancient), or an older English, or Latin (another language at which Stephen is tested and which has a long history in Ireland). The imposition, correction, and restoration of these make the linguistic politics of an "Irish" writer as complex as any in the twentieth century, with or without an overt recognition of this position as belated, imposed, or postcolonial.

The memory of a past language can easily tilt to nostalgia for a language lost, and this longing easily may become a figure, a synecdoche for a culture lost or suppressed. The rapidity of the equations or substitutions that arrange a childhood memory, ancestral languages, and cultural integrity no doubt obscures historical processes and complexities. In the place of historical description of changes in language use and users, today's talk about old words fashions a map that excavates, partially and piecemeal, the sites of ancestral language, which themselves are understood to have been overwritten by imposed language, that thick stratum of the invader or conqueror or of the amnesia or break with the past that modernism is thought to represent. The linguistic politics of contemporary Ireland, as Crowley, Deane, and McQuillan demonstrate in this volume, are no such transparent mapping. The Anglo-Irish may recall a forgotten word, but it is still English, and the return of a language, especially if it is figured as the recollection or reconstruction of childhood, seems at best a pleasant memory.[2] In a number of poems, Heaney does play the philologue, searching out forgotten Irishisms, but he more frequently summons tokens of memory that are more durable, more material, and perhaps less political as not linguistic. The throat-slit bog people, a piece of rock or bone, connect poet and reader to an ancestral Ireland. These poems begin from a collection of fragments of a Celtic or even pre-Celtic past; the accidental find of a body or a bit of bone or a Viking torque prompts the poem, as if *res,* the thing itself, were prior to the linguistic *signum.*[3] So the poem, that artifice of signs, may evade the issue of its own language. In this elegiac fiction, Heaney has emplotted the failures of language to constitute identity or to connect the present with a past rich in real signs. The trope seems almost Horatian or Virgilian, not because those poets saw the preliterary or sub-literary as culturally authoritative, but because they posed their own poetry as distanced revivals of song, epic after the epic age, eclogue that is postexilic, outside of and later than happy pastoral, or lyric without the Greek lyre.

Heaney's recollection of Latin turns autobiographical as he writes, more positively and more lyrically, of his experience as a schoolboy first hearing Latin. Latin is again something of a stand-in for Irish in a piece Heaney wrote about translation in the *Times Literary Supplement* in December 2001. Heaney began by remembering his first encounter with Latin, as a boy hearing the preconciliar Latin mass first thing every morning at school. For the poet this was a deeply lyrical moment: "the beginning of the last gospel sounded like the first note of god's tuning fork." Soon with a little Latin Heaney finds "that the English translation ended up having less immediately persuasive power than what I took to be the original." Jerome comes to sound "like those orb-sized words of pre-Babel speech imagined by Wallace Stevens at the end of his poem 'The Idea of Order at Key West.'" Heaney continues his peregrination for those lyrical word-globes through Octavio Paz and on to Stephen Dedalus's late realization of the legitimacy of *tundish.* I, however, wish to tarry over those first Latin words, that foundational moment of hearing *In principio erat verbum.* The act of audition marks the beginning of *poiēsis,* that is, of the tradition of creation that each auditor receives. Latin as so often plays several roles: it is the language of poetry, the language of Heaney's Catholic ancestry, decidedly not English, but a genuine language that can return one to the past or to the timeless place that is poetry, where sound and sense are one.

For the Western poet recalling his poetic *principia*, Latin seems something of a revenant, like Virgil himself continually reappearing in the literature of the West.[4] Latin can of course be the schoolboy's drone as much as the poet's lyrical language, and this double history allows Latin to represent the imposition and the emancipation that a learned language entails. For Heaney, Latin abundantly recalls the struggles for and against the restoration of Irish. By evoking an ancestral language in a piece on translation, he may also recall Brian Friel's play *Translations*, in which the death of Irish is itself overabundantly represented as the loss of a native schooling in three languages (although Heaney's preference for the material origins of a poem contrasts with Friel's delight in the talk and the play of talk amid the different languages of his characters).[5] The play is set in a hedge school whose learned master teaches the original to the genuine; that is, he imparts Homer's Greek and Virgil's Latin through the medium of Irish to the Irish folk, man and woman, old farmer and speech-impaired girl (and these are folk not pedants; the best of the students, the sexagenarian Jimmy Jack Cassie, so say the stage notes, "never washes"). English speakers lurk on the school's margins, in the form of the British military surveyors who hire the master's son to aid them in renaming the countryside, obliterating the traces of Irish as surely as the hedge school will be replaced by an English school.[6] The schoolmaster, like that father of Latin poetry Ennius, has *tria corda*, three hearts, Irish, Latin, and Greek (to Ennius's Oscan, Latin and Greek). But this Irish father of poetry, quite unlike *pater* Ennius, is no robust genitor. He stands at the end of a tradition and plays a decaying schoolmaster, besotted, imperious, nostalgic. Still, his virtuosity in the three languages and poetries sets him in stark contrast to the monoglot prose workers who can but come up with imperfect English versions of place-names. The Irish in the school engage in linguistic acts of a different order: in place of a ponderous search for English glosses, Jimmy translates Homeric lines into Irish (represented in the play by English). The play's first linguistic act has Manus teaching Sarah to speak; while he coaxes her, Jimmy recites his Homer. In fact the line announces or anticipates Sarah's success, for he recites the formulaic line in which Athena answers a prior speaker (*Odyssey* 12.420—"glaukopis Athena then answered him"). The owl-eyed or grey-eyed (or perhaps faced) may itself suit the speech-impaired Sarah. At any rate, the Irish and the Homeric coincide. The summons to reply can be more insistent and mundane as when one of the scholars imitates the drunk master himself by delivering the imperatives *responde responde*.[7] The imperative to speak a classical language animates character (the two in this scene know more Latin than English — indeed the English is mispronounced or ungrammatical) and drives the play, and troubles the playwright, who must translate all into the language of the surveyors.

Latin, Irish, and Greek then enjoy a slightly unjust advantage over English, which would be only the tool of prose workers were it not also the medium of the drama and of our understanding of all the languages of the play. The easy dichotomy that identifies some languages as languages of oppression and others as languages of liberation is also undercut by the dictatorship that is the school of language learning. The terms "liberation" and "oppression" may be conceptually inadequate to describe the processes of language acquisition and the changes in subjectivity that accompany these. In the Western school, by which I mean the school of Latin, there is an overlapping contradiction. Learning Latin removes (liberates) the individual from the familial and the local and the present, but it is an oppressive business. The school of liberal education itself forms an *imperium* replete with punishment and humiliation.[8] In the hedge school Latin may well be as much a birthright as Irish since Latin is the language of the church, the language of traditional schooling, and, more distantly, the possession of the early Irish monks with their Hiberno-Latin literature. Yet it is also the language of command, especially in the master's mouth (his son speaks to Sarah in English/ Irish while Manus intones Greek). Brian Friel is representing the past as polyglot against an impoverished monoglot present, and the three languages evoke an older, Indo-European culture (against English whose literature is only as old as *Beowulf* and against the English speakers of this play who are harbingers of the monoglots to come).

The play in fact performs not so much a search for the perfect language as a double memory, the recollection of a rich and native language learning (in school and not, as Augustine, in infancy) and the memory of language lost. The story that just a generation ago school boys and girls could speak or write or read the classical languages far better than the present iron age is an agreeable, bittersweet tale. Indeed, it is a traditional tale of the tribe that flourishes each generation in part because the community of living Latin is always just out of memory, a place and time that schooling hopes to resurrect but which of course the vernacular Europe cannot reinstate. The symbolic richness of Latin is not simply an Irish phenomenon, of course. The learning of Latin is seldom described as the acquisition of a certain set of linguistic skills. In addition to the metalinguistic skill that one might expect to be learned from the context and setting of the language learning, the student of Latin also learns stories of the language, and its effect on him or her. Latin is said to impart clear thinking or discipline or an understanding of language in the abstract. For some, the mastery of the old language promises access to the more authoritative, perished knowledge and culture of antiquity or to scripture and indeed the sacred. Because it was so long the language of school, learning Latin often represents a coming-of-age.

I present below case studies in the imagination of the power of Latin. The language has no inherent structure that dictates these reactions. Rather, traditional ways of understanding the language, encoded in literature and also performed in Latin schooling, entice each generation of students toward certain dispositions about the value and use of Latin, its variants, and of other languages. These studies, far removed in time, place, and literariness, share an image of Latin as the language of school. School practices have left a strong imprint on the understanding of Latin as the language of authenticity, power, redress, even vengeance. In fact, Latin is useful precisely because of its multiple ownership. Among latter-day users, it can be near-native, as for the Irish monks, yet this traditional language, verging on a birthright, was another's native language and must be learned with considerable toil. A user of Latin can construct and lay claim to linguistic communities in ways fundamentally different from users of a (nationalist) vernacular precisely because of the multiple ownership of the language (which signals allegiances other than the nationalist or ethnic).

The hedge master and his students, the poet Seamus Heaney, and that ill-tempered user and critic of Latin, the bishop at St. Praxed's of Robert Browning's poem, pose in verse as champions of Latin. At times they represent Latin as an unchanging, even marble language of final signification. In more banal moments we overhear the schoolmaster's recitation and wonder how language can be restored or revived. The Latin that will not come to life symbolizes both an old culture silenced and the silencing effect of an old culture. Where Latin is granted a strongly positive role as a carrier of meaning and as an index of connection between past and present, the critic may well smile at the unrecognized ideological assumptions in such attitudes. Champions of the dead language of the West wield Latin as a weapon in religious, political, social, and educational campaigns, but the recurrence of enthusiasm for Latin also attests to its strength, for some, in their own education. Even beyond a nostalgia for a childhood or youthful discovery of a world of words and thoughts, Latin figures easily what we seem to want from language, an efficacious *poiēsis* that is our own but which is not ordinary.

I have reproduced below a poem published some four months before Heaney's meditation on translation.[9]

Bann Valley Eclogue

POET: Bann Valley Muses, give us a song worth singing,
    Something that rises like the curtain in
    Those words And it came to pass or In the beginning.
    Help me to please my hedge-schoolmaster Virgil
    And the child that's due. Maybe, heavens, sing
    Better times for her and her generation.

VIRGIL: Here are my words you'll have to find a place for:
    Carmen, ordo, nascitur, saeculum, gens,
    Ferrea, aurea, aetas, scelus, Lucina.
    Their gist in your tongue and province should be clear
    Even at this stage. Poetry, order, the times,
    The nation, wrong and renewal, iron and gold.

POET: Lucina. Rhyming with Sheena. Vocative. First
    Declension. Feminine gender. The Roman
    St Anne. Who is casta Lucina, chaste
    Star of the birth-bed. And secular star,
    Meaning star of the saeculum, brightness gathering
    Head great month by month now, waiting to fall.
    You were raised on the land they drove your father off.
    You had his country accent and little to learn
    Of the facts of life when you read your first poems out
    To Octavian, feeling the length of the line
    As if you were dressing husks off a hank of tow
    Or measuring wheal for thatch. Holding your own
    In your own way. Pietas and stealth. If ex-servicemen
    Were cocks of the walk at home, hexameters
    Would rule the roost in Rome. You would understand us
    Latter-day scholarship boys and girls, on the cusp
    Between elocution and duchas. Faces that were japped
    With cowdung once now barefaced to camera, live.

VIRGIL: Whatever stains you, you rubbed it into yourselves,
    Earth mark, birth mark, mould like the bloodied mould
    On Romulus's ditch-back. When the waters break

Bann's stream will overflow, the old markings
Will avail no more to keep east bank from west.
The valley will be washed like the new baby.

POET: Pacatum orbem: your words are too much nearly.
Even "orb" by Itself. What on earth could match it?
And then, last month, mid-morning, the wind dropped.
An Avernus chill, birdless and dark, prepared.
A firstness steadied, a lastness, a born awareness
As name dawned into knowledge: I saw the orb.

VIRGIL: Eclipses won't be for this child. The cool she'll know
Will be the pram hood over her vestal head.
Big dog daisies will get fanked up in the spokes.
She'll lie on summer evenings listening to
A chug and slug going on in the milking parlour.
Let her never hear close gunfire or explosions.

POET: Why do I remember St Patrick's mornings,
Being sent by my mother to the railway line
For the little trefoil, untouchable almost, the shamrock
And its twining, binding, creepery, tough, thin roots
All over the place, in the stones between the sleepers.
Dew-scales shook off the leaves. Tear-ducts asperging.
Child on the way, it won't be long until
You land among us. Your mother's showing signs,
Out for her sunset walk among big round bales.
Planet earth like a teething ring suspended
Hangs by its world-chain. Your pram waits in the corner.
Cows are let out. They're sluicing the milk-house floor.
We know, little one, you have to start with a cry
But smile soon too, a big one for your mother.
Unsmiling life has had it in for people
For far too long. But now you have it in you
Not to be wrong-footed but to first-foot us
And, muse of the valley, give us a song worth singing.

Here the poet confronts Latin, and Latin is not so lyrical and fecund a mode as when the schoolboy first heard the Gospel of John. Instead, the poet meets Virgil whose language seems dead, even deadly, all but impossible to resuscitate. The difficulty of the necromancy, especially after Dante's daunting success, is compounded by the choice of Virgilian text Heaney dares to emulate, for Heaney's poem attempts to reprise Virgil's fourth eclogue, written in the hope of peace in 40 B.C.E. (Jérôme Carcopino in the first sentence of his *Virgile et le Mystère de la IVᵉ Églogue* [Paris, 1943] writes of the "impertinence" of trying to write something new on this poem. The line of mystics and allegorizers should make the poet wary.) Latin, lyricism, the encounter of poet with Virgil that would make Heaney into Dante, a lasting peace, all need to be resuscitated, to be given animating voice. Yet the Latin is sluggish at best. The liturgical, with its promise that language is performative and sacred, seems lost. Latin is here not the uplifting *In principio erat Verbum* but the drum roll of fragments of the hexameter:

> Carmen, ordo, nascitur, saeculum, gens,
> Ferrea, aurea, aetas, scelus, Lucina.

Heaney's eye has skimmed the first lines of the eclogue and can glean only a harsh vocabulary, although the hard *c*'s and *g*'s of his first line give way in the following line to the assonance of vowels and the final, softened, church *c,* as he pronounces it, of Lucina, "rhyming with Sheena." Here the poet plays the schoolboy again, but this memory seems hopelessly prosaic. How will poetry arise from such banality? Virgil's poem is but a series of harsh nouns with perhaps the hint of something softer and more productive, *nascitur* holding the middle of the first line, and the goddess not of partition but parturition at the end.

More Latin intrudes at the beginning of the fifth of Heaney's seven stanzas (the poet's voice speaks first and last, like Tityrus, the voice of the poet in Virgil's first eclogue; in Heaney's poem Virgil has been displaced: he gets to play the part of the exiled Meliboeus):

> Pacatum orbem: your words are too much nearly.
> Even "orb" by itself. What on earth could match it?

The Anglo-Irish voice may well take issue with the orb made pacific, for at the edge of the orb and empire he may remember the native voice of the noblest Briton of them all, Galgacus, who saw so clearly, at least in Tacitus's pages, the achievement of empire at the edges: the Romans make a devastation and call it peace (*Agricola* 30: *ubi solitudinem faciunt, pacem appellant*). To write in the vestiges of Virgil's and Augustus's monumentality, or perhaps even in the echo of Wallace Stevens, seems unattainable. Heaney means more than the commonplace, inherited from Virgil's and Horace's feigned reluctance to embrace the grand theme, that the poem cannot compass the world (especially the political world). Virgil's own words are a deadened, pacified realm. Heaney is not the first, nor will he be the last, to find Virgil, the *Aeneid* especially, an onslaught of imperial vocabulary: *pietas, ordo,* and company. This partial reading arises from the poem's self-conscious fashioning of an epic language and from a poetic persona who faces epic reluctantly. Heaney's poem, forecasting peace and seeking a language that is not simply imperial or deadly, follows Virgil on several levels, including that of the *recusatio*—the figure in which the poet represents his difficulty and reluctance in taking up the grand theme of war and state or, here, of lasting peace.

Heaney has intimated the divide between the classical and the liturgical with his own beginning:

> POET: Bann Valley Muses, give us a song worth singing,
> Something that rises like the curtain in
> Those words And it came to pass or In the beginning.
> Help me to please my hedge-schoolmaster Virgil . . .

The scriptural openings and the address to the Muses, both Hesiodic and Virgilian, hope for something better than the schoolmaster's drone. Can our language, spoken or learned, rise to the level of God's speech acts that need only name and reality, creation occurs? Can a longing for Virgilianism, that state the belated poet finds himself in, rise to the level of naming and making peace? In the immediate course of the poem and in the tradition of *recusatio,* the answer is no, or at least the technique is one of deferral, indirection, of doubt realized in language. The poet responds not as Dante to Statius and Virgil but as schoolboy to hedge master. For the moment, the poetry of peace has descended once again to a parsing drill.

> Lucina. Rhyming with Sheena. Vocative. First
> Declension. feminine gender, The Roman
> St. Anne . . .

The schoolboy's parsing corresponds to the poet's listing of Virgil's diction. Joseph Brodsky has remarked of Virgil's fondness for lists that listing seems to have been the poet's preferred mode of understanding the world, which if incomplete in the *Eclogues* and the *Georgics,* the epic *Aeneid* has rounded out. Brodsky is more sensitive than most moderns to the aesthetics of the list. He understands well the connection to empire that the inventorying and naming of parts performs, whether in triumphal parade or in the geographic course of a poem of Horace. Still, it is difficult to appreciate the aesthetic motive and effect of what seems to the modern a quintessentially prosaic act.[10] In Heaney's poem as in the translations of Virgil read by Brodsky, the list spreads before the reader, as if we needed any reminding, all the drudgery and ordinariness of language learning. Reading poetry is a labor, an act of division, a mundane school algebra where words are individual items to be cataloged or at best to be glossed—thus we find the local substitute for the untranslatable, Lucina is St. Anne. The poetic persona of Heaney's poem, of course, plays the fool, the school dunce here: he is one of the latter-day scholarship boys. Yet the posturing as a schoolboy, indeed the inset scene of a successful encounter with Latin, recalls another literary student, Stephen Dedalus, subjected to a test of his Latinity.

In a poem so transparently Virgilian, Irish has more presence (even though like Friel's "Translations" through the ventriloquism of English) than it did in Heaney's autobiographical schoolboy memory of hearing the Latin mass. The poet's imitation of Virgil extends to the use of his native language. Irish place-names, an Irish word, and Hiberno-English assume the role of the Latin or Italic in Virgil's *Eclogues;* that is, where Virgil fashions a poetic landscape from Greek literary predecessors and Italian themes and terms, Heaney has Irish to match Virgil's Latin, Latin to Virgil's Greek. Where Virgil began with Sicilian Muses, Heaney has invoked Bann Valley Muses. The river Bann divides Protestant East Ulster from Catholic West Ulster, but the selection of Muse is more significant still. Bann Valley may well recollect the name for the Muses elsewhere in the *Eclogues* (3.59). Camenae, the Latin gloss for Muses, which substitutes Italic fountain goddesses for the Greek Muses, may be echoed in the trisyllable (and rhyming) Bann Valley. It is Virgilian too to create a mixed landscape. For Virgil, native Italic and Greek literary places and character cohabit. Heaney has Romulus adjacent to Bann's stream.

> VIRGIL: Whatever stains you, you rubbed it into yourselves,
> Earth mark, birth mark, mould like the bloodied mould
> On Romulus's ditch-back. When the waters break
> Bann's stream will overflow, the old markings
> Will avail no more to keep east bank from west.
> The valley will be washed like the new baby.

The overflowing Bann may also echo Horace's second ode, where the flooding Tiber seeks to blot out fratricidal, civil strife (although Horace's poem is more flood of punishment than baptism). Still, like the classical diction of the pacified orb, there is threat and exultation. The nonclassical aspect of the diction of the pacified orb, those forms of Wallace Stevens, also combine positive wonder and negative awe. Of the orb Heaney writes, "What on earth could match it?" We might ask: What has happened to Wallace Stevens's language? Perhaps we have had the match a few lines earlier. The poet had said Virgil would understand us:

> You would understand us
> latter-day scholarship boys and girls, on the cusp
> Between elocution and duchas.

The Irish word *duchas,* the sole word of Irish allowed in this poem, is an abstract noun from the root *du,* place, cognate with the Greek *Khthon,* meaning right or inherited claim to a native place. There is an old proverb that *duchas* is stronger than education.[11] The poet and the reader of Virgil stand between native place and education, and surely the poem's progress echoes the proverb. Virgil and Virgilianism seem to recede. Earth is more present. A satisfactory gloss for *patria* has been found. A topic now for Irish Camenae, Bann Valley Muses.

The many Latins of the poem have spanned the lost language of peace, those unapproachable words of the great poet, the language of schooling that removes the lad from ignorance and yet too from his birthright, and the language of poetry itself. At the end, peace and Latin and Wallace Stevens coincide, which is to say, the poet now speaks a prophetic language. (And propitious: the poet hopes not to be wrong-footed, rather the child will first-foot us all; wrong-footed is both the religious superstitious *sinistra pede* and the metrically clumsy. The child, like Rome herself, appreciates poets. Hexameters will rule and not the politicos who make the local level such a hell.) Heaney is his most Virgilian in saluting the child to come and echoing the birdless Avernus, which heralded Aeneas's journey to death and back again. The poet says he sees an orb, a prophecy right for the Sibyl or Anchises as they glimpse better than Aeneas the empire to come. Perhaps too the echo of Virgil's description of the deadly place tempers the mimicry of the vatic role of the poet (the celebratory quality of the fourth eclogue) with a gesture of epicism. The lyrical mode here never quite shakes the sepulchral—another Virgilian or Horatian gesture. The hesitant hope of the poem is that such gestures might matter. Can the marble language still signify? Or will it simply silence our latter-day efforts? The poet presents himself intermediate between the native and the literary tradition. Latin is a complex signifier: it is not simply lyricism or epicism, poetry or silence, peace or war. Latin is both the Catholic tradition and a sign for the imposed, imperial language. Quite naturally, the use of Latin brings with it reflections on the imposition of a language. The prejudice in favor of the marble language is strong: against this one abiding language are the vernaculars whose name implies they are *vernae,* homegrown bastards of the Roman master and the (foreign) slave women.[12]

The citation of Latin in a vernacular poem seems to introduce a one-sided rivalry. The poem with inset Latin, which invokes Latin, is not simply a mixed form, like the macaronic poems of the late Roman poet Ausonius which combine Latin and Greek, sometimes even in the same word. Heaney and Browning are interested in the drama of the encounter of the living and the dead languages. Poem and poet waver between the two worlds, and the hesitation in poetic medium, which is dramatized by the play of Latin and English, attracts poetic, cultural, political, and religious implications. In part, the contest is a poetic legacy, not exclusively the iteration of the debate should one write in the vernacular, but with a different question, how can the present poem be written at all, given the presence of authoritative Latin, marble or golden or iron as Heaney recalls Virgil? Ultimately, the author's pose of diffidence, this form of writerly *dubitatio,* may stem from Roman poets reflecting on the ability of Latin to match genres and themes well wrought in Greek. In addition, the early Roman poets had laid claim to writing a pure Latin and denigrated their predecessors for failing to achieve a perfect Latinity. The struggle to reuse and best the old words is a strong inheritance of the Roman poetic tradition (and its rhetorical theorization of the relation of the present to the past as one of rivalry, *aemulatio,* where each new author strives to be the *aemulus,* the rival lover in Roman elegy, of Lady Literature). Heaney has dramatized the contest by quoting Virgil's words and by adopting also that most contentious of forms, the eclogue of dueling poets.

More immediately, Browning, Friel, and Heaney take their ideas of a difficult, unequal contest with Latin from scholastic settings where the young Latin learner is faced with a harsh master. The agonistic traditions of Latin poetics and the agonies of learning Latin coincide. As each class has its top student, whose place is earned by his command of Latin, each genre has its top practitioner. That practitioner has read the old poets and now offers a better expression. To write in a genre requires, in short, pushing the poet from his pedestal. Such seems the schematic thinking of this strain of Latin or Latinate poetics. The drama of the boy learning Latin contributes three salient attitudes: Latin is a difficult language to learn, it is difficult to reanimate, and the language learner is at present an imperfect user whose self-worth will grow with his ability in this language. Indeed, he is at present a boy and a victim but will grow through Latin to be a man, a master of others through his mastery of the language of command. For different individuals and at different times and places, learning Latin has undoubtedly instilled different attitudes toward language. It is not invariable that the vernacular will be disparaged. Yet the history of the language (and its teaching) encourages an understanding of different grades of Latin. Certainly, the teaching of rhetoric instructed the pupil that different styles of language were appropriate for different genres, venues, audiences. But the gap between the written and the spoken language left a sense that one had to work at one's Latin for it to measure up. The long apprenticeship of Latin learning has had various ends — in practice Latin learning has been the education for all manner of professions — but the materials of education, to the degree that they follow Cicero and Quintilian, imagine that they are shaping the child into the orator. In the exercises of the Latin school from first reading the distichs ascribed to the elder Cato to the recitation of Cicero's speeches or the composition of the declamatory exercises, the young scholar plays at being an orator. The contest of language here is an *aemulatio,* a rivalry with his peers for preeminence, for writing and speaking as if he were Cato or Cicero. Educators speak of love of learning, but *invidia* rather than *amor* may well mark the subjectivity of those trained in a critical, traditional schooling, where a wrong word or even a wrong quantity will spoil the schoolboy's chances. The master gives grudging approval. The boy begrudges his peers. Cicero and stylistic strictures founded on a narrow canon begrudge later words.

The poetics of inset Latin pose an issue similar to that faced by the schoolboy orators: how to wield one's Latin and to control or limit another's. Of course, the apostrophe of the long-dead Latin poet or the inclusion of his words does not work in such a summary fashion. The old poet and poetic rivalries are not dismissed so easily. As in *Bann Valley Eclogue,* the evocation of school Latin or school poet figures the vernacular poet's belated stance and a desire for return, to an age or season of unmediated contact with poetry which is both childhood or the first encounter with the special language of poetry and that equally fictitious time, the moment of inspiration, when Muses might actually give up a song. Latin need not necessarily be a language of *invidia* or of combat; it might be a hymnic language, a sacred language that actualizes peace (as in a related valorization of its abilities, it is a hard, enduring language of permanent signification), but the presence of vernacular poetry transforms and reanimates the old generational contests of the

Latin poets. The first Latin poets, Livius Andronicus and Ennius especially, had crafted a poetic language and in doing so claimed in poetic epitaphs to have written pure Latin. The vernacular poet has to face this combative poetics from the prejudiced position that he is not even up to Latin. The inclusion of Latin in the vernacular poem is well represented by a poem of Robert Browning in which he faces the tradition of Latin writers, indeed tries to resurrect it by summoning a great practitioner. Like Heaney, this summons to the dead dramatizes the issue of whether Latin is a lyrical language, a source for poetry, or a sepulchral mode, fit for the dead or their allies, professors and rancorous clerics.

In Browning's poem "The Tomb at St. Praxed's," the chief characters, the dying bishop and his dead rival, figure well the anxiety of the author facing high style. The bishop's voice, returned to us by the poet's good service, complains of his rival's bad Latin. Gandolf, the rival, has taken the best burial place and to add insult to injury had inscribed an epitaph. Here a single Latin word gives the critical humanist bishop an opening. Like many a humanist Latinist, the bishop will mend the text with considerable disdain for the scribe and his language. There is in fact an elaborate triangulation in the linguistic claims and techniques of this poem. The English poet has written a poem that cites but one archival word, *elucescebat,* which is both the fault of Latinity that the bishop so pleasurably discovers and, the reader presumes, the actual inscribed word from which Browning has made his poem. The word means little more than "he was flourishing," although the metaphor is not of a flower blooming but a light shining, and is the term that Gandolf had used of himself. So poet reports bishop reporting rival. The bishop takes pleasure in reading this word since his rival "should" have written the plain verb *elucebat* and not the form with the inceptive suffix. In fact, such a form does occur, but in the Vulgate, not in any classical Latin text. The bishop detects the lateness of the word but not the religious context — he implies Gandolf is like the third century C.E. lawyer Ulpian and not the true classic, Cicero (Tully). So the bishop indulges in the humanists' linguistic polemic and politics. His Latin is Ciceronian, unlike the medieval mishmash of the Scholastics. He revives the ancient and authentic voice while his rival repeats the errors of late antiquity or of the Middle Ages. The poet Browning might then be like the bishop in giving authentic voice back to the dead and in speaking a high literary language, except that such a positive interpretation fails to acknowledge the religious edge to this linguistic politics and ignores the compromised, even tainted quality of the bishop's voice.

The bishop's appetite for the classics is only one manifestation of his covetousness.[13]

And I shall have St. Praxed's ear to pray   73
Horses for ye, and brown Greek manuscripts,
And mistresses with great smooth marbly limbs
—That's if ye carve my epitaph aright,
Choice Latin, picked phrase, Tully's every word,
No gaudy ware like Gandolf's second line
—Tully, my masters? Ulpian serves his need . . .

Most immediately, he longs that his sons will erect a lasting monument. Should they prove better Latinists than Gandolf and erect an error-free inscription, they will have manuscripts and mistresses, as classical as can be. The bishop's unrealized desire to leave a lasting, legitimate trace will fail despite his best efforts at linguistic purism.

Your tall pale mother with her talking eyes,   96
And new-found agate urns as fresh as day,
And marble's language, Latin pure, discreet,
—Aha, ELUCESCEBAT, quoth our friend?
No Tully, said I, Ulpian at the best!

The Bishop's *castigatio,* the renaissance term for textual emendation but also the Latin for "punishment of boys," can hardly make him chaste, or discipline his sons.[14] In addition to his moral lapses, his own language shows faults of style: turning back upon itself, it is repetitive, even illogical, perhaps veering too close to the whine of an old man, not the forceful exhortation of the orator. Finally, he has failed in his desire: neither his rival nor his sons have bothered with his words. He has no tomb. In point of fact, no monument to the bishop can be found in the Roman church of St. Praxed. Further, his literary genealogy reveals he will get no lasting stone monument but only the recollection of the satirist, for his Latin literary ancestor is Petronius's Trimalchio, who orders his tomb and rehearses its inscription, but the savvy reader knows the gauche freedman will have no loyal heirs once his money is distributed. The bishop for all his Latinizing will be no Horace, the poet, who if not exactly chaste by Protestant English standards, presented himself as *integer vitae scelerisque purus,* and was the champion of moderation, and, better than the bishop, managed to remain childless and so could claim his writing as a lasting inheritance, *exegi monumentum aere perennius.*

Browning has presented a Bishop full of *invidia,* an envy so encompassing that it hungers after fame, disparages those who have won their place, and ultimately consumes the self, stifling any genuine voice. The disparaged language is both the rival's ecclesisatical Latin and the bishop's bitter correctness. It is also the vernacular voice, the voice of bastards, and the voice of those who would ape the classical. Such too is the Catholic voice, on this partisan reading, perhaps especially an Italo-Catholic voice. The bishop's longing for a monument emerges more as southern Baroque materialism, an appetite for marble, than a northern resolve to recover the hard marble words of antiquity. The poet, after all, takes away only the inscribed error and makes of the church's beautiful stonework a crass materialism (the church has granite columns, mosaics of the New Jerusalem, and stone relics: the slab on which St. Praxedis slept, the well top where the sister saints Praxedis and Pudentilla hid the bones of martyrs, and the stone sarcophagi of these saints). The pilgrim poet replaces these real Catholic stones with a bitter longing for stone and "remembers," fabricates in their place, a tomb for the bishop.[15] Browning opposed the Catholicizing movement to reform the Anglican Church.[16] For an immediate source of his attitude toward Catholicism here, Woolford and Karlin (p. 261) suggest a review by Macaulay, in the October 1840 *Edinburgh Review,* of Leopold von Ranke's *Ecclesiastical and Political History of the Popes of Rome,* translated by Sarah Austin. After much criticism of the decadence of the court of Rome, with enumeration of the popes' objects of passion, including "newly-discovered manuscripts of the classics," Macaulay offers as an argumentative crescendo: "it was felt that the Church could not be safely confided to chiefs whose highest praise was that they were good judges of Latin compositions." Perhaps, however, Browning is simply following their lead. Is he another Cardinal Bembo, the arch-Ciceronianist who can make a poem in high style that springs from the detection of linguistic error? He certainly strives to avoid contaminating his verse with the sort of error Gandolf made. He names Gandolfo "Gandolf" and anglicized Prassede as Praxed.[17] Writing the Italian interloper out may be Browning's idea of reforming, restoring the English Church and poem; but does he create a new Latin, or is he simply elevating his own vernacular? Browning was not going to publish in Latin; the tradition of poets writing both in Latin and in the vernacular had all but died out. Latin composition was left to schoolboys. But the classical and the English are being allied. He is denying the Italian as mediator and suggesting another sort of return, but one dependent on the error of the vernacular, the entrance of illicit passion that the Italian represents, and perhaps his English is meant to discipline.

Browning had right not the "spirit" of the Renaissance and its contentious clerics, as Ruskin enthused, but the monumentality and linguistic torpor of Latinity facing the vernacular sons.[18] The inclusion of Latin in the vernacular poem can no doubt serve various functions. The inclusion of a tag, *dulce et decorumst pro patria mori,* may make the sentiment all the more traditional and suspect because it is an old saw (and so Pound slices up the line in lines eleven and twelve of "These fought in any case" as "Died some, pro patria, / non 'dulce' non 'et décor'").[19] Yet in Heaney's eclogue and in Browning's monologue, Latin ushers in a different voice. Poet invokes writer of Latin whose Latin provokes his own poem. The presence of Latin does not simply represent emulation of a past masterful language. Latin is rather at the same time authoritative language and the index of the distance of the present from that high style. It can be code for Catholicism, code for empire, or code for a chastened, recuperated language, purified of intermediaries, religious and political. In "The Tomb at St. Praxed's" the encounter with inscribed Latin and the untrustworthy intermediary replays the story of humanism and of the reformation. The inscription of Latin in the vernacular poem creates a contest of the languages that dramatizes issues of linguistic politics, wherein Latin itself has more than one value. Latin is a multiple signifier for reason of its long durée and the fluidity of form, style, and context that the history of the language and its users records. Perhaps Latin is especially rich, as it pokes its head through the vernacular, because it is almost a form of allegory, an index by its very form to differing codes. The strife of languages can then emerge from within the tradition and not be cast exclusively as an issue of the succession of one language or culture or religion over another. Latin may, as Heaney and Browning dramatize, be difficult to voice but equally will not easily be forgotten, or reduced by the grammarians and professors to a cold exercise in linguistic correctness; Latin is the shape and the stuff of memory, bringing us back to beginnings, reminding us not necessarily that the past is right and authoritative but that the present order of things is not written in stone.

NOTES

1. Tony Crowley discusses this episode from *A Portrait of the Artist as a Young Man* in chapter 7 of this volume.

2. On childhood memories of Latin, see Waquet, *Latin or the Empire of a Sign,* 116–17.

3. Bone functions as the trace of voice also in, e.g., Sean Jennett's "I Was a Labourer," where the dead man speaks, telling his reader in line 4, "broad is my speech," but in the poem's last line, "I am a brittle bone projecting from the sand." Cf. the main title of

a collection of Heaney's poems, *Opened Ground: Selected Poems, 1966–1996* (New York: Farrar, Straus, and Giroux, 1998), and poems therein such as "Bone Dreams," where the chance discovery of a bone leads the poet first to want to throw it at England, then to trace diction, Elizabethan, Norman, Latin, although what he reports from his philological archeology is *bán-hús,* and ultimately the desire to reach back before language and regret:

Come back past
philology and kennings
reenter memory
where the bone's lair
is a love nest
in the grass.

4. The history of the meaning of the use of Latin is receiving increasing attention. A rich account of the affiliations of Latin, the allegiances signaled and the ideological battles waged under its banner, is Waquet, *Latin or the Empire of a Sign.* See also Farrell, *Latin Language and Latin Culture.*

5. Seamus Deane, in discussing the stereotype that Irish drama revels in talk, that talk is somehow Celtic, and so on, notes that strong experimentalism with language has characterized Irish theater and that Friel in particular examines linguistic behavior as political action ("Introduction," *Brian Friel: Plays One,* 12–13). Deane treats this play and the larger issue of Irish authors' experimental English as a species of the difficulty, even failure of representation, in chapter 10 in this volume.

6. The soldiers are members of the British Army Engineer Corps who surveyed Ireland in the 1830s.

7. *Brian Friel: Plays One,* 390.

8. See especially Ong, "Latin Language Study as a Renaissance Puberty Rite."

9. First published in the *Times Literary Supplement,* August 10, 1999.

10. Brodsky, "Letter to Horace," in *On Grief and Reason,* 446–47.

11. See the entry under "dúchas" in Ó Dónaill, ed., *Foclóir Gaeilge-Béarla (Irish-English Dictionary).* The dictionary's translation here for the proverb is "instinct is stronger than upbringing." Peter McQuillan writes me that the range of the Irish word translated here as upbringing, *oiliúint,* is " 'nurturing, fostering, training' " (historically, in fact, it refers to the institution of fosterage). So the proverb is basically about nature over nurture. O'Rahilly, *A Miscellany of Irish Proverbs,* p. 5, gives the following useful addition: "Is sia théidheann an dúchas ná an fhoghlaim" = 'Nature goes further than education.' " Peter McQuillan treats the semantic range of this highly contestible term in chapter 3 in this volume.

12. See Farrell, *Latin Language and Latin Culture,* 100–103, for the association of the vernacular as a bastard language (who cites Byron's description of Italian as "soft, bastard Latin") and for the association of Latin with the church (more extensively treated in Waquet, *Latin or the Empire of a Sign,* 41–79).

13. The bishop has many literary ancestors, including Petronius's Trimalchio (I have discussed the relation of this poem to questions of Latinity at greater length in *La-*

tinity and Literary Society at Rome, 30–37). One particularly Puritan model for Browning was perhaps Cowper's "Progress of Error," which takes a dim view of the European tour, where the hapless young Englishman is victimized by his Catholic guide, quick to show him inscriptions. The young Englishman and his tutor are in Italy, wandering in a cathedral:

> Ere long some bowing, smirking, smart abbé
> Remarks two loiterers that have lost their way;
> And, being always primed with politesse
> For men of their appearance and address,
> With much compassion undertakes the task
> To tell them more than they have wit to ask;
> Points to inscriptions whereso'er they tread;
> Such as, when legible, were never read . . .

The problem with such youth has been declared before:

> We give some Latin, and a smatch of Greek;
> Teach him to fence and to figure twice a week;
> And having done, we think, the best we can,
> Praise his proficiency, and dub him man.
> From school to Cam or Isis, and thence home;
> And thence with all convenient speed to Rome . . .

If only youth had sufficient languages, they would not be prey to Catholic clerics.

14. For example, the title of Joseph Scaliger's emendations, *Castigationes et Notae* (Leiden, 1600). Stephanie Jed has connected the philological practice of *castigatio* to Florentine politics in *Chaste Thinking.*

15. Woolford and Karlin, eds., *The Poems of Browning,* 2:259: "Mrs. Orr (*Handbook* 247) states, probably on B.'s authority: 'The Bishop's tomb is entirely fictitious.'" The existence and site of the tomb developed into a scholarly controversy; see Woolford and Karlin, *The Poems of Browning,* 259–60; Bloomer, *Latinity and Literary Society,* 32.

16. See Greenberg, "Ruskin, Pugin, and the Contemporary Context of *The Bishop Orders His Tomb,*" 1588–94, quoted in Woolford and Karlin, eds., *The Poems of Browning,* 2:260, following K. I. D. Malsen, "Browning and Macaulay," *N&Q* 27 (1980): 525–57.

17. Woolford and Karlin, eds., *The Poems of Browning,* 2:259.

18. Ruskin lauded the poem for Browning's appreciation of the southern artists' veneration of stone and for his grasp of "the Renaissance spirit" (*Modern Painters* iv 1856, *Works,* ed. Cook and Wedderburn [1913], 6:448). Ruskin treats the English poet as a lapidary Latinist: all that the scholar had attempted to express in many prose pages Browning had got right in a few lines.

19. Quoting Horace seems to draw poets' barbs. Jonathan Swift wrote of himself (in "On the Death of Dr. Swift"), "But he laughed to hear an idiot quote / A verse from Horace learned by rote."

BIBLIOGRAPHY

Bloomer, W. Martin. *Latinity and Literary Society at Rome.* Philadelphia: University of Pennsylvania Press, 1997.

Brodsky, Joseph. "Letter to Horace." In *On Grief and Reason.* New York: Farrar, Straus and Giroux, 1995.

Cowper, William. *Complete Poetical Works of William Cowper.* Edited by H. S. Milford. London: Oxford University Press, 1913.

Deane, Seamus. "Introduction." In *Brian Friel: Plays One.* London: Faber and Faber, 1996.

Farrell, Joseph. *Latin Language and Latin Culture: From Ancient to Modern Times.* Cambridge: Cambridge University Press, 2001.

Friel, Brian. *Brian Friel: Plays One.* Edited by Seamus Deane. London: Faber and Faber, 1996.

Greenberg, R. A. "Ruskin, Pugin, and the Contemporary Context of *The Bishop Orders His Tomb.*" *PMLA* 84 (1960): 1588–94.

Heaney, Seamus. *Opened Ground: Selected Poems, 1966–1996.* New York: Farrar, Straus and Giroux, 1998.

———. "Bann Valley Eclogue." *Times Literary Supplement,* December 2001.

Jed, Stephanie. *Chaste Thinking.* Bloomington: Indiana University Press, 1989.

Malsen, K. I. D. "Browning and Macaulay." *N&Q* 27 (1980): 525–27.

Ó Dónaill, Niall, ed. "Dúchas." In *Foclóir Gaeilge-Béarla (Irish-English Dictionary).* Dublin: Baile Átha Cliath: An Gúm: An Roinn Oideachais, 1977.

O'Rahilly, T. F. *A Miscellany of Irish Proverbs.* Dublin: Tabot Press, 1922.

Ong, Walter J. "Latin Language Study as a Renaissance Puberty Rite." In *Rhetoric, Romance, and Technology: Studies in the Interaction of Expression and Culture.* Ithaca: Cornell University Press, 1971.

Ruskin, John. *Modern Painters* iv (1856). In *The Works of John Ruskin,* edited by E. T. Cook and S. D. O. Wedderburn, 6:448. London: G. Allen; New York: Longmans, 1903–12.

Waquet, Françoise. *Latin or the Empire of a Sign from the Sixteenth to the Nineteenth Centuries.* Translated by John Howe. London: Verso, 2001.

Woolford, John, and Daniel Karlin, eds. *The Poems of Browning.* Harlow: Longman, 1991.

10 Dumbness and Eloquence

A Note on English as We Write It in Ireland

SEAMUS DEANE

I

In 1947, the centenary of the Irish Famine's worst year, the Irish government asked the Irish Folklore Commission to send collectors and researchers around those parts of the country that had been most severely affected by the catastrophe and to record what memories of that time still survived. The fruit of that labor, a formidable array of large folio volumes in which those memories were recorded in both Irish and English, is now housed in the Department of Irish Folklore at University College, Dublin. Two convictions dominate what was remembered. One was that the Famine did indeed have a genocidal dimension. Genocide was of a piece with traditional British government policies towards the Irish Catholic majority. The other, sometimes felt to be compatible with the belief in genocidal intent, sometimes not, sometimes entirely independent of it, was that there must have been a radical fault in Irish civilization, most especially in the Irish-speaking civilization, that allowed it to succumb so completely to the potato blight and its attendant ills. Some of the old people interviewed—necessarily, they were on average an elderly group—believed or remembered that their predecessors had believed that the Famine was a punishment from God; and whatever the responsibility of the British government or of anybody else, that it ultimately constituted a divine judgment on a way of life that did not deserve to survive and that had to be expunged.

Victims often blame themselves; oppressed peoples are frequently absurd in their self-estimation. This material contains some classic examples of this mutilated condition. But it is interesting in other respects too. In it we see that in popular culture a new phase of the long argument of the previous two hundred fifty years about Ireland's relation to modernity and atrocity had already begun. Clearly, the beliefs recorded here were first articulated in print by John Mitchel, and have conventionally been associated with him and with a fiercely resentful republicanism of which he is considered in some circles to be an early-warning example. There is little doubt that Mitchel's characterization of the famine as an act of genocidal policy on the part of the British government informs many of these memories. To a much lesser extent, but still notably there, is also his belief that the influence of the Roman Catholic church in advising people to accept their fate and to resign themselves to God's will robbed the victims of their urge to resist and therefore allowed the export of food from the country and the evictions and clearances to take place without serious opposition. These beliefs were scarcely unique to Mitchel, although he was certainly the most vivid exponent of them. The double impact of the two imperialisms, British and Roman, on the Irish psyche was to become a favored topic in Irish writing after the Famine, most famously in Joyce's fiction.[1]

The historical debate about nationalism and colonialism, which is also a debate about the relationship between modernity and atrocity, of which the contemporary version known as revisionism is a reprise, begins with the Famine. It is a debate generated by the question of what the Famine meant. The end of "Old Ireland" and the emergence of "Modern Ireland" (perhaps)? The well-known argument that it was terrible, but in the long run beneficial, to lose so many lives and yet make economic reform and improvement possible has often been made by Panglossian historians and economists. But it has many companions.

To its left is the nationalist argument that, for all the attempts to extinguish, oppress, and degrade the Irish, their "spirit" would endure. The people's cultural durability was said to be visible in, for example, their unshakable devotion to Catholicism in the face of the dungeon, fire, and sword of the Reformation; or their retention of their warm "Celtic" sympathies and loyalties in the face of the commercialized "Saxon" selfishness of British capitalism. In sum, the Irish are a spiritual people, much given to religion, poetry, superstition, depression, alcohol, schizophrenia, improvidence, intuition, and impulse; they thereby form a startling contrast to the anally retentive, philistine, hypocritical, and coldly calculating British, with their Empire and their composite United Kingdom whose brilliantly designed flag is no more than a butcher's apron.

To its right is the antinationalist argument that Ireland was conquered and Gaelic civilization destroyed because it had indeed a fatal flaw: it was out of step with and even hostile to the March of Progress, of which capital development and the English language were identifying features. The Famine, in this view, had at least the merit of making both of those agencies central to any proposed transformation of Ireland. The version of cultural nationalism offered by the Irish Revival seemed to be a temporary rebuke to this argument, although it could be claimed that Joyce and Shaw and perhaps even Synge understood that Irish modernity was precisely a condition in which the "cultural" view of "tradition" and the "economic" view of capital development were joined in unequal combat.

A characteristic postcolonial difficulty for Ireland arose from the conjunction within these various debates of the economic issue and the so-called spiritual issue. As in the case of India, but also in keeping with many colonized territories, Ireland had claimed for itself a kind of internal independence predicated on a spirituality (National, Irish, Celtic) that distinguished it from the oppressor British system and even, in some of its more overheated supporters, was said to distinguish it from the rest of the world.[2] It was easier to do this in the late nineteenth century when there was a general countercultural movement in favor of the wisdom of the East in the metropolitan centers of the West; and Irish writers were ready to adapt this notion of Eastern spirituality in general to their own Western island in particular. Yeats is the most obvious example, but there were many gradations in the wide spectrum of Irish mysticism or, more exactly, mysticism about being Irish. But with the achievement of the Free State's independence, the claim to a spiritual domain and to a form of spiritual exceptionalism had to be sustained along with an effort to achieve that economic and material development which, as Ireland claimed, had long been thwarted by the initial colonial relationship and then by the more intricate colonial union with the neighboring island.

Independence achieved freedom from the most obvious forms of coercion, but it did not easily win freedom from long-established structures of domination and habits of dependence. Ireland's bivalve relationship with and within the United Kingdom produced anomalous conditions in which economic backwardness and modernizing projects were intermixed just as, politically, the country was alternately bribed into passivity or coerced into obedience. It was closely bound up with and clearly distanced from the federation to which it belonged and to which it was simultaneously foreign. The closest analogy is Algeria. It too had been incorporated within a metropolitan system, yet had inevitably also remained a colony of France. This intensified the bitterness of the separation between Algeria and France and between Ireland and the United Kingdom. It also intensified the difficulty of achieving independence and perhaps overstimulated the colonized country's desire for and dream of autonomy.[3] Perfect autonomy, either in politics or in economics, is a fantasy most fervently indulged by the hopelessly dependent. The pressure of this peculiar domestic-colonial, British-Irish relationship also intensified the wish for a rhetoric of separatism which had an appeal that was particular to Ireland and yet was also universal in its range. It was the only possible reply to the local/universal appeal of specific Britishness and universal, imperial pretensions to "civilization."

By the thirties, in the midst of a worldwide recession, it seemed to some Irish intellectuals, who largely ignored the recession itself, that the economic failure of the new state, which was to persist until the sixties, had its explanation in the cultural regressiveness of a polity that had rephrased spiritual supremacy into Catholic triumphalism and a provincial, censorious, and illiberal hatred of modernity. Out of this conjuncture came the new historical revisionism, led by Sean O'Faolain's two books on great Irish leaders of the past—Hugh O'Neill and Daniel O'Connell.[4] The two books are really one book, written twice with a different set of names and the same theme. Both O'Neill and O'Connell, leaders who came from the heart of the old Irish civilization, had been educated into modernity (one via the Renaissance, the other via utilitarianism) and attempted to lead their people towards those sunlit uplands. Each recognized that Gaelic civilization suffered from a fatal weakness, an implacable nostalgia for the premodern. Of the two, O'Connell was clearly the more successful. He created the Catholics as a political force, turned their faces towards the modern world, and advocated the abandonment of the Irish language as a means towards that end.

O'Connell's advocacy of English as the language of modernity reverberated even more strongly after his death in 1847. For prominent among those recorded memories of the Famine in the Department of Irish Folklore at University College, Dublin, is the reaction of the people at large against the Irish language. It was the Famine Irish who testified most damagingly to the belief that the retention of the Irish language meant death and exile, poverty and economic disadvantage. It seemed that it was in the language itself and in the later attempts to revive it that the fatal flaw resided. The weakness of a civilization that had been expelled from the modern world was audible and visible there. The weakness persisted in the hopelessly nostalgic and impractical efforts to restore the language and the values it was presumed to have realized in the past and still to hold in suspension for the future. Such beliefs are still widespread, more than one hundred fifty years later. Perhaps it is just as telling to remember that they were also widespread two hundred years earlier. As in Wales and Scotland, in Ireland it was widely believed and stated that the native language was a barrier to civilization. In Swift's words, "I am deceived, if anything hath more contributed to prevent the Irish being tamed, than this encouragement of their language, which might easily be abolished and become a dead one in half an age, with little expense, and less trouble."[5]

The disaster of the Famine combined with all the other forces of industrialization, urbanization, and educational policy to make the flight from Irish comprehensible as what Seán de Fréine calls "a millenial or utopian movement."[6] But it also involved accepting what the same author called "the ethnocentric Ascendancy viewpoint that Irish was a backward language and that even to speak it was a hindrance."[7] It is this catastrophic dimension that is, I believe, critical in any attempt to understand the intricate relationships between various forms of competence in the English language and the varied forms of "authenticity" that are often indicators of both a level of "incompetence," when that is measured against standard English, and a form of vigorous eloquence, when the standard form of English is deemed to have become featurelessly uniform. But English is not merely the language of a country or an empire or of an invading culture; it is the language of a condition, modernity. It is in relation to modernity, which is also part of the successful history of British imperial expansion, that Irish linguistic behavior is best examined.[8]

II

The relationship between the Irish and the English languages in modern Ireland, at least since the Famine, has a bearing on and may even be homologous with the wider relationship between tradition and modernity. Looking at the narrower issue may help to illuminate the wider one. If the fatal flaw lay in the Irish language and, by implication, in the whole civilization that wrote and spoke it, then it hardly matters what exposed it—the violent militarism of the British State, the emergent capitalist world system, an accident of Nature, or divine intervention. It was there, and all that vanished as a result of the exposure had to be understood, in however demoralized a spirit, as the inevitable loss that was exacted by the much-hypostasized idea of progress, as it was then known (or development, as it is now called). Yet the abandonment of a language that had such a long history, such an elaborate literature, and had been the intimate form of representation and communication for so many centuries in so enclosed an area produced problems that refused to dissolve. Among them were the inability of considerable numbers of the Irish people to speak English in a manner that was comprehensible to native English speakers; the difficulty, if not the impossibility, of understanding a past that had in many of its most influential and scholarly forms been largely represented in the abandoned language; the recognition that the abandonment of the language involved the abandonment of so much else in traditional customs, practices, and ways of thought that the security of any group identity or of what the nineteenth century called "national character" was seriously weakened, if it survived at all.

In addition, with a weakened or lost security of identity in this communal sense, came a readiness to accept a surrogate, even though that had to be concocted from a mix of political and cultural stereotypes that had been produced to serve various propagandistic purposes at different times. The caricatured barbarian Irish of the tradition of historical writing in the English language, the unmatchably civilized and aristocratic Irish of the Gaelic tradition, the Speakers from the Dock, the bel canto tenors moored behind the sleek pianos of the middle classes, the ballad singers in streets and pubs that increasingly took their material from the beshamrocked pages of the *Nation* newspaper and its almost uniformly dreadful submartial music and lyrics, the simian creatures of the British tabloid imagination, the Fenian heroes of novels and of prison literature, of badly translated sagas and fustian poetry of a quantity and quality only matched in recent times, the Celts, the Gaels, the Hibernians, the Catholics, the Rebels, and the Rapparees, Paddy the drunkard, and Paddy the Malapropist, were all huddled together into the Irish/Irish-American identity that survived deep into the twentieth century and is only now being redesigned in the virtual spaciousness of postmodern prosperity. From Thomas Moore to Crofton Croker, from Mrs. Hall to Somerville and Ross, from William Maginn to George Moore, from Mangan to Joyce, from Boucicault to Yeats, Maria Edgeworth, and Lady Morgan to Oscar Wilde and Elizabeth Bowen, we see authors attempt to find an exemplary mode of representation for an Irish community or communities that, we are told, have never before been represented properly or at all or which are only now being represented at the very moment of their departure from history. To top it all, we are also and often told that the experience of these communities or organizations defies representation.

Here I want to narrow the issue further. It is no news to anyone that Irish writing in the English language is recurrently obsessed with the problems involved in the idea of representation. Swift and Burke, Joyce and Beckett would be the four writers most plagued and yet aggravated into eloquence by the impoverished resources of the language they exploited. It is equally well known that Irish writing in English has (inevitably) but with astonishing ingenuity appropriated the contrast between provincial yet natural modes of speech and value and metropolitan yet anaemic modes. This has been a staple feature of the work of Anglo-Irish dramatists — Farquhar, Steele, Goldsmith, Sheridan, Shaw, and, with a different inflection of the same paradigm, Wilde and Synge. Since Maria Edgeworth's *Castle Rackrent* it has been a regular revenant in Irish novels, although in fiction the respective rewards for native woodnotes, wild and metropolitan accents and values have been less predictably distributed.

But the two issues — the contrast between metropolitan and provincial and the problematic issue of representation — have in common a peculiar attitude towards language. It is that language is ultimately insufficient for the purpose of representation. Metropolitan sophistication and eloquence is usually the index of hypocrisy, moral vacuity, absence; native inarticulacy, even though it is often associated with a degree of slyness or low cunning, is usually the index of authentic feeling, the more so in ratio to the degree of inarticulacy. We are all familiar with the sectarian version of this: Protestant inarticulacy versus Catholic eloquence, the one a crucial element in a set of values that comprise solidity, stolidity, even stupidity, and loyalty; the other similarly positioned in a set of values, if that is the word, comprising disloyalty, instability, cleverness, and insincerity. This often conflicts with the racist version in which the Irish Catholic is the butt of humor because he or she cannot master the English language and produces instead a comic-pathetic patois that indicates an ineducable condition of backwardness. It is not at all surprising that in any colonial situation, the mastery of the language of the colonizer, and the tense situation between that and the language(s) it displaces, should be so critical an issue for writers in particular. Further, the displacement of Irish by English, which is one of the consequences of the Famine, allies the loss of language with tragedy; but equally, it allies the loss of language with the arrival of modernity or, at least, the arrival of the conditions that made both modernization and modernity possible in Ireland. It is the combination of this set of issues with the broader problem of representation that provides much Irish writing with a distinctive problematic.

It is remarkable that literature in Irish and literature in English by Irish authors should have in common a reputation for being so technically accomplished, so given to displays of virtuosity, and so inclined to degenerate, in their weaker moments, into conditions of inane verbosity or gnomic alexandrianism. It would be less remarkable if it could be shown that each tradition of writing fed off or influenced the other. But this was only true in rare instances. Both traditions were independent one of the other, especially in the eighteenth century, when their dual coexistence became an important fact of Irish cultural life. It was equally important that Irish was the language of a weakening and English of a strengthening civilization; this reality was integral to both literatures, not an external circumstance. But it was integral to the literature in English in retrospect; it was not so evident at the time to Swift or to Burke that either the English/British civilization in Ireland or civilization in general would successfully endure, or endure in any recognizable form, the challenges it faced. In the modern period of Irish history, which may be dated from 1690, both literatures have been periodically given to the representation of cultures that seemed to have no future or a very dubious prospect of one. Gaelic civilization's prospects were dim, to say the least, after 1690; but English civilization's prospects in Ireland often seemed dim too, both to protestant alarmists for law and order and to those who found that the colonial relationship upon which it was based was paradoxically the source of its frailty. Reason and madness were near-allied in Swift's writings, not because Swift was a deeply disturbed individual, but because he was deeply perceptive about the anomalous condition of Ireland and, by extension, of any version of civilization that pretended to be anything other than local or provincial. Yet if it were no more than that, did it deserve to be known as civilization? Under what conditions, economic, moral, political, could universality (or even colonial expansion) be established and legitimized?

The baroque style of Swift's early work, particularly of *A Tale of a Tub,* and the "plain" style of almost everything he wrote in the eighteenth century proper rehearse the conflict between a particularity of detail that is overwhelming and a universality that is blandly vacuous. His adaptation of the plain style, itself the basis for the generic Enlightenment style of transparency, perfected by Voltaire and Gibbon, is deceptive because it so effectively conceals the virtuosity it seeks to satirize. Madness disguised as reason, expertise operating as a form of insanity, civilization perverted in the name of its preservation—these are some of the obsessions that Swift's writings accentuate to the point of vertigo. My concern here is briefly to acknowledge his well-deserved reputation for linguistic virtuosity and the alliance, in the critical reception given his work then and since, between that virtuosity and, on the one hand, various forms of excess, illness, psychosis, and madness and, on the other, his "patriotism." In effect, the "mad" view of Swift transferred to him all the ills and insanity that he attributed to the political and moral situation he represented in his writings; this also tainted the political reputation he gained rather than the political situation he satirized. It is the first, although the classic case, in Irish writing, of the linkages between linguistic virtuosity and a political situation that was in some respects atrocious and in others inexplicable, because it was (in Irish conditions at least) self-destructive. As in Gulliver's case, when atrocity is expressed and defended as polite common sense, when actuality is transferred into nightmare in the name of progress, or the eating of children solemnly offered as a cure for famine, the virtuosity consists in the maintenance of the syntax, grammar, and tone of the civilized and progressive European.

Burke too has been recognized as a great writer much given to excess, and the excess has often been associated with his nationality. It manifests itself in his rhetoric, of course; this is profoundly Hibernian, which is to say hysterical, strident, self-consciously empurpled, irrational. The political beliefs of a writer so defined are as difficult to summarize or even to respect as they are easy to denigrate because of the taint of "national" excess or personal incapacity. Burke was much more interesting on this topic than his denigrators when he addressed the question of language and its peculiar powers in his early treatise, *The Sublime and the Beautiful* (1757; 2d ed., 1759). There he stated the problem clearly in his critique of clarity. Adam Phillips, in his introduction to a recent edition (1990) of the famous treatise, calls attention to the implication in Burke's account of language that "it is uniquely powerful . . . because it is, unlike the realist painting of his day, non-mimetic, what we would now call an arbitrary system of signs. Words are not windows we look at the world through. And it is the absence of this visual notion of clarity that stirs our most intense feelings. Clarity, for Burke, and not its more conventional antagonist Reason, is the antithesis of passion."[9]

One of the confusing elements in Burke's essay is his assertion that the Sublime is beyond the reach of language because it has no limits; linguistically, this involves us in incoherence. Yet in art the Sublime produces delight while in Nature it stuns and paralyses. The connections between delight and paralysis are indicated but not dwelt upon at any length. Instead, Burke chooses to develop the companion connections between vigorous languages that can, by deploying the passions, give some "idea of the thing described" and polished languages, like French, which, however clear and perspicuous, "are generally deficient in strength." Here we have a foreshadowing of the Irish and English uses of language: "the languages of most unpolished people," like "the oriental tongues," have "a great force and energy of expression"; they retain their natural awe before the world and are not "critical in distinguishing" things.[10] These are conventional beliefs of the time, but Burke is disturbing the assumptions upon which they are based. The polite and civilized are eloquent, the uneducated are dumb; yet it is also the case that the "natural" are eloquent, the polished are dumb. It is the contradiction exploited but not explored in Anglo-Irish drama of the eighteenth century and then again renewed as a matter of crucial distinction between Irish and English, peasants and city-dwellers, in the Irish drama of the late nineteenth and twentieth century.

The linguistic turn Burke gives to his account of the Sublime and of representation in language undergoes modification in Kant's *Critique of Judgment* where the failure of reason to control the aesthetic response evoked by the Sublime is experienced as a sense of pain, loss, and even terror. This then leads to a characteristically Kantian assertion that such an experience is foundational for the transition from aesthetic to moral experience. Yet such a move also brings the individual from a private to a social level; morality has a social dimension that private experience lacks. The association of pain or loss with these transitions from private and individual to public and social levels is later reasserted and re-oriented in Freudian psychology with the extension of the conceptual reach of the Sublime to the theory of sublimation.[11] Under the influence of Lacan, the linguistic emphasis is revived, still in the context of a loss or sense of loss that must be redirected or compensated for. Phillips, who had read Burke's treatise in the light of his own and Burke's preoccupation with language's capacity for representation, later intensifies the argument when he speaks of psychoanalysis as "one way of speaking up for our formative linguistic incompetence, for the necessary relationship between our verbal uncertainty and our fluency; for the profit of loss."[12]

There is a consistent political implication in all of this; the speaker of a vigorous version of the new language is always someone who is unpolished, or uncivilized, or who is as yet a child. The language of reason is ineffective for the representation of childhood experiences. Another language is required, one that is less plain and more sumptuous in its rhetoric, less transparent and more opaque—the language of the unconscious. Indeed, the acquisition of language is a necessary introduction to the adult world and may have no necessary relation to those experiences that belong to the prelinguistic stage. The acquisition of language as such is different from the acquisition of a new language, but the doubt that a prelinguistic universe can be translated into language weakens the belief that one language can be translated into another. This is especially the case if the "translation" is accompanied by coercion and (sometimes) spectacular violence.

It is therefore no great surprise to find that the relationship between the condition of inarticulacy and eloquence should be so memorably represented in central works of the Irish Revival such as Joyce's *Portrait of the Artist as a Young Man* (1914) and Synge's *Playboy of the Western World* (1907). Stephen Dedalus and Christy Mahon both begin in profound inarticulacy and both end in astonishing eloquence. They do so by making an account of their acquisition of language the governing experience of their lives. Beginning in hesitation and stammering, they both achieve mastery over words and over the Dublin and Mayo cultures that they must ultimately leave for the sake of their own moral and linguistic freedom. The inherited languages they have absorbed are authoritarian in structure: they represent the claims of Roman Catholicism, British political and cultural imperialism, Irish and local patriotisms. But the two young men are, above all, sons in rebellion against parental disciplines. They both achieve a radical, individual isolation which is both a triumph and a defeat. In each case, the freedom, the linguistic independence, is created by a form of imagining, or forging, that is close to but not identical with lying.

In one sense, these works would seem to emblematize the movement from enslavement to freedom that is characteristic of the political hopes of the period to which they belong. This is partly true. But since that movement is represented by them as a linguistic evolution, it must be allowed to be highly nuanced and not at all a simple narrative of progress. Synge's play, more obviously than Joyce's novel, indicates that the greatest difference between the condition of dumbness and that of eloquence is that, in the first, lying is impossible and that, in the second, lying is both necessary and inevitable. It is again an issue that psychoanalysis dwells upon. An aphasic or an autistic person, it has been claimed, cannot lie. "Faced with the structural rigor of the real," claims John Forrester, such a person "loses all notion of the possible."[13] This gives us some clue about one of the effects of communal catastrophe, somewhat like Burke's description of the effects of the Sublime which always has terror at its heart. It paralyzes, stuns, petrifies. It robs the victim(s) of the power to imagine any other possibility. It is a reality so fierce that it cannot be denied, although the wish to deny it is as strong as any wish could possibly be.

The effect is to create a condition in which, in Ireland's case, the language of the real, in all its rigor, is Irish—and that emerges as silence; and the language of the possible is English—and that emerges in eloquence. Eloquence is as rich as imagination and possibility and the thought of the new can be. It is the language of modernity. The condition of dumbness, aphasia, or silence is the repressed condition of nonmodernity, if not indeed antimodernity, the condition of nothing new being possible and the vision of traditional life as nothing but a grinding, monotonous, and ultimately catastrophic nullity. Yet, assuming—however blithely—that the repressed always returns in some guise or shape, it could be claimed that the sweet irony about Irish eloquence is that it so often incorporates within itself the Irish language as such, or those versions of Irish incompetence in the English language which mark the gradations between the stage of "infancy" ("infans," as in Joyce's *Portrait*) and the stage of adult possibility, as when Stephen and Christy Mahon respectively turn towards exile from their dying communities. They seek freedom in some other land or territory that is not Ireland but that is truly a country of the imagination, a country of the possible although not entirely a possible country. Had they remained inarticulate, the rigor of the real and the peremptory force of authority would have quenched the possibility of possibility that is released with (even by?) their rapidly increasing ability to speak with a force, vigor, and eloquence lacking in the routinized language of the inhabitants of the controlled and submissive social realm of modernity.

Joyce and Synge were not stray voices in this regard. Yeats and George Moore, in their different ways, promoted, as part of their cultural crusades, the linguistic freedom and vigor that they believed was allied to political and social independence for Ireland. Thomas MacDonagh's *Literature in Ireland: Studies Irish and Anglo-Irish* (1916), with its significant dedication to George Sigerson, the editor of the important anthology *Bards of the Gael and the Gall* (2d ed., 1907), introduced the notion of an "Irish Mode" of literature which was neither English nor "Celtic" and was distinguished by a fusion of the Irish and English languages.[14] For all of these writers, the true language of modernity was an Irish English that fused the traditional and the contemporary, "good sense" and "fine fabling."[15] But there was also a tragic note to be heard, rarely absent in Irish poetry, drama, or fiction in the long period of revival and counterrevival from 1880 to 1950. It is audible as silence, the silence of the other language that haunts the English language, sometimes in the shape of its syntax and grammar, or of its idiom and vocabulary, sometimes merely as reference or implication. On rarer occasions, as in Beckett—for instance, in his radio play, *All That Fall* (1957)—it operates as the language for that which is unsayable in English, or simply is unsayable as such.[16] The unsayable has two realms. One is temporal. It is the realm of the prelinguistic. The other realm is historical; it is the realm of atrocity, communal immiseration, ethnocide. Language may be understood to be irrelevant to the first and incompetent for the second. Or it may be understood to be incriminated in the second, as itself part of the reason for and part of the material structure of the collapse. During the Revival, the Irish language was associated with all of these positions and the English language, in its "Irish Mode," was assigned a creative role in emancipating the Irish communities from that culturally autistic silence in which the Irish language and civilization seemed to be entombed. Although the English-language literature of the Irish Revival rarely mentions, much less deals with, the Famine that preceded it by a generation, it nevertheless meditates endlessly upon the linguistic condition that was part of that event's cultural inheritance.

"Revival" is a term that more properly applies to the immense effort expended by several organizations across a century to revive the Irish language. From the Gaelic Society (1808) to the Gaelic League (1893), the vision blurred and cleared alternately until, in the last decade of the century, it finally seemed to have found the sharp focus it needed. But what the Gaelic League did was in effect to create an organizational base (over six hundred branches by 1904) for insurrectionary politics; it certainly gave an impulse to the learning of the language, but the schism between the living language and the philological tradition that had made it an object of academic study just as the language ceased to be widely spoken during the Famine was never healed. It is still a standard feature of the linguistic condition of Irish that those who are scholars and experts in the language maintain it as an esoteric subject always threatened with contamination by those who stumblingly, inaccurately, and ungrammatically speak or try to speak it. Nothing has devastated the language more than the pursuit of authenticity by those who, in preserving this ideal, have created as its opposite a jargon or patois. The division within the Irish language between extremely sophisticated scholarship and a somewhat delinquent common speech has been part of the Gaelic tradition since the destruction of the aristocratic Gaelic civilization in the seventeenth century; it continued to be part of the extramural division between English and Irish in the nineteenth century. In each case, the paradigm was based on a contrast between the commanding skill of a literary elite and the hapless incompetence of an uneducated mass. Even the history of the Gaelic League itself has been read as the fall from a literary exclusiveness into a mass political movement in which the language was a victim of a process of degradation. Extramural disputes are more frequently conducted in racial and intramural disputes in class terms. In each case there has to be an elite and a mass; in each case there are also great traditional skills and recently and imperfectly acquired or distorted rudiments; in each case too there is, at the heart of the matter, producing these oppositions, a political trauma.

It seems even more obvious now than it did in 1980 when it was first produced that Brian Friel's *Translations* is one of the key texts for the understanding of this set of issues. It poses the question of language loss and acquisition in the light of a modernity that is founded on expertise and violence and of a traditionalism that is founded on fidelity and anachronistic pedantry. The relationship between dumbness and eloquence is variously explored. Sara begins and ends in dumbness, having had a brief entrance into the eloquence of identity. But for the present purpose, what is most interesting in the play is its critique of the very position that it most affectionately represents—that of Hugh and his civilization. The critique rests on the recognition that Hugh and the Greek-Latin-Irish culture he embodies is petrified. It has become hermetically sealed within its own universe. In fact, Friel's diagnosis here is very similar to that of O'Faolain almost half a century earlier; and of the relatives of the Famine victims making their reports in 1947. The old civilization was doomed, not only because it was economically impoverished, but also because, with all its learning and ritual and failed rebellion, it had never learned what modernity taught as its first lesson—that change, even rapid change, is an abiding principle of the communal as of the individual life. The fault lies within the old system itself and, more deeply, within the language of the old system that, because it could not undergo change, must now undergo transmogrification. Roland is the betrayer of his father's world, but, as the play keeps reminding us, betrayal is another word for translation. Hugh's world cannot be "translated" into the martial, technological world of the British Empire. All that can happen is that it might echo within it as a noise that has lost its source.

Coercion helped to kill the Irish language, and compulsion helped to abort its revival. But its more recent efflorescence is surely related to a sense of emancipation from both. The political requirement is not that we become eloquent in a language that is our own, whether that be Irish or English or both; it is to become eloquent in a language that we never had but which is believed to exist, if only because of our dumbness in it. That is the language of freedom.

NOTES

1. See Seamus Deane, "The Famine and Young Ireland," in *The Field Day Anthology of Irish Writing*, 2:115–208; Mitchel's most influential writings on the Famine are *The Last Conquest of Ireland (Perhaps)* (Dublin, 1861); *The History of Ireland from the Treaty of Limerick to the Present Time* (Glasgow, London, Dublin, 1869).

2. See, for instance, Partha Chatterjee, *The Nation and Its Fragments: Colonial and Postcolonial Histories*, 47–51.

3. On Ireland and Algeria, see Ian S. Lustick, *Unsettled States, Disputed Lands: Britain and Ireland, France and Algeria, Israel and the West Bank-Gaza*, 121–48, 303–49.

4. *King of the Beggars* (London and New York, 1938); *The Great O'Neill* (London and New York, 1942). His simple and standard contrast between pragmatism and abstract idealism also governs his earlier biography, *Eamon de Valera* (London, 1933, 1939).

5. Cited in R. D. Grillo, *Dominant Languages: Language and Hierarchy in Britain and France,* 86.

6. "The Dominance of the English Language in the Nineteenth Century," in D. O Muirithe, ed., *The English Language in Ireland,* 83.

7. Ibid., 84. See also de Fréine's *The Great Silence.*

8. See, for much valuable information and for key historical examples, Tony Crowley, *The Politics of Language in Ireland, 1366–1922: A Sourcebook;* and his forthcoming *The Politics of Language in Ireland, 1534–1998.*

9. *A Philosophical Enquiry into the Origin of our Ideas of the Sublime and Beautiful,* Introduction, xix.

10. Adam Phillips, ed., *Edmund Burke,* 160.

11. See John Cohn and Thomas H. Miles, "The Sublime: In Alchemy, Aesthetics and Psychoanalysis," 289–304; see also Meg Armstrong, "'The Effects of Blackness': Gender, Race, and the Sublime in Aesthetic Theories of Burke and Kant," 213–36. Armstrong identifies the connections between privation and excess and the achievement of mastery: "The sublime is not simply a moment of terror and privation on the way to a recovery of self-possession and mastery (or recognition of oneself within a transcendent symbolic order); rather, the sublime exceeds this drama of identification and marks the sheer ecstasy of the image of foreign bodies" (214).

12. Adam Phillips, *The Beast in the Nursery,* 49. On some of the most prominent discussions of psychoanalysis and colonialism, especially those of Fanon and Bhabha, see Robert Young, *White Mythologies: Writing History and the West,* 152–56.

13. John Forrester, *Truth Games: Lies, Money and Psychoanalysis,* 23.

14. See *MacDonagh,* 8–9. Sigerson, in turn, had dedicated his anthology to Douglas Hyde.

15. Richard Hurd, *Letters on Chivalry and Romance,* 154. Hurd is speaking here of what the Revolution of 1688 gave —"good sense"— and what it lost —"fine fabling." He is also speaking specifically of Scotland.

16. See Beckett's remark, "If you really get down to the disaster, the slightest eloquence becomes unbearable." Cited in J. C. C. Mays, ed., "Samuel Beckett," in *The Field Day Anthology of Irish Writing,* 233.

BIBLIOGRAPHY

Armstrong, Meg. "'The Effects of Blackness': Gender, Race, and the Sublime in Aesthetic Theories of Burke and Kant." *Journal of Aesthetics and Art Criticism* 54.3 (1996): 213–36.

Chatterjee, Partha. *The Nation and Its Fragments: Colonial and Postcolonial Histories.* Princeton: Princeton University Press, 1993.

Cohn, John, and Thomas H. Miles. "The Sublime: In Alchemy, Aesthetics and Psychoanalysis." *Modern Philology* (February 1977): 289–304.

Crowley, Tony. *The Politics of Language in Ireland, 1366–1922: A Sourcebook.* London: Routledge, 2000.

Deane, Seamus, ed. *The Field Day Anthology of Irish Writing.* 3 vols. Derry: Field Day Publications, 1991.

Forrester, John. *Truth Games: Lies, Money and Psychoanalysis.* Cambridge, Mass.: Harvard University Press, 1997.

de Fréine, Seán. "The Dominance of the English Language in the Nineteenth Century." In D. O Muirithe, ed., *The English Language in Ireland,* 70–87. Dublin: Mercier Press, 1977.

———. *The Great Silence.* Dublin: Foilseachain Naisiunta Teoranta, 1965.

Grillo, R. D. *Dominant Languages: Language and Hierarchy in Britain and France.* Cambridge: Cambridge University Press, 1989.

Hurd, Richard. *Letters on Chivalry and Romance.* London: A. Millar, 1762.

Lustick, Ian S. *Unsettled States, Disputed Lands: Britain and Ireland, France and Algeria, Israel and the West Bank–Gaza.* Ithaca: Cornell University Press, 1993.

MacDonagh, Thomas. *Literature in Ireland: Studies Irish and Anglo-Irish.* Dublin: Talbot Press, 1916.

Mays, J. C. C., ed. "Samuel Beckett." In Seamus Deane, ed., *The Field Day Anthology of Irish Writing,* 233–313. Derry: Field Day Publications, 1991.

Mitchel, John. *The Last Conquest of Ireland (Perhaps).* Dublin: The Irishman Office, 1861.

———. *The History of Ireland from the Treaty of Limerick to the Present Time.* Glasgow: Duffy, 1869.

O Faolain, Sean. *Eamon de Valera.* London: Thomas Nelson and Sons, [1933] 1939.

———. *The Great O'Neill.* New York: Duell, Sloan, and Pearce, 1942.

———. *King of the Beggars.* London: T. Nelson, 1938.

Phillips, Adam. *The Beast in the Nursery.* New York: Pantheon, 1998.

———, ed. *Edmund Burke: A Philosophical Enquiry into the Origin of our Ideas of the Sublime and Beautiful.* Oxford: Oxford University Press, 1990.

Sigerson, George. *Bards of the Gael and the Gall.* 2d ed. London: Unwin, 1907.

Young, Robert. *White Mythologies: Writing History and the West.* London: Routledge, 1990.

AFTERWORD

11 Philosophy and Its Languages

A Philosopher's Reflections on the Rise of English
as the Universal Academic Language

VITTORIO HÖSLE

One of the most important changes my generation is witnessing within academia is the slow but irresistible triumph of English as the universal academic language. A process that began decades ago for the natural sciences, to which it then seemed limited, extended first to the social sciences and now more and more to the humanities. The following reflections deal with the advantages and disadvantages of this process, and as reflections by a philosopher, they focus on the discipline I am most familiar with. In addition to the contingent personal reason just mentioned, there may be an objective justification for this limitation, namely, that in the traditional hierarchy of the different academic disciplines philosophy enjoyed a particular position; therefore, its linguistic fate may be symptomatic of general changes in the academic enterprise. But whatever the possible justification of my procedure, I confess from the beginning that my essay is, and is intended to be, far less "objective" than the other ones collected in this volume: It is the conceptual articulation of the basically emotional reactions of a person who in the last few years has tried, with great difficulties, to publish more and more in English instead of German, the language in which he was academically trained. (I learned German at the age of six, Italian being my native language.) Still, I hope that my musings will be of some interest for other people, particularly for those non-native English speakers in Anglo-American academia who share my situation and have to recognize that the contemporary contest of languages was won by a language which is not their own.

The linguistic process occurring now is in many aspects the inversion of the long process that led to the demise of Latin as the universal academic language and to the rise of national academic languages: A new academic lingua franca is forming, without any doubt at the expense of all other modern national languages. Since the situation we have at the beginning of the twenty-first century with regard to academic languages seems to be closer to the situation existing in the seventeenth century than to that of the late nineteenth century, it is worthwhile to look at the reasons that led to the rise of national academic languages from the thirteenth century onward. For if there were good reasons for the shift from Latin to the national languages at that time, then we will more easily find some of the disadvantages connected with the actual changes. Historical facts are not arguments, but it well befits a philosopher to try to learn from those historical events which are the result of a process guided by reasons. Therefore I deal briefly with the replacement of Latin as a universal academic language by national languages (I), before I discuss both the positive and the negative aspects of the new emergence of an academic lingua franca (II). Again, my examples are drawn mostly from philosophy.

I

Up until the thirteenth century, the only languages in which original philosophical texts were written in Europe were Greek, Latin, and Arabic. Greek is, of course, the first philosophical language of Europe and remained so for about a thousand years. The rise of a Latin form of Christianity and the split of the Roman Empire were necessary in order to prepare Latin for the role of the leading philosophical and academic language of the world, a role which it maintained from the ninth to the nineteenth century. When the Roman republic began to become interested in cultural matters, Greek was sensed as superior: The first literary achievements in Latin are translations from the Greek, and from Quintus Fabius Pictor onwards until Cato's Latin *Origines,* the first Roman historians wrote in Greek about Rome (of course, also for the political reason of explaining the Roman point of view to the Greek-speaking world). With regard to philosophical texts in Latin, it is unlikely that any existed in the second century B.C.E. (Amafinius probably was not much older than Cicero); in any case, it is only in the first century B.C.E. that two of the most impressive linguistic geniuses in the history of the Latin language created Latin as a full-fledged philosophical language. I have in mind, of course, Lucretius and the likely editor of his work, Cicero, one of the greatest, if not the greatest, Roman poet and the greatest Roman orator respectively. Despite their awe-inspiring achievements, Latin remained inferior to Greek in its philosophical expressive power until the end of antiquity. Suffice to mention that Latin lacks the definitive article, a fact which renders the translation of such a simple concept as τὸ ἀγαθόν notoriously difficult (Cicero adds "ipsum" to make it clear that he does not deal with a particular good).[1] This, along with the fact that the Latin tradition never produced philosophers of the originality of Plato and Aristotle or even of Epicurus or Zeno of Citium, explains why, for many Romans, Greek remained an attractive choice when they wrote philosophical works (even for their private use): I mention only Musonius Rufus and Marcus Aurelius. None of them, though, can claim the stylistic achievements of Seneca, who is hardly an original thinker but who certainly enriched philosophy's capacity to express various states of mind by writing in a Latin far more complex and subtle than the Greek of the other Roman Stoics.

After the conquest of Greece by the Roman Empire, not only did Romans write in Greek, but Greek native speakers published in Latin. Ammianus Marcellinus, for example, continuing Tacitus, writes his historical work in Latin. However, the knowledge of both languages is a reality for more Romans than Greeks.[2] Given the intellectual superiority of Greece, it is the Romans who have to justify themselves for not writing in Greek; it is they who have to fight to build a language as rich as Greek.[3] The inhabitants of the empire who were neither native speakers of Latin nor of Greek had to choose between the two languages for their publications; sometimes they even managed to write in both (as did Apuleius). We can call this situation an academic bilingualism of a whole culture: cultivated persons have the choice between two languages that are regarded as almost equally universal (while the many other languages spoken in the empire are excluded from academic and even literary purposes). Of course, not every intellectual was able to write in both (we do not have a general academic bilingualism on the individual level), but the ideal was certainly at least a reading knowledge of both languages. Since both were living and spoken languages, there was a tendency to write in one language if one was born in a determinate part of the empire. But this geographic criterion is not absolute and probably subordinate to a criterion which we could call the topical: Mathematical works are written in Greek (the agrimensors are not mathematicians in a scientific sense of the word), juridical books in Latin.

This academic bilingualism ends with the split of the empire and particularly with the end of its western part. Latin became the only academic language of western Europe, Greek the only one of the Byzantine Empire. An important difference, however, is that in western Europe many vernacular languages began to develop and thus Latin increasingly acquired the status of a language for special purposes (even if it was, of course, spoken by intellectuals in the monasteries and later in the universities, and it remained the language of liturgy). Thus we have a situation of bilingualism or even multilingualism, which must, however, be distinguished from academic bilingualism, since Latin was for a long time the only academic language, even if Latin texts were translated into vernacular languages already in the first millennium (I think of Alfred the Great's Old English translations of Augustine and Boethius in the ninth century and Notker Labeo's translations into Old High German in the tenth and eleventh centuries). The linguistic situation in southern Europe is even more complicated due to the Arab conquest of Spain, for now Arabic emerges as the third philosophical language on the Continent. It is both a living lingua franca and an academic language on three continents, used also by such Turks as Farabi and by Jewish philosophers such as Jehudah Halevi and Maimonides, who were both born in Spain. (Halevi's *Kuzari* was translated into Hebrew in the same century—the twelfth—in which it was written.) But, with a noteworthy exception, Arabic is not an option for the philosophers living under Christian rule: For them, one certainly cannot speak of an academic bilingualism. However, as is well known, the translation of various classical Greek philosophers into Latin occurs at the beginning via Arabic, which is studied by the Christian translators in Toledo and Segovia. The main reason why I had to mention Arabic in my context is that its importance as a philosophical language is probably linked to the first use of a vernacular European language for philosophical purposes. Why? One does not risk much if one bets that even among the most erudite scholars in the humanities, very few know which was the first modern European language in which original philosophical texts were written. This language is Catalan, and it is the achievement of a single person to have created in a very short time a philosophical language of a richness and differentiation, such as German, for example, would achieve only in the eighteenth century (by which time little if any literature was published in Catalan, which was revived as a written language only in the nineteenth century). I grant that my comparison is unfair, since Catalan, being a Romance language, could far more easily borrow its philosophical vocabulary from Latin than German. Still, that linguistic deed is astonishing. The person I have in mind is Ramon Llull (1232–1316), one of the most original philosophers of the Middle Ages as well as the founder of the first living philosophical language in medieval Europe. There are three reasons for Llull's recourse to Catalan instead of Latin. First, he was a layman without any academic education; his knowledge of Latin was poor (as prove his Latin works, even if it is often difficult to find out whether they are really written by him or are translations from Catalan by other people). Second, Llull was a poet, who before his conversion had already written love poems in Catalan and had really mastered this language. Third, Llull was confronted on Mallorca with the presence of many Arabs, and desiring to convert them, he had to learn their language very well (he probably knew it better than Latin). Now, in contrast with Latin, Arabic was not only a language for educational and academic purposes but also a language for general purposes, and this may well have contributed to Llull's choice of Catalan as his main language. (His first book, the *Libre del gentil e dels tres savis* of 1274–76, seems to be a translation from an original Arabic version written by himself; it was translated in his lifetime into French and in the fourteenth century into Spanish.) Certainly Llull's switch to the vernacular was due partly to incapacity. He knew Latin only superficially; and since he was convinced that his philosophy was based on a direct revelation from God and therefore extremely innovative and original, he was less interested in linking his ideas to an existing tradition: It is amazing how few authorities he quotes. This has, again, partly to do with his ignorance, but partly with the rationalist nature of his philosophy, which rejects authorities in the name of reasons. To this, sociolinguistic factors are connected: Llull's audience, at least at the beginning of his career, was outside of the universities, which did not take him seriously and which he himself did not regard as a natural place for his operations. (In his novel *Blaquerna,* he nevertheless recognized the importance of a universal language—which he imagined could be only Latin—for the solution of international tensions.) Of course, his choice of Catalan had a positive reason as well: his superb sense for its possibilities. Because he also wrote very lively dialogues in which the existential dimension of the discourse, aiming at a conversion of the interlocutors, is no less important than the quality of the arguments, it made perfect sense for him to choose a language with a poetic potential the Latin of the medieval philosophers lacked.

There is little doubt that an analogous positive reason played a role too in the use of the second vernacular for philosophical purposes: I mean Italian, which through Dante's *Convivio* (between 1304 and 1307) became a philosophical language. Nevertheless, for the author of the *Divina Commedia* as well, Italian is not the only or main language for philosophical debates. Not only *De monarchia,* which, aiming at a public in the whole empire, could hardly be published in another language, but also the (never completed) treatise on language *De vulgari eloquentia,* which tried to show that under certain conditions Italian could claim the same dignity and beauty as Latin, is written in Latin. In the *Convivio* Dante justified at length the use of the vernacular.[4] Commenting on Italian *canzoni,* he, first, did not deem it appropriate to write in Latin. Second, he wanted to be generous: Latin would serve fewer people; princes, barons, knights, and many other noble persons, both male and female, would be excluded from the audience.[5] Third, he mentions the natural love for one's native language.

The third vernacular used for philosophical purposes is (Middle High) German in the sermons of Meister Eckhart (1260–1329). While his main philosophical and theological treatises are in Latin, there are both treatises and sermons written in the vernacular (many of his sermons were preached in female monasteries). Even if not written for colleagues, they contain hardly less original thoughts than the Latin works, and the linguistic creativity manifested in them is simply flabbergasting. Eckhart has a clear consciousness of the innovative nature of his linguistic choice, and he justifies it with the precept of the Gospel to take care of the sick: One should teach the uncultivated, to make them cultivated.[6]

If I am right, the reasons for the tentative use of vernacular languages for philosophical purposes in the late thirteenth and the early fourteenth century are partly the linguistic capacities (or, in Llull's case, incapacities) of the authors of these texts, partly the genres used (dialogues and sermons, as closer to everyday life, being particularly prone to the use of the vernacular), partly a consideration for the public addressed. Still, all three of the above-mentioned authors wrote also in Latin, and it is not until the sixteenth century that there are philosophers who wrote exclusively in the vernacular. The two most original thinkers who come to mind are Machiavelli and Montaigne. The reasons for the rejection of Latin as the philosophical language are again very different. Of course, both are masters of their own language, Italian and French respectively, and we have to be deeply thankful for their decision in favor of the vernacular. In the case of Machiavelli, this positive reason is linked to the negative one that his Latin does not seem to have been very good (similarly, Jakob Böhme had to write in German because he did not know Latin); but in the case of Montaigne this explanation does not hold, for as a child he was fluent in Latin, which he knew far better than French.[7] The discontent with the aridity of late medieval Scholastic Latin cannot have been a motive either, for the humanists had shown from the fourteenth century onwards that there was an alternative Latin, worthy of a more modern type of intellectual. The choice of French in the case of Montaigne is certainly determined by his desire to be read not by professors but by aristocrats, to whose class he desperately wanted to belong. His courtly background is similar to that of Llull—both philosophers were acquainted with their kings—but with Montaigne there is a certain snobbishness in the fact that a man with his knowledge of Latin refuses to use it. Also, the genre issue is important. The new genre Montaigne founds—the essay—is the opposite of the scholastic treatise; it is and claims to be antisystematic, associative, and subjective. It contains many reflections on personal experiences and feelings that occurred in a French context; to render them in Latin would be to alter them and thus poison the source from which the whole enterprise derives its legitimacy. (Also Bacon's *Essays,* addressed as they are to a wider public, will be in the vernacular, even if the majority of his work is in Latin.) In Machiavelli's case, the rise of national consciousness is a further important factor for the choice of the language: A book like *Il principe,* ending as it does with an appeal to liberate Italy from foreign forces, could hardly be published in western Europe's universal language, Latin; and while the more theoretical content of the *Discorsi* would allow them to be written in Latin, the wish to form politicians and not academics favors the choice of the Italian language. Analogously, the political dimension as well as the intent to have a political impact explains why Bodin, whose *Heptaplomeres* is in Latin, wrote *Les six livres de la République* in French.

In the course of the seventeenth century, an academic bilingualism became the norm for most philosophers, at least in Italy, France, and England. A philosopher there was supposed to publish in Latin as well as in his vernacular, and many books written in either language were translated (by the authors themselves or someone else) into the other: Campanella's *La città del sole* was written first in Italian (1602 and 1611 in a revised version) and translated into Latin in 1613–14 and, again revised, in 1630–31; Bacon himself expanded and translated *The Proficience and Advancement of Learning* of 1605 into Latin in 1623; Descartes's *Meditationes de prima philosophia* of 1641 were translated into French in 1647 by Luynes and Clerselier, whose work Descartes himself supervised as he did with Picot's 1647 translation of the *Principia philosophiae* of 1644; Hobbes rendered his English *Leviathan* of 1651 in Latin in 1668 (it is possible that he had begun to write the work in Latin), Locke's *Epistula de tolerantia* of 1689 was translated into English in the same year (he wrote the *Second* and the *Third Letter* directly in English in 1690 and 1692). All of these authors were bilingual, and so it is mainly a question of genre and of public that determines the linguistic choice: Books as personal as the *Discours de la méthode*[8] or as political as the *Two Treatises of Government* could hardly be written in Latin. There are, of course, exceptions to the rule of bilingualism. On the one hand, there is someone like the great naturalist Antoni van Leeuwenhoek, an autodidact, who ignored Latin and whose texts were all written in Dutch. They found a European public, how-ever, because almost all were translated into English or Latin; in 1681 Leeuwen-hoek became a member of the Royal Society. On the other hand, not all Eu-ropean languages had yet evolved in the seventeenth century into the status of functional academic languages. This goes without saying for languages with rela-tively few speakers, such as Danish (Czech is, due to Comenius, the most im-portant exception, although Comenius thought every child should learn Latin). But it is true for Spanish and also for Russian, which only in the nineteenth cen-tury became fit for philosophical productions (the first Russian philosopher, Chaadayev [1794–1856], wrote, albeit about Russia, still in French). Even Ger-man had a wide-ranging philosophical production only in the eighteenth cen-tury. Leibniz wrote his technical works in Latin, but his works for a broader public, mainly aristocrats, were in French, the language of the German and later also the Russian aristocracy. (Frederick the Great would write all his works, even his Political Testaments for his heir, in French, which until the early twentieth century, due in part to its status as diplomatic language, enjoyed far more respect than English.) Although Frenchmen did not consider Leibniz's French to be that of a native speaker,[9] it nevertheless guaranteed a work like the *Theodicée* a Eu-ropean public. Only a few of Leibniz's texts are in German, including, naturally enough, his reflections on the improvement of the German language (*Unvor-greifliche Gedanken, betreffend die Ausübung und Verbesserung der teutschen Sprache*). Whatever Christian Wolff's philosophical merits, it is his achievement to have prepared German to become a language capable of the greatest philosophical sophistication. I wonder whether the rise of German as one of the three most important philosophical languages of Europe in the late eighteenth century is one of the factors for the decline of Italian, which, it seems to me, fewer European philosophers (I am not speaking about poets and artists) have been willing to learn at least in the past two centuries, while Hume still knew it — the time for studying foreign languages being necessarily limited, one has to make a choice. Of course, there are more important reasons inherent in the quality of Italy's cultural production that explain the demise of the appeal of Italian; but even the greatest intellectual achievements suffered from this new intellectual situ-ation. One of the many reasons for the slow reception of Vico's *Scienza nuova* in Europe was that he wrote it in the vernacular. While its predecessor, the so-called *Diritto universale,* was in Latin and was still reviewed by such European scholars as Jean Leclerc in the *Bibliothèque ancienne et moderne* of 1722, the com-plete silence Vico's masterpiece encountered was a partial consequence of the choice of language. Italy has to be grateful to Vico for this choice, for the *Scienza nuova* enormously enriched its linguistic patrimony, but Vico's fate exemplifies the intellectual isolation that the abandonment of a universal academic language usually entails for those who write in a language read only by a small minority. The incomparably greater European success of a work like Montesquieu's *De l'esprit des lois,* which is related with regard to the content, though doubtless far more superficial, has not only to do with the fact that it is far easier to grasp and can be more quickly applied to politics but also with the language in which it was written. Analogously, Kierkegaard became a European celebrity only in the first half of the twentieth century, among other reasons because his works had to be translated from a language few people outside Denmark could read.

Already in the eighteenth century most original philosophical works were written in the native language of their authors. (I ignore the works in the scholastic tradition, which at that time were no longer original.) It was in the sciences that Latin remained until the nineteenth century an important vehicle of communication: Gauss wrote his most important mathematical works in Latin, and in a particularly elegant Latin, since he had long hesitated between a career as a classicist and one as a mathematician. (He made the right choice: not yet nineteen, he discovered the construction of the regular polygon with seventeen sides.) Nevertheless, up until the nineteenth century, a professor of philosophy was expected to write occasionally in Latin. On his promotion to full professor, Kant wrote *De mundi sensibilis atque intelligibilis forma et principiis* in 1770 in Latin; and when in 1801 Hegel became *Privatdozent* at the university of Jena, he had to submit a Latin thesis (*De orbitis planetarum*). At the end of his life, as rector of the university of Berlin, Hegel again gave two public addresses in Latin (for these occasions, he needed help from a friend).[10] In fact, Hegel was firmly convinced that a living philosophy could be produced only in one's own native language, and he praised both Luther's translation of the Bible and Wolff's efforts to achieve a German philosophical language.[11] There is little doubt that Hegel's dark language emulates the poetic achievements of his friend Hölderlin — both have an extraordinarily developed linguistic self-awareness. Particularly interesting is Hegel's reaction, when during his time as the rector (headmaster) of a gymnasium in Nuremberg he was asked by his former student Peter Gabriel van Ghert in a letter of August 4, 1809, whether he would be interested in a position at a Dutch university, where courses were still taught in Latin.[12] On December 16, Hegel answered that in case something worked out, he would have to teach in Latin at first but that he would soon try to switch to Dutch, if this were allowed, for he regarded it essential for the true appropriation of a science to own it in one's native language.[13]

Even Schopenhauer, whose German differs so markedly from Hegel's, but whose style certainly is not inferior to Hegel's, decided to rewrite his work *Über das Sehn und die Farben* in Latin in 1830, when, frustrated with his neglect by the German public, he tried to gain European attention. The hierarchy of languages still in force in the mid-nineteenth century is manifest in Schopenhauer's translation in his works of quotations from English, Spanish, and Italian but never from French and Latin. (Greek quotations—sometimes also Italian ones—are translated into Latin.) Latin and French were thus regarded as those languages that a cultivated bourgeois was supposed to know, but not English. As far as I see, Schopenhauer was the last of the great philosophers who at least occasionally wrote in Latin. Some years ago this made a hoax possible: Two scholars claimed to have found a manuscript from very late in Schopenhauer's life, in which he seemed to have changed radically his philosophical view.[14] This manuscript was purported to be in Latin, and only a translation of it was offered (with a few sentences quoted in the "original"). Many people (among them, I confess it, me) were fascinated by this *trouvaille,* until it became known that it was a joke. Of course, the "text" had to be in Latin, for (particularly the late) Schopenhauer's original German is simply inimitable. Nietzsche wrote only his philological articles on Diogenes Laertius in Latin—in this discipline Latin is still an acceptable academic language today, as the prefaces to the best critical editions continue to be in Latin—while it is inconceivable to render Nietzsche's terse philosophical prose in Latin without destroying its peculiarly seductive character.

There is no doubt whatsoever that the main reason for the disappearance of Latin as the academic language in the nineteenth century is the nationalistic ideology to which intellectuals contributed so much.[15] Since nations were defined to a great extent by language, cultural policy was regarded as a core matter for the then-existing states; and since the democratic ideology aimed at educating all citizens, the rejection of Latin was inevitable. (Only the stubborn hierarchical universalism peculiar to Catholicism maintained Latin for a far longer time, until it too was dropped in the Second Vatican Council, to the chagrin not of its worst members.) The desire to differentiate one's own culture from that of one's neighbors led to the use of one's own language wherever possible; only those intellectuals belonging to small linguistic groups or to communities whose language was very difficult for non-native speakers to learn used one of the major European languages. In the first half of the twentieth century, French and German were at least as important as English as such regional academic linguae francae: The Hungarian Lukács as well as the Pole Ingarden wrote their main works in German. (While Lukács published only articles in Hungarian, Ingarden wrote his main work, *Spór o istnienie świata/Der Streit um die Existenz der Welt,* at the beginning simultaneously in Polish and German but then completed the Polish version first.) In the second half of the century, French was the elective language of the Lithuanian philosopher Lévinas, of the Rumanian Cioran, and of the Bulgarian Todorov, all of whom, however, had immigrated to France. But for those who did not live in a Francophone country, English was the only and ever more attractive alternative to their own native languages. This is difficult to understand and to accept for Frenchmen, much more so than for Germans, since the latter can interpret the rejection of German by, for example, the Dutch and the Scandinavians after World War II and its replacement with English as the just punishment for the politics of Nazi Germany. The famous Norwegian logician Thoralf Skolem stopped publishing in German and switched to English in 1940, after Germany had occupied his country, and many followed his example. Even those many German-speaking émigrés who found a harbor in the Anglo-American countries during the time of German totalitarianism began to publish in English (a fascinating exception being Wittgenstein), and many, like Karl Popper or Hannah Arendt, stayed with that language. An interesting exception is Hans Jonas, who wrote his first great book, *Gnosis und spätantiker Geist,* in German, his second, *The Phenomenon of Life,* in English, but decided to write his last and by far most successful book, *Das Prinzip Verantwortung* (1979), in German again. Being in his seventies, he was not sure whether he would have the time to complete it in English. Though he had left Germany in 1933, he still needed far more time to write good English than good German. The result was a book in a German that was somehow awkward—for Jonas had ignored the development of that language for almost half a century.[16] But there is no doubt that the archaic patina of his language, corresponding so well to the character of his thought, contributed to making his book the best-seller it deservedly became.

II

Of course, intellectuals still continue to publish in their national languages. But it is obvious that almost every professor in the world, nowadays in the humanities no less than in the sciences, is especially proud and happy when he manages to write something in English, or at least to be translated into it. (Though I speak Italian fluently, I never felt the urge to write books or essays in it, and I was far less thrilled when several of my books were translated into my native language than when my first book came out in English.) The reason is very simple: The cultural hegemony of the United States is obvious, and one has, ceteris paribus, a far greater number of readers when one publishes in English than in another language. Which German, Frenchman, or Spaniard has not heard at international conferences the question by an Indian or Chinese person, whose attention he managed to capture by some remarks related to his own research, "Do you have something in English about it?" And who does not feel humiliated when he has to answer in the negative? The function of English nowadays is thus very similar to that of Latin in the early modern period: Most intellectuals try to be (at least) bilingual, to read and write in their native languages as well as in English.

There is, however, one important exception—the native speakers of English, who often enough are monolingual and have no incentive whatsoever to learn another language. In fact, this is the major difference between the linguistic hegemony of English today and that of Latin in the past. When Latin was still a living language, in the Roman Empire, it had to vie with Greek; the Roman imperialists were more willing to recognize the superiority of another culture and language than Americans are today. I presume that this eased the Roman rule in the eastern empire, for it diminished the asymmetry that every power relation entails. And when Latin had given way to the new vernaculars, it was for all intellectuals alike an academic language distinct from the language of everyday interactions with nonintellectuals; it did not favor any particular group. (Even the speakers of Romance languages had only a limited advantage, since the grammar of medieval Italian made it more difficult to learn Latin than, for example, the Middle High German grammar.) Furthermore, since Latin was also the language of the liturgy, it enjoyed a special dignity that English, being also the language of the most vulgar forms of expression, clearly lacks. The feeling that one is entering a higher intellectual sphere probably ennobled the speakers and writers of Latin in a way hardly imaginable to us foreigners who are fighting with the English language. For English is less exclusive than Latin was. In principle, everyone is able to acquire at least a modest knowledge of this language. Indeed, English conquered the world not only because of political factors such as the Anglo-American victories in the two world wars; its triumph also has to do with the fact that this language can be learned on a superficial level quite quickly while one can continue to expand one's English vocabulary. (Russian is much harder at the beginning, but one achieves a point of saturation far earlier.)

On the other hand, English is also the language of exceptional artistic achievements, which Latin hardly was anymore, at least in the early modern age, and this creates abysmal differences in the mastery of the language by native and non-native speakers. (Joseph Conrad's and Vladimir Nabokov's successes as English authors, although they were non-native writers, are exceptions that the normal acquirer of a foreign language should not even hope for.) To give examples: Thomas Aquinas's or Spinoza's Latin are not particularly attractive, and almost every philosopher could hope to achieve that level. (Of course, the Latin of a humanist such as Erasmus is something different, but, first, few humanists were original philosophers, and, second, even their Latin usually lacks the poetic grace one can very rarely achieve outside of one's native language.) But if Hans Jonas, after having lived more than forty-five years in English-speaking countries, published his last books in German, one of his reasons might well have been the feeling that he could never write English with the elegance of Austin or Quine.

What are the advantages and disadvantages of the actual situation, and is there any possibility of enjoying the former and avoiding the latter? With regard to the advantages, it is quite clear that the rise of English as the universal academic language increased the general communicability of intellectual ideas. Everyone has to learn only one foreign language — and the native speakers of English don't even have to do that — in order that all the important texts published recently may be read by everybody interested in them. Vico and Kierkegaard had to wait a long time before they could be received abroad; in principle, today intellectual ideas are immediately available for study and criticism. This is one aspect of the phenomenon called "globalization"; one of its consequences is that not only ideas but also persons have become commodities in a universal market. This language may sound deprecatory, but it is not intended as such. I am not complaining about this aspect of late modernity, because we also had it, if in a different form, already long ago. In the Middle Ages and in early modernity, European intellectuals were indeed extremely mobile, despite an infinitely inferior system of transportation and information transfer, because they shared a common language. I need only to mention Anselm of Canterbury, Thomas Aquinas, Erasmus, Descartes, and Pufendorf, all of whom spent their lives in different European countries. The emigration of European intellectuals to the United States, first forced by political threats and then elicited by an intelligent polity of the search for excellence by the best academic institutions, seems to make this mobility, which had vanished in the age of nationalism, normal again. Even if not everybody was so rooted in his birth town as Vico and Kant, in the late eighteenth and in the nineteenth century, it was extremely difficult for a German philosopher, for example, to find a position outside a German-speaking country. That did not need to be his home state, and even after the German unification there remained universities in Austria and in the Baltic provinces of Russia where he could apply for a position, but still the area was limited. Today the linguistic hegemony of English makes not only Europe but the whole world one big market for intellectuals.

However, there is one important difference: Most European academic institutions, and even more those of developing countries, are not able to attract Anglo-American intellectuals; the brain drain goes only in one direction. I would be surprised if for every hundred Russian intellectuals who immigrated to the United States, one could find one American who immigrated to Russia. Of course, this has to do with different economic potentials, for the universalism of the market is, as we all know, compatible with great differences in income and thus in power. Again, this is not intended to be primarily a contribution to cultural criticism. To a great extent, the non-Anglo-American countries themselves are responsible for the failure of their academic institutions, which are unable to compete with the Anglo-American ones; they have refused the necessary reforms, one of which would be the introduction of English as the teaching language in order to attract able foreigners. I have argued elsewhere[17] that one of the causes of difficulties for the European Union in becoming a federal state is that it lacks a European intelligentsia, united by common interests, while Germany and Italy had a national intelligentsia long before their unification in the nineteenth century. There are incomparably fewer Frenchmen and Frenchwomen teaching in Germany (and vice versa) than there are in the United States, because the European universities are still caught in the nationalist paradigm, committed mainly to teaching in their national languages (the few exceptions are mostly private universities or special graduate programs in business and engineering). At a department of philosophy in a German university it can still be controversial among faculty whether one can accept a *Habilitationsschrift* in English, even if it deals with literature that is mostly in English and even if the persons who oppose the choice of English would themselves take pride in being translated into English.

Of course, the greatest advantage of the rise of English as a universal language is its potential contribution to the downfall of the nationalist ideology, which wreaked so much havoc on Europe in the twentieth century. In the European context, as I have just suggested, the acceptance of English as one of the languages of university education could strongly increase the probability of a federation of the European states. For it is unlikely that a Frenchman will be willing to accept a president of the federation who does not speak French, or at least not fluently, if he is not accustomed to professors who do not speak, at least not fluently, his language. However, it will be a long process before an alternative to the cherished native language will be accepted in the French universities, longer than in every other European country for reasons discussed above. And it is certainly possible that the resentment engendered by the triumph of English will create particularly aggressive nationalist reactions against it in Europe and even more in Asia.

It would be not too difficult to argue that such reactions are silly and dangerous, even if this does not entail that politicians should ignore them. But beside this political issue, there are objective disadvantages linked to the hegemony of English, disadvantages sometimes sensed even by those whose irate reaction shows that irrational factors are determining their agenda. I have already mentioned the asymmetry characteristic of the actual situation and different from the situation existing earlier with regard to Latin. Non-native speakers of English feel deprived of the expressive power they have in their own language, and they rightly fear they will be at a disadvantage in the competition for arguments by being less able than the native speakers to make their points clearly. I am not fishing for compliments if I aver that in writing this text in my miserable pidgin English, I again and again felt that I would have expressed my thoughts far more elegantly and wittily in German. Feeling at home in a language is an important factor for feeling at home in the world, and the uneasiness connected with the sensation that one cannot convey exactly what one thinks is a painful one. If the price of the universal communicability of ideas is the loss of power of persuasion of these ideas, due to their trivialization in an impoverished language, that price may well be too high. The spread of English over the globe endangers the other languages, which, even when they continue to be spoken, assume more and more English words. That is not necessarily bad, and it can even be useful when it helps to name objects which otherwise would remain inaccessible in that other language. But it can destroy the unity of the language and paralyze all efforts to find modulations and differentiations within that language itself, thus forestalling its further development. It might even happen that in the long run the general use of a simplistic pidgin English will deprive also the native speakers' English of its extraordinary elegance and complexity, because it will adapt more and more to its global environment.

My point is not only a subjective one, expressed from the perspective of a non-native speaker. For the world as such, including the native speakers of English, the actual situation may entail a deplorable loss of cultural richness. It might be that every language, at least after its vocabulary has been updated by the introduction of foreign words, will be equally fit for the expression of chemical ideas, but I strongly doubt that something similar holds for philosophy. For the nature of philosophy has not to do only with content but also with the intellectual process in which this content is presented, and this process differs according to the nature of the language in which it occurs. I am far from wanting to defend a general theory of incommensurability among different languages: In most cases, a reasonably accurate translation from another language into a sufficiently rich language is possible. There are even good English translations of Heidegger, and that is indeed an astonishing achievement. But from a genetic point of view, it seems to me quite probable that certain thoughts are more likely to be grasped for the first time in one language than in another. The categorization of the world, which assumes different shapes in the grammar and vocabulary of different languages, determines, although certainly not in an inescapable way, some aspects of our access to reality, and furthermore there are in each language concepts associated for contingent historical reasons with other concepts. (In Moscow in 1990, I met a Russian who wrote only in a far from flawless German, for his own language had been poisoned for him by the ideological texts written in it.) It seems plausible to me that the analytical way of thinking is more tuned to a syntax like the English than to a syntax like the German or the Greek, which have a greater richness in hypotactic constructions and invite a more holistic approach. Therefore the fear is justified that the triumph of English at the expense of other languages would deprive us of perfectly possible and reasonable ways of interpreting the world, and this can hardly be the aim of philosophy.

Given the positive and the negative side effects of the rise of English, how should we react? The question is somehow futile, for we cannot do much. The process is far too strong to be stopped. Essentially, our problem is only an application of the greater question of how the need for universal norms can be combined with a recognition of different cultures having their own dignity. It is not difficult to see that the two demands are not only compatible but even support each other: A plurality of cultures can survive on this planet only if there are norms respected by all of them—otherwise none could feel secure. On the other hand, the ecological consequences of monocultures are well known—they are far more vulnerable to infections than plantations with different species. Cultural diversity as well as biodiversity increases the chances of survival for humankind, and therefore a universalist ethics cannot oppose it but must foster it. Insofar as the exchange and the criticism of ideas is facilitated by one universal academic language, one has to be grateful for the emergence of it. If all people were taught English as a second language in their childhood, most of the subjective problems I have mentioned could be overcome. But if these problems disappeared because only English was left over, the objective loss of cultural richness would be appalling. We can therefore only aim at educating bilingual individuals, who are as fluent in English as they are in their own different native languages and who publish alternately in both of them. And we can only hope that more and more native speakers of English also try to become bilingual — even if they don't have to do so in order to communicate with others, they may well recognize that this supererogatory act may enrich their perception of the world, both when they read classic works in their original language and when they try to make their ideas clear in a language other than their own.

NOTES

I thank Katie Freddoso for correcting my English, Martin Bloomer for many discussions of the subject, and the Erasmus Institute, whose fellowship allowed me to write this paper.

1. *De finibus* II 5: *bonum ipsum;* III 34: *ipsum bonum.*

2. "Utraque lingua" is used for the two languages (Horace, *Satires,* I 10, 23) far earlier than the Greek equivalent ἑκατέραν γλῶτταν (Plutarch, *Lucullus* 1; speaking of a Roman).

3. See Horace, *Satires,* I 10, 20 ff. Horace even rejects the introduction of Greek words into Latin poems so familiar from Lucilius.

4. See Dante Alighieri, *Il Convivio,* ed. M. Simonelli (Bologna, 1966), 10–28 (chaps. V–XIII). The three main reasons are named in chap. V (10): "cautela di disconvenevole ordinazione; prontezza di liberalitate; lo naturale amore a propria loquela."

5. Chap. IX (18 f.): "Non avrebbe lo latino così servito a molti . . . e questi nobili sono principi, baroni, cavalieri, e molt' altre nobile gente, non solamente maschi ma femmine, che sono molti e molte in questa lingua, volgari e non litterati." The argument that the use of the vernacular reaches out to more persons can be found already in Llull: *Art Amativa,* in *Obres de Ramon Lull,* ed. S. Galmés et al., 21 vols. (Palma de Mallorca, 1906–50), XVII 6 f.

6. "Ouch sol man sprechen, daz man sôgetâne lêre niht ensol sprechen noch schrîben ungelêrten. Dar zuo spriche ich: ensol man niht lêren ungelêrte liute, sô enwirt niemer nieman gelêret, sô enmac nieman lêren noch schrîben. Wan dar umbe lêret man

die ungelêrten, daz sie werden von ungelêret gelêret. Enwære niht niuwes, sô enwürde niht altes. 'Die gesunt sint', sprichet unser herre, 'die enbedürfen der arzenîe niht.'" *Meister Eckharts Buch der göttlichen Tröstung und von dem edlen Menschen (Liber "Benedictus")*, ed. J. Quint (Berlin, 1952), 63.

7. See the end of *Essais* I 26 (*Essais,* vol. 1 [Paris, 1962], 187 f.]).

8. Descartes himself mentions at the end of the *Discours* the following further reason: Given the newness of his ideas, he does not want to be read by persons who confuse authorities with arguments. "Et si j'écris en français, qui est la langue de mon pays, plutôt qu'en latin, qui est celle de mes précepteurs, c'est à cause que j'espère que ceux qui ne se servent que de leur raison naturelle toute pure, jugeront mieux des mes opinions, que ceux qui ne croient qu'aux livres anciens" (Paris, 1951, 105).

9. See G. W. Leibniz, *Die philosophischen Schriften,* ed. C. J. Gerhardt, vol. 5 (Berlin, 1882), 8.

10. See Friedrich Förster's letter of June 22, 1830 (*Briefe von und an Hegel*, 3d ed., ed. J. Hoffmeister, vol. 3 [Hamburg, 1969], 307).

11. "Vorlesungen über die Geschichte der Philosophie," in *Werke,* Bd. 20 (Frankfurt, 1971), 53, 258 f.

12. "wo man aber (bis jetzt wenigstens) die Vorlesungen im Lateinische haltet" (*Briefe von und an Hegel,* ed. J. Hoffmeister, vol.1 [Hamburg, 1969], 291).

13. "In Ansehung der Sprache, in der die Kollegien auf holländischen Universitäten zu halten gewöhnlich ist, so würde dies in lateinischer Sprache wenigstens im Anfange geschehen müssen; wenn die Gewohnheit es erlaubte, hievon abzugehen, würde ich mich bald in der Landessprache auszudrücken suchen; denn ich halte es an sich für wesentlich zur wahrhaften Aneignung einer Wissenschaft, daß man dieselbe in seiner Muttersprache besitzt" (Ed.cit., 299).

14. F. Volpi and W. Welsch, "Schopenhauers schwere Stunde," in *Schopenhauer im Denken der Gegenwart,* ed. V. Spierling (Munich, 1987), 290–98.

15. See J. Benda, *La Trahison des clercs* (Paris, 1927).

16. *Das Prinzip Verantwortung* (Frankfurt, 1979), 10 f.: "Der Entschluß, nach Jahrzehnten fast ausschließlich englischer Autorschaft dies Buch auf deutsch zu schreiben, entsprang keinen sentimentalen Gründen, sondern allein der nüchternen Berechnung meines vorgerückten Alters. Da die gleichwertige Formulierung in der erworbenen Sprache mich immer noch zwei- bis dreimal so viel Zeit kostet wie die in der Muttersprache, so glaubte ich, sowohl der Grenzen des Lebens wie der Dringlichkeit des Gegenstandes wegen, nach den langen Jahren gedanklicher Vorarbeit für die Niederschrift den schnelleren Weg wählen zu sollen, der immer noch langsam genug war. Dem Leser wird es natürlich nicht entgehen, daß der Verfasser die deutsche Sprachentwicklung seit 1933 nicht mehr "mitbekommen" hat."

17. "Könnte die Europäische Union als Bundesstaat funktionieren? Und kann sie ein Bundesstaat werden?" in *Universitas* 56 (2001), 1234–44.

Contributors

JOSEPH P. AMAR is associate professor and director of Arabic and Syriac Studies at the University of Notre Dame and writes on the interactions of Syriac and Arabic cultures in the classical period. His most recent publication is *Dionysius bar Salibi's Response to the Arabs,* Corpus Scriptorum Christianorum Orientalium, 2005.

W. MARTIN BLOOMER is associate professor of classics at the University of Notre Dame. His publications include *Valerius Maximus and the Rhetoric of the New Nobility* (1992); *Latinity and Literary Society at Rome* (1997); and *The School of Rome: Latin Studies and the Origins of Liberal Education* (forthcoming).

SUSAN D. BLUM is associate professor of anthropology at the University of Notre Dame. Her most recent book is *Deception and Truth: Reflections of an American Anthropologist in China.*

THEODORE J. CACHEY JR. is professor of Italian and chair of the Department of Romance Languages at the University of Notre Dame.

TONY CROWLEY is professor of language, literature and cultural theory at the University of Manchester. His work includes *Language in History: Theories and Texts* (1996); *The Politics of Discourse* (second edition 2003); and *Wars of Words: the Politics of Language in Ireland 1537–2004* (2005).

SEAMUS DEANE is Keough Professor of Irish Studies at Notre Dame. Among his publications are *Celtic Revivals* (1986); *Strange Country* (1995); *Reading in the Dark* (a novel) (1996). He edited *The Field Day Anthology of Irish Writing,* 3 vols. (1991) and most recently has published *Foreign Affections: Essays on Edmund Burke* (2005).

DIMITRI GUTAS, professor of Arabic at Yale University, works on the transmission of Greek thought into Arabic in the Middle Ages and on Arabic philosophy.

His more recent publications include *Avicenna and the Aristotelian Tradition* (1988); *Greek Thought, Arabic Culture* (1998); and *Greek Philosophers in the Arabic Tradition* (2000). He is currently preparing an annotated critical edition of the Greek text and medieval Arabic translation of Theophrastus's *Metaphysics*.

VITTORIO HÖSLE studied philosophy, Greek, and Sanskrit in Regensburg, Tübingen, Bochum, and Freiburg and is now Paul Kimball Professor of Arts and Letters at the University of Notre Dame in the departments of German, Philosophy, and Political Science.

RICHARD HUNTER is Regius Professor of Greek at Cambridge University. He has published widely on Greek, especially Hellenistic literature, including *Theocritus and the Archeology of Greek Poetry* (Cambridge, 1996) and *The Argonautica of Apollonius: Literary Studies* (Cambridge, 1993).

PETER McQUILLAN teaches in the Department of Irish Language and Literature at the University of Notre Dame. He is the author of *Mood and Modality: A History of the Irish Subjunctive* (2002) and *Native and Natural: Aspects of the Concepts of "Right" and "Freedom" in Irish* (2004).

HAUN SAUSSY has published *The Problem of a Chinese Aesthetic* (1993), *Great Walls of Discourse* (2000), and many articles about poetry, poetics, interpretation, and related subjects. His current project is an interdisciplinary history of the concept of rhythm from 1880 to 1930. He is professor of comparative literature at Yale University and also teaches in the Department of East Asian Languages and Literatures.

Index

Abbāsid era, 107–9
academia
    English as the universal language of,
        255–61
    Latin replaced by national language in,
        246–55
academic bilingualism, 246–48, 251–52,
    256
academic institutions, failure of non-Anglo,
    257–58
Académie Française, and rejection of
    English terms, 137
Act for English Order, Habit and Language,
    169
A fhir théid go Fiadh bhFuinidh (Ó hUiginn),
    84–85
Africa (Petrarch), 21
Alberti, Leon Battista, 23–26
Alexander the Great, 99–100, 102–3
Alexandrian poetry, 192–93
All That Fall (Beckett), 238
Ammianus Marcellinus, 247
Amorum libri (Boiardo), 28
ancestral language, 207–8
Anderson, Benedict, 151
Anglo-Irish. *See* Hiberno-English
Aphrahat, 47
Aquinas, Saint Thomas, 257
Arab empire, 104–9
Arabic language, 48–50, 99–109, 142,
    248–49
Arab nationalism, 104–5
Aramaic language, 41–44, 50–51,
    52n.16, 100
Archaeologica Britannica (Lhuyd), 173
Arendt, Hannah, 255
Aristotle, 196, 197–98

Arnold, T. W., 106
Athens, freedom of speech in, 192
Avestan texts, loss and recovery of, 103–4

Bacon, Francis, 117, 251
"Bann Valley Eclogue" (Heaney), 212–18
Bardaisan of Edessa, 45–46, 48
Bards of the Gael and the Gall (Sigerson), 238
Beatha Aodha Ruaidh Uí Dhomhnuill
    (Ó Clérigh), 75–76
Becher, Johann Joachim, 114
Begly, Conor, 173
Belgium, Linguistic Divide between
    Flanders and Wallonia, 137
Bembo, Pietro, 32–33
Besnier, Pierre, 117–18, 131n.17
Bharatidasan, 135–36
bilingualism, academic, 246–48, 251–52,
    256. *See also* diglossia
binary notation, 125–28
Biondo, Flavio, 23–24, 34n.18
Blaquerna (Llull), 249
Blommaert, Jan, 151
Boccaccio, Giovanni, 16–18, 21–22, 27,
    36n.33
Bodin, Jean, 251
Böhme, Jakob, 250
Boiardo, Matteo Maria, 28
"Bone Dreams" (Heaney), 224n.1
Book of the Courtier, The (Castiglione), 32
Book of the Customs of the Countries
    (Bardaisan), 45–46, 48
Borges, Jorge Luis, 112–14
boundary-celebrating societies, 136, 151
boundary-disputing societies, 135–36, 151
boundary-shrugging societies, 136–37, 151
Bradshaw, Brendan, 70, 80, 82, 83

Brodsky, Joseph, 215–16
Browning, Robert, 218, 220–23, 225n.15,
      225n.18
Bruni, Leonardo, 19–20, 23–24, 34n.9,
      34n.18
Burke, Edmund, 235–36

Caball, Mark, 75, 84, 86
Callimachus, 192, 198, 200–201
Campion, Edmund, 166
Canada, tolerance of linguistic diversity in,
      135, 137
Castiglione, Baldassare, 32
Castilian dialect, 137
Catalan language, 137, 248–49
Catholic Church. See also Christianity
      Irish Famine and, 228
      Irish national identity and, 74–77, 85
      Latin in, 208–9, 220–23, 224n.13, 254
      and role in decline of Irish language, 170,
      177–78
Céitinn, Seathrún (Geoffrey Keating), 66,
      70, 75, 80–81, 82, 83
Chaadayev, Pyotr Yakovlevich, 252
Chao, Y. R., 148
China
      cultural nationalism in, 139
      language policy in
      —of Communist regime, 139, 144–45
      —literacy and, 144–45, 149
      —and Nationalist regime, 139, 143
      —and romanization, 143, 159n.39
      —and script reform, 142–43, 158n.36
      —and spoken language standard, 139,
      142–45, 148, 152–53, 154n.20
      linguistic diversity in, 135–36, 140–42,
      145–50, 152–53
      literature, linguistic issues in, 156n.26
Chinese writing system, 117
Christianity. See also Catholic Church
      Chalcedonian, 101–2
      Syriac-speaking, 44–49, 51, 101–2
Cicero, 247
Cioran, Emil Mihai, 255
Clarysse, Willy, 190

classification systems, 112–13, 123–25
coded languages (codebooks), 115, 121,
      128–29. See also cryptography
Cohn, Bernard, 74
Colvin, Stephen, 191–92
Comenius, John Amos, 252
Comento (de' Medici), 31
Commedia (Dante), 16–20, 27, 30–31
Conrad, Joseph, 257
Constantine I (Roman emperor), 100–101
constitutions, language specifications in,
      140, 149, 155nn.22–23
Contra amores (Platina), 19
Convivio (Dante), 16, 249–50
Conway, Richard, 171–72
Coptic language, 100–101, 103
Council of Florence (1438–39), 22
Countess Cathleen, The (Yeats), 180
Couturat, Louis, 130
Crisolora, Manuele, 33n.7
Critique of Judgment (Kant), 236
Croce, Benedetto, 18
cryptography, 114–20, 121. See also coded
      languages (codebooks)
Cyrene, 190
Czech, as academic language, 252

Daniel, E. Valentine, 62
Dante, 20–21. See also specific works by
Das Prinzip Verantwortung (Jonas), 255
Davies, Anna Morpurgo, 191
Davis, Thomas, 178
Decameron (Boccaccio), 17, 27
de Fréine, Seán, 231
De l'esprit des lois (Montesquieu), 253
Della Famiglia (Alberti), 24–25
De monarchia (Dante), 249–50
Dēnkard, 103
Descartes, René, 117, 251, 262n.8
"De verbis romanae locutionis"
      (Biondo), 23
De vulgari eloquentia (Dante), 16, 249–50
Dewar, Daniel, 176
"D'fhior chogaidh comhailtear síothcháin,"
      67–69

dialectical affiliation and genre in Greek
poetry, 187–88, 191–92, 198–99, 201
dialectical culture, 189–90, 197
"Dia libh a laochruidh Gaoidhiol," 70–72
Dialogi ad Petrum Histrum (Bruni), 20–22
"Dialogo intorno alla nostra lingua"
(Machiavelli), 32
"Dialogue in Hibernian Style" (Swift), 175
Dictionary of the English Language, A
(Johnson), 175
diglossia, 22–25, 142, 151. *See also*
bilingualism, academic
Dijkstra, Klaas, 44
Dinneen, Patrick S., 62, 179
Dionisotti, Carlo, 36n.33
Diritto universale (Vico), 252
Discours de la méthode (Descartes), 251, 262n.8
Discorsi (Machiavelli), 251
dispute poems, 41
diversity, culturally varying tolerances of.
See also nationalism-language
relationship; *specific languages*
boundary-celebrating societies, 136, 151
boundary-contesting societies, 135–36
boundary-disputing societies, 151
boundary-shrugging societies, 136–37,
151
China, 135–36, 140–42, 145–50,
152–53
United States, 135, 137, 151, 152, 153,
153n.3
Drijvers, Han J.W., 41
Duara, Prasenjit, 139
dúchas (dúthchas)
bunadhus link, 64–65, 76
character traits represented by use of,
87–89
in context
—of culture of origin, 63–65
—of exile, 72–74, 81–85
—interpreting, 61–62, 90
—of nationalism, 70–76
—of socio-economic change, 85–89
—of the symbolic center, 65–74
defined, 61

index of cultural unity, 84–85
in political poetry, 70–74, 82–84
Dunne, T. J., 74
Duranti, Alessandro, 62, 65
dúthaigh (dúiche), 60–63, 76–80, 84–85.
See also Irish language

Eckhart, Meister, 250
Eclogues (Virgil), 216
Eco, Umberto, 113
Ecomium of Ptolemy Philadelphus (Ptolemy),
193–94
Edessa, 42, 43–45
Edgeworth, Maria, 176
Edwards, John, 135
Egeria, 47–48
Egypt, Hellenization of, 100
"El idioma analítico de John Wilkins"
(Borges), 112–13
Elizabeth I (queen of England), 170
Elliott, J. H., 84
English, the
anti-Irish sentiment, 165–66
Gaelicization of, 168–70
Irish Famine and, 227–28
English language
Englishness and, 167–68
exclusivity and alienation in, 167–68,
256–57
hegemony of, 135, 137, 256–61
Irish literature in, 232–40
Irish mode of, 238–39
linguistic correctness debates, 175–76
as universal academic language, 245,
255–61
English language in Ireland
Catholic Church and, 170, 177–78
domination of, 137
Gaelicization of, 168–71
individuality of, 180
Irish resistance to, 170–74, 176–77
legislation enforcing use of, 168–70, 173
linguistic prejudice of English, 166,
168–70, 173, 175–76, 181–82, 207–8
present-day use of, 181, 182

Ephrem the Syrian, Saint, 47
Epistula de tolerantia (Locke), 251
Erasmus, Desiderius, 257
Erbaugh, Mary, 148
Essay on Irish Bulls (Edgeworth), 176
essays, 251
Essays (Bacon), 251
Essay towards a Real Character and a Universal Language (Wilkins), 120–23
Evans-Pritchard, E. E., 67

"Fada i n-éagmais inse Fáil" (Nuiseann), 82–85
Famine, Irish, 227–28, 229, 230–31, 233
"Fearann cloidhimh críoch Bhanbha" (Ó hUiginn), 75–76, 77–80
Ferdinand III (Holy Roman emperor), 116–17
Ferguson, Charles, 142
Fertile Crescent, Hellenization of, 100–102
Fiammetta (Boccaccio), 27
Ficino, Marsilio, 28
Fifteenth Idyll (Theocritus of Syracuse), 188–90, 192
Fitzgerald, James Fitzmaurice, 76–77
Florentine as foundation for Italian language, 16, 25–26, 31–33
Foras Feasa ar Éirinn (Céitinn), 64–65, 66, 75, 80–81
Formentin, Vittorio, 24
Forrester, John, 237
Fortes, Meyer, 67
Foucault, Michel, 112–13
French, as language of philosophy, 250–51, 252, 255
Friel, Brian, 209, 218, 239–40

Gaelic language. *See* Irish language
Gaelic League, 179, 239
garshūnī translations, 48–50, 103–4
Gauss, Carl Friedrich, 253
Geertz, Clifford, 134
German, as language of philosophy, 250, 252, 255
Ghert, Peter Gabriel van, 253–54

Gibbons, Luke, 74
Giraldus Cambrensis (Gerald of Wales), 165
Gnosis und spätantiker Geist (Jonas), 255
Gow, A. S. F., 199–200
Grammatica della lingua toscana (Alberti), 24
Grattan, Henry, 177
Greece
  dialectical culture in, 189–90, 197
  Fertile Crescent, Hellenization of, 100–102
  pagan vs. Christian culture in, 100–102
  Persia, Hellenization of, 102–4
  Sophistic movement and, 197
Greek (Hellenistic) poetry
  authenticity of language in, 200–201
  cultural politics of, 194–201
  exotic elements in, 197–98
  genre and dialectical affiliation in, 187–88, 191–92, 198–99, 201
  politics/power link to dialect and, 192–96
  restrictions on writers of, 197
  socio-linguistic consciousness of the elite and, 188–91, 198–201
  stylistic criticism in shaping of, 197–98
Greek language
  Arabic's relationship to, 100, 103–4
  Aramaic, influence on, 43, 100
  Avestan translations of, 103
  Christianity and dominance of, 100–102
  as common language (*koinē*), 187, 190–96, 202nn.9–10, 202n.1
  and Coptic language, 100
  Doric dialect and traditions in, 189–94, 198–99
  and introduction in Italy, 33n.7
  as language of philosophy, 246–47
  and link of politics/power to dialect, 188–89, 192–96
  in *Translations* (Friel), 209–10, 239–40
  and use in Syria, 41, 45–48
Gumperz, John J., 65

Heaney, Seamus, 167, 207–9, 212–18, 224n.1
Hebrew language, Aramaic displacement of, 41–42

Hecale (Callimachus), 198
Hegel, Georg Wilhelm Friedrich, 253–54
hegemony. *See also* linguistic imperialism,
   of English language
  of English language, 135, 137, 256–61
  Florentine desire for cultural, 30
Henry VIII (king of England), 168, 169
Heptaplomeres (Bodin), 251
Heraclides of Pontus, 190, 194
Hiberno-English, 175, 180–81
Historie of Ireland (Campion), 166
Hobbes, Thomas, 251
Hobsbawm, Eric, 138
Hokkien lanugage/dialect, 139, 148, 154n.20
Hölderlin, Friedrich, 253
Homer, 192–93
Homeric Hymn to Apollo (Theocritus), 194
Hong, Keelung, 154n.20
Hong Kong, multilingualism in, 148
Hooke, Robert, 124, 129
Hopkinson, Neil, 199
Horrocks, Geoffrey, 187
Hughes, Geoffrey, 89
humanist debate on vernacular vs. Latin,
   17–22, 23–26
Hyde, Douglas, 169, 179
Hymn to Demeter (Philikos), 198–99

"Idea of Order at Key West, The"
   (Stevens), 208
Iliad (Homer), 192–93
Il principe (Machiavelli), 251
Indonesia, 140
Ingarden, Roman, 255
"Integrative Revolution, The" (Geertz), 134
"Interesting Case of John Alphonsus
   Mulrennan, The" (Heaney), 167
invented language
  Essay towards a Real Character and a
   Universal Language (Wilkins) and,
   120–23
  Leibniz's binary system and, 125–28
  Micrographia (Hooke) and, 124
  Polygraphia nova (Kircher) and, 116–20

Ireland
  barriers to modernity in, 228–31
  cultural durability in, 228
  Famine in, 227–28, 229, 230–31
  habits of dependence and, 229–30
  social change in early modern, 85–89
  and Spanish ethnic origin, 63–65
Irish, the
  and allegiance to Catholicism, 74–77, 85
  colonialism's effect on, 165–70, 173,
   181–82
  as exiles in their homeland, 72–74,
   81–85
  Giraldus's description of, 165
  national identity of
  in nineteenth and twentieth centuries, 74
  political and cultural stereotypes in
   creating and representing, 231–32
  in sixteenth and seventeenth centuries,
   65–75
Irish drama, stereotype of, 224n.5
Irish English language, 180–81, 238–39
Irish language, *dúchas (dúthchas)*. *See also*
   dúthaigh (dúiche)
  and Catholic church, 170, 177–78
  colonizers' attitudes toward, 166,
   168–70, 173, 181–82
  community and, 177
  compulsory status of, 181
  decline in use of, 181
  documenting of, 181
  and economics, 171–72, 174–75,
   176–77, 178
  and education in English, 171–72, 176,
   177, 178–79, 209–10, 239–40
  evolution of, 180, 238–40
  and Famine survivors' beliefs, 230–31
  and generational shift, 174–75
  Irish alienation from, 167
  Irish mode of, 238–39
  legislation against, 168–70, 173
  modernity, 230–31, 233, 237–40
  national identity and, 177–80, 231–32
  origin shared with Spanish, 63–65

Irish language (*cont.*)
    poems about, 172–73
    post-independence, 180–81, 229–30
    pursuit of authenticity in loss of, 239
    and revival movement, 173, 179–80,
      238–39
    shame felt by users of, 179
    in *Translations* (Friel), 209–10, 239–40
Irish Language in a Changing Society, The
    (Bord na Gaeilge), 181
Irish Literary Theatre project, 179
Irish literature in English, 232–40
Islam, 48–50, 104–7
Isocrates, 196
Italian language
    Florentine vernacular as foundation for,
      16, 25–26, 31–33
    as language of philosophy, 249–50,
      251, 252
    Latin vs.
    —cultural-political context of, 22, 26–29
    —Dante's influence on, 15–16, 19,
      20–21
    —humanist debate on, 17–22, 23–26
    —and Landino's program of linguistic
      reform, 30–31
    —and movable type, 27, 32–33
"I Was a Labourer" (Jennett), 223n.3

Jakobson, Roman, 61–62
Jennett, Sean, 223n.1
Jesus, language used by, 53n.24
Johnson, Samuel, 175
Jonas, Hans, 255, 257
Joyce, James, 181–82, 207, 237–38

Kant, Immanuel, 236, 253
Keenan, Patrick, 178, 179
Keogh, John, 175
Kierkegaard, Søren Aabye, 253
Kiltartan (Kiltartanese), 181
Kircher, Athanasius, 113, 114–20, 121,
    128–29
Kong Jiesheng, 156n.26

Landino, Cristoforo, 29–31
language
    acquisition of, 210, 236–38
    neutrality in, 127–28
    perception's role in understanding,
      124–25
    social formations from, 128–30
language-power relationship
    Alexander the Great and, 101–2
    and Arabic, 99–109
    and China, 149–52
    classicism in, 111–13
    dialectical affiliation and, 187–88,
      192–96
    and Fertile Crescent, from seventh to
      ninth centuries, 101–2
    imagination of, 114
    originator-speaker form of, 128–29
    Persia, 102–4, 107
Latin language. *See also* Italian language,
    Latin vs.
    advantages to learning, 208–11
    Catholic Church's association with,
      208–9, 220–23, 224n.13, 254
    Heaney's childhood memories of, 208–9
    as language of school
    —"Bann Valley Eclogue" (Heaney),
      212–19
    —liberation and oppression in
      acquisition of, 209–11
    —"Tomb at St. Praxed's, The"
      (Browning), 220–23
    liberation and oppression in the
      acquisition of, 239–40
    roles played by, 210–11
    spoken vs. written, 22–25
    in *Translations* (Friel), 209–10, 239–40
    as universal academic language,
      246–55
    in vernacular poetry, 212–23
Lebanon, 40, 50
Leerssen, Joep, 75
Leeuwenhoek, Antoni van, 251–52
Leibniz, Gottifried Wilhelm, 125–28, 252

Les six livres de la République (Bodin), 251
Leviathan (Hobbes), 251
Lévinas, Emmanuel, 255
Lewis, D. S., 89
Lhuyd, Edward, 173
Libre del gentil e los tres savis (Llull), 249
"Life of Dante" (Bruni), 19, 20
linguistic imperialism, of English language,
    166, 168–70, 173, 181–82. *See also*
    hegemony
linguistic signs, context in interpretation of,
    61–62
linguistic tolerance. *See* diversity, culturally
    varying tolerances of
literacy and language standardization,
    135–36, 137, 144–45, 149, 155n.25
literature
    Irish, in English, 232–40
    linguistic issues in Chinese, 156n.26
Literature in Ireland (MacDonagh), 180, 238
Locke, John, 251
love, as theme in vernacular poetic
    tradition, 15–16, 18–19, 28
Lucretius, 246–47
Lukács, György, 255
Llull, Ramon, 248–51
Luther, Martin, 253
Lu Tianming, 156n.26

Mac Cana, Proinsias, 66, 67, 68
Mac Craith, Micheál, 84
Mac Crutín, Aodh, 173
MacDonagh, Thomas, 180, 238
Macedonian language, 195
Macedonian ruling class, 196
MacHale, Archbishop, 178
Machiavelli, Niccolò, 32, 250, 251
Magnes, sive de arte magnetica (Kircher),
    115–16
Mair, Victor, 146
Malaysia, 140
Mandarin language, 139, 154n.20
Marx, 111–12
Mason, Henry Monck, 177

McQuillan, Peter, 224n.11
Medici, Lorenzo de', 22, 28, 29, 30, 31
Meditationes de prima philosophia
    (Descartes), 251
memory of language, 103–4, 207–8,
    212–18
Mercury or the Swift and Silent Messenger
    (Wilkins), 121
Micrographia (Hooke), 124
Migliorini, Bruno, 22
Miscellany of Irish Proverbs, A (O'Rahilly),
    224n.11
Mitchel, John, 228
modernity
    atrocity and, 227–28
    English language in Ireland and,
        180–81, 238–39
    English as the language of, 230–31, 233,
        237–40
    in Ireland, barriers to, 228–31
Monophysites, 101
Montaigne, Michel, 250
Montesquieu, Baron de La Brède et de, 253
Moore, George, 238
Moran, D. P., 179
"Mo thruaighe mar táid Gaoidhil," 72–74
movable type, importance of, 27, 32–33
Muhammad, 104–5
Multilingualism (Edwards), 135
Murray, Stephen O., 154n.20

Nabataean Aramaic, 43
Nabokov, Vladimir, 257
nationalism
    Arab, 104–5
    in China, 139
    cultural, 139, 167, 177–78
    English dominance and decreases in,
        258–59
    European revival of patriotism and,
        82–85
    Gaelic, sixteenth-century, 70–74
    Irish, 65–77, 85, 167, 177–78, 231–32
    political, Irish vs. English, 177–78

nationalism-language relationship.
  See also diversity, culturally varying
    tolerances of
  examples of, 137–38
  intellectuals and, 254–55
  Irish language and, 177–80, 231–32
  in political poetry, 70–74, 82–84
Native American language suppression, 137
native language, use by authors, 253–54
Naturalis historia (Pliny), 29
"Necessity of De-Anglicising Ireland, The"
  (Hyde), 169
Neo-Persian language, 107
Neoplatonism, 19, 28
Nestle, Edward, 51
Nestorians, 101
Niccoli, Niccolò, 21–22
Nicholson, Rev., 174–75
Nicolson, E., 166
Nietzsche, Friedrich Wilhelm, 111–12, 254
Norman, Jerry, 141
Nuinseann, Uilliam, 82–85

Ó Bruadair, Dáibhí, 172
Ó Buachalla, Breandán, 75
O'Byrne, Feagh McHugh, 70–72
O'Casey, Sean, 181
Ó Cléirigh, Lughaidh, 75–76
O'Connell, Daniel, 177–78
Ó Corráin, Donnchadh, 67
Ó Cuív, Brian, 63–64
Ó Dónaill, Niall, 61
O'Donnell, Daniel, 230
O'Donnell, Peadar, 178
O'Faolain, Sean, 230, 240
Ó Gnímh, Fear Flatha, 72–74, 83, 88–89
Ó hUiginn, Maol Mhuire, 84–85
Ó hUiginn, Tadhg Dall, 67–69, 77–80
O'Neill, Hugh, 230
"On the Death of Dr. Swift" (Swift), 225n.19
O'Rahilly, T. F., 224n.11
Ó Rathaillle, Aodhagáin, 173
Oratio ad Graecos (Tatian), 45–46
Ó Súilleabháin Béirre, Domhnall, 63–65

Pairlement Chloinne Tomáis (*PCT*), 86–89
Papua New Guinea, 136
Passions of the Tongue (Ramaswamy), 136
Pearse, Patrick, 179–80, 182n.3
Peeters, Paul, 48
Pehlevi language (Middle Persian),
  102–4, 107
Peirce, Charles Sanders, 61
perception, role in understanding language,
  124–25
Persian language, 102–4, 107
Petrarch, Francis, 16–18, 21–22, 27
Petty, Sir William, 174
Phenomenon of Life, The (Jonas), 255
Philikos, 198–99
Phillips, Adam, 235, 236
Philodemus of Gadara, 190
Philosophical Essay, A (Besnier), 117, 131n.17
philosophical language, 113–14, 123
philosophy
  and hegemony of English language,
    259–61
  Latin replaced by national languages in,
    246–55
  native language use by authors in, 253–54
  universal language in, 245
Phoenicia/Phoenician language, 41
Platina (Bartolomeo Sacchi), 19, 34n.10
Playboy of the Western World (Synge), 237
Pliny the Elder, 29
poetry. *See also* Greek (Hellenistic) poetry;
    specific poems
  Alexandrian, 192–93
  "dispute" genre of, 41
  dúchas (*dúthchas*) in, 70–74, 82–84
  of exile, 73–74, 82–85
  Gaelic political, 70–74
  of Heaney, 208
  Latin and, 209
  pre-Islamic Arabic, 104
  Roman tradition of, 218
poetry, vernacular. *See also specific poems*
  and competition of 1441, 26
  Latin used in, 212–23

love as theme in, 15–16, 18–19, 28
Raccolta aragonese and, 30
Troubadours' inauguration of, 18
Politian (Angelo Poliziano), 30
Political Anatomy of Ireland, The (Petty), 174
Polygraphia nova (Kircher), 114–20, 121
Popper, Karl, 255
Portrait of the Artist as a Young Man (Joyce),
167, 181–82, 207, 237
Posidippus of Pella, 194–95
Principia philosphiae (Descartes), 251
Proficience and Advancement of Learning, The
(Bacon), 251
*Proposal for Correcting, . . . the English
Language* (Swift), 175, 176
Prose della volgar lingua (Bembo), 32
Ptolemy Philadelphus, 193–96

Qu'rān, Arabic as language of, 104–7

Raccolta aragonese, 30
Ramaswamy, Sumathi, 136
Rees, Alwyn, 66
Rees, Brinley, 66
reflection-theories of language, 111–14
religion-language relationship. *See specific
religions*
Renan, Ernest, 138
Richardson, John, 174
Romaine, Suzanne, 136
Roman poetic tradition, 218
Ruijgh, C. J., 199
"Ruin of Education in Ireland and the Irish
Fanar, The" (MacHale), 178
rule-based languages, 129. *See also* invented
language
Russian, as language of philosophy, 252

Salutati, Coluccio, 20–21, 33n.7
Sapir, Edward, 61
Sasanian empire, 102–4, 107–8
Schmitz, Thomas, 192
Schopenhauer, Arthur, 254
Schott, Gaspar, 118–19

Scienza nuova (Vico), 252–53
semaphore, 115, 121
Seneca, Lucius Annaeus, 247
Sepúlveda, Juan Ginés de, 81
Sigerson, George, 238
Silverstein, Michael, 60, 62
Simms, Katherine, 84
Singapore, multilingualism in, 148,
155n.25
Skolem, Thoralf, 255
Smith, Anthony D., 60
social formations from language, 128–30
Society for the Preservation of the Irish
Language, 179
Southeast Asia, linguistic issues in, 140,
156n.26
Spanish, 63–65, 137, 248–49, 252
Spenser, Edmund, 165, 168–69
Spinoza, Benedict de, 257
Sri Lanka, Tamil vs. Sinhala in, 137
Stafford, Thomas, 63
standardization and literacy concerns,
135–36, 137, 144–45
Stanihurst, Richard, 166, 170
Steinberg, Jonathan, 151
Stevens, Wallace, 208, 217
Stillman, Robert, 122–23
Sublime and the Beautiful, The (Burke),
235–36
Sun Yatsen, 138–39
Swift, Jonathan, 175, 176, 225n.19, 231,
234–35
Synge, J. M., 237–38
Syriac language
discovery of texts documenting, 50
dispute poems in, 41
first known use of, 53n.24
geographic expansion of, 43–44, 46, 47
Hellenization of, 101–2
Islamic era and, 48–50
Jesus' use of, 53n.24
scholarly interest in, 40, 51
survival factors of, 44–49, 50–51,
101–2

Taiwan / Taiwanese language (Hokkien
  or Southern Min), 139, 154n.20
Taiwanese Culture, Taiwanese Society
  (Hong and Murray), 154n.20
Tale of a Tub, A (Swift), 234
Tamil language, 135–36, 137
Tatian, 45–46
Tavoni, Mirko, 24
Theocritis of Syracuse, 188–94, 198, 199
Theodicée (Leibniz), 252
Theodoret, 47
Thirteenth Iambus (Callimachus), 200
Thucydides, 192
Todorov, Tzvetan, 255
"Tomb at St. Praxed's, The" (Browning),
  220–23, 225n.15
Topographia Hibernica (Giraldus), 165
Tour in Ireland, A (Young), 175
translation
  Abbāsid movement of, 102, 108
  of Avestan texts, 103–4
  in Landino's program of linguistic
    reform, 29
Translations (Friel), 209, 239–40
*Treatise Containing a Plain and Perfect
  Description of Ireland* (Stanihurst), 166
Trovato, Paolo, 22
Tuscan aspiration to Italian vernacular, 30
Twelfth Idyll (Theocritus), 191

Über das Sehn und die Farben
  (Schopenhauer), 254
Umayyad era, 106–8
United States, tolerance of linguistic diversity,
  135, 137, 151, 152, 153, 153n.3

universal empire through language,
  129–30
universal language, 116–20, 126–30, 245,
  249, 255–61

vernacular
  as bastard language, 218, 224n.12
  movable type and resurrection of, 27
  philosophical language and development
    of, 248
  and use in philosophy, 249–51
vernacular poetic tradition, 15, 18–19, 28.
    See also poetry, vernacular
Verschueren, Jef, 90, 151
Vico, Giambattista, 252–53
View of the Present State of Ireland, A
  (Spenser), 168–69
Vindication of the Antiquities of Ireland
  (Keogh), 175
Virgil, 212–19
Vita nuova (Dante), 15
Voloshinov, V. N., 90

Wales, bilingual education in, 155n.25
Webster, Noah, 180
Wilding, Nick, 119
Wilkins, John, 112–14, 120–25, 128–29
Wittgenstein, Ludwig, 255
Wolff, Christian, 252, 253

Yeats, William Butler, 179–80, 182n.3,
  238
Young, Arthur, 175

Zoroastrianism, 102, 103, 107